Word Study that Works for All Learners

Words Their Way® Services for Educators

Words Their Way® for Teachers: Self-Paced Course

This self-paced, interactive, professional development workshop is designed to help K–10 educators, as well as reading specialists, literacy coaches, facilitators, and staff development trainers master the methodology of the Words Their Way® word study approach for their students.

The Words Their Way® for Teachers: Self-Paced Course gives you:

- **Personal Training** – provides self-paced practice on your own time.
- **Individual Instructional Path** – tailors the workshop specifically to your grade level or role in your school.
- **Interactive Practice** – features authentic classroom video, student spelling and writing samples, plus routines, methods and assessment activities.
- **Immediate Feedback** – includes an assessment module that tracks your responses to guide your mastery of the Words Their Way® approach to word study.

Learn more & view the introduction at **www.pearsonlearningsolutions.com/online-learning/words-their-way-online-workshop**

Words Their Way® Training for Teachers

Words Their Way® Training for Teachers is a three-day, face-to-face workshop that will help educators and literacy coaches unlock the potential of word study and enhance learning in phonemic awareness, phonics, vocabulary, spelling, fluency, and comprehension.

Key features include:

- High-quality training on the research-based book, *Words Their Way®*, developed in conjunction with the Words Their Way® author team
- The opportunity to learn how to effectively implement the Words Their Way® approach in their classrooms
- Tailored to grade bands (K–1, 2–3, 4–5, 5–8) to ensure instruction meets the needs of students at various developmental spelling levels

Words Their Way® Training for Teachers: Fused Online Course

Words Their Way® Training for Teachers: Fused Online Course is travel-free, schedule-friendly, and allows teachers, administrators, and specialists to build their capacity through interactive learning modules that provide videos of classroom implementation, teaching tips, and insight from Pearson's authors and education experts.

Words Their Way® Coaching and Modeling

Words Their Way® job-embedded coaching offers intensive support for schools wishing to build capacity. An experienced Pearson consultant works directly with educators and coaches to analyze data, review lessons, and address areas of student need.

Words Their Way® Overview: Self-Paced Course

Words Their Way® Overview: Self-Paced Course is a bundle of self-paced, online modules that help educators implement the Words Their Way® word study approach and include videos, practice, performance assessments and quizzes to assess learning.

Learn more at **www.pearsonpd.com**

Words Their Way® Series

The word study approach that more than half a million educators trust! Based on years of research into invented and developmental spelling, the classroom-proven framework of this successful series is keyed to the five stages of spelling and orthographic development. Teachers everywhere have grown to love its no nonsense method for studying words. Each stage-specific companion volume features a complete curriculum of reproducible sorts and detailed directions for teachers working with students in each stage of spelling development, from emergent through derivational relations.

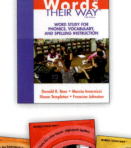

Words Their Way®: Word Study for Phonics, Vocabulary, and Spelling Instruction

This Fifth Edition features updated activities, expanded coverage of English learners, and emphasis on progress monitoring. All new classroom videos, an enhanced assessment application tool, as well as games and interactive word sorts and picture sorts are available on the PDToolkit web resources site and offer teachers even more tools that will enhance their word study instruction.

Words Their Way® Companion Volumes

These 5 companion volumes are targeted to the word study instruction of an individual stage of spelling development outlined in the core book, and, with reproducible sorting pages and directions, the books provide a plan of action for motivating and engaging your students.

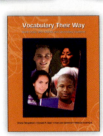

Vocabulary Their Way®: Word Study with Middle and Secondary Students

With a focus on developing vocabulary with students in intermediate, middle, and secondary grades, this book offers research-tested ideas for helping students use word patterns to puzzle out meaning to content area vocabulary. It also provides much needed assessment information to help teachers gauge where to begin instruction as well as hands-on opportunities for teachers to keep students' attention and interest as they build vocabulary.

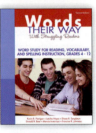

Words Their Way® with Struggling Readers: Word Study for Reading, Vocabulary, and Spelling Instruction, Grades 4–12

This resource provides specific guidance, strategies, and tools for helping struggling students catch up with their peers in literacy. The thrust is intervention – specifically, utilizing word study with its hands-on, assessable approach to aid students struggling with the vocabulary, fluency, and comprehension load of middle and secondary classrooms. This book will help you determine student needs, provide you with the strategies to guide each student toward success in content area comprehension, and even outline ideas for fitting these strategies into your crowded schedule.

Words Their Way® with English Learners

Based on the same solid research, *Words Their Way® with English Learners,* Second Edition, helps you determine what your students bring with them from their home languages, where their instruction in English orthography should begin, and how best to move these students through their development. The Second Edition includes the *PDToolkit for Words Their Way®* which provides word study teaching scenarios to allow teachers to see how to engage in word study with English Learners.

Words Their Way® Companion Volumes for Spanish-Speaking English Learners

These new companion volumes begin with a series of picture concept sorts that teach students how to sort, providing guidance to help you make sorting meaningful in your classroom. All words are selected based on their phonetic properties as well as their usefulness in reading, speaking, and understanding grade level content. Start your readers with the *Emergent Sorts* and move to *Letter-Name Alphabetic* and *Within Word Pattern Sorts*. You'll find something for all ability levels in these new resources, with sorts tailor-made to fit new learners, older students, or even advanced ELLs who need more concept and vocabulary support.

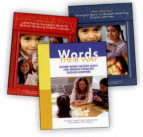

Words Their Way
for PreK-K

Words Their Way for PreK-K

Francine Johnston
University of North Carolina at Greensboro

Marcia Invernizzi
University of Virginia

Lori Helman
University of Minnesota

Donald R. Bear
Iowa State University

Shane Templeton
University of Nevada, Reno

PEARSON

Boston • Columbus • Indianapolis • New York • San Francisco • Upper Saddle River
Amsterdam • Cape Town • Dubai • London • Madrid • Milan • Munich • Paris • Montréal • Toronto
Delhi • Mexico City • São Paulo • Sydney • Hong Kong • Seoul • Singapore • Taipei • Tokyo

Acquisitions Editor: Kathryn Boice
Executive Development Editor: Hope Madden
Editorial Assistant: Carolyn Schweitzer
Executive Marketing Manager: Krista Clark
Production Editor: Janet Domingo
Editorial Production Service: Electronic Publishing Services Inc., NYC
Manufacturing Buyer: Linda Sager
Electronic Composition: Jouve
Cover Designer: Diane Lorenzo
Illustration: Francine Johnston and Electronic Publishing Services Inc., NYC

Photo credits: Pearson Education

Credits and acknowledgments borrowed from other sources and reproduced, with permission, in the textbook appear either here or on the appropriate page within text.

Library of Congress Cataloging-in-Publication Data

Johnston, Francine R.
   Words their way for preK-K / Francine Johnston, University of North Carolina-Greensboro, Marcia Invernizzi, University of Virginia, Lori Helman, University of Minnesota, Donald R. Bear, University of Nevada-Reno, Shane Templeton, University of Nevada-Reno.
      pages cm
   Includes bibliographical references and index.
   ISBN-13: 978-0-13-243016-6 (pbk.)
   ISBN-10: 0-13-243016-9 (pbk.)
  1. Word recognition.   2. English language—Orthography and spelling—Study and teaching.
3. Reading—Phonetic method—Study and teaching (Early childhood)   4. Vocabulary—Study and teaching (Early childhood)   5. Language arts (Early childhood)   I. Title.
LB1050.44.J64 2014
372.6'049—dc23

                                                                        2013046496

V011
10 9 8 7 6 5 4 3 2 1

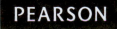

ISBN 10: 0-13-243016-9
ISBN 13: 978-0-13-243016-6

ABOUT the AUTHORS

Francine Johnston

Francine Johnston is a former first grade teacher and reading specialist who learned about word study during her graduate work at the University of Virginia. She is retired from the School of Education at the University of North Carolina at Greensboro, where she taught literacy courses and directed a clinic for struggling readers. Francine continues to work with regional school systems as a consultant. She is a co-author of the *Words Their Way*® series of books and materials.

Marcia Invernizzi

Marcia Invernizzi is the Henderson Professor of Reading Education at the Curry School of Education at the University of Virginia. Marcia is also the executive director of the McGuffey Reading Center, where she teaches the doctoral internship in the reading clinic. Formerly an English and reading teacher, she works with Book Buddies, Virginia's Early Intervention Reading Initiative (EIRI), and Phonological Awareness Literacy Screening (PALS). She is a co-author of the *Words Their Way*® series of books and materials.

Lori Helman

Lori Helman is an associate professor in literacy education in the Department of Curriculum and Instruction at the University of Minnesota and co-director of the Minnesota Center for Reading Research. Her research and writing have focused extensively on the literacy development of students learning English as a new language, including other *Words Their Way*® instructional materials. Lori taught bilingual kindergarten for ten years in Santa Cruz, California.

Donald R. Bear

Donald R. Bear is a professor in literacy at Iowa State University and co-directs the Duffelmeyer Reading Clinic. Donald is involved in innovative professional development grants. He is an author and co-author of numerous articles, book chapters, and books, including *Words Their Way*, Fifth Edition, and *Words Their Way with Struggling Readers: Word Study for Reading, Vocabulary, and Spelling Instruction, Grades 4–12*. Donald is involved in numerous studies that examine literacy learning, including studies of orthographic development in second languages.

Shane Templeton

Shane Templeton is Foundation Professor Emeritus of Literacy Studies at the University of Nevada, Reno. A former classroom teacher at the primary and secondary levels, his research has focused on developmental word knowledge in elementary, middle, and high school students. He is co-author of *Words Their Way*, *Vocabulary Their Way*, and, with Kristin Gehsmann, *Teaching Reading and Writing: The Developmental Approach*. Since 1987, Shane has been a member of the Usage Panel of the *American Heritage Dictionary*. He is educational consultant on *The American Heritage Children's Dictionary* and wrote the foreword to the recently published *Curious George's Dictionary*.

BRIEF CONTENTS

CONTENTS

chapter 5

Word Study for Phonics and Spelling 99

chapter 6

Concept of Word in Text 138

This brand new text brings the phenomenon of *Words Their Way*® to the youngest readers. Why word study with preK and kindergarten students? Because the hands-on approach motivates them, keeps them engaged, and helps them build early literacy skills. The word study approach as outlined by renowned *Words Their Way*® authors is a developmentally driven instructional method. It remains a sound and popular method because of its concrete and research-supported approach for teaching children phonics, vocabulary, and spelling skills.

Through word study, students examine, manipulate, and categorize sounds, letters, and words. Using this approach, teachers create tasks that focus students' attention on critical features of words: their sounds, patterns, and meanings. This new text takes that time-tested, classroom-proven approach and focuses on the needs of emerging readers.

Using the same systematic approach to word study, guided by an informed interpretation of spelling errors and other literacy behaviors, *Words Their Way for PreK–K* offers a responsive, child-centered plan for vocabulary growth and spelling development appropriate for children just beginning school. Step by step, the chapters in this text explain and model exactly how to provide effective instruction in the fundamentals of early literacy.

As you'll see when you meet the wonderful prekindergarten and kindergarten teachers in the pages of this text, the literacy diet can be implemented in a fun, engaging, and developmentally appropriate way. Good teachers integrate vocabulary and concept development, alphabet knowledge, phonological awareness, phonics, concepts about print, and concept of word into all aspects of the school day. This book features diverse classrooms, including students who are learning English as a new language, and the preK and kindergarten teachers who are highlighted demonstrate many valuable techniques for developing language and literacy. The text guides you to integrate the essential elements of literacy instruction—Read To, Read With, Write With, Word Study, and Talk With (RRWWT)—with your students. Students who have a balanced diet in each of these areas develop the foundational skills needed to become successful readers and writers. This structure not only allows you to integrate the critical elements of literacy instruction, but also aligns with the proficiencies presented in the *Common Core State Standards*.

Predictable chapter structures contextualize literacy content inside a real preK or kindergarten classroom before covering the chapter's core concept in depth. Chapters then focus on how to plan instruction around that concept, including step-by-step lesson plans and dozens of activities to take directly into the classroom. Chapters also look closely at how to best assess your students' skills in a specific area—concepts about print, concept of word and word identification, phonological awareness, and more. There's also a complete chapter to help you organize your classroom for making the most of word study.

The appendix provides reproducible materials such as pictures, game templates, sample sorts, and assessments—materials you'll need to implement these strategies with your students and get your classroom up and running. Finally, chapters include notes to direct you to the PDToolkit online resource (http://pdtoolkit.pearson.com), where you'll find videos of word study in preK and kindergarten classrooms, as well as games and materials you'll find most valuable for young readers.

You'll have everything you need to ensure that your prekindergarten and kindergarten students are able to learn words *their* way and become successful readers.

PDToolkit for *Words Their Way*®

Accompanying *Words Their Way for PreK–K* is an online resource site that, together with the text, provides you the media tools you need to carry out word study instruction that will motivate and engage your students and help them succeed in literacy learning.

The PDToolkit for *Words Their Way*® is available free for 12 months after you use the password that comes with this book. After that, it is available by subscription for a yearly fee. Be sure to explore and download the resources available at the website. The following resources are currently available:

- Classroom video footage brings you into the classrooms of teachers using word study at different stages of development.
- Assessment tools provide downloadable inventories and feature guides as well as interactive classroom composites that help teachers monitor their students' development throughout the year.
- Prepared word sorts and games for each stage will help you get started with word study in your classroom.
- A Create Your Own feature allows you to modify and create sorts by selecting words or pictures to be used with the word sort templates.

To learn more, please visit http://pdtoolkit.pearson.com.

Acknowledgments

We would like to thank the many wonderful preK and kindergarten teachers we have learned from over the years. We appreciate the teachers, administrators, students, and parents who permitted us to observe and document the excellent practices going on in schools in Minnesota, Virginia, Nevada, and North Carolina. Jackie Dagenet creates an exemplary literacy-rich classroom at Colfax Elementary Elementary School in Guilford County North Carolina for four-year-olds. Kilee Christnagel is an inspiration to kindergarten teachers everywhere and is accomplishing amazing things with her students. Nee Xiong helps us to see what is possible with very young English learners. A special thank you goes to Linda Woessner at Hancock Elementary in St. Paul, Minnesota, and Darl Kiernan with Washoe County School District in Nevada for sharing their ideas with us. Thanks also to Virginia Coffey from Albemarle Country Schools and the many teachers who participate in the summer McGuffey Reading Center.

We would like to thank the reviewers of the manuscript for their careful reading and perceptive comments: Karen Gooch, Miami University; Luisa Palomo Hare, Liberty University (NE); Jeri Powers, Riverview Elementary (KS); and Pamela Sullivan, James Madison University.

Finally, we thank the many wonderful individuals in the publishing world who supported this book, including Linda Bishop Montgomery, who encouraged us to frame such a book for the preK and kindergarten audience; Aurora Martínez Ramos, who supported it to fruition; Hope Madden, for her caring and uncanny ability to guide us and marshal resources; Kathryn Boice, who helped us to put the finishing touches on this book; and Barbara Strickland, who shepherded us through the paperwork.

Introduction

Jackie Dagenet is a master at integrating literacy into daily routines, play centers, and thematic units as well as carefully planned language arts activities. A good example of this integration is a spring unit that revolves around the life cycle of birds, particularly ducks. Jackie is sensitive to children's interests and abilities so her themes vary from year to year, but the wonder of hatching eggs and the appeal of baby ducks mean that this unit is one that she uses often with her preschool class.

Jackie's curriculum is designed to meet a wide range of diverse needs. There are students learning to speak English, children with developmental delays and physical disabilities, and many children from homes with limited incomes. By spring most children are able to participate for 20 minutes or more during group time, as long as listening and discussions are balanced with music and movement. Jackie gathers the children on the rug by leading them in songs, including a new one they have been practicing for several days, "Five Little Ducks." Here are the words to the first verse of the song and the finger play that can accompany it.

Five little ducks went out one day [Hold up five fingers.]
Over the hills and far away. [Wave hand up and down, then hold hand over eyes to
     look far away.]
Mother duck said, [Use hands to imitate bill of a duck.]
"Quack, quack, quack, quack."
But only four little ducks came back. [Hold up four fingers.]

The song repeats as fewer ducks return each time, until finally no little ducks come back. The last verse resolves the problem.

Sad mother duck went out one day [Make a sad face.]
Over the hills and far away.
Mother duck said, [Use hands to imitate bill of a duck.]
"Quack, quack, quack, quack."
And all of her five little ducks came back. [Hold up five fingers.]

INTRODUCE THE BOOK. A copy of the big book of this traditional rhyme illustrated by Pamela Paparone is displayed on a stand. Once everyone is settled, Jackie draws their attention to the book cover and asks them what they notice. Immediately the children begin talking about the picture, which shows a large duck watching as little ducks move up and over a hill. Jackie poses her usual question when introducing a book, "What do you think this book will be about and why?" The children readily agree that it must be about the same five little ducks they have sung about. Jackie then points out the title, "Here is the title of the book and these words say . . ." She pauses to encourage the children to respond. . . . "Five Little Ducks." She points carefully to each word in the title and asks the children to repeat it again. Then she goes on to explain that it is an old rhyme that their parents and grandparents might have known and that it has been illustrated by Pamela Paparone. She pauses to think aloud and point to the letters in the name as she says, "Hmm, Pamela Paparone—her name has a lot of *P*'s in it!"

Because the children have already learned the words to the song, Jackie focuses most of their attention during the first reading of the big book on the illustrations. Every two or three lines of text have a full-page illustration that shows Mother Duck busy about the house: raking leaves, hanging up wash, ironing, and picking apples. In a smaller illustration on the opposite page, the little ducks are shown crossing hills to find gardens, farm animals, and woodland animals. Jackie reads the simple repetitive text as she turns each page. But she encourages the children to talk about the pictures, especially the ones that show the passage of time and the return of the little ducks to enjoy the apple pie made by Mother Duck. Although the words of the song are repetitive and may not offer unfamiliar vocabulary, the pictures can be used to introduce many words. Jackie supplies vocabulary such as "rolling out the dough" or "hanging up quilts on the clothesline" to describe things that might not be familiar to her students. She also poses questions to invite discussion, such as "How do you think Mother Duck is feeling?" and "Where do you think the little ducks went?"

Jackie leaves the big book out for the children to look at during center time. Many of the children gravitate to the book, eagerly looking at the pictures and finding even more things to talk about. Jackie or her assistant stops by and encourages them to describe what they see, eliciting more oral language.

CONCEPTS ABOUT PRINT. The next day Jackie plans a group lesson that shifts more attention to the printed word. As she turns each page, she uses a short stick to track the words and she points out some special features of print. She models how reading starts at the top left of the page and moves to the right, followed by a return sweep—ideas known as **concepts about print**. *Five Little Ducks* offers a good opportunity to highlight the rare letter *Q*, so Jackie calls on several children to come up and find the capital *Q* and lowercase *q*'s. Another child is asked to point to the *Q* on the alphabet chart so that the children make the connection that the letters on the chart are the same as the letters they see in books. Jackie also draws their attention to the rhyming words: "I am going to pause and let you say the words that rhyme. 'Five little ducks went out one . . . (day), over the hills and far . . . (away).' What are the words that rhyme? Yes, *day* and *away* rhyme because they sound alike at the end." This is repeated with attention to *back* and *quack* as rhyming words.

FOCUS ON SENTENCES. Jackie then displays a pocket chart with the first verse of the song written out on five sentence strips, one for each line. She explains to the children that they are going to read the words with her. She slows down, reading and not singing, as she points to each word; she encourages the children to read along with her in a choral fashion. After reading the strips, she passes them out to five children as she explains, "Yusef, this is your sentence. These words say, 'Five little ducks went out one day.'" Then, with the children's help, the five children rebuild the first verse of the song. "How does the song start? Who has that sentence with those words?" She might repeat this with different children while letting others go off to centers. The strips are left in the pocket chart, and Jackie encourages the children to stop by during center time to use the pointer and track the words on their own.

FOCUS ON WORDS. The big book is read again on a third day, and the children once more have a chance to talk about things they have noticed in the pictures. Jackie encourages them to use some of the vocabulary she introduced earlier by saying, "What is Mother Duck doing in this picture? What is she hanging on the clothesline?" Again the children chorally read the sentence strips as Jackie points to the words, and she gives several children a chance to point as she observes how well each is able to track the print. Jackie has prepared an extra sentence strip of the first line. As she reads each word, she cuts it off and then says, "Let's see how many words are in this sentence." Together they count the words. Jackie poses a challenge: "Our words are all mixed up. Can we put these words back in order? What is the first word in the sentence? How can we find that word? What is the first sound in *Five*? The first letter in *Five*?" The words *out* and *one* are both three-letter words that begin with sounds not commonly associated with the letter *O*, so they are potentially confusing. Jackie is very direct about this: "The next word is *out*, and it is hard to find. But listen to the last sound in *out*. I hear a *T* at the end of that word and I see a *T* at the end of this word. I can also look up here at this sentence and check my words."

After rebuilding the sentence together and reading to check for accuracy, Jackie lets most of the students go to centers and keeps a small group of six to work with for a few more minutes. She passes out the words and invites the children up to put the words in order under the model sentence. As they work she asks them to explain how they figured out where to put the words, and then the sentence is read to check. Once more the big book, sentence strips, and now word cards are left out, and children stop by to play the role of teacher as they point to the words and rebuild the verse and first line. Few children in preK are likely to fully develop the ability to point accurately to a line of memorized text, a skill known as **concept of word**, but Jackie looks for insights she has modeled and talked about, such as moving the pointer from left to right and top to bottom.

Jackie has started with a whole text—or, in this case, a song as well as a book—and gradually worked with smaller pieces of it: sentences, words, and letters. We call this a **whole-to-part** instructional framework, which introduces children to reading in a very supportive way. The final step in the whole-to-part model is to work on letter–sound correspondences. To do this, Jackie pulls out a collection of pictures for words that start with *F* and *D*, because several words in the song begin with one of these two consonants. She also has cards with capital and lowercase letters for *Ff* and *Dd*. Jackie typically introduces letter sounds with the whole class but then plans follow-up lessons with a smaller group for those who are ready for this step.

FOCUS ON LETTERS AND SOUNDS. Jackie holds up an alphabet card for *F*, pointing out the capital and lowercase forms. Jackie then asks the children whether they can find some words in the song that start with *F*. She reminds them that they will have to look at both capital and lowercase letters at the beginning of words. The first word, *Five*, is an easy one. Jackie points to the *F* and explains, "The first letter in this word is *F*." The word *far* takes a little more work and the children are proud when they find it in the second line by watching carefully as they chorally read together. Jackie then explains, "Listen to the first sound in these words: *ffffive* and *ffffar*. They both begin with the same letter and the same sound." Jackie repeats this for the letter *D*, and the children find the words *duck* and *ducks* three times as well as the word *day*. Then Jackie puts up the letter cards for *D* and *F* in a pocket chart and explains that there are a lot more words that begin with those letters. Jackie holds up the picture of a fish and says, "Listen to the first sound in *fish. Ffffffish*. Say it slowly with me: *fffish. Fish* starts with *F*, so I will put it beside the letter *F*. Here is a duck. *Duck* starts with *D*, so I will put it beside the letter *D*. Let's name these other pictures and sort them under *D* or *F*. Here is a dog. Listen: *dog, fish.* Do they start with the same sound? *Dog-duck.* Do they start with the same sound? *Dog* starts like *duck*, so I will put it under *D*." Each new picture is compared to the **key words** *duck* and *fish*. After sorting the pictures in columns, Jackie and the children name them to emphasize the beginning sound: *duck, desk, dish, dog, doll,* and so forth. If there are children in the class whose name begins with *D* or *F*, their names (or pictures) are added to the sort. The sort is repeated. This time Jackie might pass out the pictures to individual children, who take turns coming up to sort.

EXTENSIONS. Jackie extends her *Five Little Ducks* lesson in several ways. Earlier, she had the class find the letter *Q* in the book and on the alphabet chart. She now continues to highlight that rare letter, demonstrating how to make the capital and lowercase *Q* on a large piece of chart paper, explaining that the children should first make a circle starting at the top and then add a "kickstand" so it does not roll away. She leaves a marker there for children to practice throughout the day. Jackie also supplies props to act out the song and reads additional books about ducks, including another version of

Five Little Ducks by Ian Beck in which the little ducks end up in the care (or control?) of a fox. It is not clear whether the fox has good or bad intentions, making it an issue children might debate. *Make Way for Ducklings* by Robert McClosky is a realistic story that can be compared to the two versions of *Five Little Ducks*. There are also many excellent information books about ducks. These read-alouds can lead to a discussion of real and make-believe and a concept sorting activity that contrasts pictures of real ducks with fantasy ducks dressed in clothing and engaged in activities such as baking and cleaning. The study of ducks can also be extended to the study of other water birds, and children can learn about their habits and life cycles as well as the differences between ducks, geese, and swans.

THE LITERACY DIET. Jackie integrates vocabulary and concept development, alphabet knowledge, phonological awareness, phonics, concepts about print and writing, and concept of word—what we call the literacy diet—into all aspects of the school day. In the following chapters each part of the diet will be explored in greater depth, but it is important to understand that they are not taught in a prescribed sequence but overlap and work together. Each day, all the elements of the literacy diet should be addressed in preK and kindergarten classrooms during five essential literacy activities: Read To, Read With, Write With, Word Study, and Talk With—summed up as the acronym *RRWWT*. In the process of carrying out these activities, all of the kindergarten-level Common Core State Standards (CCSS) for English Language Arts (2010) can be met in a developmentally appropriate way. These standards, which have been adopted by nearly all states, describe a set of foundational skills for reading and language. It is very likely that the expectations in your local school districts will be similar. Each aspect of RRWWT is related to CCSS proficiencies, as noted in the lesson plans in this text. The literacy components, as shown in Figure I.1, will help students develop the foundational skills needed to become successful readers and writers.

Throughout this text, we will be visiting the classrooms of talented preK and kindergarten teachers. We want to thank these teachers for the ideas and inspiration they have given us and introduce you to them.

- Jackie Dagenet is a National Board certified teacher who has worked for 23 years in the Greensboro Public Schools as a preschool and kindergarten teacher. She is an adjunct instructor for the department of teacher education and higher education at the University of North Carolina at Greensboro.

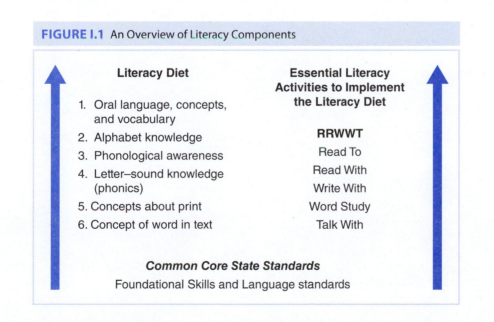

FIGURE I.1 An Overview of Literacy Components

Literacy Diet

1. Oral language, concepts, and vocabulary
2. Alphabet knowledge
3. Phonological awareness
4. Letter–sound knowledge (phonics)
5. Concepts about print
6. Concept of word in text

Essential Literacy Activities to Implement the Literacy Diet

RRWWT

Read To

Read With

Write With

Word Study

Talk With

Common Core State Standards

Foundational Skills and Language standards

- Kilee Christnagel has been an elementary teacher and literacy coach in the Minneapolis Public Schools for 16 years. She currently teaches kindergarten at Marcy Open School.
- Kristen Polanski works in the Saint Paul Public School system, where she has taught multilingual students learning English at the kindergarten and other grade levels for 11 years.
- Lori Helman (coauthor of this text) taught bilingual kindergarten for 10 years in Santa Cruz, California, where she put many of the activities in this book into practice in English and Spanish.
- Nee Xiong is a preK teacher at Saint Paul City School in Saint Paul, Minnesota, where she teaches four- and five-year-olds in a multilingual, urban setting.
- Regina Smith, a featured kindergarten teacher, has been a literacy coordinator, reading specialist, and classroom teacher. She is currently an assistant professor and coordinator in the Early Childhood Education Program at East Central University in Ada, Oklahoma.

Oral Language, Vocabulary, and Concept Development

Kristen Polanski is working with a group of eight kindergarteners who are learning vocabulary related to the weather. Most of the students are learning English as a new language, so Kristen wants to make sure that they are comfortable with the new words before she engages them in a sorting task together. Students chant along as Kristen holds up a picture card, says the name of the object, and asks students whether they know what it is. When she holds up a picture of a thermometer, one student suggests "piano" because it resembles the keys of a piano. Another student says "amotheter." Kristen says "good try" and asks the students to repeat the word after her, gently guiding them to stick out their tongues at the beginning and chant the word beat by beat with her as in "ther-mom-me-ter." Then she asks, "What does a thermometer tell us?" One student notes, "It tell are you cold or are you hot." Kristen responds by affirming the student: "It tells if it's cold or hot."

PD TOOLKIT™
for Words Their Way®

Watch Kristen Polanski conduct a vocabulary lesson with her English learning students at the PDToolkit. Click on Videos and select Emergent. Scroll to find "Vocabulary Development and Concept Sorting."

In this brief vignette, Kristen's lesson opens the door to many of the topics we will discuss in this chapter: Why are vocabulary, oral language, and concept development so critical to long-term literacy development? What approaches to instruction will assist teachers in ensuring that all of your students have access to the language they will need to grow and succeed academically? And, how might teachers like Kristen create a word-learning classroom that builds on the language resources that students bring with them from their families and communities?

Language Is Fundamental

Michael Halliday reminds us, "Language has the power to shape our consciousness and it does so for each human child, by providing the theory that he or she uses to interpret and manipulate their environment" (Halliday, 1993, p. 107). The preschool years are a time of intense growth in language development. From the moment they are born, children learn to communicate with the people in their lives. Beginning with crying and cooing, they practice the sounds, inflections, and communication patterns they experience with caregivers. In the first few years of life, very young children develop foundational understandings of the sound system of their home language (phonology), the way it is put together into meaningful messages (syntax), what it means (semantics), and how to appropriately communicate to others (pragmatics). Early language development continues to amaze those of us who watch it unfold in the children with whom we work or live.

Variation in Students' Vocabularies

Preschool and kindergarten children bring many language resources with them to school when they arrive. Most of them can communicate their needs and ideas in their home languages, understand the meanings of thousands of words, and interact with others to share information and learn together. By the time they enter first grade, most children have learned an average of 14,000 words (Carey, 1978). This means that many four- and five-year-olds are acquiring 1,000 to 3,000 words a year, or as many as eight words a day! However, this is not true for all children.

Children come to school having had very different language experiences (Biemiller & Slonim, 2001). Although language learning is a process wired into all humans, individuals learn from the people with whom they interact and from the experiences they have had. In a classic study, researchers estimated that by three years of age, some children had heard three million more words than other children, and by the time they enter school, some children have heard 30 million more words than others (Hart & Risley, 1995). It is not just the number of words heard that is striking—it is the different contexts in which these words are used and the different types of interactions with adults (Hart & Risley, 1995; Verhoeven, van Leeuwe, & Vermeer, 2011). The unfortunate reality is that these differences may be primarily related to children's socioeconomic environments. By the age of three, children from high-poverty backgrounds have heard fewer than one-third of the words that children from professional families have heard. In addition, many children today live multilingual lives and are learning one language at home and a different one at school. Although students may bring rich oral language resources with them to school, their strengths may not be supported within a classroom environment that only recognizes language development in English. It is incumbent on the educators in the classroom to help connect the students' knowledge in their home languages with the words and concepts they need to learn in English.

It is clear that students within early childhood classrooms will have a range of language resources to build on, and teachers will need to focus explicitly on developing their oral language and vocabulary skills. Only in this way will educators begin to close the tremendous oral vocabulary gap that exists between children who bring extensive vocabulary and oral language skills in English to the classroom and those who do not (Biemiller, 2005; Dickinson, McCabe, & Essex, 2006).

Different Kinds of Vocabularies

As new parents soon learn, young children understand much more of what they hear than they are able to produce. Words that a person understands when used by others are their **receptive vocabulary**. The words a person is comfortable using are **productive vocabulary**. The productive vocabularies of young children are considerably smaller than their receptive vocabularies. As a child learns to read, a **sight word vocabulary** of recognized printed words is acquired. In this chapter, our focus is on oral vocabulary and how to enhance the number of words in a child's receptive and productive vocabularies, with the ability to use the vocabulary being the ultimate goal.

Vocabulary Learning Goes Hand in Hand with Concept Development

Young children are constantly learning about the world and how it is categorized (conceptual knowledge) and labeled (vocabulary knowledge). Sit near a preschooler and his or her caregiver at a park or in a restaurant and you are likely to hear conversations that involve pointing and identifying objects (e.g., "See the doggy? He's a nice doggy."), instructing about new topics (e.g., "That's a bee, it can sting us."), and information gathering by the child (e.g., "What's that?"). Words are the tools that help us understand new ideas. That is why learning a new topic often involves learning new vocabulary, and learning new vocabulary is often dependent on understanding something about the world. For example, when learning about African animals, the word *giraffe* will make a lot more sense if the student has seen a giraffe at the zoo, in a book, or in a movie. Conversely, a child who sees a giraffe for the first time will want to know, "What is *that*?" To teach the word *giraffe* to a child who has never seen a giraffe or used the word before involves teaching a concept as well a new word. Children who know the word for giraffe in their home language do not need to learn the concept; they need only to connect the word in English to the word they already know in another language.

Building a Language-Learning Classroom

A well-developed vocabulary is an essential part of school success (Cunningham & Stanovich, 2003; Duncan et al., 2007) and is dependent on the richness and frequency of verbal interactions with peers and adults, along with exposure to new objects, experiences, and ideas. Adults should engage children in conversation at every opportunity and intentionally use language that includes new vocabulary and more complex sentences, as well as visuals or other materials that make the new vocabulary clear. Classroom environments that are well managed and positively oriented invite peer interaction that results in greater language use—a primary goal in early language and literacy development (Mashburn, Justice, Downer, & Pianta, 2009). Students who are learning English as a new language need to be explicitly taught the words and structures of the new language, and they make connections to what they already know in their home language. This chapter will describe strategies to introduce, contextualize, and exercise oral language along with concept development.

Word Selection

Word selection is critical for ensuring that all students have access to the curriculum being studied in class, but there are so many possible words to be studied that it is often hard to know where to begin and how to select the right words. It is easy and tempting to look for hard words, but the hardest words may not be the words children are most likely to hear again, retain, and use on their own. They also may not be the words that will give children with smaller vocabularies in English the opportunity to catch up to their peers in learning class content. We suggest four criteria for selecting words: (1) utility or instructional potential, (2) concreteness, (3) repetition in text, and (4) thematic or topical relatedness.

UTILITY OR INSTRUCTIONAL POTENTIAL. When thinking about utility, consider words that can be used regularly in the classroom or words that will show up in other books or lessons being taught in class. For example, the book *Don't Let the Pigeon Drive the Bus* by Mo Willems includes many opportunities to hear and discuss the words *bus* or *driver*, both important words that are likely to come up very frequently in classroom interactions. After focusing on these words in reading aloud, make a point of using them in other contexts. You might ask students, "Did you come to school on a *bus* today, or in a car, or walking? Who was the *driver*?"

CONCRETENESS. It is not surprising that the majority of the words young children first acquire are nouns, because nouns often can be referenced concretely (e.g., *tractor, crayon, turtle*). An analysis of early semantic knowledge revealed that 40 percent of words learned in the early years are nouns, 25 percent are verbs and adjectives, and only 15 percent are pronouns or prepositions (Bates et al., 1994). It is useful for teachers to be aware of these percentages as they select words to teach. Objects are the easiest words to teach because you can show them to students or provide a picture. However, you can make verbs, adjectives, and adverbs concrete by modeling them with facial expressions, acting them out, and using them in context. Prepositions or position words should also be explicitly taught and used repeatedly. Jackie Dagenet uses a stuffed animal and directs her preK children to place it in various positions. For example, "Put Lucky in front of the house." On the playground, she often lays out a jump rope and gives children directions such as "Stand behind the rope" or "Jump over the rope."

REPETITION. Also consider what words are used more than once in a story or lesson: These will offer repeated exposure in a meaningful context. For example, the words *drive* and *driver* are used multiple times in *Don't Let the Pigeon Drive the Bus*.

THEMATIC OR TOPICAL RELATEDNESS. As you review your teaching topics or classroom themes, think about the vocabulary that will be important in understanding key concepts; choose words that can be clustered in a semantic category (Whitehurst, 1979). For example, while studying about the body, books will feature body parts such as *head, hair, eyes, nose, mouth, ears, hands, feet, legs, stomach, back, arms, shoulders,* and so on. Other important thematic vocabulary during this topic may relate to healthy behaviors such as *eating, sleeping, washing,* and *exercising.*

Repeated Exposure

Simply mentioning the meaning of words or doing lots of reading aloud is not enough to enhance the vocabulary learning of those students who need it the most (Beck, McKeown, & Kucan, 2002, 2013). When new words are introduced, children should be asked to repeat them, use them in phrases and sentences, and answer questions about them. For example, after reading the phrase "around and around he whirled" (from *Whistle for Willie* by Ezra Jack Keats), the teacher might pause briefly to draw attention to the word *whirled* and ask children to act out the verb. After reading the book, the word should be discussed again: "Say the word *whirl*. What do you think it means? Would you whirl on the grass? Would you whirl fast or whirl slow? Tell your partner how you would fill in this sentence: 'I whirl when I _____.'" Beck, McKeown, and Kucan (2002, 2008) describe how to plan repeated exposure to words in different contexts to help students learn the meaning and use of new vocabulary.

Planning Instruction for Vocabulary

Vocabulary develops in a supportive environment with lots of exposure, modeling and explanation, guided practice, and independent use. (Table 1.1 lists some general principles of vocabulary instruction.) Each unit of study or instructional goal involves new vocabulary that will be needed in order to understand the concepts being taught. For example, while Kilee's kindergarteners are involved in a study of maps, some of the key words they learn are *community, map, globe, neighborhood, birds-eye view, directly above, above, below, behind, near,* and *far.* It is important for Kilee to identify these key terms before she plans her lessons. She should provide many opportunities for students to hear and learn about the words in a number of contexts, practice using the words in structured interactions, and then encourage their use in independent settings. This follows the gradual release instructional continuum that you will see in chapters throughout this text: (1) expose and explain, (2) recognize and identify, and (3) produce or apply (Fisher & Frey, 2008; Pearson & Gallagher, 1983).

TABLE 1.1	**General Principles of Vocabulary Instruction**

1. Select words that are useful in the world and important to understanding the classroom curriculum. Targeted vocabulary instruction should enhance what students already are beginning to understand.

2. Introduce new vocabulary in meaningful contexts, such as during a real-life experience or during a shared book activity. Be ready to define the word in terms children will understand. Use drawings, photos, or body motions to develop the children's understanding of the word.

3. Plan for repeated use of selected words and provide many opportunities for children to try out new words in guided settings. For a word to move from receptive to productive vocabulary, children will need to be able to use it themselves.

1. *Expose and explain.* As noted in Table 1.1, new vocabulary is best introduced in meaningful contexts. This includes real-life events such as building or cooking projects, short trips around school or the neighborhood, or through the use of visual texts or Internet-based materials. As a key term is introduced, make sure students see a picture, an object, or a pantomime of it so they can make a meaningful connection. For students learning English as a new language, consider previewing the least-familiar and most-essential vocabulary before presenting it to the whole class so they have an extra dose of its meaning (Helman, Bear, Invernizzi, Templeton, & Johnston, 2009). Provide examples of the key term in various contexts until students understand its unifying characteristics. For example, when studying the term *map,* students need to see many types of maps such as a wall map, a road map, a map of directions to a friend's house, and a map of land formations and water.

2. *Recognize and identify.* There are many ways to provide opportunities for students to work with the key vocabulary terms you are studying, such as through picture sorts (e.g., sort "maps" versus "not maps"), games that relate to the terms (e.g., bingo with map-related pictures), or additional texts or poems that feature the vocabulary. Guide students to "Point to the map on this page." Or ask, "What do we call this illustration?"

3. *Produce or apply.* As students become more familiar with the new vocabulary, the teacher gradually give them responsibility for demonstrating their understanding and using the vocabulary independently. This might include creating their own dictated stories using the terms or drawing and labeling their own pictures. Depending on the concept being studied, children may display their knowledge through projects, conversation, or group work. The goal is for students to use the new words and ideas appropriately and regularly so they become a part of their interactions in the world. For example, students may be asked to draw a map of part of the classroom and explain it to a friend.

To help students develop the deep and wide vocabulary knowledge they will need to succeed in their academic studies, teachers can't just teach vocabulary for a few minutes a day. Rather, vocabulary and language learning must become an integral part of all aspects of the early childhood classroom. In this section, we discuss many ways to build a language-rich environment that will support all students' vocabularies and advance oral language and concept development. We describe how classroom routines can be a context for word learning, how to use read-alouds, how to get students talking and using language, and how to develop big ideas and language through concept sorts.

Developing Language through Classroom Routines and Conversations

To create a language-rich classroom, engage children in talk throughout the day in many different activities. Greet children by name and ask them a question to start the day. Visit children in centers and during free play; engage them in talk about what they are doing. Snack time and lunchtime provides an opportunity to sit down in a small group and engage students in an extended conversation. Model how to introduce topics: "Do any of you have a pet at home?" or "What do you like to do at bedtime?" In Nee Xiong's preK classroom, she posts reminder cue cards at the tables to encourage the adults to create conversations with the children. The cards have questions and prompts such as, "Could you explain your answer?" and "Who can add on to what was said?" By modeling higher-level conversational skills, she demonstrates how to be a good listener who responds and probes for more information. This also builds conversational skills for children to use as they talk with each other during play time and lunchtime.

Sophisticated Words

Throughout the day, teachers have opportunities to model the use of "sophisticated" words for familiar concepts. Young children are usually delighted to use such "big" words (Beck, McKeown, & Kucan, 2013) and this emphasis helps to develop children's motivation to learn and enjoy words, their meanings, their sounds, and their pronunciations (Scott, Skobel, & Wells, 2008; Stahl & Stahl, 2012). For example, Lane and Allen (2010) describe how a kindergarten teacher begins the year by asking the "weather watcher" to report to the class using terms such as *sunny, cloudy,* or *warm.* Over time, the teacher gradually introduces new terms. After several weeks, for example, the appointed "meteorologist" was expected to *observe* the weather *conditions* and report her *forecast* using words such as *overcast, brisk,* or *frigid.*

Teachers should be on the lookout for, gradually teach, and consistently use more sophisticated synonyms for content studies; but they should also consider the common language of everyday routines. For example, students can *distribute, dispense,* or *allocate* materials. During discussions, encourage *participants* to *contribute* and *elaborate* their ideas and those of others. Before walking outside, the children may be asked to *assemble adjacent to* or *parallel to* the wall, and then to *proceed* in an *orderly* fashion. Compliment the children for being *courteous, amiable, agreeable, gracious,* and *considerate.* When children have learned the primary colors, introduce more nuanced color words such as *beige, maroon, lavender,* and *teal.*

As you work with young children, you should consciously take opportunities throughout the day to elevate your language, while always making sure that your messages are comprehensible to them. Provide appropriate explanations, repeated exposure, and opportunities for children to use that sophisticated vocabulary. Table 1.2 provides some possible terms for familiar concepts. Be selective about the ones you might want to include in your classroom.

Language in Centers

During center time, teachers should move about to observe and support children's play. McGee and Richgels recommend that teachers "sit and stay" for a few minutes to model language and engage children in conversations about what they are doing (McGee & Richgels, 2012, p. 196). As they build with blocks, make comments such as, "I see you used the larger block on the bottom and then the smaller block on top." As children work to put a puzzle together, provide them with language that helps them accomplish the task: "If you think the puzzle piece goes there, try turning it around." At the sand table you might reinforce the word *sift* in its various forms: "Here is the *sifter.* I am going to *sift* this dry sand. Would you like to try *sifting*?" Or you might describe what you see the child doing and ask questions: "I see you have been *constructing* something here. Can you tell me about it?" Note that this simple modeling addresses Common Core State Standard (CCSS) Language: 4, Vocabulary Acquisition and Use.

for Words Their Way®

At the PDToolkit, watch Jackie introduce vocabulary as children assemble a puzzle. Click the Videos tab and then choose Emergent Stage. Look for "Sealife Puzzle and Vocabulary."

McGee and Richgels (2012) also suggest keeping a list of words posted in centers as a reminder of vocabulary to use with children. Add to the lists as more words occur to you and save them from year to year. Encourage assistants or classroom volunteers to refer to the list of target vocabulary also. West and Cox (2004) list "spotlight words" for over three hundred play centers. Table 1.3 lists some examples related to particular centers that might be regularly incorporated into your informal conversations for repeated exposures over time.

Recasts, Expansions, and Questions

Two well-researched practices to use with young children to improve both syntax and vocabulary are recasts and expansions (McGinty & Justice, 2010). A *recast* acknowledges what the child says, but also provides corrective feedback without being negative. For example, in the vignette at the beginning of this chapter, the student said, "It tell are you cold or are you hot." Kristen recasts the sentence as, "It tells if it's cold or hot." An *expansion* involves repeating what the child says but adding just a bit more: "The thermometer tells us if it is hot or cold." Children are not asked to repeat what you say but they may often do so spontaneously.

Questioning is a way to encourage language, but be sure to use open-ended questions such as "What do you want to build with the blocks today?" rather than yes-no questions such as "Do you want to play with blocks?" Use the familiar WH question

TABLE 1.2 **Sophisticated Synonyms to Use in PreK–K Classrooms**

move/walk	pass out	tell/show	think
assemble	distribute	share	reflect
approach	deliver	*contribute/contribution*	imagine
proceed	allocate	assistance	consider
navigate	dispense	benefit	assume
progress		*respond*	ponder
advance		*participate*	infer
hustle		demonstrate	*identify*
		indicate	respond
		comment	*conclude/conclusion*
		observe	
		elaborate	

happy	nice	smart	tired
content	pleasant	brilliant	weary
relaxed	polite	bright	exhausted
calm	agreeable	clever	drowsy
pleased	considerate	sharp	fatigued
delighted	compassionate	intelligent	sluggish
thrilled	thoughtful	knowledgeable	
ecstatic	caring	on the ball	
appreciative	courteous	skillful	
grateful	understanding	capable	
	sociable		
	sensitive		

make	mad	collect	active
design	angry	gather	energetic
create	upset	*obtain*	vigorous
construct	annoyed	*select*	bouncy
build	cross	remove	lively
achieve	aggravated	replenish	calm
coordinate	frustrated		relaxed
cooperate	irritated		
illustrate	furious		
	enraged		
	infuriated		

Note: Italicized words can be found on the academic word list in Coxhead (2000).

TABLE 1.3 **Vocabulary Development in Centers**

Sand and water play	grains, gritty, damp, moist, clumps, sift, trickle, ripples, scoop, liquid, droplets, texture, measure, volume, mold, mounds, impression, containers, sieve, strainer
Blocks	construct, create, erect, assemble, organize, reorganize, elevate, destroy, dismantle, design, increase, shambles, elaborate, entrance, exit, reproduce
Restaurant	customers, servers, waiter/waitress, chef, delicious, recommend, suggestion, appetite, request, menu, expensive

starters—*Who, What, Where, When,* and *Why*—to engage children in a language exchange. "What is happening here? Why did you choose that? What do you notice? How can you solve that problem?" are all examples of open-ended questions. In Nee's preK classroom, students learned about germs and were asked how to prevent spreading germs. Students responded to this open-ended prompt with many good ideas, including washing with soap, brushing teeth, taking showers, and not touching things. The photo shows one child's effort to write a response. The teacher rewrote his statement below: "I learned if we don't wash our hands we get sick germs."

Show and Tell

Most children enjoy having time in the spotlight. Show and Tell provides an opportunity for children to get to know each other better, to use expressive language, and to respond to questions and comments from their peers. However, it needs to be carefully planned and conducted. Limit the time to three to five minutes total. That way, listeners will not be expected to sit for extended periods of time. Consider having only one or two students share per day. If you have a special student of the day, sharing could be that person's privilege. Also, keep in mind that some students may be homeless or have limited possessions to share. Encourage children to bring in whatever might be special to them or to share a favorite book or something from the classroom to avoid the perception that Show and Tell is about showing off new possessions (Otto, 2010). You can also encourage children to bring something to school related to a theme you are studying—but have a few extra items to share with students who do not have something to bring from home. This can be a good way to gather the materials for a concept sort (described later). Imagine the different ways you might sort stuffed animals brought from home: by size, color, clothing (versus no clothes), types of eyes, how well loved they look, and so on.

Reading Aloud to Enhance Vocabulary

There are many good reasons to read quality literature to children, not the least of which is to develop a love of books. Plan to read from a variety of genres with themes and topics appropriate for young children. Informational texts about seasons, weather, transportation, and how seeds grow provide new vocabulary and develop background information, especially when

I learned if we don't wash our hands we get sick germs.

included in thematic units of study (Pentimonti & Justice, 2010; Zucker & Landry, 2010). Through read-alouds, children are exposed to new words and more complex sentence structures, so it is not surprising that research has established that read-alouds are a source of vocabulary growth in young children (Biemiller & Boote, 2006; Whitehurst, Zevenbergen, Crone, Schultz, Velting, & Fischel, 1999).

SELECTING BOOKS. The best books for vocabulary development will offer more than simple repetitive language. Instead, consider books that offer rich language and enough complexity to enhance children's listening comprehension. Save simple books like *Brown Bear, Brown Bear, What Do You See?* by Bill Martin for shared reading, described in Chapter 4, an activity in which children are expected to memorize the text and approximate the act of reading by reading chorally with you. This distinction is important. A steady diet of simple text may not encourage the development of book-related vocabulary, exposure to literary language, or the development of comprehension strategies to the same extent as more complex literature.

Select books on topics that appeal to young children and that introduce vocabulary that is not likely to occur in everyday interactions. For example, books like *Corduroy* or *A Pocket for Corduroy* offer engaging stories to which young children can relate, but also include words like *escalator, amazing, palace,* and *enormous*—words that are good candidates for explicit instruction. Select read-alouds from a variety of genres: realistic fiction like *A Chair for My Mother* (Vera B. Williams), fantasy like *Harold's Purple Crayon* (Crockett Johnson), folk tales like *The Three Billy Goats Gruff* (Paul Galdone), information books like *Building a House* (Byron Barton), and poetry like *The Spider and the Fly* (Mary Howitt). Some books will be related to themes of study like animals or friendship, and others will be selected for pure pleasure.

REREADING. Young children love to hear their favorite books read and reread, and there is good reason to indulge them. Favorites become like old friends that are fun and comfortable to be with. More than that, repeated readings help to secure the syntax or sentence structures and vocabulary children have heard into their own memories. When Ellie was only three she spontaneously retold *Curious George* (H. A. and Margret Rey), pointing to the picture where George fell off the ship and saying, "George is struggling in the water." That was probably the only place she had heard the word *struggling,* but she had heard the book read many times and she naturally included the language in her retelling.

In busy classrooms you may feel that there is not enough time to reread books more than a few times, but you may ask classroom volunteers or older students to reread books that children request. (This can be a good opportunity for older students to practice reading books at a lower reading level that might not be acceptable in their

own classroom.) You can record favorite books or use commercial recordings so that children can listen to them again in a listening center. Students in Kilee Christnagel's kindergarten class enjoy listening to books on tape and then responding to writing prompts about their favorite parts, as shown in the photo. This encourages them to revisit the language introduced in the book. You can also send home books for parents to read. Jackie has a collection of favorites in plastic bags that children can check out to take home. Each bag contains a book as well as ideas for parents such as extension activities and questions for discussion.

SHARING BOOKS THROUGH MEDIATIONS. When sharing books with the very young, it is often the case that little reading actually occurs. Instead parents, caregivers, and teachers "talk through" a book in an interactive way known as *mediation.* These mediations reflect the adult's personal knowledge of what the child knows.

They are adapted to the child's interests and attention span. Like read-alouds, mediated sharing offers many opportunities to introduce new vocabulary words. Direct children's attention to pictures by labeling ("There's an elephant") or questioning ("Can you point to the lion?"). Encourage the child to respond by (1) labeling things in the pictures ("What is that?"), (2) talking about what is happening ("What is the zebra doing?"), and (3) making connections with his or her own life ("Have you ever been to the zoo?"). For young children, concept books that teach numbers, colors, opposites, and so forth are ideal because they have clear illustrations and limited amounts of text (one or two sentences to a page). They can be shared in small groups and one-on-one. When you do read the text, you might simplify the language or substitute words you think children are more likely to know.

This mediated experience is also valuable for children who are learning English. In small groups, children will have many more opportunities to participate, and you can monitor their attention and make adjustments as needed. The preK students in the photo formed an impromptu group around one student who was engaging in conversation about her book with an educational assistant. Although each student had a book of her or his own, they were pulled into the interesting questions and conversations being shared.

Four-year-olds will come to preschool with varying amounts of experience with books and differing tolerances for sitting still to listen to a read-aloud. Less-mature listeners with little book experience still need mediation in a small group or individual setting as described previously, and you might use classroom assistants and volunteers to help with these students. Other students will be able to listen to a reading for an extended time. Your ultimate goal will be that all the children develop the attention span to benefit from the group read-alouds. Invite all children to participate in the large-group session, but also allow children to leave if their ability to concentrate is not sufficient for the experience. You may find that previewing the book in a small group with English learners or students who are just building listening stamina prior to reading a book aloud will help them maintain their attention.

ENRICHING THE READ-ALOUD EXPERIENCE. There are several ways to make the read-aloud experience more productive in terms of vocabulary acquisition. Keep the principles listed in Table 1.1 in mind as you consider the following suggestions.

Adding Words to Simple Text

Even a simple text with limited words offers the potential for introducing new vocabulary as you discuss what is happening in the illustrations. For example, though *The Cat Sat on the Mat* by Brian Wildsmith is characterized by very simple predictable language, the cat experiences quite a range of emotions—from contented, to uneasy, to agitated, to furious—as more and more animals gather on the mat. Discussion of this book should include how the cat feels, with opportunities to introduce many synonyms for *happy, sad,* and *mad*—words that the children are likely to suggest. Discussing the illustrations will benefit English learners, in particular, who will be relying on those illustrations to understand much of the story. This is also an excellent opportunity to look up some of the synonyms in their home languages; *content* and *furious* turn out to be *contento* and *furioso* in Spanish!

Interactive Read-Alouds

Reading to children will often be done in an interactive way that stimulates lots of conversation as children respond with comments and questions and point out things they notice in the illustrations (Barrentine, 1996). This means that the teacher does not simply read as a performer, but as a facilitator of conversation, stopping as needed to encourage children's participation while keeping the flow of the book going. Although interactive read-alouds are the preferred way to share books, you may want to read through some books without interruptions the first time and then read them a second or third time in a more interactive way.

Extending Knowledge of Target Words

After selecting target vocabulary to develop before, during, and after a read-aloud, it is necessary to think about how to develop deeper and more extensive knowledge underlying these words (Templeton & Gehsmann, 2014). Beck and her colleagues (Beck, McKeown, & Kucan, 2002, 2008, 2013) suggest that we may do this by relating words to children's own experiences, associating new words with known words, and having children complete ideas that include the target vocabulary words. For example, in reading and rereading aloud to children a selection about artists and musicians, Regina Smith selected the target vocabulary words *important, combinations, ease,* and *rhythm*. She discussed them with the children in the context of the selection, defined them in kid-friendly language, and, over the course of a few days, engaged them as follows:

Relating Words to Children's Own Experiences

- "Which are *combinations* of foods—carrots and celery, or apples?"
- "Name three things that you can do with *ease*. Why are they so *easy* for you?"
- "What are some things that are *important* to you? Why are they important to you?"
- "Do you hear *rhythm* when you hear a cat meowing or when you listen to music?"

Associating New Words with Known Words and Phrases

- "Which word means something that matters a lot? (*important*)"
- "Which word means being able to do something that isn't hard? (*ease*)"
- "Which word describes what you have when you mix together different colors to make new colors? (*combinations*)"
- "Which word tells what you hear when we clap together to a song? (*rhythm*)"

Completing Ideas

- "You make a *combination* of things when you . . ."
- "You were able to finish your work with *ease* because. . ."
- "My little brother doesn't have *rhythm* when he dances because . . ."
- "The school assembly was *important* because . . ."

Anchored Vocabulary

Printing out words on cards that will be the focus of vocabulary instruction during a read-aloud is a way to anchor the meaning of the word to its sounds and spelling (Juel, Biancarosa, Coker, & Deffes, 2003). Supplement words with pictures to enhance meanings. (Use search engines to find images that you can electronically insert on the word card before printing.) These vocabulary cards will also serve as a reminder to review the words over time and in different contexts. Lesson 1.1 outlines the steps and provides an example that would be most appropriate in kindergarten. Two dictionaries for young children that are excellent resources for kid-friendly definitions are *The Longman Elementary Dictionary* (2010) and *The American Heritage First Dictionary* (2007). When Nee's preK class was studying about spring, the text she planned to read aloud provided an opportunity to introduce and practice many new words that were relevant to the season. She first introduced some of the vocabulary from the book using pictures. Then, during the reading of the text, the children were asked to notice when a key word was mentioned, and respond by enacting a quick body movement. They were also encouraged to talk about the illustrations using the key words. Nee periodically restated the kid-friendly definition or asked a relevant question as needed.

LESSON 1.1   Anchoring vocabulary

Reading *How Do Dinosaurs Say Good Night?* by Jane Yolen and Mark Teague provides an excellent opportunity for young children to learn verbs describing different types of behavior (e.g., *pout, mope, sulk*) and to become familiar with the written forms of frequently occurring words in speech and in print (e.g., *say, throw, about*). (CCSS Language: 4, Vocabulary Acquisition and Use)

Materials

A copy of *How Do Dinosaurs Say Good Night?* by Jane Yolen and Mark Teague and prepared cards such as *mope, swing,* and *demand.*

Step 1. Preview

Read *How Do Dinosaurs Say Good Night?* ahead of time and select a few words whose meanings may not be known to all of your children. Remember to focus on words that are important to the meaning of the story but are also likely to come up again in other stories. Write the words you select on cards in neat block letters and attach pictures when possible.

Step 2. Introduce the words

Before reading the story aloud, introduce the words along with a picture or object that illustrates each word. If the word is not a concrete object, act it out or create an icon that will help the group make a meaningful connection. Ask students whether they know the word or have an experience with it. Always try to use kid-friendly definitions with accessible language. For example, the word *mope* may be defined and acted out as "to be unhappy and move around very slowly."

Step 3. Anchor the word in memory

Do this by pointing to the word as you say it slowly, highlighting its beginning sound; then have the students repeat it with you. Point out the beginning sound and letter, saying, "*mope* begins with *m*: /mmmmm/ /ōp/."

Step 4. Read aloud

During the read-aloud, when you come to the word, hold up the card and briefly draw attention to it to remind students of its meaning and letter–sound properties. Ask someone to point to the word on the page of the book.

Step 5. Review immediately

After reading, go through the word cards once more and ask students to say the words, define the words, and perhaps use the words in a sentence that also recalls events in the story. For example, you might hold up *swing* and say, "What did the dinosaur swing from side to side?" Ask questions that use the words, such as "Would you ever *demand* something? Why?"

Step 6. Review over time

New word cards can be added to a growing set to be reviewed over time. Keep them handy and pull them out when you have a few minutes to spare and go through them. It is this continued exposure that will ensure that the words are retained over time. If children notice the anchored words in new contexts, make it a cause for great celebration. You can be deliberate in selecting new read-alouds with similar words such as *Where the Wild Things Are* (Maurice Sendak) and informational texts about dinosaurs: such texts provide excellent support for learning words related to parts of the body, size and amount, characteristics, and habitat. Children could also do concept sorts (described later in this chapter). During a unit on dinosaurs, for example, and learning some of their characteristics, the children may sort them by characteristics such as those that walk on two legs and those that walk on four legs.

EXTENDING THE READ-ALOUD EXPERIENCE. After sharing books with children, activities such as discussions and retellings will enhance their enjoyment and understanding of the story and offer opportunities to use some of the new vocabulary they have heard.

Retellings with Books

After children have heard a story in the context of a read-aloud, you may ask them to retell it. This process will encourage the use of new vocabulary and language patterns. To facilitate retellings, you will want to reread favorites and keep those books available so that children are able to revisit and explore them on their own. Children need to be taught how to do retellings. Begin by modeling: "When you revisit this book and look at it on your own, try to retell the story. Watch how I do that by looking at the pictures." Retell the story using the illustrations, several of the words and phrases in the story, and your own words. When you finish, go back through the book again, page by page, and call on different volunteers to talk about each page. You may need to prompt with some questions. Consider audiotaping the children's retellings; children love to hear themselves, and you might find that they are more eager to do a retelling when they are recorded so that they may listen to themselves afterwards.

A well-researched intervention, *dialogic reading,* is designed to stimulate children's oral language and enhance their ability to retell stories (Whitehurst, Arnold, et al., 1994). When parents and teachers of at-risk preschoolers have used dialogic reading, children grow in expressive and receptive language (Justice & Pullen, 2003; National Early Literacy Panel, 2008). In dialogic reading, children are gradually given more responsibility for retelling the story until they are able to retell with little or no assistance. Parents may be trained in dialogic reading, and books that have been read and discussed in class can be sent home with the children. After reading a book aloud, follow up with small groups or individual children to help them become the teller of the story. Morgan and Meier (2008) suggest the following steps, known as the PEER sequence, to support children's ability to retell:

P *Prompt* the child to say something about the book. Use open-ended questions. For example, while pointing to a picture in the book *Llama Llama Misses Mama* (Anna Dewdney) in which Llama Llama is pulling clothes out of the dresser, ask "What is Llama Llama doing?" The child says "Getting dressed."

E *Evaluate* the child's response: "That's right!"

E *Expand* the response by rephrasing or adding information to it: "He's going to put on the red sweater."

R *Repeat* your prompt, and ask the child to expand on it: "Tell me what Llama Llama is doing?" The child then replies, "He is getting dressed and putting on the red sweater."

You may use additional prompts to stimulate children's talk, such as the following:

1. Ask *what, when, where, why,* and *how* questions.
2. Leave a blank at the end of a sentence for the child to fill in.
3. Ask the children to *retell* what happened so far or at the end.
4. Ask the children to *describe* what they see happening in the pictures.
5. Ask the children to *make connections* with their own experiences.

Building a "Tower of Talk"

This activity models *how* to engage in a sustained conversation for preschool and kindergarten children by adding a block as each participant talks (Templeton & Gehsmann, 2014). Lesson 1.2 offers an example for introducing this activity to children.

LESSON 1.2   Tower of talk

Children do not always understand the turn taking and contributions expected in a conversation. The concrete use of Unifix cubes, blocks or other colored counting objects can help children master these concepts. (CCSS Speaking & Listening: 1a, 1b, and 3, Comprehension and Collaboration)

Step 1. Explain and model

Show children how this activity works in a "fishbowl" setting by choosing two or three children to model in the middle while the other children watch. Choose a topic that is interesting and familiar to the children, such as a recent field trip, the gerbil babies that suddenly appeared this morning, or a favorite read-aloud book. Tell the children, "In this activity, we will be working on listening to each other and taking turns talking. When someone adds to our conversation, they will add a Unifix cube to our Tower of Talk."

Pass out two or three Unifix cubes to each child who will be in the fishbowl with you. Each child should have his or her own color. Begin the conversation: "We discovered eight gerbil babies in the gerbil cage this morning!" While you are speaking, put your Unifix cube on the floor in front of the children.

Step 2. Invite participation

Ask the children to reply to what you just said with another statement or a question. When each child responds, he or she adds a cube to the Tower of Talk. You may need to remind the children how important it is to take turns and not speak over each other. Children may be reluctant to contribute to the conversation, so you will also model how to invite them into the conversation: "I've noticed that Darrell hasn't added to our conversation lately, so I'm going to ask him a question: Darrell, what did you think when you first saw our gerbil babies this morning?" After Darrell shares, ask him to add one of his cubes to the tower. If Darrell doesn't share, however, you may lean over and whisper a possible comment into his ear, encouraging him to add it to the conversation. Your goal is to keep the conversation going until all the children's Unifix cubes are gone.

Step 3. Reflect on the process

After the fishbowl demonstration, talk with all of the children about what they noticed as they listened to your conversation. Emphasize the importance of mentioning what someone else has said or building onto what they've said.

Step 4. Extend

Provide all the children the opportunity to try out the Tower of Talk activity with a buddy or a small group. Children usually are excited and delighted to see their tower grow—it's not long before they will be requesting more Unifix cubes so they can really grow their Towers of Talk! Once children have practiced this activity several times, remind them about using these "acknowledging and extending" skills in other contexts such as in a discussion of a read-aloud or during Show and Tell.

Turn and Talk

This activity is an excellent way to increase opportunities for children to exercise language, thought, and vocabulary use through oral interaction. Assign partners, and ask children to turn and talk to their partner during a discussion or read-aloud. In contrast to the traditional practice of calling on one child, through Turn and Talk every child has the opportunity to respond to a question, share

an experience, make a prediction, summarize, and so forth. Children who are reluctant to speak in front of a larger group (because they are less verbal, shy, or learning the language) are usually more comfortable when talking with a partner. The steps are as follows:

1. Model your expectations for Turn and Talk with another adult. Demonstrate how partners will take turns, and suggest ways to encourage a partner who is reluctant to talk: "Tell me what you think"; "It's your turn now"; or "You go first this time." You may also call on two children who do a particularly good job together to model for the rest of the group. Children should turn knee to knee and eye to eye, and talk softly so as not to distract others. In Nee's preK classroom, each partnership in a Turn and Talk has two Popsicle sticks—one with a mouth pictured and one with an ear. Students who hold the ear first are the listeners, and the ones with a mouth on their stick are the talkers. After a short time, the children change sticks and take a different role. This scaffolding ensures that all students are practicing both speaking and listening.

2. Partners could be selected before the read-aloud or other shared experience begins, or you may allow children to pick their own partners on the way to the group and then sit down together. When selecting partners, take into consideration children's language competence and confidence. A more verbal child may provide a model for a less verbal child, but he or she might also dominate the conversation, so watch to see how pairs work out and be ready to intervene with suggestions about ways to give the less verbal child an equal opportunity. The same partners might be established for a week or longer. This can save organizational time.

3. Bring Turn and Talk time to a close by offering a countdown warning. Slowly and steadily count down: "5, 4, 3, 2, 1." As children notice, they should stop their conversations and put attention on the teacher. How much time you allow will vary but bring Turn and Talk time to a close before children lose their focus and get off the assigned topic; this will typically be only a couple of minutes.

4. As children talk with their partners, listen in to monitor their conversations. When everyone is back together, you may call on one or two children to share what they talked about. Because the less verbal or shy children have already been sharing their ideas with their partners during Turn and Talk, they may now be more confident in speaking before the larger group.

Think Pair Share

Another way to enhance oral language interactions is Think Pair Share. Once students learn to do Turn and Talk, this will be an easy variation that provides think time to engage with a topic at hand and ends with the opportunity to share ideas in the larger group. The steps are as follows:

1. *Think*. During a read-aloud or discussion, instead of immediately raising their hands to answer a question, make a prediction, share an experience, or define a word, the children are asked to think of their own response for a few moments.

2. *Pair*. Students then turn and either talk to a partner or their small group. As with Turn and Talk, you might assign partners or groups in advance; they may stay together for a week or more. You should, however, observe the pairs or groups to make sure all children are participating.

3. *Share*. After everyone has had a chance to talk, you may call on individual or groups to report back to the larger group. As you listen in on the groups, you might identify ideas or examples that seem particularly worthwhile, and request that the children who came up with them share with the larger group.

Turn and Talk and Think Pair Share activities provide excellent extensions to read-alouds or other experiences. When children understand their format, they may apply them as they interact with their peers and apply their understanding of concepts and vocabulary in other planned activities such as cooperative learning formats or centers (Wasik, Bond, & Hindman, 2006). These and other engaging activities that prompt children to report and retell encourage them to use new words and more complex sentence constructions (Ward, 2009).

Creative Dramatics

Like dramatic play centers (such as housekeeping or the post office) where children invent their own scenarios, creative dramatics are a way to encourage children's self-expression as well as vocabulary development. During creative dramatics, children act out memorable scenes from stories they have heard. This is first done under adult direction with the aim of retelling the story and involving lots of children as actors or audience. You will want to brainstorm with children about what characters will be needed and what each character will do. Then walk through your dramatization, posing questions and prompting language. Children are encouraged to add dialog or scenes to add to the story. Many children's picture books work (folktales are particularly good), but the following two compilations have brief stories ready to read to children with scenes to dramatize.

- Siks, G. B. (1958). *Creative dramatics: An art for children.* New York, NY: Harper & Row.
- Ward, W. (1952). *Stories to dramatize.* Anchorage, KY: The Children's Theatre Press.

Children can also be encouraged to make up their own stories. Bhattacharyya (2010) describes a kindergarten classroom in which children dramatize familiar personal narratives and fairy tales as the basis for composing their own stories, both oral and written.

Stimulate retellings and dramatizations by supplying props such as puppets, flannel board cutouts, objects used in the story, or plastic figures. After you model the use of props or puppets with the whole class, place them in a center or make them available during activity time for children to use on their own. However, props are not always necessary in creative dramatics. To prepare for dramatizing a story, follow these steps:

1. After listening to a story, ask students to select a character and think about how that particular character acts—roaring like a lion after hearing *Leo the Lion,* or stirring the pot of pasta like Anthony in *Strega Nona* (Tomie dePaola).
2. Reread a short scene from a story; then have three or four students act out the scene through movement and recalling a few lines.
3. Ask children who were observing to share what they liked, as well as what might be improved the next time.
4. Ask another three or four students to try the same scene.

Acting Out Meanings

Young children love any type of movement activity. As they encounter new words through read-alouds and your use of sophisticated words (see page 13), take advantage of opportunities to act out the children's developing understandings (CCSS Language: Vocabulary Acquisition and Use: 4a, 5a, 5b, 5c, and 6, Vocabulary Acquisition and Use). For example, to support children's understanding of different types of words describing the act of walking after discussing the word *saunter* in Ezra Jack Keats's *A Snowy Day,* you may first demonstrate the terms *saunter, stroll, trot, meander, march, stride, tiptoe,* or *sashay* and then invite the children to do these actions (Templeton & Gehsmann, 2014). In so doing, you are supporting their developing awareness of the shades of meaning, or nuances, among words (Common Core State Standards, 2010). Verbs such as *walk, stroll,* and *march* are a good starting point because they are the easiest for children to distinguish between. Adjectives are just a bit more challenging, so begin with the frequently occurring ones such as *happy, sad, tiny, enormous,* and invite children to demonstrate them through facial expressions and bodily movement. This is particularly effective with children learning English.

Antonyms

Support children's explicit understanding of the relationships between words and the concepts they represent through an exploration of *antonyms*—words that are opposite in meaning. Begin by sharing concept books about opposites such as Eric Carle's *Opposites* or *Exactly the Opposite* by Tana Hoban, which feature colorful illustrations. Then engage children in acting out antonyms as they follow along with your directions and modeling. Call out commands such as these:

- Take a **big** step. Take a **little** step.
- Walk **fast**. Walk **slow**.
- Point **up**. Point **down**.
- Clap your hands **loudly**. Clap your hands **quietly**.
- Point to a **light** place in the room. Point to a **dark** place.
- Put your hand **over** your head. Put your hand **under** your chin.
- Make a **happy** face. Make a **sad** face.
- **Open** your mouth. **Close** your mouth.
- Raise your **right** hand. Raise your **left** hand.
- Come **here**. Go **there**.
- Show me how you feel when you are **hot**. When you are **cold**.
- Pretend to lift a **heavy** box. Pretend to lift a **light** box.
- Stand **on** the rug. Stand **off** the rug.
- Go **in** the door. Go **out** the door.

Once children are good at following your directions, challenge them by saying, "Show me the opposite of happy. Show me the opposite of fast." Watch for different ways that they act out the opposites.

Experiences and Conversation

Reading aloud to children provides virtual experiences that can stimulate oral language and vocabulary learning, but real experiences with cooking, science experiments, special visitors, classroom pets, field trips, and so on are especially engaging and provide opportunities for verbal interactions. These experiences will be particularly important for English learners, but the presence of the "real world" is engaging for all young children. It is easy to think that experiences and conversations just happen, and, to a certain extent, they do; but planned experiences with careful attention to vocabulary and concepts are more likely to be fruitful. Even better, combining read-alouds with experiences supports the necessary repetition of targeted vocabulary and promotes linkages that facilitate learning. Because it is important for children to encounter new words and concepts in different ways, planning experiences that promote vocabulary learning and help maintain that vocabulary over time is critical.

Let's say you have conducted a series of read-alouds about animals that make good pets, and you have decided to get a hamster for the classroom. The concepts and vocabulary that you could develop and use over time might include *hamster, male, female, habitat, nutrition, diet, exercise, bedding, gnaw,* and *nocturnal.* These words represent conceptual understandings you can develop about hamsters and are words children can then use in their daily conversations about hamsters. Use the same criteria outlined earlier to select words: utility, concreteness, opportunities for repetition, and relatedness to theme. An experience like caring for a classroom pet can lead to lots of reading and writing activities as well. You might create labels with the students' help for the cage, water bottle, and exercise ball. Students might dictate their observations and insights about hamsters in the language experience approach (described in Chapter 6) or participate in an interactive writing activity (described in Chapter 4). In addition, you might ask students to illustrate and write about hamsters in their own journals.

Concept Sorts: Developing Big Ideas and Language

The human mind works by using a compare-and-contrast categorization system to develop concepts and establish relationships between concepts. Through comparing and contrasting objects and their features or attributes, children are able to create groups or categories (Clark, 2003). This process is the foundation of critical thinking (Gillet & Kita, 1979). At all levels of development, learners categorize objects, pictures, words, or phrases in what we call **concept sorts**. The ability to categorize demonstrates maturing thinking, but this thinking needs to be developed through children's conversations about why and how they are categorizing objects and pictures.

Children's vocabulary grows and becomes more precise as they develop more complex concepts. You play an important role by labeling objects, actions, events, and feelings in meaningful contexts (Otto, 2010). For example, a young child might call any ride-on plaything a "bike" and point to a tricycle when asking for a turn. Your response might be, "Do you want to ride the tricycle? Tricycles have three wheels." By supplying labels as well as the distinguishing characteristics, the child's conceptual web or **semantic field** for "playthings with wheels" can grow to include big wheels, tractors, wheelbarrows, wagons, and scooters.

Concept sorts can develop deeper understanding about underlying concepts and the words that label these concepts, as well as how these concepts/words relate to other concepts and words within a semantic field. For example, a picture sort of vehicles might be used to extend a child's concepts by assigning things with motors into one category and things that needed to be pedaled, pulled, or pushed into another. See Figure 1.1 for how such a sort might look along with labels agreed on by the children. The same pictures could also be sorted by the number of wheels (one: wheelbarrow; two: bicycle, scooter, and motorcycle; three: tractor and tricycle) or by those that have handles and those that have steering wheels. By attending to features such as wheels, motors, handlebars, and pedals and talking about these during the sorting process, children acquire more precise concepts as well as labels. Basic concept sorting tasks are a surprisingly simple way to engage English verbal interactions (Bear & Helman, 2004).

FIGURE 1.1 Concept Sort for Vehicles

CONCEPT SORTS WITH CONCRETE OBJECTS. For young children, we begin sorting activities with concrete objects, then move to sorting activities with pictures. Concrete sorting activities (see Lesson 1.3 for an example) may involve, for example, pasta, buttons, or miniature dinosaur figurines. These objects are sorted by size, shape, color, or other attributes that children may notice. Using such concrete objects is an excellent way to introduce children to the idea or process of sorting. Importantly, they become aware of particular attributes and develop the ability to categorize objects according to those attributes through their growing awareness of comparison and contrast. At first, it is difficult for most young children to stay focused on a single attribute—they may start off sorting by shape and then, in the middle of the activity, switch to color. As children have the opportunities to sort real, concrete objects that have different features, encourage and support them in *talking about* why they are sorting the objects the way they are. By beginning with concrete sorts, you are setting the stage for moving to picture sorts and eventually phonics sorts, described in Chapter 5.

The children may sort many different types of concrete objects—including themselves—and there are many ways of exploring the different types of categories and their attributes or features. Here are some additional possibilities:

- Children: male/female, age, favorite color, wearing pants/shorts/dresses
- Bottle caps: material (plastic or metal), size, color, print/no print, texture
- Buttons: two holes/four holes/no holes, shapes, colors, size
- Shoes: girls'/boys', right/left, tie/Velcro/slip-on
- Mittens and gloves: knit/woven, right/left
- Lunch containers: boxes/bags, plastic/metal/nylon
- Legos: color, shape, number of pegs, length
- Food: sweet, sour, bitter, salty, fruits, vegetables, grains

LESSON 1.3 Pasta sort

Sorting different types of pasta according to the basic attributes of size, shape, or color is an excellent way to introduce the idea of concrete concept sorts. (CCSS Language: 5a, Vocabulary Acquisition and Use)

Materials

This sort will require three to six types of pasta that vary in size and in shape. You may either buy two or three different colors of pasta or you may dye your own: Shake the pasta in a jar with a tablespoon of alcohol and a few drops of food coloring, then lay it out on newspaper to dry. Make sure that each color has a variety of shapes and sizes. Children can sort the pasta on paper divided into columns as shown in Figure 1.2, or simply into piles.

FIGURE 1.2 Paste the Pasta

Step 1. Invite students to sort and assess

Give each child a handful of pasta and a sorting paper. Ask children to come up with their own way of grouping the pasta. This will provide you the opportunity to evaluate which children understand attribute sorting and which will need more guidance. When they finish their first sort, ask the children to share their groups. Discuss *how* they decided to place different pieces of pasta in different groups or categories. Emphasize the different ways—the different features or attributes—by which they can sort.

Step 2. Model

If most or all of the children do not appear to understand how to come up with their own groupings, then you will model one possibility: "Hmmm . . . Let's see: Are all of our pasta pieces the same color? What different colors do we have? I wonder . . . What do you think? Could we sort our pasta by the different colors? We could? Let's try that!" You could then model how to begin the sort, saying "I'm going to look first for all of my red pieces of pasta. . . ." and so on.

Step 3. Ask the children to re-sort

Decide on a category different from the first one to sort again. To conclude the lesson, as well as have a concrete example and reminder of their sort, have the children glue the pasta onto their paper by categories; then label the sort. At first, you may label them, but, depending on the children's knowledge about print and the alphabet (see Chapters 2, 3, and 4), you may encourage them to write their own label.

for Words Their Way®

Watch Kristen do a concept sort with weather-related words at the PDToolkit. Click the Videos tab and then choose Emergent Stage. Look for "Vocabulary Development and Concept Sorting."

CONCEPT SORTS WITH PICTURES. Pictures are used in concept sorts to expand children's vocabulary and to encourage rich verbal interactions. For example, after talking and reading about concepts related to weather, children can sort pictures of mittens, sandals, sunscreen, jackets, and galoshes. Teachers should model and use the language of comparison and contrast: *bigger than, smaller than, not as large as,* and so forth. This explicit attention to language helps children unpack what they tacitly know about the concepts underlying the labels, and becomes part of their own discussions about words and concepts. Concept sorts for English learners are particularly worthwhile because pictures can be sorted into categories without knowing the English terms. At the same time, native-English-speaking partners can supply unknown words, and, in the process of talking about the sort, new vocabulary is learned and exercised.

Pictures may be glued down into categories and children can be encouraged to label the pictures and categories, spelling as best they can as shown in Figure 1.3. In addition they should have the opportunity to write about their sorts and what they are noticing and learning. After exploring animals and comparing and contrasting farm animals with zoo animals, one kindergarten teacher helped the children create their own animal books. In addition to drawing pictures of their favorite animals, the children were asked by their teacher to write about an animal or animals. Their efforts ranged from scribbles and random letters to "readable" text—for example, I LIK THE LINS N TGRS.

The pictures used in concept sorts may be words that are new to students, and they need to be directly taught. It will be important to talk about the meaning of the word and to use the words repeatedly each time they are used in sorting. For example, when sorting birds and animals, it may be helpful to stop and talk about the meanings of the words *claw* and *hoof*. English learners may also be acquiring the names of more common objects, such as *pig* and *duck*. As they sort, the children should be encouraged to name the pictures; this provides additional practice, and the words become more familiar as the children hear one another pronouncing the new words. The children should then be asked to describe their categories.

BOOKS AND CONCEPT SORTS. Concept sorts are also an easy way to extend read-alouds and provide additional exposure to new vocabulary (Carpenter, 2010). After listening to *Are You a Butterfly?*, children are provided picture cards to sort into three groups: butterflies, caterpillars, and eggs. Through this type of categorization activity, children move beyond their basic awareness of butterflies to an understanding of the life cycle of egg to caterpillar to butterfly to egg. This book also presents an excellent opportunity to develop oral language with creative dramatics as children re-enact events in the life cycle of a butterfly. Lesson 1.4 offers an example using the picture storybook *Froggy Gets Dressed* (Jonathan London), and Lesson 1.5 is based on a book about colors.

> **Read more about encouraging children's writing in Chapters 3 and 5.**

LESSON 1.4 Concept sort for clothing

Froggy Gets Dressed, by Jonathon London, tells the story of a young frog who wants to go outside and play in the snow but needs to put on his winter clothing first. He has plenty to remember, and children will giggle along as he forgets essential pieces of clothing. (CCSS Foundational Skills: 1b, Print Concepts; 2d, Phonological Awareness; 3a, Phonics and Word Recognition; CCSS Language: 5a and 5c, Vocabulary Acquisition and Use)

Materials

Collect real objects or pictures of items suggested by *Froggy Gets Dressed*—for example, socks, boots, hats, scarves, mittens, and pants. Also have on hand objects or pictures of items that children would not wear out in the cold, such as a bathing suit or sandals.

Step 1. Invite students to sort

After reading *Froggy Gets Dressed,* the children can be introduced to a concept sort. Gather together around a large table or pocket chart, and ask them to choose the items they would need to put on before going out in the snow. Place those items in one pile. Place items that are not appropriate for cold weather in a separate pile.

(continued)

LESSON 1.4   Concept sort for clothing (*continued*)

Step 2. Sort, check, reflect, and re-sort

After the items have been sorted, ask the children to describe how the items in each category are alike. Then ask them to think about a word or words that "we can use to describe or label each of our groups." They might describe the categories as "for the cold" and "for a warm day," for example. Print their selected words on cards, making sure they can see you as you write. Say each word slowly and talk about the sounds you hear in the words and the letters you need to spell them. You might also give each child in the group a card to label one of the individual items in a group, sounding out the name as best as they are able.

Step 3. Individual sorting

Keep the items and key word cards available so that children will be free to redo the sort on their own or with a partner at another time, perhaps during free time or center time. Encourage them to talk as they sort.

Step 4. Paste and label

Divide a section of a bulletin board or a large sheet of paper into two sections, each labeled with a key word. If children work independently, a sheet of paper may be folded into two sections. Children may be asked to draw items, or they might be given a collection of magazines or catalogs to search for pictures to cut out and paste into the correct category. You will need to model how to look through magazines and catalogs at first: Turn each page slowly, spending time looking at each page, encouraging the children to name what they see, then deciding whether the pictures fit their categories. Encourage them to write and label the pictures.

Step 5. Extend

Froggy Gets Dressed is a great introduction to healthy dressing habits. The same pictures the children have drawn or cut out can serve as the beginning pictures for categories such as "What can cover my legs, chest, or head?" You can also sort clothing by color, design, or fabric.

LESSON 1.5   Concept color sort

Concept books are designed around a single topic like colors, opposites, shapes, or numbers and provide an excellent introductions to concept sorts. To introduce a color sort, start with a book like *Mary Wore Her Red Dress and Henry Wore His Green Sneakers* (Merle Peek), *Is It Red? Is It Yellow? Is It Blue?* (Tana Hoban), or *White Rabbit's Color Book* (Alan Baker). (CCSS Language: 2d, Conventions of Standard English; 5c, Vocabulary Acquisition and Use)

Step 1. Share the book

Because concept books are primarily illustrations and have little text, engage children in discussing what they see. Then provide the appropriate labels: "This is a book about colors. Here is a picture of a toy school bus. What color is the school bus? Yes, the school bus is yellow. Now it's your turn. What do you see here?"

Step 2. Sort objects or pictures

If you've not already done so, get in the habit of collecting objects or pictures of objects that you may use for your sorting activities. When preparing for your children's sorting based on color, you should be able to find real objects around the classroom such as toys, markers, and books. Explain to the children that they are going to help you sort the objects by color. Model how you will do this, using complete sentences: "Here is a red ball. I will put the ball with the other things that are red." After the sort is completed, support children in making generalizations such as, "How are all these things alike? Yes, all the things in this category are *red*."

Step 3. Label

With help from the children, make labels for each category: "Boys and girls, I am going to label this category by writing 'red' on this card. What letter do you think I need to write down first? Listen, *rrrr*-ed...."

Step 4. Independent work

Place sorts where children can easily access them on their own, preferably with a partner, and encourage them to talk as they sort. In addition, students can look for more pictures in magazines or catalogs that fit the categories. They may also draw pictures, cut them out, and then paste them into their categories. Importantly, they should be encouraged to write the name of each category.

THEMATIC UNITS AS A STARTING POINT FOR CONCEPT SORTS. Concept sorts in the context of thematic units of study provide a rich opportunity for introducing, reviewing, and extending the learning.

Animal Concept Sort

This sort is an excellent way to introduce a thematic unit. You will need plastic animals or animal pictures.

Ask children to think of ways that the animals can be grouped together. They may notice different possibilities, such as fur or feather coat, dangerous or not dangerous, and color. Children will often realize that some animals may be grouped in more than one way. If your unit is based on exploring animal *habitats,* then you will guide the children in sorting animals according to the places they live. If you are studying the food chain, you may guide the children in sorting the animals according to meat eaters, plant eaters, and those that eat both. In addition to the great vocabulary that will come up related to animal and food names, children will also develop an important concept that later in their academic experience will help them access the more sophisticated labels of *carnivores, herbivores,* and *omnivores.*

Fruit and Vegetable Concept Sort

Bring a collection of real or plastic fruits and vegetables to share or use pictures of fruits and vegetables. This sort may be introduced through books featuring food.

1. Display the pictures and invite the children to think of those that might go together. Encourage them to think of several possibilities. Record the ideas on a chart. Some possibilities include big/little, fruit/vegetable, peel it/don't peel it, green/not green, and tastes sweet/doesn't taste sweet.
2. Sort the produce by the identified categories, and talk about why each item is sorted into a particular category: "An apple is a fruit, so I will put it with the orange and grapes."
3. After discussing different categories, have the children decide the suggestion they each liked the best. Give kindergarten children construction paper to label their categories. They can then draw or cut out pictures for each category. Encourage them to label their pictures and categories, as shown in Figure 1.3.

FIGURE 1.3 Fruits and Vegetables Sort

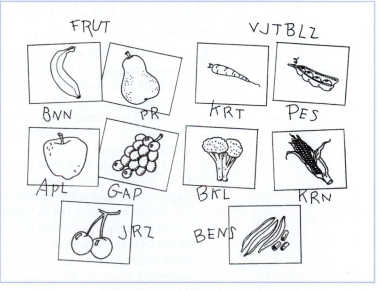

Keeping Track of Vocabulary Growth

Instructional activities described in this chapter such as retellings and concept sorts can also be used to measure progress in children's vocabulary growth. Teachers can note increases in word use by tallying the number of ideas, facts, or concepts expressed in the retelling or in the explanation of the sort. Retell assessments have been shown to be authentic, valid, and reliable means of assessing understanding (Fuchs, Fuchs, & Maxwell, 1988). Noting the number of objects, pictures, or items correctly sorted into conceptual categories can also yield a reliable means of assessing depth of receptive vocabulary (Ward, 2009). Other developmentally appropriate ways of assessing receptive vocabulary growth in emergent learners include pointing to pictures that answer direct questions (e.g., "Which picture is the veterinarian?") or answering sets of yes/no questions (e.g., "Is an acorn a seed?" "Do plants grow from seeds?" "Do all seeds look the same?"). Kearns and Biemiller (2010/2011) have validated a simple vocabulary measure that asks children to get two yes/no questions correct for a particular word to assess their knowledge of it. For example, to assess the word *season*, you might ask, "Is fall a season when leaves turn brown?" (yes) and "Is it an example of a season when I go to bed?" (no).

Connecting with Families and Communities

There are many ways that parents can support vocabulary learning (Templeton, 2009). Figure 1.4 provides an example of the kind of letter you might want to send home. In addition, remember to translate letters so they can be understood by families of children learning English as a new language.

Frequently Asked Questions about Bilingual Language Learning

Many teachers and parents have questions about how using students' home languages affects their learning of English. They often fear that working with two or more languages will confuse children or cause them to be delayed in their language learning. In this section we briefly address some of the questions that have come up in our work with early childhood educators and families regarding oral language learning in more than one language.

1. *Are children likely to experience confusion or language delays because of exposure to two or more languages?* De Houwer (1995) clearly outlines the research base: There is no evidence that students who operate in multilingual worlds are any more likely to experience language delay or become confused in their language acquisition. Instead, the use of the home language can provide great support for the acquisition of a new language. In addition, becoming bilingual can be a socially and intellectually empowering experience.

2. *What if a student uses more than one language within the same sentence or conversation?* Code switching (or moving between languages or registers within languages) can happen in many ways—at the level of the conversation, the sentence or phrase, or even within a word. For example, a student who is explaining an event that occurred may introduce a word that is unique in one language because there is no direct translation or it holds special cultural meaning (e.g., "My *tío* came to visit."). As students learn language they can also play with its forms, such as when one student added *-cito* (showing affection) to the end of his friend's name in class (*Briancito*). These creative

FIGURE 1.4 Letter to Parents

Dear Parent,

You play an important role in helping your child develop vocabulary and learn new things about the world through oral language. This knowledge is the foundation for the more advanced reading and writing your child will do throughout the grades.

Talk with your child. Explain what you are thinking or doing ("I'm hungry. It's time to fix some lunch."). Ask questions that require more than a yes or no response ("What shall we make?" rather than "Do you want a peanut butter sandwich?"). Use new words ("Let's make something *delicious*."). Share observations ("I saw a squirrel stealing bird food this morning."). Invite your child to respond ("Why do you think he is taking the seeds? Maybe he will store them up for winter.") You do not need to teach children how to talk, but you need to model your own talk and encourage them to talk.

Teach your child nursery rhymes, jump rope jingles, and songs that you remember from your own childhood. Explain what any unusual words mean. Change the words in the songs or make up your own songs or rhymes with your child's name.

Read to your child from a variety of books. Take the time to point out things in pictures and explain the meaning of words they might not understand. Encourage your child to ask questions and say things about the story. Reread favorite books and take turns letting your child "read" to you. Pretending to read is an important first step in learning to read.

Tell your child stories and encourage your family to tell stories. Storytelling is a way that cultures have passed on values and traditions for millions of years and it is a way to build relationships with others. Families often have their own collection of stories to share, like the time Granddad lost his glasses in the snow or the time Aunt Crissy brought home a lost puppy. Children love to hear about the things you did as a child or the things they did when they were younger. In addition you can tell traditional stories like folktales and fairy tales instead of reading aloud.

uses of language should not be seen as errors, but rather as children's meaningful application of multiple language systems.

3. *As a teacher, should I ask parents to speak in English at home with their children?* Basically, the answer to this question is no. Children need their parents to speak to them in the language they know best, and as educators we want to encourage the multilingual potentials of our students. When students learn words and concepts in their home languages, educators can build on that conceptual knowledge in English at school. Children who learn rhymes and stories in their home languages will be better able to appreciate others in English. Children who suddenly experience a withdrawal of a home language are likely to experience emotional and psychological difficulties (De Houwer, 1995). Encouraging parents to use only the language of schooling also decreases the self-esteem and bilingual capacities of the child.

4. *What if I don't speak the home languages of my students?* In today's linguistically diverse classrooms, even bilingual teachers are unlikely to speak the languages of all their students. There are still many things you can do to help your students use their home languages to learn English, and you can show your interest by learning about their home languages.

   • Ask students to teach you words from their home languages.
   • When you teach a new word, ask students to share what it is called in their home language.

- Allow students to translate ideas into their home languages for each other.
- Encourage students to tell or write stories in their home language.
- Bring in print or audio materials in students' home languages.
- Invite family members or community representatives who speak other languages to come to the classroom.
- Send notes to families in students' home languages so that classroom ideas can be discussed in a familiar language.
- Get excited about the many languages you hear in your classroom, and notice their commonalities and unique aspects.

Multilingual Resources

There are many web-based resources available to support you in learning about and including multilingual materials from a variety of heritage languages in your preK or kindergarten classroom. A quick search of "rhymes in _____" (language background), or "cultural information about _____" (ethnic or cultural group) will lead to plenty of examples that will open doors to new perspectives and understandings. Sometimes even this small amount of information will help you in framing questions and conversations with students and their families. In addition, school districts that experience a substantial influx of students from particular linguistic backgrounds often post dictionaries, cultural information, and translations of parent education materials on their websites. Look online for the UCLA Language Materials Project for background information and teaching resources for more than 150 languages. In the current digital age, knowledge about the worlds our students come from is literally at our fingertips.

Alphabet: Letter Recognition and Production

he traditional simple song known as "Bingo" is easily taught to four- and five-year-olds and can be used to help them learn the alphabet. The song goes like this: "There was a farmer had a dog and Bingo was his name-oh. B-I-N-G-O, B-I-N-G-O, B-I-N-G-O, And Bingo was his name-oh." The verse repeats, but instead of naming the first letter, the children clap for the *B*: [clap]-*I-N-G-O. On* the third round the first two letters are replaced with claps and the last verse replaces claps for all five of the letters. (There are many versions of this on YouTube if you don't know the song.)

After teaching children the song "Bingo" over several days, Jackie lays out large alphabet cards for each of the five letters, explaining to her preK class that the letters spell the dog's name. The children work together to put the letters in order to spell Bingo, and then children line up to take turns stepping from card to card as the letters are called in the song. As the song progresses to the next round, a letter is turned over to indicate a clap until all the letters are face down. (Children could also be given the letter cards to hold up as it is named, turning each card around when it is to be replaced with a clap.) Jackie has created an additional version of the song featuring her dog Lucky. The song then goes like this: "There was a teacher had a dog and Lucky was his name-o. L-U-C-K-Y . . ." Children whose names are spelled with five letters could also be featured: "There was a teacher had a boy and Jacob was his name-o." Additional versions give children practice with additional letters. After modeling this with a large group, Jackie makes the letter cards available during free play time and children do the activity independently. A similar activity can be done with the song "Old MacDonald Had a Farm" using letter cards for the traditional E, I, E, I, O or a variation such as A, E, I, O, U.

FIGURE 2.1 Direction Matters in Print

Alphabet knowledge is the strongest early predictor of later reading success (Adams, 1990; Snow, Burns, & Griffin, 1998). This should not be too surprising when you consider that visual familiarity with the letters and the ability to distinguish between them is necessary to make sense of printed words. However, there is a lot to learn about the alphabet itself. Letters have names, sounds, shapes, a set order, upper- and lowercase forms, and they must be written in particular ways.

The letters of the alphabet are arbitrary abstract symbols that can take children several years to learn completely. Of the 26 capital and 26 lowercase letters, there are only 12 whose upper and lowercase shapes are identical or almost so (*Ss, Xx, Pp,* etc.), leaving 40 distinctive shapes to learn (Ehri & Roberts, 2006). Letters that share common visual features, such as *m* and *n* or *i* and *j*, may be confused for some time. And, unlike other aspects of life, directional orientation is vital. In the three-dimensional world, a cup is a cup whether you approach it from the left or from the right or the top, as shown in Figure 2.1. Not so with letters: A *b* is a *b* and a *d* is a *d*. Direction makes a difference in print.

Letter Names and Letter Recognition

The first step in learning the alphabet for most children is learning the letter names in sequence as they sing the traditional ABC song. A list of these letter names can be found in Table 2.1. Note that many letter names share similar sounds and are often confused. The letter name *B* or /bee/, for example, shares the ending **vowel** sound with /dee/, /tee/,

TABLE 2.1   **Names of the Letters of the Alphabet**

A	ay	H	aich	O	oh	V	vee
B	bee	I	ie	P	pee	W	double yoo
C	see	J	jay	Q	kyoo	X	ecks
D	dee	K	kay	R	are	Y	wie
E	ee	L	el	S	es	Z	zee
F	ef	M	em	T	tee		
G	gee	N	en	U	yoo		

/pee/, and so forth. The letters *G* and *J* start with the same sound (/jee/ and /jay/), as do *Q* and *K* (/kyoo/ and /kay/). (Slash marks indicate the sound of the letter or letters inside.)

To reduce the memory load and possible confusions, some literacy programs avoid teaching students the names of the letters (Reading Mastery or Distar, for example). There is no strong evidence to support this practice though, and learning to associate just a sound with a symbol may be much more difficult than a name (McBride-Chang, 1999). Sounds make poor labels (Ehri & Roberts, 2006). For one thing, consonant sounds are often hard to make in isolation. Just try to say the sound for *B* without adding a vowel sound as one does in /buh/. In addition, some letters, such as *C,* have more than one sound. Would we call it /k/ or /s/? Both are already sounds for other letters! Many children learn the letter names at home before school, so it seems artificial to avoid using the names in school. And there is no well-known ABC song with just sounds!

We believe that names are useful labels when talking to children about letters, and research has established that children who know the names of letters learn the letter–sound associations more readily than those without letter–name knowledge (Kim, Petscher, Foorman, & Zhou, 2010). This is probably because most letter names offer clues to at least one sound (Share, 2004; Treiman & Kessler, 2003). Consider the list of letter names in Table 2.1. Children learn sounds of letters more readily when those names begin with consonant sounds such as *K* (/kay/) or *T* (/tee/) than those beginning with vowels such as *F* (/ef/) or *L* (/el/) (Evans, Bell, Shaw, Moreti, & Page, 2006; Treiman, Weatherston, & Berch, 1994; Kim et al., 2010). A few letter names do not offer clues to the sounds they represent. The letter name for *W* is "double u"; for *Y* it is "wie"; and for *H* is "aich". However, the name for *H* does end with the /ch/ sound, and young spellers may spell *chin* as HN. To summarize, letter names fall into four categories:

1. Some letter names begin with an initial consonant letter sound: *B, C, D, G, J, K, P, Q, T, V, Z*
2. Some letter names begin with a vowel sound (often short *-e*) and end with a consonant letter sound: *F, L, S, X ,M, N, R*
3. Vowel letter names are the same as the sounds for long vowels: *A, E, I, O, U*
4. Some letter names offer no clue to the consonant sound: *H, W, Y*

The names of letters serve as a reference for children when they first begin to invent spellings, even before formal schooling, and initial sounds are most likely to be represented first (Henderson, 1981; Read, 1971). Young writers rely on letter names to spell phonetically

FIGURE 2.2 Ellie's Writing Attempt: "When are you coming?"

See Chapter 5 for more information about how children develop as spellers.

or alphabetically. See Figure 2.2 for an example of a child's early writing attempt ("When are you coming?"). As Ellie wrote a note to her sister Meg, she spelled *are* as R and *you* as U. According to letter name logic, there is no need to add vowels because they were already part of the letter names. When you say the name of the letter *Y* ("wie"), you can feel your lips moving to make the shape of /wuh/, the sound we associate with *W. Consequently*, Ellie quite logically spelled *when* as YN. Long vowels that "say their names" are usually the first vowels used in writing. For example, children might spell *cake* as KAK. We have noticed that Spanish speakers often use vowels in their spelling earlier than English speakers. This may be because Spanish is a syllabic language in which the vowels stand out more (Helman, 2004). Nevertheless, there is a reciprocal relationship between learning letter names and letter sounds in most alphabetic languages. That is, learning either one supports the acquisition of the other.

Learning about the Alphabet

Many children will have learned letters at home from parents and siblings, who pointed out the shapes and provided them with the letter names while eating, dressing, playing, bathing, reading, shopping, and traveling. Magnetic letters on the refrigerator door, alphabet puzzles, alphabet blocks, alphabet books, and alphabet games are staples in many print-rich homes (Adams, 1990). One study found that middle-class four-year-olds knew an average of 54 percent of the letter names and five-year-olds knew 85 percent (Worden & Boettcher, 1990). This means that children who come to preschool and kindergarten without exposure to the alphabet from home or daycare are already well behind their classmates in terms of alphabetic familiarity. They need teachers to help them develop a variety of concrete connections with the letters in a direct but game-like manner, such as the "Bingo" song activity described previously.

Children tend to learn the letters in their own names first (Bloodgood, 1999; Treiman & Broderick, 1998). This is probably because names are part of their identities. Children are excited to see their names on labels, nametags, or lunch bags. The order of learning the remaining letters can be influenced by several factors. Kindergarteners master capital letters most readily. Capitals are considered more visually distinct; are easier to form; and are featured in games, books, and curricula for preschoolers. Parents and caregivers emphasize children's names and refer to them in discussing letters—especially the first letter, which is capitalized (Levin & Aram, 2004, Evans et al., 2006). *V, W,* and *Y* are the hardest of capital letters to learn, perhaps because they all look alike or because, in the case of *W* and *Y,* their names do not reflect their letter sounds.

Research indicates that some letters are harder to learn than others, which may mean that they require more attention in the classroom. The lowercase letters that are easiest to learn are the ones most similar to their capital forms, such as *Cc, Xx,* and *Zz* (Huang & Invernizzi, 2012; Turnbull, Bowles, Skibbe, Justice, & Wiggins, 2010). The lowercase *g* is one of the hardest to learn, perhaps because there are two distinct lowercase forms (g, g) and neither of them bears a visual relationship to the capital *G. Lowercase* letters *b, d, p,* and *q* provide well-known difficulties because of their similarities; however, *p* is not as readily confused as the others, perhaps because it is visually similar to capital *P.* The lowercase *q* is the hardest of all letters to name (Evans et al., 2006), perhaps because children seldom encounter it and confuse it with *p.* No single characteristic explains why some letters are easier than others. *X,* for example, is rare in reading materials and children's names but is one of the first to be learned, probably because of its visual distinctness. *O* is also one of the easiest—this may be because circles show up early in children's first drawings and the round *O* is therefore a familiar shape.

Writing the Alphabet

The ability to write the letters is an important skill that is highly correlated with literacy learning in preschool children (Puranik, Lonigan, & Kim, 2011). Writing a letter from memory (not just copying) requires that the student retrieve its visual representation and then coordinate the fine motor movements needed to produce it (Berninger, 1999). There is good evidence that the motoric act of letter formation helps to secure the visual representation of the letter in the brain (Bara & Gentaz, 2011), and children who can write letters with ease can give more attention to spelling and composing as they learn to read and write (Graham, Berninger, Abbott, Abbot, & Whitaker, 1997).

Although there are different handwriting programs and different materials used to teach the physical act of writing (including varying pencil sizes and types of paper), research has not established the superiority of one over the other (Asher, 2006). However, there are good reasons to teach young children proper pencil grip as well as efficient, accurate letter formation so that they do not develop bad habits that are hard to break later (such as starting letters at the bottom or retracing lines). Consistency and some focused practice on one letter or similar letters are important as children are first learning letter formation (Asher, 2006). In addition, children benefit from the chance to experiment with different writing tools and writing surfaces (Mayer, 2007).

Some letters will be more difficult than others for children to produce. Letters with slanted lines, like *Y* and *K*, seem especially challenging. Kaitlyn's attempts to write the first letter in her name when she was four years old is shown in Figure 2.3. It was not until kindergarten that she was able to produce a more conventional *K*.

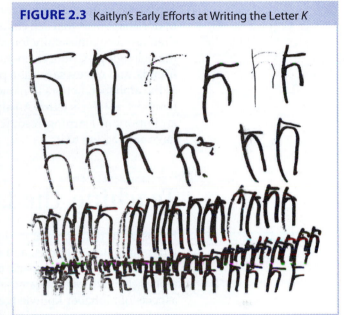

FIGURE 2.3 Kaitlyn's Early Efforts at Writing the Letter *K*

Font Variations

There are many styles or fonts that exist in the world of print, and these variations add to the difficulty of learning to identify letters. For example, the letters *A* and *G* have two distinctly different lowercase forms (a versus ɑ and g versus ɡ), and children may think these are different letters if variations are not explicitly pointed out. Children eventually come to see the regularities of letter shapes by noting the salient, stable characteristics of letters in many contexts and as represented in different fonts, sizes, shapes, and textures. By extracting the "M-ness" across all the variations of different *M* font styles, an essential concept of *M* is formed (see Figure 2.4). Additional encounters with *M* add new attributes to the concept of the letter, and explicit talk about these variations helps students remember the visual features that are characteristic of particular letters.

FIGURE 2.4 Font Styles

M ℳM **M m** M **M M** ℳ M

m **m** m **m** **M** m m m m m

No More Letter of the Week!

Letter of the week activities have been a longstanding staple in many early childhood classrooms, but we have several concerns about this approach. Studying one letter at a time overlooks the importance of comparing and contrasting letters—children need to learn what something is not, as well as what it is. Reutzel's research (2008) showed that it was better to teach a new letter each day than to spend an entire week on a single letter. Letter of the week activities do not serve the needs of children who come to kindergarten already knowing all, or most, of their letters and who are ready for more challenging activities than pasting macaroni in the shape of the letter *M*. And for children who do not already know most letters, one letter a week for kindergarten is much too slow. There are 26 letters and approximately 36 weeks in the school year, so a letter a week sets a very slow pace. Expectations in many school systems are that kindergarten children will acquire a sight vocabulary and be reading simple, patterned texts by the end of the year. To meet these goals, complete alphabet knowledge is required long before the last 10 weeks of school.

Instead of approaching the alphabet as one letter per week, we suggest that four- and five-year-olds be immersed in the study of letters—all the letters. Alphabet immersion can be accomplished in many ways, but one activity we especially like (and describe later in this chapter) is to teach children the letters in classmate's names and then have the children use the names daily for taking attendance, making choices, taking turns, or identifying belongings. Children are highly motivated to learn their own names and the names of friends, and names serve as a powerful springboard to recognizing and writing the letters of the alphabet. Letters in names take on the personalities of the owners: *K* is Kaylee's letter and *T* is Tyler's letter. An alphabetic display of classmates' names and photos becomes an important learning resource in the classroom and should be posted where children have easy access to it.

Teaching the Letters of the Alphabet

Exposure to the alphabet is nicely accomplished as you share alphabet books, talk about letters in many contexts, and teach children to track the letters as they sing the alphabet sound. However, explicit instruction and extended practice are needed as well. The alphabet activities and games described in this chapter are designed to develop different aspects of alphabet knowledge, including letter naming, letter recognition (both capitals and lowercase), and letter production. Learning the sounds associated with letters begins here but is more thoroughly addressed in the chapter on phonics, Chapter 5.

In preK some teachers might prefer to start with capital letters, but the world of print is full of both capital and lowercase letters, so introduce children to both as soon as possible. When working with children, use the terms *capital* (or uppercase) and *lowercase*. The terms *big* and *little* are confusing because some capital and lowercase letters are the same height (*B/b, L/l, F/f*) and because the letters children will see around them vary in how large they are printed. Alphabet charts should include both capital and lowercase letters.

Getting Started with the Alphabet

Learning the alphabet song is the traditional first step in learning the letters. The rhythm and rhyme will help children master it with relative ease. However, children may not realize that the song refers to individual letters unless you point to letters as you sing.

Learn the Alphabet Song and Track the Letters

Teach the alphabet song to the tune of "Twinkle, Twinkle, Little Star" and sing it every day until everyone knows the sequence by heart. You may have recorded versions, or you may find animated versions online that you can play for the children. The song teaches the names and the order of the letters, serving as a point of reference for years to come. (Some adults still find themselves humming the song when trying to find something in alphabetical order!) While singing the song, point to the letters on an alphabet strip large enough for all to see. Once children learn the sequence, let them follow along on the posted strip, or provide each person with an individual alphabet strip (found in Appendix B) so students can begin to match what they are saying to the letters. Separate the sequence of "LMNOP" and slow it down so children hear each letter. Pointing to the letters will help children understand that "LMNOP" is five letters and not one long word.

Talk about Letters in the Environment

Letters are everywhere in the environment, so take the time to draw the children's attention to letters in your classroom and around the school building. Look for the *X* in *exit* and talk about what *exit* means. Point out the difference between the first letters in *girls* and *boys* on the restroom doors. Try to find every letter of the alphabet someplace in your room or in the school building. Take digital photos of signs to make an electronic slide show or to add to a class alphabet book.

Alphabet Books and Extensions

Sharing alphabet books provides a context in which the forms and features of print, including letters, can be discussed with young children (Smolkin, Yaden, Brown, & Hofius, 1992). Reading alphabet books aloud also has the potential to support children's development of beginning phonemic awareness as well as alphabet knowledge (Murray, Stahl, and Ivy, 1996). However, some ABC books have better potential for learning letters than others, and how teachers use the books will influence student learning.

Although some alphabet books serve as a way to teach letter identification and letter sounds to young children, many alphabet books are designed for other purposes and a range of ages. Some are in the form of a storybook, such as Wanda Gag's classic *ABC Bunny*. Sometimes they showcase the art of the illustrator, such as *Alphabet City* by Stephen Johnson or *The Z Was Zapped* by Chris Van Allsburg. Other books offer content information and new vocabulary words, such as *The Underwater Alphabet Book* by Jerry Pollatto. Some of these books are appropriate for young children just learning the alphabet; others are best used with primary or even upper elementary students. Table 2.2 lists some of the factors to consider when selecting books. One research study found that teachers were most likely to focus on comprehension when using alphabet storybooks and did not talk about the letters and sounds much at all (Bradley & Jones, 2007).

It is actually rather hard to find a basic alphabet book with easily identified pictures that represent the prominent sound or sounds of each letter. One example is *26 Letters and 99 Cents* by Tana Hoban, which offers one familiar object for each letter. When selecting alphabet books for the purpose of teaching beginning sound associations, there are some cautions to keep in mind. Look for books that feature familiar objects that students can name so that they are saying the correct label to go with a letter (i.e., not saying *cow* for a yak). Many publishers of little books such as Rigby and The Wright Group have a book for each letter of the alphabet and, because they are designed specifically to teach letter–sound correspondences, the pictures are of everyday objects that the children are likely to know and name accurately. These types of books are especially useful for English learners who need to master basic vocabulary words.

TABLE 2.2 **Alphabet Book Selection**

When choosing alphabet books for letter instruction, try to find books that have the following qualities.

- Show clearly recognizable capital and lowercase letter forms in a simple font style
- Use pictures of common objects that young children can name accurately
- Avoid using consonant blends or digraphs for initial sounds
- Avoid a confusing array of sounds for the vowel letters and words in which the vowel is part of a letter name (Children only hear the *n* in *Indian*, the *l* in *elephant*, and the *r* in *artist*—not the vowel that comes before.)

Many letters have more than one sound, so some ambiguity is hard to avoid in alphabet books. You will often find hard and soft sounds for *G* (*goat* and *giraffe*) and *C* (*cat* and *circle*) mixed together on the same page. **Digraphs** like *sh* (*shell*) and *ch* (*chicks*) may be found on the *S* and *C* pages. This can be confusing to children because the sounds of /sh/ and /ch/ are different from the letter sounds for the single consonants *S* and *C* respectively. Words beginning with **blends**, such as *dr,* do not offer the best exemplars for a letter sound. For example, *dragon* might be found on the *D* page, but the initial consonant sound is really more like the sound of *J,* as in /jragon/, than *D. Vowels* represent many sounds, so *apple, ape,* and *artist* may appear on the same page representing the short, long, and *r*-controlled sounds of *a* respectively. *X* usually sounds like *Z* when at the beginning of words. At some point, these variations are welcome. But to children who do not yet know how to read or spell, the word *elephant* begins with "L," not a short *e,* and the word *inch* starts with "N." It's important to be aware of these confusing examples and be prepared to discuss them explicitly with your students. For example, Lois Ehlert's *Eating the Alphabet: Fruits and Vegetables from A to Z* features *jicama* and *jalapeño* on the *J* page. This provides an opportunity to recognize that the *J* in Spanish is pronounced like the English *H*—an important point if you have a child named José in your classroom. Likewise, if you have a Cynthia or Georgio, you will want to point out pictures that have the soft sound for *C* or *G* and explain that some letters have more than one sound.

Don't worry if an alphabet book isn't perfect. Just be prepared to address the complexities as you share the book with your children. Start with books that are more straightforward until children become familiar with the letters; then introduce more challenging books.

SHARE ALPHABET BOOKS. Collect a variety of age-appropriate alphabet books to share with your students and keep in your room. Some of our favorite titles appropriate for preK and kindergarten are in Table 2.3, but new ones are published all the time and there are too many to list. If you want children to benefit from examining alphabet books independently, it is important that you model how to use them. Show children how to touch and name the letters: "Here is capital *B* and here is lowercase *b*"; then form sentences such as "*B* is for *bear*" or "*Bear* starts with *B.*"

Share alphabet books as part of read-aloud time, and then make them available for children to look at on their own—perhaps in the alphabet center described later in the chapter. If the book is in the form of a story, read it in an interactive way. Solve puzzles such as finding the letters hidden in the illustrations. If the book features language play,

| **TABLE 2.3** | **Annotated List of Alphabet Books for Young Children** |

Anno, M. (1975). *Anno's alphabet.* New York, NY: Crowell.	Objects are hidden in the borders of this book
Base, G. (1986). *Animalia.* New York, NY: Harry Abrams.	Letters are not prominently displayed, but children can have fun searching for all the pictures that begin with the target letter
Bayor, J. (1984). *A: My name is Alice.* Illustrated by S. Kellogg. New York, NY: Dial.	This lends itself to interesting variations, but some words are obscure (e.g., Nancy is a nutria and Ned is a newt)
D.K. Publishing. (1997). *My big alphabet book.* New York, NY: DK Preschool.	A classic format with capital and lowercase along with several easy-to-identify photographs for each letter
Dragonwagon, C. (1992). *Alligator arrived with apples : A potluck alphabet feast.* New York, NY: Aladdin.	Includes some unusual names of foods

Ehlert, L. (1989). *Eating the alphabet: Fruits and vegetables from A to Z.* San Diego, CA: Harcourt Brace.	Includes some rare words (e.g., *kohlrabi* for *K*), but illustrations are outstanding
Ernst, L. C. (1996). *The letters are lost.* New York, NY: Scholastic.	Alphabet blocks are lost along with objects that share their letter; for example, *F* took a swim with some fish
Fain, K. (1993). *Handsigns: A sign language alphabet.* New York, NY: Scholastic.	Nicely illustrated, but some pictures are obscure (e.g., *vixen* and *lynx* for *V* and *L*)
Folson, M. (2005). *Q is for duck: An alphabet guessing game.* New York, NY: Houghton Mifflin Harcourt.	A puzzle book for children who already know their letters (*A* is for *Zoo*. Why? Because zoos have animals.)
Gág, W. (1933). *The ABC bunny.* New York, NY: Coward-McCann.	A simple rhyming adventure story for reading aloud
Hoban, T. (1995). *26 letters and 99 cents.* New York, NY: HarperCollins.	One side opens to letters and the other to numbers; easy-to-name objects for most letters
Hobbie, H. (2000). *Toot and Puddle: Puddle's ABC.* Boston, MA: Little Brown.	An alphabet book inside a story: Puddle tries to teach a friend how to write his name but then finds he must teach the letters of the alphabet
Horenstein, H. (1999). *Arf! Beg! Catch! Dogs from A to Z.* New York, NY: Scholastic.	A favorite for dog lovers, but words are often actions (e.g., *C* for *catch*) or not clearly cued by pictures (e.g., *F* for *friends* and *G* for *good dog*)
Johnson, S. (1999). *Alphabet City.* New York, NY: Puffin.	Each letter is hidden in a realistic painting of city scenes
Kitamura, S. (1992). *From acorn to zoo and everything in between in alphabetical order.* New York, NY: Scholastic.	Lots of objects are featured for each letter and are labeled
Lobel, A. (1981). *On Market Street.* New York, NY: Greenwillow.	Familiar objects are used to create people, such as a man made of zippers
MacDonald, S. (1986). *Alphabetics.* New York, NY: Trumpet.	This Caldecott Award book offers striking graphics of letters transforming into objects; for example, the *K* acquires a string and becomes a kite
McPhail, D. (1989). *David McPhail's animals A to Z.* New York, NY: Scholastic.	Features capital letters and illustrations with a variety of objects, such as a gorilla playing a guitar or a goose with glasses
Miller, J. (1987). *The farm alphabet book.* New York, NY: Scholastic.	Features objects found on a farm, beginning with apples
Musgrove, M. (1976). *Ashanti to Zulu.* New York, NY: Dial.	This Caldecott winner tells about African tribes as it goes through the alphabet
Rankin, L. (1991). *The handmade alphabet.* New York, NY: Scholastic.	A large hand signs the letter on each page accompanied by an object
Seuss, Dr. (1963). *Dr. Seuss's ABC: An amazing alphabet book!* New York, NY: Random House.	A rollicking text in the Seuss style
Shannon, G. (1996). *Tomorrow's alphabet.* Illustrated by D. Crews. New York, NY: Greenwillow.	Is in all capitals and is potentially confusing, but features familiar objects with a twist; for example, *T* is for bread, tomorrow's toast
Slate, J. (1996). *Miss Bindergarten gets ready for kindergarten.* Illustrated by A. Wolff. New York, NY: Scholastic.	In this story of a teacher preparing for the first day of school, all her students are introduced in alphabetical order, starting with Adam the alligator and ending with Zach the zebra
Tyron, L. (1991). *Albert's alphabet.* New York, NY: Atheneum.	In this wordless book, a carpenter duck builds capital letters out of a variety of materials

enjoy the rhythm and rhyme. Just be sure to also take the time to involve children in naming the letters and pictures that begin with each letter as you go through the alphabet book. In some cases, the pictures may be familiar things like cats or butterflies; other times, they may be unfamiliar words like *dromedary* or *mercat*. Do not expect children to learn all these new words, but take the opportunity when possible to expand their concepts and vocabulary—especially when the new words will prove useful in the classroom curriculum. ABC books such as Mary Azarian's *A Farmer's Alphabet* can be incorporated into thematic units, as new words will be encountered in other contexts and are more likely to become new vocabulary.

ALPHABET BOOK FOLLOW-UPS. Some alphabet books lend themselves to many extension activities. *Miss Bindergarten Gets Ready for Kindergarten* is featured in Lesson 2.1.

LESSON 2.1 *Miss Bindergarten Gets Ready for Kindergarten*

This storybook written by Joseph Slate and illustrated by Ashley Wolff is great to share at the beginning of the year, as it features a teacher getting her classroom ready on the first day of school while her students are simultaneously getting ready at home. Miss Bindergarten is a border collie and her students range from Adam the alligator to Zach the zebra, reflecting each letter of the alphabet. There is limited text, so students should be involved in talking about the pictures. As the clock on the wall shows, this remarkable teacher gets her room prepared in just two hours! (CCSS Foundational Skills: 1d, Print Concepts; 2a and 2b, Phonological Awareness; CCSS Language: 5c and 6, Vocabulary Acquisition and Use)

Materials

Copy of *Miss Bindergarten Gets Ready for Kindergarten* and a set of alphabet letters on cards.

Step 1. Introduce

Show students the front and back covers of the book and ask them to speculate about what is going on. They will see children playing while Miss Bindergarten has her arms full with school supplies. Point to the words in the title as you read it, clap the syllables in *Bindergarten,* and name the author and illustrator. You might ask children to identify the capital letters in the title. Talk about the pictures on the title page that show Miss Bindergarten waking up and getting ready to leave for school. Point out the cockatoo and tell them to watch out for what the bird does throughout the book.

Step 2. Read aloud

Read the book aloud to enjoy the story and talk about what Miss Bindergarten does in the pictures. Then read it again to focus more on the children as they are introduced, pausing to let children supply the ending rhyme for each sentence. You may want to use the key in the back of the book to help you identify some of the rare animals like Noah the newt or Vicki the vole.

Step 3. Reread

Read the story again on a second day. Because the letters do not play a prominent role in the format of the book, pass out letter cards and make each child responsible for holding up his or her letter when the animal whose name and species starts with that letter is introduced. Help children identify an animal that

▶

begins with the same letter as their name and brainstorm more animals. Damian's name starts with a *D* and *D* is for *dog,* but also *duck, dolphin,* and *dinosaur.* Follow up with all kinds of names activities.

Step 4. Extend

Talk with your students about how they get ready for school and create a **language experience approach** dictation with a repetitive language pattern such as "Anna gets out of bed. Benjamin puts on his shoes. Lisa has juice." Creating a class dictated response such as this might take several days if you include all the students in your class, or you can do it individually or in small groups. Children can be asked to illustrate their sentence, and the pages can be compiled into a class book entitled something like "Our Class Gets Ready for Kindergarten."

> **Read more about dictations in Chapter 6.**

Chicka Chicka Boom Boom

This book by Bill Martin and John Archambault has become a classic alphabet book for good reasons. Letters become characters in the rhyming story. The lowercase letters climb up a coconut tree until it bends under their weight and dumps them on the ground. Capital letters then come to soothe their pains. After reading the story, spread out a collection of letters and have children find the letters as they are named in the story, putting them in order and matching capitals to lowercase. You can create a large coconut tree on the side of a metal filing cabinet so that children can act out the story and match capital and lowercase forms using magnetic letters. The supplement *Letter and Picture Sorts for Emergent Spellers* (Bear, Invernizzi, Johnston, & Templeton, 2010) has more ideas and materials to use with *Chicka Chicka Boom Boom.*

Create Class Alphabet Books

After enjoying a variety of alphabet books, involve children in creating their own. For preschoolers this might be a class alphabet book in the form of a big book or an electronic presentation (made with a tool such as PowerPoint) that includes photos of the children. A book focusing on actions might include photographs and sentences such as "Samantha sifts in the sand. Jason and Julie jump. Martin plays on the monkey bars."

For kindergarten students, individual alphabet scrapbooks can be an ongoing project. (See Figure 2.5.) Prepare a blank book for each child by stapling together seven sheets of paper folded in the middle. Here are some different things that can be added over time:

1. Provide digital photos of classmates to add to appropriate pages.
2. Practice writing a few capital and lowercase forms of the letter on each page.
3. Paste in letters in different sizes and fonts cut from magazines and newspapers.
4. Draw and label pictures that begin with the letter's sound.
5. Cut out and paste magazine pictures that begin with the letter's sound. These pictures, too, can be labeled.
6. Add words to create a personal dictionary.

FIGURE 2.5 Alphabet Scrapbook

LETTER FORMATION. Children need to learn to produce letters as well as recognize them. Teaching letter formation early helps children to develop good habits and directionality. Fink-Chorzempa, Graham, and Harris (2005) offer some guidelines appropriate for preschool and kindergarten:

1. Talk aloud as you trace a letter, describing the strokes. In forming a capital *F,* for example, say, "Start at the top and pull down. Go back to the top and slide right. Then go to the middle and slide right."

TABLE 2.4 **Practicing Letter Formation**

1. Draw letters with fingers in trays or flat box tops with a thin layer of sand, rice, salt or grits. Color the rice or grits by shaking in a tablespoon of alcohol and a few drops of food color and then spreading it out to dry. Ground-up colored chalk can be used to color sand and salt, or you can find colored sand at a craft store.
2. Write letters in chocolate pudding, shaving cream, or finger paints. A spoonful of finger paint can be sealed inside a zip lock bag for repeated use.
3. Shape letters out of play dough, clay, pipe cleaners, Wikki Stix, or other materials. Laminated letter cards can be used as a template on which to form letters.
4. Look for textured letters in school supply catalogs or make them by cutting letters out of medium grit sandpaper, felt, or foam and gluing them to cardboard. Students trace the letters with their fingers.
5. Do rubbings of sandpaper letters. Use clothespins to clip lightweight paper in place while children rub with the side of a broken unwrapped crayon.
6. Paint letters with water using large brushes on chalkboards or sidewalks and watch them disappear on a sunny day.
7. Write letters on classmates' backs using a finger to see whether they can guess it.

2. Ask the children to imitate you as you model the strokes and to verbalize their movements.
3. Provide visual models with arrows that show the order and direction of strokes.
4. Talk about the visual features of letters and how letters are alike and different. Point out, for example, that capital *B* and lowercase *b* begin with a line and then curve, whereas lowercase *d* begins with a circle before the line.

As students trace or write letters, guide them to follow a standard series of strokes. Check with the primary teachers in your school or local school system for the letter formation system that is used. You can also search the Internet for "letter formation" or "manuscript handwriting" to find directions. There are different systems and they do not all agree. But what seems most important is to decide on a system and use it consistently as you model and direct children.

Although handwriting instruction during preschool may be informal with a focus on learning to write one's own name, children in kindergarten should have more systematic instruction with plenty of practice writing all the letters. Encourage the children to write letters on unlined and lined paper, white boards, magna doodles, and magic slates using markers, chalk, pencils, crayons, and brushes. From time to time, ask them to select their best-formed letter. Give feedback as needed and pull aside children who need more practice. Provide a variety of writing media to enhance their multisensory experiences, and encourage children to write in centers and during play. Table 2.4 lists some creative ways to get students practicing their letter formation with sensory materials.

for Words Their Way®

At the PDToolkit, watch Jackie talk about children's names and then work with Fabiola as she learns to write her name. Click the Videos tab and then choose Emergent Stage. Look for "Names and Handwriting."

LEARNING LETTERS WITH CHILDREN'S NAMES. The names of children in your class are an ideal point from which to begin the study of alphabet letters because children are naturally interested in their own names and their friends' names. Pat Cunningham has described many activities based on children's names (Cunningham, 1988), and creative teachers have come up with more of their own.

Name of the Day

We like the idea of a "name of the day" so much better than a "letter of the week," because more letters are covered in a much shorter time. Teachers of young children find that it can be difficult to break young children of the habit of using all capitals to write their names, so we recommend using lowercase letters from the start. The basic format for name of the day is described in Lesson 2.2, and there are many possible variations and extensions.

LESSON 2.2   Name of the day

This lesson is repeated every day until all the children in your class have been featured. You can add names of classroom pets or special stuffed animals if you want. (CCSS Foundational Skills: 1, 1b, and 1d, Print Concepts; 2b, 2e, Phonological Awareness; CCSS Language: 1a and 2c, Conventions of Standard English)

Materials

Prepare cards with names of children written in neat block handwriting; have blank ones available. Put all the names in a box, gift bag, or decorated can. A pocket chart is handy for displaying the names and letters.

Step 1. Introduce the name and talk about its features

Each day, with great fanfare, a name is drawn and becomes the "name of the day." The teacher holds up the card and begins with a very open-ended question: "What do you notice about this name?" Children will respond in all sorts of ways, depending on what they know about letters: "It's a long name." "It has three letters." "It starts like Tommi's name." "It has an *O* in the middle." If children don't offer any ideas, be ready to model your own by saying something like, "I notice that there are two letters in the middle of this word that are the same." Develop **concepts about print** by asking questions such as "What is the first letter? What is the last letter? Which letter is a capital?" Say, "Let's count to see how many letters are in the name. Let's clap to see how many syllables are in the name."

Step 2. Chant the letters

Lead the children in a chant as you point to each letter. A cheer led by the teacher can go like this:

Teacher: "Give me a *K*."	Children: "K"
Teacher: "Give me an *I*."	Children: "I"
Teacher: "Give me an *M*."	Children: "M"
Teacher: "What do we have?"	Children: "Kim!" (Repeat three times)

Step 3. Cut apart the letters and reorder

On a separate card, write the name of the child as the children recite the letters again. Then cut the letters apart and hand out the letters to children in the group. The children are asked to put the letters back in order to spell the name correctly. This can be done in a pocket chart or on a chalkboard ledge and repeated many times. We recommend starting with a capital letter and using lowercase for the rest.

Step 4. Write the name

In kindergarten, children should attempt to write the featured name. This might be done on individual whiteboards, chalkboards, or pieces of paper clipped to cardboard. This is an opportunity to offer some handwriting instruction as you model for the children. Discuss the details of direction and movement of letter formation as the children imitate your motions. Prior to kindergarten you might elect to focus on just the first letter in a child's name for children to practice as a group activity.

Step 5. Compare names

The featured name is added to a display of all the names that have come before. Names can be arranged in alphabetical order and updated as new names are added. As each name is added, it can be compared to previous names with questions such as "*Kim* has an *m* at the end. Who else has an *m* in their name? *Kim* has three letters. Who else has three letters in their name? Do you see another name with an *i* in the middle?"

Literature Connections

Read aloud stories that feature names and name writing such as *Puddle's ABC* by Holly Hobbie, *Miss Bindergarten Gets Ready for Kindergarten* by Joseph Slate, *Chrysanthemum* by Kevin Henkes, and *Leo the Late Bloomer* by Robert Kraus.

Initial Sound Substitution

Speculate about how other names would sound if they all started with the same letter as the featured name of the day. What if everyone's name started with *K* like Kim's? Jason would be Kason! Leslie would be Keslie. Change the words of Raffi's *Willoughby Wallaby Woo* song accordingly, as described in the next chapter, on page 69.

Make Up More Names

It is unlikely you will have a child for every letter of the alphabet. Consider naming classroom pets or stuffed toys with unused rare letters (Zoe the guinea pig or Queenie the fish) and include them in the activities! If a new pet is introduced during the school year, challenge children to come up with a name that starts with an unused letter.

Research the First Letter

Look for the first letter in the featured name in other places. Find it on an alphabet chart. Pass out alphabet books and ask children to find the letter in the book they have and report on other words that start with that letter. Look for interesting variations in print styles.

Name Grids

Some children need quite a bit of scaffolding to learn to write their own name, especially if their early writing experiences have been limited. One way to provide structured support is to provide laminated paper divided into a grid as shown in Figure 2.6. In the first row, the child's name is printed. In the second row, the child places letter cards into each box to match the name written in the top row. In the third row, the child writes each letter into the corresponding box in each column. These name grids can be put into a names center, as described later in the chapter.

Guess the Name

Once all the children's names have been introduced and displayed, you can play Guess the Name. Offer children five clues, beginning with the broadest and narrowing down the possibilities. This game, which

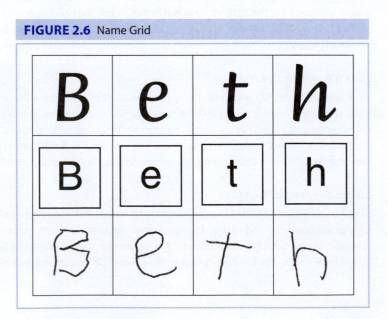

FIGURE 2.6 Name Grid

Letter Searches

Environmental print is especially rich in creative lettering styles. A good way to get practice with letters in many sizes, colors, and font styles is to send children on letter searches:

1. Ask students to look through magazines, junk mail, advertisements, catalogs, and newspapers to find and cut out as many font variations as they can for a particular letter. Students might work together initially. Have the children collect the letters in labeled paper bags, baggies, shallow boxes, or trays and use them to create a class bulletin board, a class alphabet book, or individual alphabet scrapbooks.
2. Do a search of the room. Provide a pencil and clipboard. Assign a letter for students to find—one that they are learning to recognize or write perhaps. Let them move around the room and write the letter every time they find it.
3. Give students a page from the newspaper and a colored highlighter. Ask them to highlight a particular letter every time they find it—another good way to work on letters they need to learn. Provide a different color and ask them to look for another letter.

The PDToolkit has some prepared font sorts to print. Click on the Sorts and Games tab, type "font" into the keyword box, and hit "apply."

Fonts

Create font sorts as described in Lesson 2.3. Collect letters from newspapers, catalogs, magazines, and other print sources or search your computer fonts and print out letters in the largest size possible. Cut the letters apart, mount them on small cards, and laminate for durability. Use both capitals and lowercase, but avoid cursive styles for now. Focus on no more than five letters at a time. After modeling the

---

LESSON 2.3   Sorting letters by case and font style

Decide on two to four letters to study at a time. Create a collection of letters as described in the preceding list (item 4). You can simply sort on a table or carpet, or a manila folder can be divided into columns and placed in a center with the letters needed for sorting stored inside. This lesson will focus on *C* and *D*. (CCSS Foundational Skills: 1d, Print Concepts)

Step 1. Discuss the letter *C*

Lay out your collection of letter cards in a random fashion. Hold up a card with the capital *C* and say something like this: "Here is the capital *C. It* looks like a circle with the side missing." Trace the letter as you say this. "Here is a lowercase *c*. It looks just like the capital *C* but is smaller. I am going to start a column here with these letters and look for more *C*'s. I notice this *C* has thick lines instead of skinny lines, but it still looks like a circle with the side missing. It looks a little small so I think it is a lowercase *c*. Can someone find another *C* and tell us about it?" Find several more and help the children talk about any special visual features and decide whether each is a capital or lowercase letter.

Step 2. Discuss the letter *D*

Hold up a capital *D,* trace it, and say something like this: "Here is a capital *D. It* has a straight line and then a curve that looks like a big belly. Here is a lowercase *d*. Hmmmm, it doesn't look much like the capital *D*, does it? It is as tall as the capital *D* but has a circle and then a straight line. I will put the capital and lowercase *D*'s in a column over here. I am going to look for another capital *D. This* letter has thick lines and is sort of leaning but it still has a straight line and a big curve. Can you help me find some *D*'s and tell me about them?"

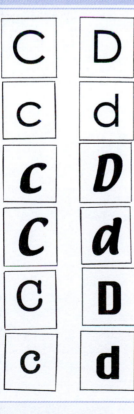

FIGURE 2.8 Font Sort with *C* and *D*

(continued)

LESSON 2.3 Sorting letters by case and font style *(continued)*

Step 3. Sort

Sort all the letters into the two groups, as shown in Figure 2.8. If you have time, do a second sort, but this time create four columns and sort the capitals separate from the lowercase letters.

Step 4. Summarize

Say something like this as you point to examples: "Letters come in lots of different styles and sizes. They may have thick lines or skinny lines; they might lean; they might have little lines added here and there; they might be fancy or plain. Sometimes the lowercase letters look just like the capital letter and sometimes the lowercase letters are different. Today you have learned about *C* and *D.* You can do this sort by yourself in the alphabet center during playtime."

sort with a group of children, place the materials in a center where the children can work independently. *Words Their Way: Letter and Picture Sorts for Emergent Spellers* (Bear, Invernizzi, Johnston, & Templeton, 2010) has letters to use for font sorts.

Valentine's Day

This holiday offers a special opportunity to focus on names and letter learning, and it is celebrated in most schools. Provide specific directions to avoid children's cards being signed and addressed by their parents in cursive handwriting:

1. Send home a list of names carefully printed in a large simple font. Also send directions for parents to help their children sign their name on all their valentines and address them with their classmate's names. This might take several sittings but the motivation will be high.
2. If you think some children might not purchase valentines (due to cost or the fact that it is not a holiday celebrated in their culture) be ready to provide alternatives. You can send home some red and white paper and simple directions for how to make cards, or you might make cards in school as an art project instead of expecting parents to provide them. Some teachers buy discounted valentines on February 15 and save them for the next year to be sure that all children will have some to send.
3. Prepare individual valentine mailboxes, bags, or pockets with each child's name clearly printed. When children bring their valentines to school, they should "mail" all the cards themselves. Sometime prior to opening the valentines you may want to check and see that all the cards ended up in the right place or ask the children to check before they begin to open them. For example, cards for Jeremy and Jenny are likely to be confused.
4. If children have been learning and using their classmates, names all year, they should be able to read those names as they open their valentines.

ALPHABET GAMES. Simple games are a way to provide additional practice in an engaging way and can be used independently in centers (once modeled) or supervised by volunteers (parents or older students) and assistants. Although many of the activities described previously are game-like, we include a few additional games that are easy to create and play. Many follow traditional game formats such as concentration or bingo. You may choose to target particular letters in these games for children who are still mastering the alphabet. Consider the level of challenge your students can handle. As a general rule when preparing games, mix in letters your students know with letters they are learning so some initial success is ensured. Competition and winning should not be emphasized when playing games with young children. Focus on participating and working together.

FIGURE 2.9 Alphabet Eggs

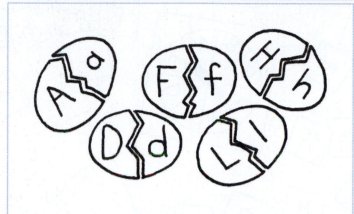

Alphabet Eggs

Create a simple set of puzzles designed to practice the pairing of capital and lowercase letters. On poster board, draw and cut out a four-inch egg shape for each letter in the alphabet. Write an uppercase letter on the left half and the matching lowercase letter on the right portion. Cut the eggs in half using a zigzag line (see Figure 2.9). Make each zigzag slightly different so the activity is self-checking. Children should say the letters to themselves and put the eggs back together by matching the capital and lowercase form.

There are many other shapes that can be cut in half for matching. In October, for example, pumpkin shapes can be cut into two; in February, heart shapes can be cut apart the same way. There is no end to the matching possibilities. Acorn caps can be matched to bottoms, balls to baseball gloves, frogs to lily pads, and so on. These matching sets can also be created to pair rhyming words or pair a letter with a picture that starts with that letter. Pictures can be found in the appendix.

Alphabet Concentration or Memory

Create cards with capital and lowercase forms of the letters written on one side. You can use the letter cards from Appendix B (page 224), but run them on colored paper or glue them to cardstock to be sure they cannot be read from the back side. Select both familiar and not so familiar letters. Avoid using too many letters at a time; 8 to 10 pairs is probably enough. Place pairs of letters face down in a scrambled order. Players turn up two cards to find a match. If the cards match, the player names the letter and keeps the cards.

To introduce this game or to make it easier, play it with the cards face up or use just capital letters. As letter sounds are learned, matching consonant letters to pictures that begin with that letter sound can change the focus of this game.

Letter Spin

Make a spinner with six to eight spaces, and label each space with a capital letter. Write the lowercase letters on small cards, creating five or six cards for each letter (see Figure 2.10). The arrow on the spinner can be cut out of soft but rigid plastic like that used in milk jugs. Make a hole in the middle of the arrow using a hole punch so that it turns freely around a brad. Push the brad through a slit in the base so that it does not turn. A square of foam core board or mat board makes a sturdy base that will not bend and can be easily held by the children. Inserting a washer between the arrow and base ensures that the spinner turns freely.

Lay out all the lowercase cards face up. Each player in turn spins and lands on a capital letter. The player then picks up one card that has the corresponding lowercase form, orally identifying the letter. Play continues until all the letter cards have been picked up.

Alphabet Bingo or Lotto

Divide 8½ inch squares of cardboard, cardstock, or paper into 9, 16, or 25 equal spaces. (Use fewer spaces for younger children.) Print or glue a letter into each square, making each bingo card random and creating a different card for each player. Laminate the cards if desired. Use paper squares, buttons,

FIGURE 2.10
Letter Spin

PD **pd** TOOLKIT™
for Words Their Way®

The PDToolkit has "Alphabet Eggs Matching" and "Alphabet Spin" in PDF file format. Click the Sorts and Games tab and select Emergent Stage. Type "games" in the search box and hit the Apply button. Scroll down to find games.

poker chips, or any kind of small object as markers. Make a set of letters to pull from a box or bag. These can be the same as the letters on the board or might be lowercase or capital pairs.

The teacher, a child, or an assistant pulls a letter and calls it aloud. Show the letter if needed for extra support when children are learning the letters. When a child covers all the letters in a row, they call "bingo" and then must name all the letters as the markers are removed. A variation is black-out bingo, in which all spaces must be covered before anyone can call bingo.

Name bingo is a variation to play once children have had a chance to learn each other's names. Prepare 4- by 4-inch bingo cards by writing in the names of students in the class, making each card different. Use a set of name cards to pull from a bag or box. The players will cover up a student's name when it is called.

Alphabet Draw

Print letters in the upper left corner of cards or cardstock cut into 2- by 3-inch pieces. Create pairs such as capital and lowercase letters for matching. Include a card with a star or other shape as a wild card. Make at least 10 pairs (20 cards) so, when playing with three or more players, each player can be dealt six to seven cards. During a player's turn, any pairs should be laid down. Players not holding a pair draw a card from the person to their left. If they make a match with a card in their hand, they can lay it down. Play proceeds until all the cards are laid down.

PD **pd** TOOLKIT™
for Words Their Way®

At the PDToolkit, click the Assessment Tools tab and then choose Emergent Stage. Look for "Alphabet Recognition."

Assessing Letter Recognition and Production

To determine what students know about letters, teachers can use several tasks of increasing difficulty that assess different aspects of alphabet knowledge. Written forms and directions for alphabet assessment may be found in Appendix A and online.

1. *Sequence of letters.* Sing the alphabet song to the tune of "Twinkle, Twinkle, Little Star" as a class. Take note of who knows the song and can handle *LMNOP* as separate letters.

2. *Recitation and pointing.* Ask students to point to an alphabet strip as they recite the letters in order. If they get tripped up on *LMNOP,* see whether they can self-correct and get back on track. If they are singing the song and pointing, you might suggest that they say the alphabet and slow down on *LMNOP.*

3. *Random recognition.* The letters can be shown randomly to assess letter recognition, starting with the capitals that students are most likely to know first. Students can be asked to identify letters printed on a single sheet of paper (see page 192) where they have been randomly reordered, or you may want to use letter cards and hold up one letter at a time for children to name. Note how easily and quickly students name the letters. If they have to stop and think about a name (perhaps by reciting the ABC song to themselves), that is a sign that they do not know it automatically.

4. *Letter production.* Call letters aloud, in or out of order, for students to write. Seat children where they cannot refer to an alphabet strip for this assessment. Consider not only whether the child is able to create a recognizable form of the letter but also whether they write it in a standard direction. By kindergarten, children should be learning how to form letters in conventional ways to develop handwriting fluency.

5. *Name writing.* Take note of how well children can write their names and whether they use all capitals or a mix of capital and lowercase letters.

> A name-writing task that is scored developmentally is described in Chapter 4.

6. *Sounds.* Knowing the sound or sounds associated with a letter is also part of alphabet knowledge. We will discuss assessing letter sounds in more detail in Chapter 5, but you can simply point to letters and ask the children for the sounds instead of the names. If you have students who come to your class having learned sounds instead of names, this will give you important information.

Benchmark Scores

According to research conducted with hundreds of thousands of kindergartners using Virginia's PALS assessment, most kindergartners recognize and name, on average, 19 lowercase letters (presented in random order) in the fall of the year, and nearly all of them by the end of kindergarten (Invernizzi & Huang, 2011). Four-year-olds know 12 to 21 capital letters and 9 to 17 lowercase letters by the spring of preschool. End-of-year first graders who read on or above grade level were shown to have recognized 21 to 22 capital and lowercase letters, on average, at the end of their 4-year-old preschool year (Invernizzi & Huang, 2011).

Instant and accurate recognition matters, and rapid naming tasks that measure speed in letter naming have long been another strong predictor of early literacy achievement. Although some literacy assessments record how many letters children can name in one minute, these are best used as a screening measure, to find out who is above or below a grade-level benchmark. One-minute timed assessments of alphabet recognition do not cover the entire alphabet, and it is important to find out what specific letters children need to learn. For this reason, we prefer alphabet recognition assessments that inventory the entire corpus of letters.

Working with Parents

There are many ways that parents can support learning of the alphabet. Figure 2.11 provides a possible letter that you might want to send home. In addition, you might want to send home copies of alphabet cards, like those in Appendix B, printed on heavy colored paper so families have letters to work with.

FIGURE 2.11 Parent Letter

Dear Parents/Guardians,

Your child is learning the letters of the alphabet. Attached to this letter are sheets of letters that you can cut apart and store in an envelope to use with your child. Below are some ideas about how to help your child learn their letters. Keep it fun, and do only as much as your child is interested in.

- Find out what letters your child knows. Start with the capital letters. Lay them out in order and ask your child to name and touch each one. Then mix up the letters and see which ones your child can name. Make piles of the ones they know and the ones they don't know. Repeat this with the lowercase letters.
- Print a model of your child's name using one capital letter and the rest lowercase on an index card or ordinary paper. Pull out letter cards for the letters in your child's name and ask your child to put the letters in order to make his or her name. Provide help as needed until your child can do it alone. Repeat with the names of other family members or friends.
- Help your child put the letter cards in order from A to Z. Start with the first ten letters in capitals, then move on to the whole alphabet. After your child learns the capital letters, add the lowercase letters.
- Lay out all the letters face up and call out letters for your child to find. You might focus on four or five letters that your child does not know. Name the letter and ask your child to find it. Give clues like "Find the C. C is like a circle, but it has an open mouth."
- Use the letter cards to play Concentration or Memory. Select four to eight letters with both the capital and lowercase forms. Scramble them face down. Take turns trying to make a match as two cards are turned over. If they match, keep them. If not, turn them back over in the same place before the next player goes.
- Point out letters in books you read that your child is learning. Begin with the letters in their name.
- Look for alphabet books to read and share. If there are just letters and pictures, say something like "Here is a capital A and here is a lowercase A. Apple (or whatever it pictures) begins with A." Help your child name other things that start with a letter.
- Ask your child to look for a particular letter on road signs or in the grocery store. Give them a pad and paper to write it each time they find it.
- There are many Internet resources for alphabet learning, including free games and videos. There are also alphabet apps for a small fee. Some good ones are iWrite Words, Fish School, and Interactive Alphabet.

Please let me know if you have any questions.

Sincerely,

Phonological Awareness

Jackie has been teaching her four- and five-year-olds to recite nursery rhymes. One day she uses a puppet named after her dog Lucky to teach children a sense of rhyme. She starts by explaining: "Lucky wants to learn some nursery rhymes and I want you to help him. Will you say 'Jack Be Nimble' for him?" The children eagerly recite the rhyme while Lucky listens attentively. "Do you think you can say it now?" Jackie asks Lucky. He nods eagerly and recites: "Jack be nimble, Jack be quick, Jack jump over the candle holder."

"No, no," exclaim the children, "that's not right."

Jackie explains to Lucky, "It has to rhyme. Does *quick* rhyme with *holder*, boys and girls? Let's say it again." The children repeat the rhyme and Jackie reminds Lucky that he has to say *candlestick*. Then Lucky tries it: "Jack be nimble, Jack be fast. Jack jump over the candlestick."

The children laugh and say, "No, no."

"But I said *candlestick*. What's wrong?" asks Lucky.

Jackie points out that *fast* and *stick* don't rhyme. "You have to say rhyming words." She asks the children to try once more to teach Lucky the rhyme, and they emphasize the rhyming words. This time the puppet says it correctly and the children clap. "Does *quick* rhyme with *stick*, boys and girls? Yes, *quick* and *stick* are rhyming words. Let's teach Lucky another nursery rhyme. What shall we teach him next?"

They try "Jack and Jill" next. Lucky struggles again, saying, "Jack and Jill went up the mountain to fetch a pail of water." Then, on his next try, Jack fell down and broke his head. When Lucky asks what is wrong, the children can now explain, "It has to rhyme!" or "Those words don't rhyme." Later, during center time, Jackie observes several children playing with Lucky and acting out the same interactions, telling the puppet, "You have to say the rhymes right."

for Words Their Way®

At the PDToolkit, watch Jackie doing a similar activity to develop a sense of rhyme. Click the Videos tab and then choose Emergent Stage. Look for "Learning about Rhyme."

The Sounds of Language

Children delight in the sounds of oral language, and through language play they become sensitive to sounds before they are aware of them at a conscious level. Children detect the difference between *tackity tack tack* and *rackity rack rack* as they repeat those silly phrases, but they probably would be unable to describe what makes them alike or different. That's because becoming aware or conscious of something requires a kind of cognitive distancing that does not come easily to young children. Children can hear and use speech sounds easily at a tacit, or subconscious, level—they can talk and can understand when others talk to them. But bringing tacit awareness of individual speech sounds to the surface to be examined consciously and explicitly, apart from their communicative intent, is developmentally more difficult. Jackie exposes her children to rhyme in numerous ways. Then, by explicitly comparing words that rhyme and words that do not rhyme, she helps them understand more consciously what rhyme is all about.

The ability to pay attention to, identify, and *reflect on* various sound structures of speech is known as **phonological awareness**. It is the umbrella term for a range of conscious understandings about speech sounds, including syllables, rhyme, alliteration (the repetition of the same beginning consonant sound, as in *fee fi fo fum)*, and the ability to blend and break apart the sounds of words orally. Phonological awareness has been widely identified as a critical understanding needed to progress in literacy (Goswami, 2001; Metsala, 2011; National Reading Panel, 2000; Snow, Burns & Griffin, 1998).

Phonological awareness develops gradually over time and progresses from a sensitivity to big chunks of speech sounds, such as whole words, syllables, and rhyme, to smaller parts of speech sounds, such as the individual sounds or **phonemes** within words (Pufpaff, 2009; Pullen & Justice, 2003). **Phonemic awareness** is a subcategory of phonological awareness and refers to the ability to identify and reflect on the individual phonemes. Segmenting *sit* or *thick* into three sounds (/s/-/i/-/t/ or /th/-/i/-/ck/) is an example of phonemic awareness. Emergent learners in preschool and early kindergarten typically develop partial phonemic awareness, such as detecting and separating the initial consonant sounds of words. By late kindergarten, some children will have full phonemic awareness: the ability to separate all the sounds in a word, including blends and the medial vowels (/s/-/t/-/e/-/p/).

In general, phonological awareness activities should move from playing with larger speech units such as words and syllables to smaller speech units such as individual phonemes; however, there is really no hard and fast rule about this. You can find opportunities throughout the day to talk about a variety of speech units. When lining up, you might call the students by the number of syllables in their names; when reading a book aloud, you might have the students listen for the beginning sound in the title. The first step in developing children's phonological awareness is to draw their attention to units of sound at every opportunity and, in doing so, familiarize them with terms such as *word, rhyme, syllable,* and *beginning sound.*

Planning for Instruction

Phonological awareness activities should progress from exposure and explanation by the teacher, to recognition and identification, and finally to production by the child (Duffy, 2009; Fisher and Frey, 2008; Pearson & Gallager, 1983). This gradual release and developmental continuum is reflected in the ordering of the activities described as follows using rhyme as an example:

1. *Exposure and explanation.* Children first hear and join in saying jingles or singing songs that feature rhyme. Next, the teacher points out and explains "rhyme" as a concept. For example, after reciting Jack and Jill several times, a teacher might say, "I hear some rhyming words in this poem. Jack and *Jill* went up the *hill* [emphasizing those words]."
2. *Recognition and identification.* Children identify or match words that rhyme. The teacher might say, "Can you find two more words that rhyme in 'Jack and Jill'?" Or, given pictures of a man, a pan, and a frog, the children are asked to pick the two that rhyme.
3. *Production or application.* Children produce or generate words that rhyme. The teachers might pause while reading to allow children to supply a rhyming word or ask, "Can you think of some more words that rhyme with *Jill*?"

Phonological awareness activities in preschool and kindergarten classrooms should be engaging whole-group language activities that benefit all students, using a variety of instructional strategies that have been identified as successful and effective (Blachman, 1994; Lundberg, Frost, & Peterson, 1988; Smith, Simmons, & Kame'enui, 1995). Because it is such a critical prerequisite for beginning reading, however, it is important to assess and plan explicit small-group lessons for students who need additional support. In addition to the activities discussed in this chapter, Table 3.1 lists more resources for teachers.

Syllables and Words

A large sound unit to address first with young children is the **syllable**, because syllables have a physical reality that other units of sound do not. Each syllable corresponds to a release of breath and can therefore be segmented fairly easily in oral speech. Although they are sometimes referred to as *beats* or *claps*, we suggest that you teach children the term *syllable* from the beginning.

EXPOSURE AND EXPLANATION. Children often delight in long words, so take the time to point them out when they come up, especially during a read-aloud. *The Gingerbread Man* (by various authors), *The Very Hungry Caterpillar* (by Eric Carle), *Miss Bindergarten Gets Ready for Kindergarten* (by Joseph Slate), and *Chrysanthemum* (by Kevin Henkes) are

| TABLE 3.1 | **Teacher's Resources for Phonological Awareness** |

Adams, M. J., Foorman, B. A., Lundberg, I., & Beeler, T. (1998). *Phonemic awareness in young children.* Baltimore, MD: Paul H. Brookes.

Blevins, W. (1997). *Phonemic awareness activities for early reading success.* New York, NY: Scholastic.

Ericson, L., & Juliebo, M. F. (1998). *The phonological awareness handbook for kindergarten and primary teachers.* Newark, DE: International Reading Association.

Fitzpatrick, J. (1998). *Phonemic awareness: Playing with sounds to strengthen beginning reading skills.* Cypress, CA: Creative Teaching Press.

Opitz, M. F. (2000). *Rhymes and reasons: Literature and language play for phonological awareness.* Portsmouth, NH: Heinemann.

just a few examples of books with multisyllabic words in the title. Point to the word itself as you say the syllables so that the children can see the printed connection. Then parse out the syllables as you clap, tap, slap, drum, stomp, jump, or move in other ways. You can also raise a finger or push a counter for each syllable, making it easy to go back and count the syllables in longer words.

Words are another large unit of sound, and they are easily confused with syllables until children actually learn to read. How does one know that *Once upon a time* is four words and that *grasshopper* is only one unless you know the printed words? Nevertheless, you can begin to draw attention to words without expecting children to read them. The key concept in the beginning is for children to understand that syllables are not equivalent to words—some words, like *grasshopper,* have more than one syllable. What's important is that each word refers to one thing, one person, one action, one emotion, or one description, and so on; word meanings are essential in differentiating words from syllables. But word meanings can also get in the way. Young children are very concrete thinkers, so it is not surprising that they often associate the length of a word with the size of its referent (Ferreiro & Teberosky, 1982). Although *caterpillar* is a fairly long word, it refers to a relatively small creature, and so it is common to find that children think the word *caterpillar* is smaller than the word *cat,* because cats are bigger than caterpillars! Emergent learners have difficulty attending to the sound structure of a spoken word apart from its meaning.

TEACHING RECOGNITION OF SYLLABLES AND WORDS. In addition to talking about words and syllables as they turn up in books and other contexts, you should also plan activities such as Lesson 3.1 that focus on these different units.

LESSON 3.1   Big words and little words

One way to help children develop an awareness of spoken words as a unit is to take two concrete "short" words and make them into one "long" compound word (e.g., *snow+ man = snowman*). The steps described in this lesson demonstrate how to move from attending to the meaning of words to also attending to their sound, a necessary step in developing the idea of written word size. By attending to the number of syllables in spoken words, children begin to understand that the size of words in print has to do with their sound, not necessarily their meaning. **(CCSS Foundational Skills: 2b, Phonological Awareness)**

▶

Step 1. Look at pictures

Show a picture of snow and another picture of a man, as shown in Figure 3.1. (Find images for this in Appendix C or find digital images online and display them on a computer or whiteboard. See Table 3.2 for a list of other compound words for which you can find images.) Discuss the meaning of each word separately. Then place the two pictures side by side and ask children to say each word in succession: "snow-man." Talk about how the one word *snowman* is made of two words, *snow* plus *man.* Next, replace the two separate pictures of snow and a man with one picture of a *snowman* and discuss again how the word *snowman* is made up of two words: *snow* and *man* (Cabell, Justice, Kaderavek, Pence, & Smith, A., 2009).

FIGURE 3.1 Compound Word

| snow | man | snowman |

Step 2. Attend to spoken syllables

Hold up the picture of *snow* and ask children to clap as they say the word *snow.* Next, hold up the picture of the *man* and ask the children to clap as they say the word *man.* Finally, hold up the picture of the *snowman* and ask the children to clap for each word in *snowman.* Discuss how the word *snowman* is longer than either the word *snow* or the word *man* because *snowman* has two syllables, whereas *snow* and *man* have only one! *Snowman* has more claps, so it is a longer word. What is a snowman? A man made of snow.

Step 3. Compare printed words

Hold up the printed word *snow* and compare it to the printed word *snowman.* Count the letters and talk about which word has more letters.

Step 4. Compare spoken words

Say, "I'm going to say two short words and you tell me what long word those two short words make. Ready? *Bath* [pause] *room.* What longer word do those two smaller words make? Yes, they make the word *bathroom!* Let's clap out the syllables in *bathroom* [clap clap]. What is a bathroom? A room where you can take a bath! Ready for another one?" Repeat with other concrete compound words such as those listed in Table 3.2.

TABLE 3.2   **Compound Words That Can Be Pictured**

basketball	skateboard	bedroom	butterfly
sunflower	lipstick	rainbow	wheelchair
fingernail	sunglasses	raincoat	pancake
football	mailbox	handbag	starfish
keyboard	doghouse	horseshoe	ponytail
sandbox	cupcake	pancake	trashcan
cowboy	ladybug	hairbrush	moonlight

Syllables in Names

Several important concepts can be developed by clapping the syllables in names. First, children become aware that even though each name refers to a single person, each single person's name may have more than one syllable. The second important concept addressed in this activity is that although *Shameeka* may be smaller than *Tay,* her name is longer. This fact can be further emphasized by counting the number of letters in each name as children compare them in print. Throughout the year, highlight the number of syllables in children's names in different ways. Create graphs, first by calling children to form groups by the number of syllables in their name and then by arranging names or photographs on a chart to make a bar graph. Call children to gather for a story or line up by syllables (e.g., "If your name has two syllables, come sit on the rug.").

> **Chapter 2 describes many activities that focus on children's names.**

Counting Words and Syllables

The concrete comparison of spoken words to printed words can be accomplished through a variety of activities. Children can add a Lego or Unifix cube for each word in a line as they repeat it. The cubes represent words and can be counted and compared to the number of words in a printed line. Sentences or lines can be compared. "Which sentence or line is longer? How can you tell? Yes! Longer sentences have more words—so more Legos!" When there is disagreement, check by clapping out the syllables in the word and compare it to the printed word unit in the line of text. For example, children may count seven words in "Old MacDonald Had a Farm" as they repeat it, but then count five words when they see it in print. The teacher can help them clap out the syllables to each word as she points to it, and in so doing, they discover that MacDonald has three syllables even though it is only one name. The big idea is to use speech to count words, to use print as a "check" on the accuracy of the number, and to use syllable clapping to resolve the mismatch between the two.

Sorting Pictures by Syllables

Another way to develop an understanding of syllables is to sort pictures of objects by the number of syllables. You can probably think of lots of concrete words with one and two syllables, but Table 3.3

TABLE 3.3 **Concrete Words with Three to Five Syllables**

THREE SYLLABLES		FOUR SYLLABLES	FIVE SYLLABLES
butterfly	potato	caterpillar	hippopotamus
banana	cucumber	watermelon	refrigerator
strawberry	tomato	alligator	
popsicle	rectangle	helicopter	
lollipop	triangle	motorcycle	
tricycle	elephant	automobile	
bicycle	kangaroo	television	
rollerblades	octopus	elevator	
telephone	grandmother	escalator	
gingerbread	umbrella	kindergarten	
hamburger	basketball	aquarium	
valentine	xylophone	kaleidoscope	
peppermint	hamburger	unicycle	
piano	newspaper		

lists some with three, four, and five syllables. You may want to start with just one- and two-syllable words. Use number cards as headers for this sort, or use cards with one to five dots. Say something like, "Here is the picture of an apple. Listen to the syllables in *apple* as I clap them, *ap-ple.* I hear two syllables, so I will put the apple under 'two.' Here is a peach. Listen: *peach.* I only hear one syllable in *peach,* so I will put it under 'one.' Now help me sort the rest of these pictures. Where will we put the carrot? Clap and count!"

Teacher, May I?

In this game, the traditional "Mother, may I?" is changed to "Teacher, may I?" Line up the children on the playground or in the gym. You can stretch out a rope to mark the starting line. Teach children the game first. The leader calls a name and says something like "Latisha, you can take two [baby, giant, or regular] steps". Before Latisha steps out she must say "Teacher, may I?" and be told "Yes" by the leader. To adapt to syllables, the leader would say something like "Silvio, step the syllables in *kangaroo.*" Silvio must then say, "Teacher, may I?" and take three steps. If a child forgets to say "Teacher, may I?" or if the player takes the wrong number of steps, he or she must go back to the starting line. The first one to touch the leader is the winner and becomes the next leader. To help the leader recall longer words, you might use a set of pictures from the last activity. Children can also step out the syllables in their name. Kim may be allowed to take one giant step whereas Joshua takes three baby steps.

Rhyme

The world of young children is filled with rhyme in many forms—poems, nursery rhymes, songs, jump rope jingles, and playground chants—so it is easy and natural to expose children to rhyme. To develop phonological awareness, however, you must plan activities that help children to focus *consciously* on rhyme. Many children develop a sense of rhyme easily, whereas others need more structured activities that draw their attention to the nature of rhyme, especially the location of the rhyme within words. Technically, one-syllable words are composed of two smaller units, an onset and a rime. The **onset** can be one initial consonant letter such as *b*, or a cluster such as *ch* or *br*. The **rime** is made up of the vowel and what follows, such as the *-ite* in *bite* or the *-ight* in *bright*. Words such as *bright* and *bite* are considered rhyming words because they sound the same at the end. Children will later study word families that share a rime (the *-at* in *cat, hat, fat,* and *mat*) and learn to analyze the letters that spell the onsets and rimes. But the first step is to identify rhyming words orally without reference to spelling pattern.

To read more about word families, look at Chapter 5.

English learners may not be as familiar with rhyme for several reasons. First, a sense of rhyme comes with lots of exposure to poems and songs that are common in English-speaking early childhood environments, and English learners may not have this common language embedded in their background experiences. Although Spanish does have rhyming words, rhyming is also identified as a stress on the vowel patterns in words. For example, in a simple Spanish poem the words *cuero* and *fueron* would be considered rhyming even though they do not end in the same way. The vowel pattern is so strong that it carries the weight of the rhyme and overrides the final consonant. Developing a sense of rhyme may take longer for English learners than native speakers. Because of this difference, difficulties with rhyme awareness should never hold English learners back from working on other phonological awareness skills.

EXPOSURE AND EXPLANATION WITH RHYMING BOOKS, JINGLES, AND SONGS. Singing songs is a fun way to develop a sensitivity to rhyme and teach the concept of rhyme. It's best to sing the song through several times before drawing attention to the rhymes. Be explicit as you teach children about rhyme: "*Fox* and *box* are rhyming words. Listen: *box/fox.* Rhyming words sound alike at the end." Books and picture storybooks provide a particularly good way to expose children to rhyme while enjoying colorful pictures and an engaging story. The traditional story of "Henny Penny" features Cocky Locky, Goosey Loosey , Turkey Lurkey, Ducky Lucky, and Foxy Loxy. This is an easy story to tell and act out. You may like Vivian French's version, in which the animals do not get eaten by the fox in the end. Picture books such as *Llama Llama Red Pajama* and other books in the series by Anna Dewdney or books about Bear by Karma Wilson and Jane Chapman are favorites written in rhyme that feature familiar topics such as bedtime, seasons, friends, and the first day of school. *Is Your Mama a Llama?* by Deborah Guarinao invites student participation, with each line cued by an illustration. As you reread books like these aloud, pause to allow the children to supply the rhyming word. Some favorite rhyming books are listed in Table 3.4, but there are many more.

NURSERY RHYMES. Traditional nursery rhymes provide an excellent source for developing many important literacy concepts, including rhyme. Despite the old-fashioned language, children enjoy the playful sounds of *Hickory Dickory Dock* and the nonsense of a cow that jumps over the moon. But there are other reasons to teach young children these traditional rhymes. Nursery rhymes introduce children to story structure in its most basic form. There is a setting or orientation: Jack and Jill are going up a hill to fetch water. There is a problem: Jack falls down and breaks his crown. And there's a resolution: Jill comes tumbling after. Children can recite and easily act out many nursery rhymes with simple plots.

TABLE 3.4	**Rhyming Book List**

Ahlsberg, J., & Ahlsberg, A. (1978). *Each peach pear plum: An "I Spy" story*. New York, NY: Scholastic.

Cameron, P. (1961). *I can't, said the ant*. New York, NY: Putnam Publishing.

Crews, D. (1986). *Ten black dots*. New York, NY: Greenwillow.

Degan, B. (1983). *Jamberry*. New York, NY: Harper.

Dewdney, A. (2005). *Llama Llama red pajama* New York, NY: Viking Juvenile. Look for more books in this series, including *Llama Llama mad at Mama* (2007) and *Llama Llama misses Mama* (2009).

French, V. (2006). *Henny Penny*. New York, NY: Bloomsbury.

Guarina, D. (1989). *Is your mama a llama?* Illustrated by Steven Kellogg. New York, NY: Scholastic.

Hoberman, M. A. (2003). *Miss Mary Mack*. London, England: Little Brown Books.

Langstaff, J. (1991). *Oh, a-hunting we will go*. New York, NY: Aladdin.

Martin, B., & Archambault, J. (1987). *Here are my hands*. New York, NY: Holt and Co.

Raffi. (1999). *Down by the bay*. New York, NY: Crown Books.

Seuss, Dr. (1965). *Hop on pop*. New York, NY: Random House. Also see *There's a wocket in my pocket* and *Fox in socks*.

Shaw, N. E. (1997). *Sheep in a jeep*. Boston, MA: Houghton Mifflin. Look for other books in this series, including *Sheep out to eat* (1995).

Strickland, P., & Strickland, H. (1994). *Dinosaur roar!* New York, NY: Scholastic.

Walton, R. (1998). *So many bunnies: A bedtime ABC and counting book*. New York, NY: Scholastic.

Wilson, K. (2002). *Bear snores on*. New York, NY: Margaret K. Mcelderry. Look for more titles in this series, including *Bear wants more* (2003) and *Bear's new friend* (2006).

Wilson, S. (2003). *Nap in a lap*. New York, NY: Henry Holt.

Wood, A. (1995). *Silly Sally went to town*. Boston, MA: Houghton Mifflin Harcourt.

Nursery rhymes also introduce children to a cast of characters who are likely to reappear in literature throughout their school years. You won't fully appreciate Ahlberg's *Each Peach Pear Plum* if you don't already know Mother Hubbard. Beautifully illustrated collections of nursery rhymes have long been a staple of children's literature and should be shared with young children. The illustrations not only add to the fun but also help children develop an understanding of the events and teach vocabulary. Comparing different illustrators' styles and interpretations of the same nursery rhyme can be a source of interest and discussion. Finally, the nursery rhymes provide short, simple, copyright-free texts that can be used to develop concepts about print and concept of word. Although some educators worry that nursery rhymes contain old-fashioned language, others believe their rhyme and rhythm provide excellent material for emergent readers who are developing phonological awareness. Language structures that are difficult for English learners to make sense of should be clarified with simple language and dramatic play. Take some time to explore the many nursery rhyme resources available on the Internet. On YouTube you can find animated versions to bring the rhymes to life. Laura Smolkin's website, Webbing into Literacy: A Head Start Program, provides many ready-to-print materials and teaching ideas.

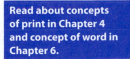

Read about concepts of print in Chapter 4 and concept of word in Chapter 6.

When selecting rhymes to use with your students, you may consider the following guidelines:

- Do your students have adequate English language skills to be able to repeat the rhyme from memory after several exposures? If the language and sentence structures are so unfamiliar to a portion of your students that they have difficulty repeating the language, look for rhymes that have more common language and simple sentence structures. Otherwise, you will only be teaching to the more advanced students in your class.

- If you have students who are learning English, seek out rhymes that offer sentence patterns that could be built on through variation. For example, "Jack and Jill went up the hill to fetch a pail of water" uses somewhat old-fashioned language, but the structure "X and X went ___ the ___ to _____" could be transformed to "Ahmad and Rosita went down the street to find a pair of glasses." Use the structure of simple nursery rhymes to help build students' oral language skills and teach important and useful vocabulary.

- If you have a significant number of students from a particular language background, talk to parents to find out more about children's rhymes in their home language. If possible, see whether any translations of these rhymes exist to use in class. Students' home languages and cultures can serve as a scaffold into learning the less familiar nursery rhymes of Mother Goose.

Acting Out Nursery Rhymes and Songs

Singing and acting out nursery rhymes like "Hey Diddle Diddle" will reinforce new vocabulary and provide the backdrop for playing with rhyme. Choose rhymes such as "Jack and Jill," "Old Mother Hubbard," "Little Miss Muffet," "Jack Be Nimble," or "Pat-a-Cake." Adding movement and props to reciting rhymes or singing songs will be especially important for children learning English. If possible, display an illustrated version and take the time to discuss the meanings of words like *pail* (bucket), *fetch* (go get something and bring it back), *crown* (the top of your head), and *tumble* (fall down).

Choose a child to help you act the rhyme out with simple props. Show how Jack falls down and breaks his crown by gingerly falling to the floor. Have your partner show how Jill comes tumbling after. Divide your students in pairs and have one be Jack and another be Jill, and ask them to act out the plot as they recite the rhyme or sing the song. Then leave out the props for children to act out nursery rhymes during free play time.

Activity

PD TOOLKIT™
for Words Their Way®

Go to the PDToolkit to see children acting out "Humpty Dumpty" and learning concepts about print as they work with the rhyme. Click on the Videos tab and select Emergent Stage. Scroll to find the clip entitled "Humpty Dumpty."

After singing and acting out a nursery rhyme, you can play "I'm Thinking Of": a rhyme guessing game. For example, you might say, "I'm thinking of a medicine that you swallow that rhymes with hill" (pill).

Playing with Rhymes and Jingles

Once children have memorized a nursery rhyme, you can begin to use it as the basis for language play. Begin by pausing at the rhyming words to let the children fill in the blank: "Little Bo Peep has lost her . . . ." Try alternating the lines: You say a line and the children say the next, or split your group up and alternate lines. You can also substitute nonrhyming words, as was done with Lucky at the beginning of this chapter, as a way to reinforce the concept of rhyme. Try to substitute words that are synonyms, or close to them, that can actually help children understand the meaning of some of the unusual words: "Little Miss Muffet sat on the grass," or "Hey diddle diddle, the cat and the violin." You can also create new versions of rhymes. In some cases, you may substitute nonsense words and then pause to allow the children to supply a real rhyming word, as in this example using the simple jingle "Little Bo Peep has lost her sheep."

> Little Bo Buppy has lost her . . . puppy.
> Little Bo Bitten has lost her . . . kitten.
> Little Bo Babbit has lost her . . . rabbit.
> Little Bo Balligator has lost her . . . alligator!

To offer some support, supply models or pictures of animals from which to choose the rhyming word, and then begin to involve the children in making up the nonsense word: "What would you say for *cow*?" (Little Bo Bow)

Reading Rhymes

As children build a repertoire of memorized songs, nursery rhymes, and jingles, record these on charts and read them aloud together for shared reading. Shared reading of familiar texts provides the support that emergent readers need to develop concepts about print and a concept of word as preparation for conventional reading. Having a printed copy of a song or rhyme offers you a chance to point specifically to where rhyming words occur at the ends of lines and even to point out how they are spelled the same at the end. Make the charts available during free time and encourage children to recite them as they attempt to point to the words. In kindergarten you may want to create a notebook to which children can add their own copies of rhymes and jingles.

> For more information on shared reading and personal readers see Chapter 4 and 6.

RHYME ACTIVITIES. There are many simple games and activities that will engage children in identifying, isolating, and producing rhymes.

Matching and Sorting Rhyming Pictures

Working with rhyming pictures gets children actively involved in identifying rhymes and provides extended practice when the activity is repeated in centers. Start with activities in which students only consider two or three pictures at a time. A simple rhyming extension to *Silly Sally Goes to Town* could focus on a single word such as *dog*, one of the featured animals. Simply collect a few pictures whose names rhyme with *dog (log, frog, hog)* and some whose names do not rhyme (*cat, goat, tree*). You can compare two words by holding up both pictures and saying, "Does *log* rhyme with *dog*? *Log, dog*? Yes, they sound alike at the end, so they rhyme." Or set up a choice with three pictures—two words that rhyme and one that does not (*duck, bag, truck*)—and ask students to find the two that rhyme, as in Figure 3.2. Keep the number of choices to a minimum when you first introduce rhyme so that children can be successful. Page 67 lists rhyming pictures that can be found among the pictures in Appendix B.

Once children get good at identifying two pictures that rhyme, you can teach them how to sort. Set up two or more categories and lead the children in sorting objects or pictures by rhyming sound. For

FIGURE 3.2 Odd One Out Rhyming Task

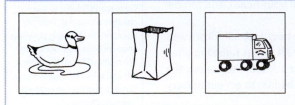

example, set out pictures of a plate and a bee as headers and sort other pictures in turn under the correct header (gate, skate, tree, key). See Lesson 3.2 for an example.

LESSON 3.2 Rhyming sort with *Here Are My Hands*

The book *Here Are My Hands* by Bill Martin and John Archambault (illustrated by Ted Rand) features rhymes that name parts of the body. Prepare a set of pictures: nose, hair, and head to serve as headers, and toes, hose, rose, bear, pear, chair, bed, and bread as the rhymes. A copy of this sort can be found in Appendix B. (CCSS Foundational Skills: 2a, Phonological Awareness)

Step 1. Read aloud

The book describes what we do with different parts of the body in simple rhymes. After reading it through once, reread it and pause to let children fill in the rhyming words.

Step 2. Model rhymes

Set out the pictures of the head, toes, and hair and explain that you are going to find words that rhyme. Hold up a picture such as the bread and say, "Listen to how I find the rhyming word: *Bread, nose;* they don't rhyme. *Bread, head;* those rhyme, so I am going to put the picture of the bread under the head." Model a few more, showing how to compare each word with the headers. Then invite children to help you sort the rest. (See Figure 3.3.)

Step 3. Check the sort

Emphasize the rhymes by reading down each column. Reiterate that the pictures rhyme because they sound alike at the end. Leave up the headers and pass out the rest of the pictures to the students. Sort again, letting each child decide where to place his or her picture. If errors are made by the students, leave them; but check the sort at the end and, if there is a picture out of place in a column, ask children to find it.

FIGURE 3.3 Rhyming Sort

Step 4. Let the children sort

Put the pictures in a center for the children to sort. You can create a sorting folder by gluing the headers in place and storing the pictures in an envelope or plastic bag inside the folder.

As children become more adept at listening for and matching rhymes, they can play a variety of other categorization and matching games. Traditional games such as bingo and concentration, in which picture cards or objects are matched to other picture cards that rhyme, are always winners.

for Words Their Way®

The PDToolkit has prepared sorts and gameboards for rhyming bingo. Click on the Sorts and Games tab, select Emergent, type "rhymes" in the search box, and hit the Apply button. You can also make rhyming sorts by following directions on the Create Your Own button at the top right of that tab.

Rhyming Bingo

Prepare enough bingo game boards for the number of children who will participate (small groups of three to five children are ideal). An appropriate game board size for young children is a 6- by 6-inch board divided into nine 2- by 2-inch squares. Copy sets of pictures and paste all but one of each rhyming group in the spaces on the game boards. (Each game board must be arranged differently.) You might laminate the boards for durability. Prepare a complementary set of cards on which you paste the remaining pictures from each rhyming group. These will become the deck from which rhyming words are called aloud during the game. You will need some kind of marker to cover the squares on the game board. These may be as simple as two-inch squares of construction paper, plastic chips, bottle caps, or pennies. Once the bingo boards are made, each child receives a game board and markers to cover spaces. The teacher or a designated child is the caller, who turns over cards from the deck and calls out the name of each picture. Each player searches the game board for a picture that rhymes with the word that was called out. Players can cover the matched picture with a marker to claim the space. The winner is the first child to cover a row in any direction or the first player to fill the entire board, depending on how long you want the game to last.

Rhyming Concentration

This game is played like traditional Concentration or the more current Memory games. Assemble a collection of 8 to 10 rhyming pairs of pictures. Paste the pictures on cards and laminate them for durability. Be sure the pictures do not show through the backside. Once your cards are prepared, shuffle them and lay them face-down in a 3 by 4 or 4 by 4 array. Players take turns flipping over two pictures at a time. If the two pictures rhyme, the player keeps the cards until the end of the game. If they do not rhyme, the cards are turned back over in place. The winner is the child who has the most matches at the end of the game. As children get better, try a 4 by 5 or 5 by 5 array.

Inventing Rhymes

Thinking up rhyming words is quite an accomplishment, requiring not only a good sense of rhyme but an extensive vocabulary. Children are likely to need support in their first efforts to generate rhymes, and nonsense frees them from the restraints of thinking of real words. Dr. Seuss was a master of pure nonsense, and one example of this is *There's a Wocket in My Pocket,* which takes readers on a tour of a home in which all kinds of odd creatures have taken up residence. There is a *woset* in the closet, a *zlock* behind the clock, and a *nink* in the sink. After reading this aloud, ask children to imagine what animal would live in their cubby, under the rug, or in the lunchroom. Their efforts should rhyme, but anything will do: a *rubby, snubby,* or *frubby* might all live in a cubby.

The Hungry Thing

Another book that lends itself to the invention of rhyme is Jan Slepian and Ann Seidler's *The Hungry Thing*. This story tells of a creature that comes to town begging for food but has trouble pronouncing what he wants. He requests *shmancakes* (pancakes), *feetloaf* (meatloaf), and *hookies* (cookies), but only a small boy can figure out what he wants. After reading this aloud, plan a follow-up activity that teaches how to invent silly rhymes. Put a collection of pictures of food or everyday objects on a table or the floor while the children sit around them. The teacher models how to imitate the Hungry Thing by making up a nonsense word and then invites the children find the rhyming object. For example, the teacher says, "The Hungry Thing wants a weet. Can you find a weet [beet]?" In response to "Where is a *mapple*?," someone would select an apple. After seeing the teacher model this, children can take turns making up their own nonsense labels. With this preparation, children may be ready to act out the story with their own food choices. As each takes the part of the Hungry Thing, the child must come up with a rhyming word for the food he or she wants, such as *monuts, bandwich,* or *smello*. The story continues in *The Hungry Thing Returns* and *The Hungry Thing Goes to a Restaurant*. These books may be out of print, but look for them in your school library or used book sources.

Variations on Songs

Songs by Raffi have been around for years and can now be downloaded as MP3s. Some of them are particularly well suited for language play. Silly rhymes are featured prominently in the song "Willoughby Wallaby Woo" from the collection *Singable Songs for the Very Young*. The song features a rhyme starting with *W* for everyone's name and can be easily adapted for the children in your class. The teacher sings the initiating phrase changing the first letter of a name to *W* (e.g., "Willoughby Wallaby Werry"), and children sing the next phrase, naming the appropriate child ("An elephant sat on Kerry"). A stuffed elephant can be passed around if you have one. Later on, this song can be revisited to focus on alliteration by holding up a particular letter to insert in front of every word. *B*, for example, would result in "Billoughby Ballaby Boo," and *F* would produce "Filloughby Fallaby Foo." Some other Raffi favorites that lead to inventive fun with rhymes include "Apples and Bananas" from *One Light One Sun*, and "Spider on the Floor" and "Down by the Bay," both from *Singable Songs for the Very Young*. Some of Raffi's rhyming songs are also available in book format, including *Down by the Bay* and *Wheels on the Bus*.

LESSON 3.3   Making up rhymes

Children who need more explicit instruction in rhyme will benefit from building rhymes. (CCSS Foundational Skills: 2a, Phonological Skills)

Step 1. Introduce a rhyming element

Ask your children to say *at*. Explain that you are going to make words that have *at* in them. Hold up a picture of a cat; ask the students to say the word *cat* and listen for the *at* at the end of *cat*. Emphasize the rhyme in a whole word. Say *c-at*, emphasizing the *at*. Ask children whether they can hear the *at* in *c-at*.

Step 2. Introduce pictures

Hold up a picture of a hat. Ask the children to tell you what it is. Tell them that *h-at* has an *at* in it. Hold up other pictures (mat, rat, etc.) and ask whether they can hear the *at* in *m-at, r-at, s-at*, and so on.

Step 3. Identify the sound

Ask students whether they can tell what sound is the same in *cat, hat, mat, fat*, and *sat*. Emphasize the *at* in each of these words. Explain that *cat, hat, mat, fat*, and *sat* rhyme because they all have *at* at the end.

Step 4. Brainstorm

Ask students to brainstorm other words that rhyme with *cat: bat, that, pat, flat*, for example. Make other rhymes in a similar fashion: *an, ack, ap, est, in, it, ick, op, ot, ock, ump*, and so on.

Phonemic Awareness: Alliteration and Beginning Sounds

Children must understand that speech can be divided into smaller segments of sound or phonemes in order to learn letter–sound correspondences, and they must learn some of the terminology used to talk about these sounds. Without understanding that words are made up of sounds and that those sounds have certain positions in words, phonics instruction will meet with little success. Directions such as "Listen for the first sound" may mystify young children. In response to the question "What sound does *dog* start with?" one puzzled child responded by barking! However, phonemic awareness activities at the emergent level help children attend to beginning sounds and learn to label and categorize these sounds in various ways.

Phonological awareness, and phoneme awareness in particular, is not language specific. Research has shown that phonemic awareness developed in one language will transfer to another (August & Shanahan, 2006; Durgunoglu, Nagy, & Hancin-Bhatt, 1993). At the same time, English learners—even at the very beginning stages of learning English—benefit from the phonological awareness activities described here, as long as the material is comprehensible to them. They may require additional instruction to keep up with the phonemic awareness development of the native English speakers. In addition, we should be mindful of the fact that emerging bilinguals may experience more difficulty with segmenting initial consonant sounds that may not occur in their native language because they are learning to identify these sounds in English.

PLANNING INSTRUCTION FOR PHONEMIC AWARENESS. In choosing tasks and activities to develop awareness of initial consonant sounds, be aware that all sounds and all tasks are not created equal. Continuant consonant sounds—those that can be pronounced with a continuous stream of breath, like /s/, /f/, or /m/—are easier to isolate and segment than stop consonant sounds, like /t/, /d/, or /p/. This is because continuant sounds can be "held" without distorting the sound, as in *sssssssssun* or *sssseeeeed*. The /s/ sounds the same in all of these beginning contexts. Not so with stop consonants that are formed by "stopping" the flow air through the mouth and cannot be "held" without distortion. (Try saying the first sound in *tap*. Notice how your tongue "stops" the sound and then releases it quickly as it merges with the vowel sound that follows.) In teaching children to isolate sounds, begin with continuous consonant sounds at the beginning of words, because these sounds can be held for emphasis.

The activities we ask children to do also vary in difficulty. It is easier for young children to identify and match beginning sounds than it is to isolate and segment them from the rest of the word. Segmenting or separating sounds is harder than blending sounds, and substituting or manipulating beginning sounds to make new words is even more difficult. This doesn't mean we shouldn't ask children in preschool and kindergarten to do these tasks. But we should be mindful of their difficulty as we plan the scope and sequence of our instruction. It's best to allow young children to become facile with easy tasks before attempting more challenging ones. Consider the increasing difficulty of the following tasks related to phonemic awareness:

1. "Do *mmmmoon* and *mmman* begin with the same sound?" (The child is asked to recognize alliteration or the same initial phoneme.)
2. "Can you find a picture of something that starts with /m/?" (The child is asked to discriminate or match phonemes.)
3. "Say these sounds together to make a word: *mmmmmm–oooon*." (The child is asked to blend given phonemes.)
4. "What is the first sound in *mmmmoon*"? (The child is asked to isolate a phoneme.)
5. "Can you think of a word that begins with /mmmm/?" (The child is asked to generate words with particular phonemes.)
6. "Can you say *moon* without the /m/? Can you change the /m/ in *moon* to /s/?" (The child is asked to identify, isolate, and manipulate phonemes.)

EXPOSURE AND EXPLANATION FOR ALLITERATION. Activities that play with **alliteration** focus children's attention on the beginning sounds that mark word boundaries in print. Awareness of beginning sounds supports children as they learn to separate the speech stream into individual words. Just as rhyming books can be used as a catalyst to spring into rhyming activities, books built around alliteration are helpful to develop children's awareness of beginning sounds. Many alphabet books feature alliterative phrases. A well-known example is the classic *Dr. Seuss's ABC,* which celebrates alliteration in the famous Seuss style. You can also share selections from books of tongue twisters. See the book list in Table 3.5.

TABLE 3.5	**Alliteration in Children's Books**

Base, G. (1986). *Animalia*. New York, NY: Harry N. Abrams.

Bayer, J. (1984). *A my name is Alice*. New York, NY: Dial Books.

Berenstain, S., & Berenstain, J. (1997). *The Berenstain's B book*. New York, NY: Random House.

Bottner, B. (1992). *Bootsie Barker bites*. New York, NY: Putnam.

Brown, M. W. (1996). *Four fur feet*. New York, NY: Hyperion.

Cole, J. M. (1993). *Six sick sheep: 101 tongue twisters*. New York, NY: Morrow.

Dragonwagon, C. (1987) *Alligator arrived with apples: A potluck alphabet feast*. New York, NY: MacMillan.

Edwards, P. D. (1997). *Four famished foxes and Fosdyke*. New York, NY: HarperCollins. Also see *The Worryworts* (2003) and *Clara Caterpiller* (2004).

Jonas, A. (1997). *Watch William walk*. New York, NY: Greenwillow Books.

Kirk, D. (1990). *Miss Spider's ABC*. New York, NY: Scholastic Press.

Pomeranz, C., & Marshall, J. (1989). *The piggy in the puddle*. New York, NY: Aladdin.

Raschka, C. (1992) *Charlie Parker played be bop*. New York, NY: Orchard Books.

Rovitch, L., & McNeil, S. (2006). *Ook the book and other silly rhymes*. San Francisco, CA: Chronicle Books.

Schwartz, A. (1972). *Twister of twists*. NewYork, NY: HarperCollins. Also see *Busy buzzing bumble bees and other tongue twisters*.

Seeger, L. V. (2007). *Walter was worried*. New York, NY: Roaring Brook Press.

Seuss, Dr. (1963). *Dr. Seuss's ABC*. New York, NY: Random House.

Shaw, N. (1991) *Sheep in a shop*. Boston, MA: HMH Books.

Activities for Alliteration. Plan activities that specifically draw attention to the beginning sounds in words and engage children in repeated practice as they learn to recognize, segment, and blend sounds.

Using Children's Books

When sharing books, tongue twisters, or jingles that feature alliteration, it is important to be explicit about what children should listen for. To make phonemes more concrete, talk about how the sounds feel or look in your mouth. Say something like this: "Many mice make music. I hear a lot of words that start with /m/. [Say the sound, not the letter.] MMMMany mmmice mmmmake mmmmusic. Look at me. When I make the sound for /m/, I feel my lips pressing tightly together. Say /m/ with me. Now let's say 'many mice make music.'" You will need to repeat this many times with other sounds. You can also model how to think about and isolate sounds as you write for children during interactive writing, described in Chapter 4. For example, if you want to write the word *we*, model how to stretch out the sounds (/wwwwweeeee/) and then isolate the first sound ("I hear /wwww/ at the beginning of *we*, and I feel my lips push out to make that sound"). To make this stretching-out process more concrete, some teachers stretch out a large rubber band as they say the word.

Puppet Play to Blend and Isolate Initial Sounds

Beginning-sound segmentation and blending games can be played with puppets or stuffed animals that have a funny way of talking (Treiman, 1985). The puppet teaches the children how to either blend phonemes or to isolate the initial phoneme from the remaining portion of the word. The children are then asked to repeat what the puppet said. The children get to manipulate the puppet themselves as they segment words given by the teacher. For example, Pat the Puppet first says "p-ig," and the students repeat by saying "p-ig." Then the teacher says *pick* and asks the students to say the word like Pat the Puppet would say it in "puppet talk." The children respond with "p-ick." To teach blending, ask students to respond to Pat by saying the word naturally. If Pat says "p-ig," the children respond with "pig." Using animal puppets such as Maggie the Moose, described in Lesson 3.4, can help children become aware of initial consonant sounds

Nursery Rhymes

Rhymes and jingles can also be used to build the awareness of beginning consonant sounds. "Peter, Peter, Pumpkin Eater" features a series of /p/ sounds in the first line. Consider the alliteration in "Goosie Goosie Gander" and "Betty Botter Bought Some Butter." Reading books and nursery rhymes that repeat initial consonant sounds is a great segue into activities that scaffold children into producing their own alliterative pairs.

Deleting Initial Sounds

Set out an array of objects or pictures of objects. Hold up one at a time as you ask, "Is this an *og*? [while holding up a picture of a dog]. No? What is it then? What sound did I leave off at the beginning of that word?" Repeat this with other objects and pictures such as "ock" (rock), "ish" (fish), and "ell" (shell). Pair this with a read-aloud of Ravich's *Ook the Book: And Other Silly Rhymes,* which features characters whose names are missing the beginning sound, such as Ug the bug and Ow the cow.

LESSON 3.4 Puppet play with beginning consonant sounds

Materials

Give an animal puppet an alliterative name such as Maggie the Moose (or Bobby Bear, Cassie Cat, Peggy Pig, etc.). You'll need an assortment of pictures or objects, some of whose names start with the /m/ sound (money, mittens, map, mat, man, mop, moon, mouse) and some of whose don't (corn, sandwich, pan, house). (CCSS Foundational Skills: 2, Phonological Awareness)

Step 1. Introduce Maggie

Explain that Maggie the Moose likes things that start with the same sound as her name, /m/. So Maggie likes milk and macaroni because *milk* and *macaroni* start with the /m/ sound just like *Maggie* and *moose.*

Step 2. Display the pictures

Show two pictures at a time (one that starts with an /m/ sound, such as money, and one that doesn't, such as leaves) and ask, "Which one would Maggie the Moose like?"

Step 3. Brainstorm

Have children brainstorm other things that Maggie the Moose would like. They may volunteer such things as marshmallows, morning, or mom.

I Spy with Initial Sounds

Teachers can use hints in games such as I Spy or I'm Thinking of Something to accentuate initial sounds. "This thing I'm thinking of begins with *mmmmm.* This thing is small and gray. It is an animal." As the children respond "mouse," the teacher asks them to exaggerate the beginning sound. As children become proficient at playing this game, they create their own riddles.

Playground Chants, Songs, and Jingles

Songs are useful in building the concept of alliteration as a string of words that all begin with the same sound. "The Name Game," originally sung by Shirley Ellis, has been passed into the oral tradition and may be known by some members of your class. Sing the song over and over, substituting the name of a different child on every round. The song builds on concepts of both rhyme and alliteration.

> Sam Sam Bo Bam, Banana Fanna Fo Fam, Fee Fi Mo Mam, Sam!
> Kaitlyn Kaitlyn Bo Baitlyn, Banana Fanna Fo Faitlyn, Fee Fi Mo Maitlyn, Kaitlyn!

Street rhymes and jump rope jingles that play with children's names are also useful for calling attention to beginning sounds. Children can clap or jump rope as they chant "My name is (child's name) and my friend is (name). We live in (place) and we sell (item)." For /m/, for example, the chant would be "My name is Marcia and my friend is Marge. We live in Martinsville and we sell marshmallows!"

Sorting by Initial Sound

Alliteration is further developed as children sort objects and pictures by beginning sound under a corresponding letter, an activity that will be described in Chapter 5. At this point, oral language activities designed to teach phonemic awareness cross over into the learning of letter–sound correspondences. This is known as **phonics**.

See Chapter 5 for more information about teaching letter–sound correspondences.

Full Phonemic Awareness

Phonemic awareness continues to develop from partial to full as children engage in a variety of literacy tasks, especially in kindergarten. We see evidence of this in children's invented spellings as they attempt to represent sounds in more than the initial position of words. Note the development of phonemic awareness in the spelling attempts for the word *bed:* B, BD, BAD. When children start to represent the medial vowel and blends (SKP or SKEP for *skip*), they are developing full phonemic awareness. The movement from partial to full phonemic awareness hinges on the convergence of several early literacy skills, including alphabet and letter–sound knowledge, awareness of initial consonant sounds, and the development of a concept of word in text (Morris, Bloodgood, Lomax, & Perney, 2003). Although phonemic awareness does not involve matching sounds to letters (a phonics skill), there is nevertheless good evidence that letters serve as concrete references that may enhance children's ability to listen for and identify sounds within words (Ehri, 1993).

WRITING AND LISTENING FOR PHONEMES. Full phonemic awareness is appropriately taught in the context of writing, because the effort to compose a message or express an idea offers an authentic reason to listen for and identify the sounds in the words you want to write. There are levels of support for segmenting phonemes during writing as you gradually release the responsibility to children. This can be done in a group setting first (such as interactive writing) and then individually as you work with one child.

Read more about interactive writing in Chapter 4.

1. *Demonstrate and explain.* Model how to slowly say the sounds in words, break the word down into individual phonemes, supply the letters, and then blend the sounds back into a word. This is best done initially with words that have two or three continuant phonemes (e.g., *mmm-eee* or *ssss-uuu-nnnn*). After isolating the sounds, supply the letter: "Listen to me say the word slowly: *Mmmeeee*. I hear /mmm/ at the beginning of *me* and that is spelled with an *m. Mmmmmeeee*. I hear *e* after the /m/." If you are writing a long word, you will first need to break it down into syllables. After writing the letters, go back and model how to say the sounds as you touch the letters and then run your hand under them to model blending.
2. *Participate.* Ask children to say a word slowly with you and isolate the sounds. See whether they can tell you what letter can be used to spell that sound. This goes beyond phonemic awareness because writing requires letters.
3. *Practice and apply.* Ask the child to identify the sounds in a word: "What sounds do you hear when you stretch out the word?" Encourage children to write for themselves, spelling as best they can. This will exercise and develop their phonemic awareness in the very best possible way. Chapter 5 will describe in detail the fascinating insights children develop and the special logic behind some of their unconventional attempts at writing during preschool and kindergarten.

Blending All the Sounds

Once children are fairly proficient at blending initial sounds with the rime that follows (as in *p-ig*), challenge them to blend three and even four sounds. This can be done with a puppet who talks in a funny way, as described previously. Pat the Puppet might say *sssss-uuuuuu-nnnnn,* and the children would be asked to blend the sounds into a word: *sun.* You can also call children to group time or to line up by saying their names in a stretched-out fashion. It can be difficult to segment the phonemes in long names like Casandra, so you might segment some names into syllables (*Ca-san-dra*) and some into phonemes (*Wwwwww-iiiiii-llllll*).

Sound Boxes

One of the early researchers of phonemic awareness was the Russian psychologist Elkonin (1973), who devised the strategy of providing boxes for each sound in a word (see Figure 3.4). Children were trained to push a counter into each box as they segmented the sounds. Other researchers and teachers have created variations of this (Blachman, Ball, Black, & Tangel, 1994; Clay, 2001), but the basic idea remains the same. The number of boxes is a clue to the number of sounds that need to be isolated, making the segmentation process more concrete and defined. This can be done as an isolated activity, as described in Lesson 3.5, but it can also be done during writing. Keep a small chalkboard or whiteboard handy. Simply draw the number of boxes needed for the word and model how to segment a sound for each box. Then go back and write in a letter or letters for each sound. If you are segmenting a word with a digraph like *sh* or *ch*, you would write both letters in one box. *Ship* (*sh-i-p*)and *dish* (*d-i-sh*) have three phonemes each. Be selective and do this only with one-syllable words that are straightforward like *go* or *wish,* and not with words like *laugh* or *February.*

FIGURE 3.4 Sound Boxes

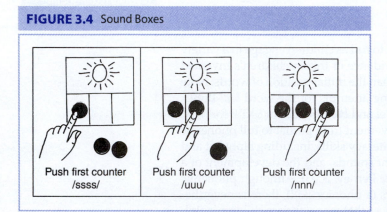

LESSON 3.5   Sound boxes

Materials

Prepare a collection of pictures with three phonemes that can be easily segmented. Some examples with beginning and ending continuants include *sun, moon, mouse, yes, mom, man, fuzz, fan, van, well, thin, seal, nose, room,* and *roof.* Words that begin with a continuant and end in a stop consonant (as in *ssss-iiiii-t*) also work fairly well (e.g., *mad, sad, rag, map, red, sit, lid, wig, zip, fog, log, mop, rock, sock, ship, feet, seed, fish, dish*). Avoid words that end in *r,* as it may be impossible to separate the vowel (e.g., *far*). Find or draw a simple illustration of the word and then draw three boxes below as in Figure 3.4. Counters can be buttons, pennies, chips, tiles, blocks, or just about anything you have available. (CCSS Foundational Skills: 2d, Phonological Awareness)

Step 1. Show the picture of the moon and name it

Explain: "Listen while I say *moon* slowly: *mmmmooooonnn.* I hear three sounds in *moon.* Watch how I say each sound and push a counter into each box. *mmmm-ooo-nnn, moon.*" Ask the children to repeat after you, perhaps pushing their own counters for each sound.

Step 2. Simplify as needed

If three sounds are difficult, drop back to words with just two phonemes (*zoo, me, shoe, moo, my*). At some point, with children who are beginning to study letter–sound matches, you might substitute letters for the counters. This might be magnetic letters or letter cards. Three-letter words are best when you begin to use letters. You can also use fewer sounds (*zoo, moo, me, shoe*) or move on to words with blends, in which case you would need four boxes (as in *stop* or *fast*).

Beginning-Middle-End

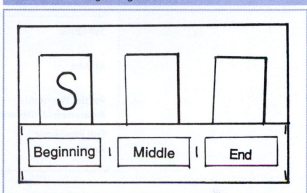

FIGURE 3.5 Beginning Middle End

Here is a variation of sound boxes that focuses on identifying the position of the sound in the word, using a song sung to the tune of "Are You Sleeping, Brother John?" Create a simple three-pocket folder like the one shown in Figure 3.5. A good size can be made from stiff 8½- by 11-inch paper or tagboard with letter cards that fit into the pockets.

1. Place the letters needed to spell a three-letter word in the pocket turned over so the children cannot see the letters. Announce the word, such as *sun*. Choose words from a familiar book, poem, or dictation when possible.
2. Sing the song to the tune of "Are You Sleeping, Brother John?"

   > *Beginning, middle, end; beginning, middle, end*
   > *Where is the sound? Where is the sound?*
   > *Where's the ssss in sun? Where's the ssss in sun?*
   > *Let's find out. Let's find out.*

3. Children take turns coming forward to pick the position and check by turning the letter card.

··················

Assessing and Monitoring Phonological Awareness

To plan instruction for phonological awareness, it is necessary to find out what children know about speech sounds and where they are along the continuum between identification/recognition and to production/use. Because phonological awareness develops from awareness of larger sound units (such as syllables and rhymes) to smaller sound units (such as beginning consonant phonemes), it is helpful to know where children are along this progression as well. We describe a series of assessments starting with hands-on interactive tasks that involve the manipulation of picture cards or counters. Unlike tasks given orally, pictures offer support so young children do not need to hold words in memory to make judgments.

As shown in Table 3.6, assessment is organized into four parts: syllable, rhyme, partial phonemic awareness of initial consonants (alliteration), and full phonemic awareness. Each section contains two levels exploring children's ability to *recognize or identify* the specific sound unit of interest (level 1) as well as children's ability to *produce, generate, or apply* those insights (level 2). Assessment forms and detailed directions can be found in Appendix A of this book or at the online PDToolkit. Some tasks can be group administered as a paper and pencil task; others must be individually administered. Scores can be compiled on the Assessment Summary Sheet. In general 80 percent can be considered sufficient mastery of a task. Children who score below 50 percent should get additional support in individual and small-group settings. Teachers should use their judgment about students whose scores fall between these.

Phonological awareness tasks similar to these have been scientifically validated by Invernizzi and her colleagues with thousands of children screened in Virginia with Phonological Awareness Literacy Screening (PALS) (Invernizzi, Justice, Landrum, & Booker, 2004) assessments at the preschool and kindergarten levels. This research has established that by early kindergarten most children, on average, can identify 8 out of 10 rhyming pairs and 7 out of 10 beginning sound pairs. By the end of kindergarten, students are likely to miss no more than one. Four-year-olds attending a preschool program can, on average, identify 8 out of 10 pairs based on rhyme or alliteration by the end of their preschool year (Invernizzi & Huang, 2011). Monitoring the development of children's phonological awareness during preschool and kindergarten helps to identify children who need

for Words Their Way®

Go to the PDToolkit to find copies of assessment materials. Click on the Assessment Tools tab and select Emergent Assessments. Scroll to find the different tasks.

	RECOGNITION WITH VISUAL SUPPORT	PRODUCTION IN AN ORAL TASK
Syllables	Sort pictures by number of syllables	Say and segment syllables
Rhyme	Odd one out with rhyming pictures	Produce a rhyme
Partial Phonemic Awareness/Alliteration	Find a match for beginning sounds with pictures	Puppet talk to segment initial sound
Full Phonemic Awareness	Push and segment the sounds with pictures	Spelling task (see Chapter 5)

TABLE 3.6 **Phonological Awareness Assessments**

additional instruction. The assessments we provide are adapted from the PALS assessments. If your school requires a more standardized assessment of phonological awareness, we recommend using PALS-PreK for preschoolers and PALS-K for kindergarteners. (See the PALS website at the University of Virginia.)

Working with Parents

Although many parents teach their children the letters of the alphabet, it is less likely that they will know to teach their children how to listen for sounds and talk about sounds in words. Terms like *phonological awareness* will be quite mystifying to them unless you have a chance to explain and give examples, so it is a good topic to cover at an open house. Figure 3.6 is a sample letter to parents that will offer some explanations about phonological awareness and some ideas about things they can do at home. You may also want to send home copies of songs, rhymes, and other jingles the children are learning so parents can reinforce what they are learning in school.

FIGURE 3.6 Parent Letter for Phonological Awareness

Dear Parents/Guardians,

Your child is learning about the sounds in oral language, including syllables, rhymes, and the smallest single sounds, which are known as *phonemes*. The ability to pay attention to and talk about the sounds in words is known as *phonological awareness*. It becomes important when children begin to learn about how sounds match to letters—or phonics. You can play an important role in helping your child develop phonological awareness using some of the activities described below.

Here are some ways to help teach about syllables and words:

• When you come across a long word, perhaps in a book or on a sign, point it out by saying something like "*Helicopter* is a long word. Let's say it slowly and clap the syllables in it. Now let's say it fast."

- Clap the syllables in family members' names to find out who has the longest name. Count the letters in family names. The one with the most syllables may not have the most letters!

Here are some ways to help teach your child about rhyme:

- Teach your child to recite and sing poems, nursery rhymes, jump-rope jingles, and songs that you remember from your own childhood. Once they are familiar, pause before rhyming words to see whether your child can supply what is missing.
- Many children's books are full of rhyming words. Books by Dr. Seuss are especially rich in rhyme. As you read such books, take the time to identify and label rhyming words: "I notice that *fall* and *tall* rhyme." Then begin to ask your child to find the rhyming words: "Listen for some rhyming words. What rhymes with *fall*?"
- Look for rhyming games online and apps that you can download. You will find lots of them and many are free.
- Create your own rhymes and have fun playing with sounds, even if they make no sense. Many parents make up silly names for their children such as Ellie-Jellie or Ready-Teddy.

Here are some ways to help teach children to pay attention to beginning sounds in words:

- Read alphabet books with your child and take the time to talk about the pictures that begin with the sound of the letters. Say things like: "*Moon* starts with *M*. Listen: *mmmmmmmoon* [emphasizing and stretching out the first sound]. Can you find something else that starts with that sound?"
- Look for examples of alliteration or tongue twisters in songs and poems, such as "Suzy sells seashells down by the seashore." Help your child repeat after you, but also take the time to talk about how the words are alike: "These words all start with the *ssssss* sound."

Sincerely,

Concepts about Print
and Writing

Jackie carefully scaffolds name writing over the year so that by spring nearly all the four- and five-year-olds in her prekindergarten classroom can write their names. In September, students signed themselves in each day when they entered the room by finding their name and picture on a card and moving the card from the "Out" side of a pocket chart to the "In" side. After a few weeks their pictures were removed from the cards so that they had to rely on the print. By January most could copy their names from a card, usually with instructional support. By April students write their names on a clipboard each morning as a record of attendance (referring to a model if needed). They also sign up for their favorite centers (like block, computer, and painting), what they want for lunch, and class jobs like feeding the classroom guinea pig. Through these routines and others that help Jackie run her classroom, young children learn about the forms and functions of literacy.

Jackie also plans many activities that feature names. Kaitlyn and her classmates are greeted one day in a group activity singing a version of "Where Is Thumbkin?" that goes like this:

> **All:** Where is Kaitlyn? Where is Kaitlyn?
> **Kaitlyn [stands and sings]:** Here I am, here I am.
> **All:** How are you today?
> **Kaitlyn:** Very well, I thank you.
> **All:** Please sit down, please sit down.

The song has been written on sentence strips in a pocket chart, and each child's name is inserted in turn. By March most children can read each other's names and are eager to see who will stand and sing next. As they repeat these lines many times, native English speakers and English learners adopt the phrases and conventions of these polite greetings.

In Jackie's prekindergarten classroom, just about every song, jingle, rhyme, or portion of patterned text that the children memorize is written on charts or sentence strips. Jackie models how to move a pointer from left to right to model **directionality** as the children sing or chant together. Sometimes Jackie points out features of print such as the question marks in the song. Children also get a chance to **track** or point to the words. The charts are posted around the room so that students can revisit them during free play.

Few of the children in prekindergarten learn to accurately track the words to "Where Is Thumbkin?," but the chart helps them to see that oral language may be captured in printed form, that writing is processed from left to right and top to bottom, and that print has particular shapes and conventions—understandings that are known as **concepts about print**. Gradually, students' pretend reading will grow to resemble real reading as they come to understand how letters help them find the words on the page. "Real" or conventional reading does not happen for most children until middle or late kindergarten, but these four-year-olds understand many concepts about print that provide fundamental insights into the nature of text.

Experiences such as these lay the groundwork for later success in literacy (Justice, Kaderavek, Fan, Sofka, Hunt, 2009; Piasta, Justice, McGinty, & Kaderavek, 2012). Even in the preschool years, children begin to experiment with these forms and functions of print at home and at school. Creating a shopping list serves an important function, and after seeing Mom write down *broccoli* and *macaroni*, children may try to add their own scribbles for *ice cream*. Figure 4.1 shows a note by a four-year-old who used letter-like symbols intentionally in an effort to influence adult behavior.

Teachers in early childhood classrooms create print-rich environments that include books, charts, signs, labels, games, posters, a picture and word sorting station, a word wall, an alphabet strip, writing center, job chart, number chart, and more. These materials

FIGURE 4.1 Kaitlyn's Note: "I don't want no people to babysit me"

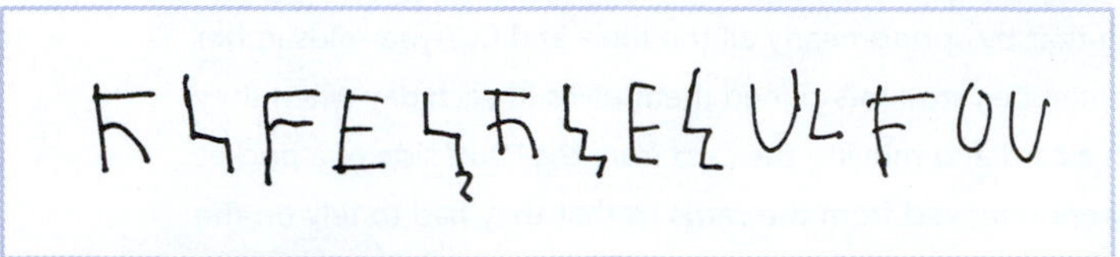

are selected to support purposeful literacy activities in the classroom. Throughout this book, we describe the routines that integrate the use of these materials into daily classroom reading, writing, and other activities. We begin the current chapter with a look at how print awareness and early writing develop and why the activities in this chapter are so important.

See Chapter 6 for more information about routines and organizing a print-rich environment.

The Forms and Functions of Print

The world of print has its own special forms and functions. Although children might be surrounded by letters in books, on signs, and on labels, they need to have adults show them what purposes print serves and the special ways in which the visual forms of print are organized. This happens when Daddy points to words on a box of cereal and explains, "That says *corn flakes*" or when their teacher prints the words to "Happy Birthday" on chart paper and points to the words as the children sing along.

Functions of Print

Language, both oral and written, serves many purposes. The list in Table 4.1 outlines a variety of purposes with examples young children would understand for using print.

Children will have observed parents making "to do" lists, signing greeting cards, labeling packages, using the computer, or reading books or newspapers at home. Classrooms provide opportunities for teachers to model and explain these same functions of print; for children who have experienced less literacy in the home, this is particularly important. Children engage in the various functions of text when teachers model and provide materials such as a cookbook or recipe cards in the housekeeping area, letter writing materials in a post office center, or menus and notepads to take orders in a restaurant play center. The key for teachers is to use print referencing: to think aloud, explain, and draw children's attention in explicit ways to written language (Justice & Ezell, 2004). One example of print referencing might be the following: When the principal announces an assembly for one

TABLE 4.1 **Functions of Print**

FUNCTION	EXAMPLE
To satisfy our needs and wants	"Let's make a list of what to buy at the store."
To control others	Child writes a "Stay out" sign on the bedroom door
To create interactions with others	Child writes a birthday card or a love note to family member
To express one's thoughts and opinions	"My favorite color is pink."
To create imaginary worlds by writing stories	"One day the elephant went to the fair."
To seek information	"Why do cats have whiskers?"
To record and communicate information	"My bean plant grew two inches over the weekend."

Source: Based on Halliday (1975, 2002).

o'clock, a teacher might say, "Boys and girls, we need a reminder. I am going to write a note here on the chalkboard. What do we want it to say?" As the children begin to develop writing skills, a student might be recruited to write the note. As the time for the assembly nears, be sure to refer back to the written reminder to show that it serves a real purpose.

Forms of Print

Print has special visual characteristics and conventions that are foundational to reading and writing (Clay, 1985). For example, there are capital and lowercase letters, which are ordered left to right and are grouped to forms words and sentences, accompanied by punctuation marks. Research has demonstrated that children's concepts about print are moderately correlated with reading ability in the primary grades (Hammill, 2004; National Early Literacy Panel, 2008; Snow, Burns, & Griffin, 1998). When teachers use a print referencing style as they read and write, (such as naming or pointing out letters, asking questions about print, and pointing to words), their students show growth on measures of concepts about print, letter recognition, and name writing (Justice et al., 2009). Table 4.2 provides examples of how teachers might reference print as they work with young students.

TABLE 4.2 **Concepts about Print (CAP) and Examples of Print Referencing**

FUNCTIONS AND FORMS OF PRINT	EXAMPLES OF PRINT REFERENCING
Functions	
Print is speech written down and, once written down, it does not change	"I'm going to write down what you say and then we can read it back."
Print is different from illustrations	"You look at the picture while I read what the words say over here."
Print carries a message	"Can you find the box with the word *scissors?*"
Print serves many purposes	"Here is the recipe for play dough. Let's read and find out what ingredients we need to add to our shopping list."
Forms	
Parts of books such as title, author, illustrator, cover, title page, dedication, poem, song, beginning, and end	"Let's look at the cover of the book to see what it might be about. We have read another book by this author. Where do we look for the author's name?"
Book-handling skills: start with the cover and turn from front to back	"Let's turn to the next page to find out what happens."
Directionality: print is oriented left to right with a return sweep and top to bottom	"This is the top of the page, where I will start reading. Then I will go to the next line. Show me where to go next."
Units of print such as letters (capital and lowercase), numbers, words, sentences, and lines	"There are four letters in this word. Let's name them. The first letter needs to be a capital because it is a person's name."
Units of sound such as syllable, beginning and ending sounds, and rhyme match to units of print	"This is a long word. Let's clap the syllables in *caterpillar*. Can this word be *rug*? What is the first sound in *rug*?"
Punctuation and special print: periods, question marks, exclamation marks, quotation marks, bold print, and italics	"Listen to how I read this sentence. It ends with an exclamation mark, so I want to sound excited."
Words are composed of a string of letters separated by spaces (concept of word)	"Watch while I point to the words in this sentence. We need to leave a space here before we write the next word."
Words can be identified in different contexts (word identification)	"Here is the word *cat*. Can you find the word again on this page? What will you look for?"

Source: Based on Justice, L. M., Kaderavek, J. N., Fan, X., Sofka, A., & Hunt, A. (2009). Accelerating preschoolers, early literacy development through classroom-based teacher child story book reading and explicit print referencing. *Language, Speech, & Hearing Services in Schools, 40,* 67–85.

Development of Emergent Writing

Emergent writing is a developmental process that begins when children make their first marks on paper and continues until they invent spellings based upon letter–sound correspondences. Observing children's writing over time reveals their developing understanding of concepts about print as well as their growing awareness of the different functions of print. It is important to observe and to take note of what children say about their writing and drawing to understand their intentions and message.

As emergent writers, children initially must learn how to hold and control a pencil, crayon, or marker. Their scribbles may have no communicative intent other than to leave their mark on paper. With practice, they develop more control; but they do not differentiate between drawing and writing, and their scribbles bear no resemblance to letters. However, scribbles can signal intentionality (McGee & Richgels, 2012), as shown in Figure 4.2(a). We have observed children orally composing stories as they write, weaving well-developed narratives while scribbling happily across the page, confident that they are recording those ideas in print.

A significant milestone is reached when children recognize that pictures and print are separate symbol systems. When one considers the sea of print, artwork, designs, logos, and signs in which children live in the modern world, this insight should be recognized as a major achievement. Scribbles evolve into representational drawings separate from what children might identify as writing. Figure 4.2(b) shows how Ellie drew a figure and explained, "This is a hand" and then added the marks to the left and said, "I write my name."

Emergent writing may take on a linear quality, but marks may be produced from right to left as readily as left to right. It takes some time for consistent left-to-right directionality to become established. Some children experiment with various forms of what has been called "**mock linear**" writing (Clay, 1985; Harste, Woodward & Burke, 1984). A string of loops may imitate cursive writing (which many children see adults using), or separate letter-like forms may have the lines and circles characteristic of print. Note in Figure 4.2(c) the linear scribbles in the note to Daddy.

As children learn the alphabet and numbers, their writing may become a random string of letters mixed with numbers in a "symbol salad." Often the first letters children use in their writing are the same as the letters in their name (Bloodgood, 1999) because these are the ones they see frequently and learn to produce first. Usually these strings of symbols are done with intention and identified as writing by the child. They may even ask an adult "What does this say?" Even though it is impossible to read, children are demonstrating that they know print carries a message that can be read by others.

One of the most exciting breakthroughs in children's literacy development happens when they realize that the letters they choose to use in their writing cannot be random, but instead must match to speech sounds in a systematic way. This sound–symbol connection is the **alphabetic principle**. Some children seem to develop this insight on their own and use their knowledge of letter names to invent spellings with letter–sound matches (Read, 1971). Most likely, however, this awareness develops through interactions with adults, siblings, or literate peers as children receive simple instruction or are given feedback to their questions. Collin asked his aunt Ellen how to write her name on a valentine he was creating. Ellen replied with the name of two letters: *L*, *N*. Collin seemed to think about this for a moment and then said, as though suddenly enlightened,

FIGURE 4.2 Examples of Early Writing

a. "This says I love you."

b. "This is a hand. I write my name."

c. "Note to Daddy"

d.

"Oh, yeah, *L N* for Ellen!" This brief interaction was a breakthrough for Collin and he began to listen for other sounds in names that he could represent with letters: EN for his friend *Ian,* KT for *Katie,* and JK for *Jake.* Of course, Collin was already using letters and letter-like forms, so he was ripe for the kind of response that would nudge him in the direction of using letters to represent sounds. How we respond to children's questions about writing will depend on where they are in the developmental progress illustrated in Figure 4.2 (Cabell, Tortorelli, & Gerde, 2013).

Children often begin by representing only one sound in a word or syllable, such as the sample in Figure 4.2(d), in which the child has labeled the drawing of pumpkins as PK. These partially phonetic efforts reveal that children know at least some of their letters and how to produce them; they are able to slow down their speech and attend to sound units such as syllables or phonemes; and they select appropriate letters to represent the sounds. These partially phonetic efforts, sometimes called **invented spelling**, are employed by young writers who are using what they know about letters and sounds to record words. Some educators call this writing *temporary spellings*, perhaps as a way to assure doubtful parents that they will be replaced by correct spellings over time. We prefer the term **developmental spelling** because it highlights the idea that students are progressing in their knowledge of conventional writing.

These initial efforts at representing sounds in words represent quite a cognitive achievement that should be respected and encouraged. However, developmental spelling has sometimes been attacked and often misunderstood, so you need to be prepared to talk to parents about it. The letter–sound matches are at times unconventional but show children's growing ability to analyze sounds and match them to letters. These efforts are a signal that children are ready to benefit from systematic instruction in phonics that will serve them well as they progress in conventional reading and writing.

> **See Chapter 5 for a description of the early stages of spelling and how to plan systematic instruction in phonics.**

Planning for Instruction

To develop concepts about print, instruction begins with exposure and explanations and then moves to identification and eventually production. As in all learning, there is a gradual release of responsibility (Duffy, 2009; Fisher & Frey, 2008, Pearson & Gallagher, 1983) that begins with modeling and leads to children's independent work. Observations of how well students demonstrate their knowledge or apply it in writing is an excellent source of ongoing, or formative, assessment.

1. *Exposure and explanations.* Point out features of print and introduce the terms needed to label them. ("This mark at the end of a sentence is a question mark; listen to how I read it" or "The first letter in your name needs to be a capital letter" as you write the child's name)

2. *Identification.* Ask children questions to demonstrate their knowledge. ("Who can find the question mark on this page? What do we call this kind of letter? Can you find this word somewhere else in the sentence?")

3. *Application and production.* Ultimately, our goal is for children to use the concepts about print as they read and write, but they will need support and reminding. "Who can make a question mark? Don't forget to leave spaces between your words when you write."

Environmental Print

The modern world is full of what is known as **environmental print**: billboards, food labels, commercial logos, packaging, catalogs, and traffic signs—not to mention electronic images beamed from televisions, computers, and notebooks. Over 30 years ago, researchers found that young children could read environmental print before they could read conventional texts (Harste, Woodward, & Burke, 1984). However, young children who identify the golden arches as "McDonalds" or the red octagon sign as "stop" are probably using colors, shapes, and context cues rather than the print. Children must learn to pay close attention to the letters themselves to benefit from the use of environmental print in the classroom.

Environmental print is concrete and familiar to young children and can be used to develop concepts about print beginning with exposure and explanation. As you read to children, write with students, and engage in other activities throughout the day, take the time to point out features of print and the many functions it serves. Jackie does this as she talks with children in the housekeeping corner about the labels on cans of food: "Here is a can of peas and here is the word *peas*. Do you see how the word *peas* starts with the letter *P*?" When students come to school with messages on their T-shirts, Jackie takes the time to read and comment on the shirt; she also uses it as a chance to point out the difference between numbers, which are common on sports team shirts, and words with letters. Other activities are listed here.

Reading and Making Signs

Books with vivid photographs that celebrate the world of print include *I Read Signs* by Tana Hoban, *City Signs* by Zoran Milch, and *Signs in Our World* by DK Publishing. Share the books with the children, reading the signs and interpreting symbols while you talk about where you might find the different signs. Compare signs with and without words, and help the children see that although both communicate information, they cannot be read in the same way. Some signs, like a yield sign, offer an opportunity to teach a new vocabulary word that can then be used intentionally in other contexts. For example, when you are moving through the school and encounter another group of students you might say, "Boys and girls, we need to yield to this group."

You may have traffic signs in your block area or in the tricycle area on the playground. Be sure to read these signs together and talk about what they mean; continue to refer to them over time. If you do not have such signs, create them with the children's help. Provide small shapes of tagboard or cardboard that children can use to make their own signs in the block center. Keep books such as *I Read Signs* and *City Signs* in the block area as a source of ideas for signs they might want to make.

Read Signs around School

Your building is probably full of signs that label restrooms, offices, and other classrooms. Take the time to read them as you move around the building, and talk about any special features. Don't just do this once, but repeatedly until children can tell you what the signs say. A class project might be to collect digital photographs of signs around the school; the pictures can be made into a book that even young children can read. It is especially easy to make these in an electronic presentation format such as PowerPoint and then print them out, two slides to a page, to cut apart as pages.

Sort and Match Environmental Print

Collect labels and signs from a variety of sources. These can come from actual packaging such as cereal boxes or soup cans, from the Internet, or from pictures you take around your neighborhood and school building. You might send a letter home to parents and enlist their help in creating a collection. Be accepting of print in languages other than English, packaging for foods from other cultures, and signs for activities that are culturally distinct from your own background. This is an opportunity to show your students that you are interested in their lives and their home experiences, and it will help connect the world of school to learning opportunities outside of school.

Mount pictures or labels on tagboard, or create an electronic display such as an interactive whiteboard. Brainstorm with children the different ways they might sort the labels into categories: (1) signs and labels with words separated from those without words; (2) product labels grouped according to whether the item is food, clothing, or a personal care item; (3) signs sorted by where they are from (restaurants, stores, streets, or the school building); or (4) labels grouped by beginning letters (e.g., macaroni, masa, and M&M's). These might be added to alphabet scrapbooks. Write out in simple manuscript form (using lowercase letters) some of the words on the labels and signs you have collected, and challenge children to match them to the original. This helps them see that the printed word remains the same in different contexts and with different print styles or fonts.

Read Environmental Print

Talk with children about how they are learning to read, and pull out examples of familiar environmental print for them to identify. Create an open-ended sentence such as "I can read _____." or "I go to _____." and substitute different logos at the end of the sentence such as "I can read Cheerios." Repeat this with other logos to create a patterned dictation that children can reread while pointing to the words. These can be the basis for a class book.

Label the Room

Labeling objects, storage bins, shelves, and areas around the room creates meaningful print and helps students take responsibility for keeping the classroom well maintained (Reutzel & Wolfersberger, 1996). However, a label such as "door" or "window" will probably be ignored unless it serves some useful purpose. If possible, children should be involved in the process by asking them what should be labeled and enlisting their help in writing the labels (Soderman, Gregory, & McCarty, 2005). Labels can then be used to draw attention to the features of print. A teacher might say, "Can you find the box for the scissors? What letter will be at the beginning of the word *scissors*?" Simply posting signs all over your room to which you never refer will not help children learn that print should serve useful functions.

Teach Children How to Identify and Write Their Names

Many educators have marveled at all that's in a child's name: lowercase letters, capital letters, letter sounds, letter shapes, letter formation movements, and the most important thing of all—a child's very identity! For this reason, more than one scholar of children's early writing development has entitled a book or article "What's in a Name?" (Bloodgood, 1999; Treiman & Broderick, 1998). You will want to post names and photos, sort names by initial letters and the number of letters or syllables, and distinguish between capital and lowercase letters as you teach children how to form the letters in their names.

> **See Chapter 2 for more ideas about using children's names to teach the alphabet.**

Reading with Children to Explore Concepts about Print

In addition to reading *to* children, described in Chapter 1, you should also plan activities in which children will read *with* you, from memory, after hearing you read to them. Don Holdaway first described **shared reading** of big books or other enlarged text as a way to "extend the lap" (Holdaway, 1979), and the process has proved to be a developmentally appropriate way for children to participate in reading at an early age (Slaughter, 1993). During shared reading, children engage in a socially supported reading-like experience. They are not expected to read in a conventional way (although some might), but they gradually transition to conventional reading as they develop a concept of word and the ability to identify some words. Students learn many things during shared reading activities, but here we introduce shared reading as a literacy activity that can be used to help children develop concepts about print.

SHARED READING. During shared reading, you will do many of the same things you do during read-alouds (making predictions, talking about new or unusual vocabulary, making connections, etc.), and both methods can include a great deal of print referencing. However, shared reading differs in two important ways from read-alouds. First, shared reading uses simple, memorable text that children can easily recite after hearing it read aloud several times. Books like *Brown Bear, Brown Bear, What Do You See?* (by Bill Martin) are known as **predictable** books. Their simple patterned repetitive language makes it easy to anticipate the words on the next page. Table 4.3 lists some favorite predictable books that can be used as early as preK. Familiar rhymes, jingles, and songs or a portion of text such as the memorable refrain from the "The Gingerbread Man" ("Run, run, as fast as you can. You can't catch me, I'm the Gingerbread Man") can also be used for shared reading because they are easily committed to memory.

TABLE 4.3 **Examples of Predictable Books That Work Well for Shared Reading**

Carle, E. (1997). *Have you seen my cat?* New York, NY: Aladdin.

Christalow, E. (1991). *Five little monkeys jumping on the bed*. New York, NY: Clarion.

Fox, M. (1991). *Hattie and the fox*. New York, NY: Aladdin.

Hill, E. (1980). *Where's Spot?* New York, NY: Putnam.

Hutchins, P. (1987). *Rosie's walk*. New York, NY: Aladdin.

Keats, E. J. (1971). *Over in the meadow: A counting rhyme*. New York, NY: Scholastic.

Langstaff, J. (1974). *A-hunting we will go*. New York, NY: Atheneum.

Martin, B. (1992). *Brown Bear, Brown Bear, what do you see?* New York, NY: Henry Holt and Co.

Neitzel, S. (1994). *The jacket I wear in the snow*. New York, NY: Greenwillow.

Paparone, P. (1997). *Five little ducks*. Orlando, FL: Harcourt.

Peek, M. (1988). *Mary wore her red dress*. London, UK: Sandpiper.

Tafuri, N. (1984). *Have you seen my duckling?* New York, NY: Scholastic.

Ward, C. (1988). *Cookie's week*. New York, NY: Scholastic.

Westcox, B. (1993). *I know an old lady who swallowed a fly*. New York, NY: Harcourt Brace.

Wildsmith, B. (1982). *The cat on the mat*. New York, NY: Oxford University Press.

Williams, S. (1992). *I went walking*. London, UK: Sandpiper.

Wood, A. (1992). *Silly Sally*. New York, NY: Harcourt Brace.

Wood, A. (1994). *The napping house*. New York, NY: Harcourt Brace.

The second distinguishing characteristic of shared reading is that students see an enlarged copy of the text that teachers point to as they read. Children are then asked to read along chorally during repeated readings and might be asked to read by themselves as they attempt to point to the words. Big books are especially popular for shared reading, and many favorites are available commercially in enlarged formats that make it easy for children to see features of the print such as letters and punctuation. You can find collections of nursery rhymes on posters. But you can also write the words from songs, poems, or portions of text on chart paper or project them on an interactive whiteboard (Gill & Islam, 2011). In some cases, you may want to create sentence strips to put in a pocket chart. Use a neat consistent style of manuscript writing to create such charts and strips.

Many teachers set up a special place in the room with a bookstand or easel where big books and charts are displayed. Children are encouraged to return during free time to "be the teacher." They imitate what they saw the teacher doing as they recite the familiar reading materials introduced earlier and try to point to the words. Some teachers have a collection of special pointers, but unsharpened pencils or chopsticks also work well. You can make a longer pointer with a 24-inch dowel rod, available at home supply stores, tipped with a pencil eraser. Big books are available from many suppliers including Rigby, Wright Group, Scholastic, Kaplan Early Learning Company, and Lakeshore Learning Materials.

Shared reading should take place daily as a whole-group activity because all children in preK and kindergarten classrooms will benefit. While some children are learning that print carries a message and is arranged linearly across the page (directionality), others are learning to recognize words that they have seen repeatedly. There is something in shared reading for everyone, and this makes it a particularly valuable part of the day. Many of the *Common Core State Standards* for kindergarten are addressed during shared reading. The basic steps for shared reading are outlined in Lesson 4.1.

LESSON 4.1   Steps in a shared reading activity

Present a big book as you would any read-aloud, taking the time to make it interactive. You may want to focus a first reading on the vocabulary, interpretation, and understanding of the book, or simply enjoy the rhythm and rhyme of a poem. If you are using a song or rhyme, it is best to teach it orally before showing children the printed form on a chart. Throughout the reading, and on subsequent readings, talk about features of the print as suggested in Table 4.2. (CCSS Foundational Skills: 1a, 1b, 1c, Print Concepts; 3c, Phonics and Word Recognition; CCSS Language: 2b, Conventions of Standard English)

Materials

Big book, chart, sentence strips, or some other enlarged selection of text.

Step 1. Before reading

(Start here if you use a book.).

- Discuss the cover and illustration. Model how to interpret the picture to make a prediction about what the book will be about: "The cover of this books shows a bunch of rabbits that are different sizes, so I think this will be about a family of rabbits. What else do we think might happen in this story?" Prompt children to do this in a similar way.
- Next, discuss the title and again think aloud how the title offers a clue to the content of the book: "The title says 'The Lost Bunny,' so I think maybe the rabbit family is going to have to look for the bunny." Point to the words as you read the title and talk about distinctive features. This can include beginning letters, alliteration, or long words with many syllables such as *gingerbread*. Take time to clap the syllables in long words and model how you point to each syllable.
- Read the name of the author and illustrator. Explain what authors and illustrators do and talk about other books the children might know by the same author or illustrator. Even young children can begin to notice the distinctive style of artists such as Eric Carle, Tomie dePaola, or Pat Hutchins. Read the title page and then have children repeat the title with you.

Step 2. During reading

(Begin here if the material is a rhyme or song. Introduce the title and author and explain the origin of the piece.) Point out where you begin reading and point below each word as you read.

- Briefly explain any new or unusual vocabulary as you encounter the words, and make connections to the children's lives. Accept comments and questions as you would for any read-aloud.
- Reference print. Point out just a few features of print on a first reading, such as, "Let's go to the next page" or "Here is a new sentence." More features can be discussed with successive readings. Remember to first label and explain, and then progress to asking children to identify and label.
- Have the children finish sentences or join in with repeated phrases when they are ready.

PD TOOLKIT™
for Words Their Way®

At the PDToolKit, you can watch Jackie use "Humpty Dumpty" with her preK students to develop concepts about print. Click the Videos tab and then choose Emergent Stage. Scroll to find the clip entitled "Humpty Dumpty."

Step 3. After reading

Allow time to talk about and revisit the book or rhyme.

- Ask the children to share their reactions as you would with any read-aloud.
- Reread the story, poem, or chant. Children join in or supply missing words when you pause. **Echo read**, with the children reading each line or sentence after you. **Choral read** by asking children to read with you. Reread again over the next few days.
- Add more references to features of print. (See Table 4.2 for ideas.)

(continued)

LESSON 4.1 **Steps in a shared reading activity** *(continued)*

- To focus on phonological awareness, emphasize words that rhyme. Pause for children to finish lines that rhyme (e.g., "Jack and Jill went up the _____ [hill]"). Point out long words, and have children clap as you touch each syllable in the word.
- Have children find words by using beginning letters and sounds. Ask "Can you find the word *tiptoe*? What letter would you look for at the beginning?"

Step 4. Extend

Shared reading can be extended through additional activities using sentence strips, words cards, and a copy of the text for each child. Other ideas include acting out the story, writing your own version of the story with the children's help, and having the children draw their own illustrations.

> Ideas about extending shared readings to develop a concept of word and word identification are described in Chapter 6.

Writing with Children to Explore Concepts about Print

Writing consists of two basic processes: (1) composition, or the generation and organization of ideas, and (2) recording those ideas into print. Here we will focus on the process of producing print. (See Table 4.4 for some recommended resources for teaching young children about composition.) Many of the recommendations of the *Common Core State Standards* are met in writing activities.

Writing with children offers an excellent chance to model the use of the alphabet, phonemic awareness, letter–sound matching, concept of word, and conventions such as capitalization and punctuation—all in the context of a meaningful group activity. As the teacher writes on a chalkboard, chart paper, or overhead transparency, children see oral ideas transformed into print. Writing with children helps them develop several broad understandings:

- What you say can be written down.
- What a person writes is captured permanently and can be returned to over and over.
- Writing serves many functions.
- Writing has special forms and conventions.

Whenever you write with children, consider the gradual release of responsibility. Start by modeling and explaining: "We just wrote a question, so we need to use a

TABLE 4.4 **Recommended Resources for Enhancing Writing with Young Children**

Bhattacharyya, R. (2010). *The castle in the classroom: Story as springboard for early literacy*. Portland, MI: Stenhouse.

Calkins, L. (2003). *Units of study for primary writers: A yearlong curriculum*. Portsmouth, NH: Heinemann.

Horn, M., & Giacobbe, M. E. (2007). *Talking, drawing, writing: Lessons for our youngest writers*. Portland, MI: Stenhouse.

Ray, K. W. (2008). *Already ready: Nurturing writers in preschool and kindergarten*. Portsmouth, NH: Heinemann.

Reid, J., & Schultze, B. (2012). *What's next for this beginning writer? Minilessons that take writing from scribbling to script*. Portland, MI: Stenhouse.

question mark at the end" or "We have to leave a space between each word." Move to asking students to demonstrate what they know: "Show me where to start the next sentence. What do we do if we run out of room at the edge of the page? What do we put at the end of a sentence? What kind of letter do we need here?" Work for application and production of features—under your supervision first: "Who can add a question mark? Can you write a capital *W* in the first word?" Take note of who answers readily and has learned targeted concepts about print, and who still needs support. More advanced children can serve as models by demonstrating what they know, but try to involve everyone in some way.

Be accurate when describing different forms of writing. It is easy to fall into the habit of saying "Let's write a story about . . ." but stories have special elements (characters, problem, solution) that are not present in most classroom writing. When you are recording observations made on a windy day, it might be best to call it a report, dictation, or a description. Teach children labels for many kinds of writing as you explore the different functions writing serves.

Ahmad

My worm is going to my fruit.

SUPPORTING WRITING. There are different levels of support to use when writing with children. Print referencing can take place during all of these as you talk about words, letters, sentences, capitalization, punctuation, spacing, and so forth, as described in Table 4.2. The level of support will depend on where students are in their development, your learning goals, and the allotted time you have for writing. The four levels follow a gradual release of responsibility but can take place concurrently. For example, in the same day you might write a note while children watch, take a dictation from an individual child in the art center, do a large group interactive writing lesson to list the characters in a folktale, and expect children to write a journal entry independently.

Write for Children

Model as you write down your own message while thinking out loud about what you are doing and why. Involve students when possible. For example, you might say to your class, "I am going to add paper plates to my shopping list. What letter do I need to spell the first sound in paper?"

Shared Writing or Dictations

Ask the children to tell you what to write as you serve as the scribe for their ideas (McKenzie, 1985). Taking a dictation, which is later used for reading material, is called the **language experience approach** (Stauffer, 1980). Print referencing can take place as you model, think aloud, and ask for help: "We need a question mark at the end of this sentence. It is a curvy line with a period underneath. Can you make it in the air with me? We start at the top, go around and down, and add a dot underneath." You may want to take individual dictations on a rotating basis, especially with children who need the extra support. This can be as simple as writing a caption to go with a child's drawing and then rereading it several times. Individual dictations can be shared in the larger group and added to a collection called a **personal reader**.

See Chapter 6 for more information about taking dictations and personal readers.

Interactive Writing

During interactive writing, the children and teacher decide what to write, and the pen is passed so that children participate in the actual writing to the extent they can (Button, Johnson, & Furgerson 1996; McCarrier, Pinnell, & Fountas, 2000). The teacher may ask a child to write just one letter or, with increasing skill, a child might write the entire word. Print referencing can include attention to numerous functions and forms of print: "We begin a letter to someone by saying 'Dear.' Who wants to come up and make a capital letter *D*? Remember to start the letter at the top." Table 4.5 describes the steps and offers tips about how to make interactive writing a productive instructional strategy.

TABLE 4.5 **Interactive Writing**

During interactive writing, the teacher and a group of children work together to compose and record ideas.

Materials: chart paper, whiteboard, or some other writing surface; markers; white-out tape or "boo boo" tape; and ready access to alphabet strip, word wall, and children's names

1. Decide with children's help on the content of the writing. Do not rush through this step, as it offers a chance to engage children in oral language and to introduce or revisit new vocabulary. When planning for their end-of-year picnic, Jackie brainstormed with her students about the toppings they wanted to buy for ice cream.

2. Model how to break sentences into words and words into syllables (when appropriate). Draw attention to phonemes by stretching out the sounds. Then model how to match the sound to a letter: "I hear the sound /mmmmm/ at the beginning of *my*. What letter will we need to write for that sound?" Refer to the alphabet posted nearby at a level children can reach. You might call on a child to point to the letter needed to represent a sound.

3. Ask a child to come forward and do the writing. In some cases, individual children may provide only one letter, or they might write the whole word. Exercise your judgment about what is a good use of instructional time. Be ready to simply provide some letters—especially vowels and silent letters—and, in some cases, simply write the letters or word yourself. For example, if the sentence is "We rode the bus to the aquarium" kindergarten children can probably come up with all the letter sound matches in *we* and *bus,* some of the sounds in *rode,* and few in *aquarium.*

4. Show children how to use resources in the room to find and copy words instead of always sounding them out. Trying to figure out how to spell *Wednesday* is probably not time well spent. The word is right on the calendar for easy reference. Children will have to think about some of the sounds in the word to find it in a posted place, so they still exercise some letter–sound knowledge. Encourage the children to write high-frequency words like *the* and *to* from memory or by referring to a word wall.

5. Through modeling and questioning, draw attention to capital letters, spaces between words, returning to the beginning of the next line, punctuation, and other concepts about print. We have seen some teachers assign a child to be a "space man" who uses his hand or two fingers to space between words. Introduce a new feature of print such as an exclamation point by explaining its purpose and showing students how to make it. Or you may ask students to produce previously introduced features, such as asking what is needed at the end of a question.

6. After each word is added, reread from the beginning to recall the next word and then reread the entire sentence before going on to the next. Limit the length of the writing to correspond with children's attention spans. In preK and early kindergarten, that might be just a few words in a list or a single sentence. Over the course of the kindergarten year, children can sit still for longer periods and create longer messages. If necessary, work on the list or message over several days.

7. At the end, reread the entire message chorally and review some of the teaching points you made. For example, if you have introduced or reviewed the use of an exclamation point, go back to it and rename it, ask students to say it with you, and then read the sentence with emphasis. Encourage children to use the features in their own independent writing.

Keep white correction tape (sometimes called "boo boo" tape) handy to correct mistakes. Use a small whiteboard or an additional piece of paper as a "practice page" or "practice space" where you can model letter formation or work out the spellings of words before children add them to the message (Williams, Sherry, Robinson, & Hungler, 2012). By kindergarten, you may want to give every child his or her own whiteboard or clipboard and ask the class to attempt the next word before you call on someone to come forward and add it to the chart. This requires every child to think about and practice what they are learning, and offers you ongoing assessment as you observe what individual children are able to do. Once the correct writing has been completed on the chart, ask children to correct their own.

Independent Writing

Although young children's first efforts at writing may be scribbles or limited to drawings, they should be treated as writers even in preschool. A child who retells the adventures of Clifford the dog using letter-like scribbles understands that print captures ideas and may exhibit left-to-right and top-to-bottom directionality. Children can be given journals and asked to write in them every day for a short period of time. They can also write at a writing center or in play areas set up with writing props like cards and envelopes. Opportunities to write should be preceded and supported with teacher modeling.

GETTING READY TO WRITE WITH CHILDREN. The traditional way to write with children is to use lined chart paper that comes in 24- by 36-inch and 24- by 16-inch spiral bound tablets. The written products can be saved and displayed on an easel or chart stand. You can also use chalkboards, overhead projectors, document cameras, interactive whiteboards, or any means that allow children to watch and participate in the writing process. Seat children so they can easily see the writing, an alphabet strip, and any displays of words you might use such as a list of classmates' names or a word wall of high-frequency words. Use the same standard manuscript style of writing that you want your children to learn. Talk about and model correct letter formation. When you are supervising a writing experience, the final written product should be spelled correctly, but you can occasionally model how to correct mistakes by crossing out letters, inserting words, or covering up errors with white tape.

> **See Chapter 6 for a description of word walls.**

WHAT TO WRITE ABOUT. Because print serves many functions, you should model a variety of purposes as you write with children. Consider these options:

- Create charts for classroom rules, notes, reminders, labels, directions, schedules, or brainstorming. You may want to make lists of questions for a class visitor or a shopping list.

- Write a message each morning about upcoming events or create a class message at the end of the day to summarize the day's happenings.
- Record science experiments, observations, recipes, summaries, retellings, reactions, thank-you notes, letters, invitations, stories, and innovations on familiar texts or rhymes.
- Graphic organizers are also a form of writing that has a real purpose in the classroom. You may create story maps, Venn diagrams, charts, or graphs.
- Model the writing you want your children to do independently. Show children how to write in a journal or learning log. Introduce new ideas for the writing center (such as making valentines) by modeling first as a group activity.

Lesson 4.2 describes a favorite form of group writing in which the teacher and children compose sentences that report on daily home and school events that are of importance to the class. Concepts about print are easily developed in this all-important daily routine.

LESSON 4.2   The morning message

Each morning, the teacher talks with the entire group to discover bits of news that can be part of the morning message. In preschool or early kindergarten, this may be only one sentence. Over time, it can grow to be as long as the teacher and children desire. An alternative to Morning Message might be the Afternoon News, when the discussion can serve as a summary of the day's events. (CCSS Foundational Skills: 1a, 1b, 1c, Print Concepts; 2d, Phonological Awareness; 3a, 3b, Phonics and Word Recognition; 4, Fluency; CCSS Language: 1a, 1f, 2a, 2b, Conventions of Standard English)

Materials

Chart paper; markers; correction tape; and ready access to alphabet strip, word wall, and children's names.

Step 1. Oral Language Production

Chat with children informally, sharing news from home or the classroom. Oral language should come first, with lots of children offering up their ideas. Take ideas from several children and then seek their agreement as to the word or sentence that captures a combination of ideas. Sometimes you may ask a child to hold on to an idea for later. In this way, more oral language is generated and you show children

(continued)

LESSON 4.2   The morning message *(continued)*

that writing should involve evaluating several possibilities and not just writing the first thing that might pop in your head. Select a piece of news to record such as "We got a new gerbil."

Step 2. Record the message

Recite the sentence together with the children to decide how many words it contains, holding up a finger for each word. Then draw a line for each word on the board or chart. Repeat each word, emphasizing the sounds as they are written, and invite the group to make suggestions about what letters are needed: "The first word we need to write is *we*. Wwwwwweeeeee. What letter do we need for the first sound in *wwweee?*" A child might suggest the letter *Y*. "The name of the letter *Y* does start with that sound. Does anyone have another idea? *We* starts like *William*. What letter does *William* begin with?" Every letter in every word need not be discussed at length. Focus on what is appropriate for the developmental level of your students. You can do the writing in the beginning, but as children learn to write their letters you can share the pen. Let children take turns writing, usually just one child per letter or word at this level. White correction tape can be used as needed but be ready to accept less than perfect letter formation when you do interactive writing with young children.

Step 3. Print referencing

Model and talk about concepts about print such as the left-to-right direction, the return sweep, capitalization, punctuation, and letter formation. Clap the syllables in longer words, spelling one syllable at a time.

Step 4. Reread

After a sentence is written and the punctuation is decided on, read the sentence together as you point to the words or as a child does the pointing. If your sentence contains a two- or three-syllable word, touch it for every syllable, helping children see how words break into syllables. Decide on the next sentence and continue. The length of the dictation will depend on the topic and especially on the attention span of the children. If there is a lot to record or interest is waning, take over the writing and spend less time asking questions.

Step 5. Review and reflect on the process

After the writing is complete, take time to ask the children whether there are any things that they notice about the text. Model as needed: "I notice that we wrote two words that start with *G* (*got* and *gerbil*), but the *G* has different sounds in each word." Modeling gives way to questioning and then spontaneous observations by children as they learn what it is they might be looking for.

Step 6. Post and share

The morning message should be left up so that children can stop by to read it for themselves. Some children may want to copy it and it might be reread the next day. A collection of all the morning messages for a week can be sent home on Friday as a summary of class news that children will have a good chance of proudly reading to their parents.

OTHER WRITING IN THE CLASSROOM. Opportunities abound in the classroom for writing. Some will arise spontaneously, and others can be planned. Here are a few of our favorite ideas for developing concepts about print.

What Were You Saying?

Add speech balloons to photos you take of your students or to pictures cut from magazines. Explain that the picture shows what is happening, but the speech balloon shows what was said. Talk about what someone in the picture might be saying. Then record it using the strategies for interactive writing in Table 4.5. Read back what it says in the speech balloon. Cut speech balloons out of paper and put them in the writing center to encourage independent writing after the activity has been modeled with a group. To further children's understanding of how speech balloons work, you can share comic strips or children's books that feature speech bubbles such as books by Mo Willems (*Don't Let the Pigeon Drive the Bus* and *Nuffle Bunny*) or Peggy Rathman (*10 Minutes till Bedtime* and *Goodnight Gorilla*).

Pattern Writing or Innovations on Text

A more structured approach to writing with children involves the use of patterned or predictable sentences in which children only supply a few words. For example, the book *Mary Wore Her Red Dress and Henry Wore His Green Sneakers,* illustrated by Merle Peek, is a simple repetitive story in which friends come to celebrate Mary's birthday party wearing different clothing in different colors. After enjoying the story, children can dictate similar sentences about what they are wearing (e.g., "Thea wore her pink T-shirt.") Many predictable books will lend themselves to this kind of follow-up pattern writing. For example, *Things I Like* by Anthony Brown suggests the simple sentence frame "I like _____."

An experience can also be used as the basis for pattern writing. After a trip to the zoo, the pattern sentence might include the child's name: "Ansel's favorite animal was the _____." Such dictations can easily be turned into a book, with each child illustrating their sentence. This kind of pattern writing is especially helpful to English learners, who will benefit from the repetitive language and supportive context. These patterned writings work well for dictations as well as interactive writing and independent writing.

Journal Writing

Journals for young children can be simply constructed by stapling several sheets of paper together with a construction paper cover that the students can decorate and label with their names. The children might get a new journal each week so that they do not have to wait too long to take their journal home. In kindergarten, you might use lined paper and make journals long enough to last several weeks or a month. Staple a copy of the alphabet and word wall words inside the front cover and have children add to the list so that they have a ready reference for high-frequency words useful in their writing. You can also add words that individual children request. In Figure 4.3(a), you see such a list; "Lucky" (Jackie's dog) has been added. Kaitlyn referenced this to write her entry in Figure 4.3(b): "Dear Journal, I goed to

Read more about learning high-frequency words in Chapter 6.

FIGURE 4.3 High-Frequency Words and Journal Entry

a.

A	in	see
and	it	the
at	I	to
all	joy	up
by	look	was
cat	Mom	yes
can	man	zoo
Dad	not	
end	no	Lucky
go	off	
if	on	
is		

b.

D R GROL
I GO DTO
JES HSOS
TO SEE LUCKY

Jackie's house to see Lucky." Although you might supply high-frequency words and special words that children request, it is important to encourage children to spell as best they can during journal writing. This frees them to write about any topic of importance to them and pays off in terms of their literacy development. Table 4.6 offers some guidelines and tips for journal writing.

Writing Centers

Setting up an attractive writing center where materials change over time also encourages children to write independently. When new materials are put in the center, it is important to model how they might be used. For example, in February red and white paper might be supplied along with a list of the

---

TABLE 4.6 ## Guidelines for Journal Writing with Young Children

- *Sharing your own journal.* Have a journal ready with several different entries; read aloud what you have written. Write about ordinary things that happen at home and at school and illustrate the entries just like you want the children to do. Children love to learn that their teacher orders pizzas to be delivered just like they do or that he overslept and didn't have time to walk the dog. You may want to add another quick entry each time your children write. Use this as a way to introduce new ideas that they can write about—but do not assign topics. Assigned topics might be appropriate for other writing during the day but journals, by definition, focus on topics of personal interest. At first, some children may copy words or sentences from around the room, or they will write about the same things they see you or others write. With time, modeling, and encouragement they will develop confidence in their own ideas and their ability to express them by spelling "the best they can," so they will not feel compelled to only write words they see in class. Figure 4.4 shows how Lee progressed in her daily writing over time as she reported on her favorite play center ("I like housekeeping"). Collections like these journal entries document development.

- *Drawing and labeling.* Some children might be intimidated at the idea of writing but feel more comfortable drawing a picture. They should be encouraged to talk about their drawing and to label at least a few things in the picture. Model this for children as an acceptable alternative for journal entries but also gently nudge children to move to complete sentences.

- *Conferring.* As the children write, move around the room, asking them to read what they have written. Sometimes you might transcribe what some children have written to help you keep track of their ideas—especially those whose scribbles or random letters are indecipherable. Some teachers do this on the bottom or back of students' papers; others prefer not to write on the children's own work and use a sticky note. It is a good idea to develop a schedule so that you meet with each student over the course of the week. Conferencing can be a place to stretch composing skills by asking questions to stimulate more writing. For example, Linny wrote, SADZ MI D ("Sadie is my dog") in her journal, and the teacher responded with, "What does Sadie like to do? Could you write another sentence that tells us more about Sadie?"

- *Print referencing during conferring.* Identify the concepts about print that children use in their writing ("I notice that you remembered to use a period here at the end of the sentence") and also remind them to use additional conventions that you have talked about during shared or interactive writing ("Don't forget to leave a space before the next word"). You can also model how to stretch out sounds in words or give a quick handwriting lesson ("Do you remember how to make the capital *G*? Let's look it up on the alphabet chart.").

- *Sharing children's journal entries.* Writing time should not be a quiet time. Children are eager to talk about what they are writing with their friends and they may seek help from each other as they write. This should be encouraged, because children can learn a great deal from each other. In addition, set aside a few minutes when children can share their journal entries. Children may sit in small groups around a table or on the floor and take turns sharing. You can also select a few children each day to share with the whole group in an author's chair. As children share what they have written or drawn, they serve as models for others, and their success is a powerful incentive for those who are hesitant to write.

- *Storing journals.* Store journals in a special bin or shelf where children have access to them in case they want to do more writing. It is helpful to have a small bin for every four to six children so they do not have to dig through a whole class's set to find their own journals. Color-coding the journal covers by group is helpful for organization.

- *Helping children collect ideas for writing.* If children come to you during the day with something to share, you might suggest that they record it in their journal. When journal writing happens regularly, children will begin to anticipate and plan in advance. Rachel brought in a slip of paper with the name of the racetrack (Eastside Speedway) she had visited with her father over the weekend tucked away in her pocket.

FIGURE 4.4 Lee's Journal Writing

"I like housekeeping" "I like housekeeping"

TABLE 4.7 **Materials for a Writing Center**

Alphabet chart posted at eye level	List of children's names
Sight words or word wall chart	List of thematic words
Different kinds of lined and unlined paper	Index cards and Post-it notes
Chalkboards or whiteboards	Rubber stamps and stamp pads
Blank cards, stationery, and envelopes	Typewriter
Colored pencils, markers, pens, and chalk	Highlighters
Speech balloons cut from white paper	Picture dictionaries
Pictures from magazines and glue sticks	Message board
Clipboards and other writing surfaces	Staplers, paper clips, and tape
Blank books made from paper folded in half and stapled	Stickers and blank stick-on labels
Commercially available place mats with letters, numbers, or simple lists of words (e.g., the planets, animals, colors)	

children's names in the class. The teacher should model with the whole group how to make valentines or sit down at the center with several children at a time. You might have specific assignments for the writing center or allow it to be used in an open-ended way. Table 4.7 lists some things to include in the writing center (Wolfersberger, Reutzel, Sudweeks, & Fawson, 2004). Some of these things may stay in the center all year; others should be switched in and out for variety.

Model activities that will be available in the writing center with the whole class or small groups. Writing ideas for the writing center include the following:

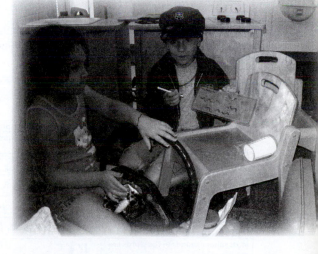

1. Select an interesting picture you have cut out of a magazine; write about the image.
2. Select a sticker and use it like a rebus in a sentence: "I see a pretty [butterfly sticker]."
3. Supply a frame sentence for children to complete: "I like _____ because _____."
4. Thematic writing can begin with a sentence frame: "My favorite animal is a _____ because _____."

Writing in Play Centers

Be sure to include writing supplies as props in play areas and thematic centers. Police officers write tickets, doctors write prescriptions, road builders require signs, and gardeners label their vegetables. Before expecting children to do this highly functional kind of writing, you must model it for them either in the whole group or in the center. When Jackie stopped by the block center one day to talk with a group of girls about what they had built, she suggested that they needed a sign. One child ran off to the supply center—which is always open for them—to get some construction paper and a marker.

Activity

FIGURE 4.5 Scoring Guide for Name Writing Assessment

Feature	Example
1. Name is separate from drawing	
2. Linear scribbles or waves	
3. Segmentation into at least two units	
4. Letter like forms	MM+I/OQ/-IXI
5. First letter of name present	
6. Uses at least half the letters in name	SAH
7. Includes all letters – may be backwards, out of order and contain reversals	SARAH
8. Left to right with no reversals	SARAH
9. Child can name all letters	
10. Appropriate use of capital and lower case letters	Sarah

Source: Based on Invernizzi, M., Sullivan, A, Meier, J., & Swank, L. (2004). Phonological awareness and literacy screening preK. Charlottesville: University of Virginia Printing Services.

FIGURE 4.6 Scoring Examples for Name Writing

	Name Separate from drawing	Linear	Segmentation into units	Letter-like forms	First letter	At least half of letters	All letters	Left to right with no reversals	Names letters	Capital and lower case letters used	Total Points
HARAS	I	I	I	I	I	I	I	I			7
IIハ?Sへ	I	I	I	I	I						5
Sarah	I	I	I	I	I	I	I	I	I	I	10

Source: Based on Invernizzi, M., Sullivan, A, Meier, J., & Swank, L. (2004). Phonological awareness and literacy screening preK. Charlottesville: University of Virginia Printing Services.

FIGURE 4.7 The Assessment of Writing

Feature	Example
Marks are clearly writing or child identifies it as writing	"I wrote a note for Mommy"
Child assigns a message to the writing or message is readable	"This says buy bananas." Or child can respond when asked what it says
Linear orientation - may go left to right or right to left	
Separate symbols -may be letter-like forms)	
Letters and/or numbers – may be mixed in a "symbol salad'	7JTUAM
Most salient sounds in the words are represented	KKS (*I like housekeeping*)
Most beginning and ending sounds represented	ILKHSN (*I like housekeeping*)
Some vowels included	ILIKHSKEPN (*I like housekeeping*)
Spaces between words	I LIK HSKEPN (*I like housekeeping*)

Jackie showed the children how to create a sign by folding the paper three ways so it would stand up without support. Then she helped them to write "Princess Palace," taking the opportunity to explain that she was using all capital letters because it was a sign. After modeling this on several occasions, children began to make their own signs.

Assessment for Concepts about Print

Concepts about print can be assessed informally whenever you ask children questions and as you observe what they do when they write. There are also more formal methods that use checklists and prepared texts. Appendix A has prepared forms and an individual score sheet that can be used across the year to monitor progress.

Name Writing Assessment

A progression of development in the writing of one's name was first described by Hildreth in 1936 and has been researched more recently by others (Bloodgood, 1999; Puranik, Lonigan, & Kim, 2011; Treiman & Broderick, 1998). You may want to collect samples of students' name writing over the year. Figure 4.5 is a scoring guide to assess children's names adapted from the PALS preK assessment used throughout the state of Virginia (Invernizzi, Sullivan, Meier, & Swank, 2004) and from an assessment system developed by Puranik and Lonigan (2011).

Provide a sheet of unlined paper and say to the children, "Draw a picture of yourself and then write your name." If the children respond that they do not know how to write their name, encourage them to "do the best they can," or "pretend." Before collecting the papers, ask each child to point out his or her name on the paper and, if the child has written letters, ask to identify the letters. Some children memorize how to write their name as a series of shapes and may not have any knowledge of the constituent letter names. Use the guide in Figure 4.6 to assign points and record scores on the CAP assessment form in Appendix A.

Assessment of Writing

Collecting children's unassisted writing over time tracks their growth in literacy and provides a record of their concepts about the forms and functions of print. Many teachers keep a weekly or monthly sample of writing in a portfolio to share with parents and to document development. The writing assessment shown in Figure 4.7 can be used to assign points similar to the assessment for names.

FIGURE 4.8 Scoring Samples for Writing

	Identified as writing	Message assigned	Linear orientation	Separate symbols	Letters/numbers used	Salient sounds	Beginning and ending sounds	Some vowels	Spaces between words	Total
ℳℯℳ (I love you)	1	1	1							3
ICD (I see a duck)	1	1	1	1	1	1				6
I SE A DK (I see a duck)	1	1	1	1	1	1	1	1	1	9

Clay's Assessment of Concepts about Print

Marie Clay (1993) developed a method for assessing children's concepts about print that has become widely used. In that assessment, teachers pose a series of questions while sharing simple picture books. A checklist based on Clay's work can be found in Figure 4.8. In addition to conducting the assessment in a structured manner, you can observe children informally in various settings to gather this information, posing questions during shared reading and interactive writing. Many school systems and state departments of education have variations of this checklist that teachers use in preK and kindergarten to meet state and local standards. You can watch different examples of this assessment online at the YouTube website by just typing "concepts of print" in the search box.

> Chapter 5 describes spelling inventories used in kindergarten to gather more information about children's letter–sound understanding or spelling knowledge.

Concept Sorts to Identify Concepts about Print

Another way to assess students' concepts about print is to ask them to categorize samples of pictures, letters, words, and sentences. See Appendix A for a prepared sort. Enlarge the sort and cut it apart to model with a group before you assess individual students. Introduce the headers: *picture, letter, word,* and *sentence*. Say something like "Here is picture of a shoe and here is the word *shoe.* Words have letters that we read. Select another card and model how you will sort it." "Here is a letter; there's just one letter, so I will put it underneath the letter card. Here is a sentence. I can tell it is a sentence because there are words with spaces between them." Then call on children to take a turn at selecting a card, deciding where it should go, and explaining why it goes there. Help the children use as many terms connected to print as possible. When describing a sentence, for example, they might mention its length, the spaces between words, and the punctuation. You can also ask children to find a short word such as *dog* and a long word such as *caterpillar* or to find a sentence with a question mark or period.

Working with Parents

Parents can be encouraged to do many things at home to develop children's concepts about print, but it may not be something they do naturally. This may be a topic to cover in an open house or parent workshop setting. Figure 4.9 is a sample of a letter that you might want to send home.

FIGURE 4.9 Parent Letter for Concepts about Print and Writing

Dear Parents/Guardians,

Your child is learning about the world of print and developing the understanding that print has a message and many purposes and forms. You play an important role in helping your child learn about print through reading and writing. Encourage your child to write—even if it is just scribbles. You will see how the scribbles change over time to letters that represent some of the sounds in words. You were excited when your child first tried to say *Mama* or *Daddy,* and you did not expect him or her to say words correctly or in complete sentences. Reading and writing will develop in similar ways with practice and encouragement.

Here are some things you can do when you read books:

- Point to each word in the title as you read the title aloud.
- Read the name of the author and illustrator.
- Find other books by the same author that your child enjoys.
- Occasionally point to the words in a sentence. Point out familiar letters such as the letters in your child's name.

Here are some things you can do to encourage writing:

- Supply paper and pencils, markers, or crayons.
- Draw and write together at the same time; talk about what you are doing as you draw and write.
- Show how and why you write notes, letters, emails, recipes, and so on.
- Keep a shopping list and have your child help you add items and then check them off as you find them.
- When your child does a drawing, ask him or her to dictate a sentence or two, which you then write underneath the drawing. Display these around the house. Point to the words as you read the dictations back.
- Ask your child to add to greeting cards or letters that you write to friends and relatives— even if the writing is scribbles. Ask your child to sign the card.

Here are some ways you can point out words all around us:

- Talk about all the different kinds of things you read and why: magazines, newspapers, books, cookbooks, bus schedules, travel guides, and so on.
- Point out labels on packages such as cereal, pasta, and cake mixes and read them to your child.
- Demonstrate how you follow written directions to make things.
- Point out signs and tell your child what they say.
- Ask your child to help you find items while shopping by reading the labels.

Sincerely,

Word Study for Phonics and Spelling

After introducing the traditional rhyme "Oh A'Hunting We Will Go" and reading it on a chart and sentence strips, Regina Smith pulls a small group of her kindergarten children to sort pictures that begin with *F* and *B*. These letters were selected because the words *box* and *fox* are rhyming words in the sentence, "We'll catch a fox and put him in a box, and then we'll let him go." She holds up a letter card for *B* and asks the children to find a word in the rhyme that starts with *B*. When the children have found the word, she writes "box" on a card. She repeats this with *F* and "fox." Then she sets out a collection of picture cards and explains that many more words begin with these same letters. She then models how to say the name of a picture and determine the letter–sound match: "Here is a fox. What sound do you hear at the beginning of *fox*? Listen: *fffffox*. I hear /ffff/. We will put the fox under the letter *F*." After modeling several more pictures this same way, Regina asks the children to help her sort the rest under either *B* or *F*. Together they name each picture and compare it to the key pictures: "Does *bed* start like *box* or *fox*?" After sorting, they name all the pictures under each letter (box, bed, boat, ball, belt) to emphasize the beginning sound and to check whether all the pictures are in the right place. Their sort looks something like Figure 5.1.

The next day, after rereading the rhyme, they repeat the picture sort again as a group. Then Regina gives each child his or her own collection of pictures to sort. She asks the children to check their work by reading down the column of pictures under each letter. The third day, after quickly sorting their pictures again, Regina passes out an alphabet book to pairs of children and asks them to find the B page and report to the group something they found that begins with *B*. The children find words like *baboon, bubbles,* and *burritos,* which Regina records on a chart. They repeat the alphabet book search with *F*. After reading each list of words for the children as a review, Regina assigns them the task of drawing pictures of things that begin with *B* and *F*. She encourages them to label their pictures, spelling as best they can.

FIGURE 5.1 Picture Sort for Beginning Sounds

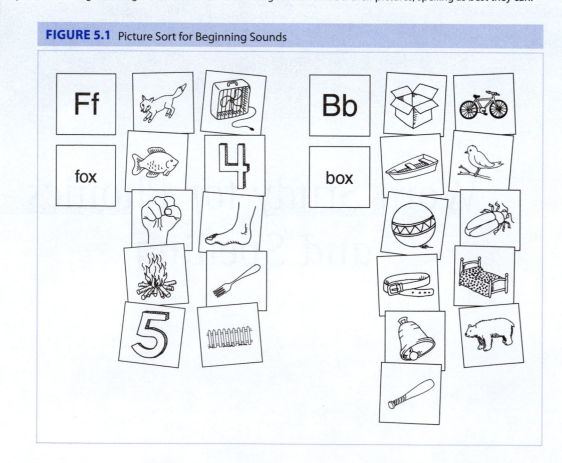

Learning to Spell: The Developmental Perspective

Alphabet knowledge (letters) and **phonemic awareness** (sounds) are two of the most powerful predictors of success in learning to read (Lonigan & Shanahan, 2009). In this chapter, we look at how children combine these as they learn the **letter–sound correspondences** needed for phonics and spelling. **Phonics** is usually associated with reading words (or decoding) whereas spelling is associated with writing words (or encoding). But the two are best thought of as complementary processes that depend on knowledge of the systematic match between letters and sounds (Ehri, 1997).

> **Chapters 2 and 3 describe the development of alphabet knowledge (letters) and phonemic awareness (sound).**

Characteristics of Spelling in Prekindergarten and Kindergarten

Early writing may consist of scribbles and random letters used to convey a message. Such pretend writing does not really involve spelling. Children begin to spell when they understand the **alphabetic principle**—that the letters they write must correspond to the sounds in the words they want to represent. Their first efforts are known as **invented spelling** or **developmental spelling** because young writers generate the spelling for words whose written forms are not stored in their memory, and they must do so based on the speech sounds or **phonemes** they are able to distinguish and match to letters.

Invented spelling has probably been around for as long as children have had access to paper and pencil, but adults gave it little attention until Charles Read (1971) investigated preschoolers' writing from a linguistic perspective. Read determined that the seemingly bizarre spellings produced by young writers represented a special logic based on the names of letters and the manner in which speech sounds are produced or articulated in the mouth. At about the same time, Edmund Henderson and his graduate students at the University of Virginia were collecting spelling samples across a range of ages and were able to use Read's insights to analyze and categorize spelling efforts as windows into children's developing word knowledge (Henderson, 1981). From this work, a developmental model of spelling came into being. In this model, development progresses from the emergent stage and the letter name–alphabetic stages of early childhood to the within word pattern and upper-level stages into adulthood. These stages and an instructional approach called **word study** have been described in *Words Their Way: Word Study for Phonics, Vocabulary and Spelling Instruction* (Bear, Invernizzi, Templeton, & Johnston, 2012). Most children in preschool and kindergarten will be found in the emergent and letter name–alphabetic stages.

EMERGENT STAGE. Children in the **emergent stage** generally range in age from infancy to six years old and may not have experienced any formal instruction in phonics and spelling. Nonetheless, children as young as two or three leave their mark by producing scribbles. At first, children at this young age may not differentiate between writing and drawing, but by the middle of this stage they produce arrays called **mock linear** writing, consisting of scribbles or letter-like forms that are separated from their drawing. As they learn about letters and how to produce them, their pretend writing may incorporate these letters in random strings. This writing is called **prephonetic** (Henderson, 1981) because children do not understand that letters represent speech sounds in a systematic way. In prephonetic spelling, young children are not really spelling; they are mimicking what they see around them. These early efforts at pretend writing show a surprising amount of understanding of how print works. See Figure 5.2 for examples of emergent spelling.

By the late emergent stage, you will begin to see evidence of tentative letter–sound matches. Some children develop this insight into the alphabetic principle on their own,

FIGURE 5.2 Characteristics of the Emergent Stage

Early emergent	Children make marks on the page that may consist of scribbles and drawing mixed together.
Middle emergent	Children create linear arrays of scribbles or letter-like forms and begin to include random letters and numbers as they are learned. Pretend writing is separated from drawing.
Late emergent *IPTH*	Children begin to use some letters that match the most salient sounds in words (usually the initial sound) but do not leave space between words.

but most will have had at least some modeling and explanations from family or teachers. Because words are made up of a series of phonemes that are difficult to separate, the youngest spellers with only partial phonemic awareness may put down just one letter to represent the most prominent sound: D for *duck*, S for *sun*, or perhaps N for *on* (Henderson, 1981; Read, 1971; Richgels, 2001). They might represent each syllable in longer words such as BD for *birthday*. It is interesting that some children will put down one sound and then random letters (DMP for *duck*), as though they know that words are not spelled with a single letter but are unable to determine what those other letter–sound correspondences might be. These first efforts at spelling can be quite difficult to interpret unless the child tells you what they say.

In Figure 5.3 you will see an example that reveals some of the special logic used by young writers. Lee has spelled "Once upon a time" with 1SPNTM, paying attention to the most forcefully articulated sounds. She used the numeral 1 with S quite logically to represent *once*. When trying to spell *elephant*, she used the names of the letters *L* (el) and *F* (ef), to spell it as LFT—one letter for each syllable. However, her spelling of *strawberry* is reduced to just an S. VN may seem like an odd way to represent "the end" until you compare the /th/ in *the* and the /v/ in *ve* and feel how the air between your front teeth and lips create a bit of friction in both. The N of *end* is both a letter name and the most obvious

FIGURE 5.3 Lee's Elephant Story

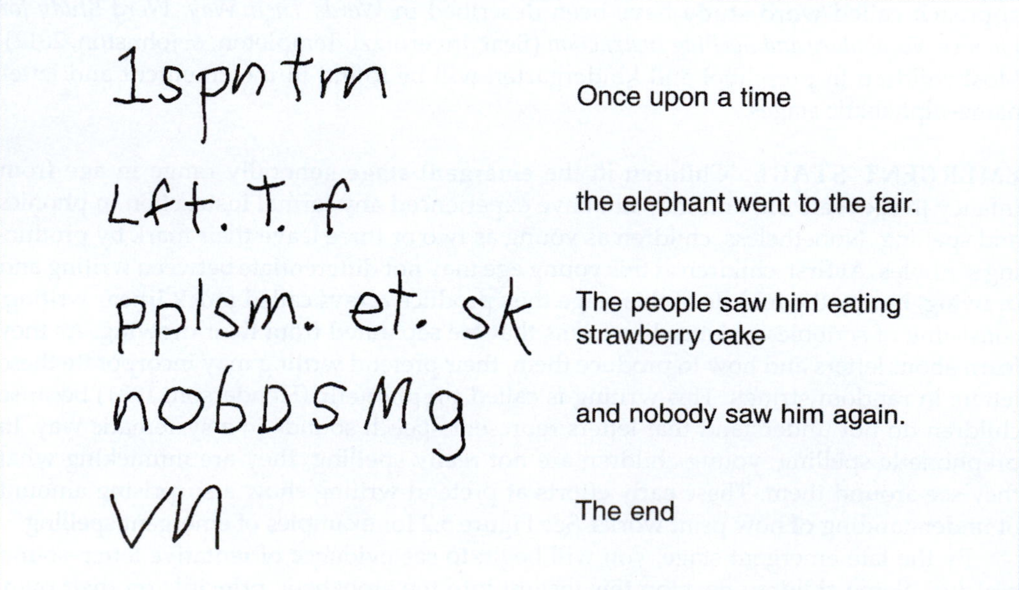

1spntm	Once upon a time
Lft. T. f	the elephant went to the fair.
pplsm. et. sk	The people saw him eating strawberry cake
nobDSMg	and nobody saw him again.
VN	The end

sound in the word. Lee has paid careful attention to the feel of spoken language in her mouth, representing those sounds that are the most obvious, or **salient sounds**.

Letter Names. Letters have both names and sounds, and it is worthwhile to spend a little time here talking about both. Children who have never had formal phonics instruction but who know the names of the letters turn to the alphabet for sound matches when they try to spell. Many letters have clues to the **consonant** sounds that they represent, either at the beginning (*B* = bee, *K* = kay) or the end (*F* = ef, *L* = el), and some are named by their **long vowel** sounds (*A* = ay, *O* = oh). There are a few letters that offer no clue to their respective sounds, such as *H* (aich), *W* (double-yoo), and *Y* (wie), but they do suggest substitutions for sounds that children are likely to make. This is why a child might spell the word *witch* as YH, using the beginning of *Y* (wie) and the ending of *H* (aich).

> **See Chapter 2 (particularly Table 2.1) for more information about letter names.**

Production of Letter Names and Sounds. How sounds are formed has important implications for how children will perceive the phonemes that they are trying to represent with letters. Without being told to do so, children appear to pay attention to where sounds are produced in the mouth (place of articulation), how they are produced (manner of articulation), and whether they are voiced or unvoiced (Read, 1971). A pronunciation chart of consonants is shown in Table 5.1. Read across each row saying the sound of the letters (/b/, /p/, /m/) to see how those sounds share the same place of articulation—on the lips. Then see whether you can detect the difference in how the sounds of /b/, /p/, and /m/ are articulated. Place the palm of your hand in front of your mouth as you say the letter sounds for *b, p,* and *m*. The lips produce a short explosion of air for "buh" and "puh," but not for "mmmm." In making the letter sound for *M*, the air passes through your nose instead of your lips, creating a **nasal** sound. Letter sounds also differ in the degree to which the vocal chords vibrate. Place two fingers on your throat to feel the difference in the sounds /b/ and /p/. The sound for *B* is **voiced** because the vocal chords vibrate, whereas the sound for *P* is **unvoiced** because there is very little vibration.

Study of the production of speech sounds may seem technical, but it explains so many of the interesting things young children do, as they apparently pay attention to physical sensations when they try to spell. For example, they are likely to confuse a voiced sound with its corresponding unvoiced sound, such as /b/ and /p/. This confusion may result

---

TABLE 5.1   **Pronunciation of Consonant Sounds**

	PLACE OF ARTICULATION		MANNER OF ARTICULATION		
		Voiced	*Unvoiced*	*Nasal*	*Other*
Lips together		b	p	m	
Lips rounded		w	wh		
Top teeth touching lips		v	f		
Tip of tongue touching teeth		th (*that*)	th (*thin*)		
Tip of tongue and roof of mouth		d	t	n	l
Tongue and roof of mouth		z	s		
Sides of tongue and teeth			sh		y
Sides of tongue and roof of mouth		j	ch		r
Back of tongue and throat		g	k	ng (*sing*)	
Throat (not really articulated)			h		

in the spelling of *pet* as BT or PD and explains why a child might substitute *J* for *ch,* spelling *chin* as JN. Understanding speech sounds will also help as you work with children to teach letter–sound correspondences. You will understand their confusions ("Yes, *B* and *P* are alike") and can talk about how sounds are produced ("I make the sound for *T* with the tip of my tongue").

To summarize, three factors account for the sometimes unusual spellings created by children in the early stages: (1) their limited phonemic awareness, which restricts the number of sounds they will try to represent; (2) their tendency to rely on letter names for sound matches; and (3) the confusions they encounter when they attend to how sounds feel in their mouth. Consider why a child might spell "I fell and hurt my chin" as IVLNRMIJN. The child is using a letter name strategy to represent the most salient sounds and is confusing sounds that are made in the same place in the mouth but in a different manner or voice (e.g., *f* and *v*). A fourth factor comes into play if children are learning English. They are likely to be unfamiliar with some of the sounds of English, and other languages may not differentiate between sounds that are in close proximity to each other in the same way that English does. As a result, children will substitute sounds and letters closest to their primary languages and alphabets. See Table 5.2 for some of the consonant confusions English learners may experience.

Hopefully this discussion will help you appreciate the special logic of young children's developmental spelling as well as how innovative and insightful young children can be as they puzzle through the spelling system and develop their own theories about how it works. Instruction will help them learn the correct associations and move them toward accurate spellings. But just as we take pride in children's first fumbling efforts at talking, eating, and walking and expect that they will make mistakes along the way, we should value these developmental spellings as their best efforts to participate in the world of writing. Parents may often feel concerned and confused about developmental spelling, so it is important to talk to them about why you accept and encourage writing that is not spelled conventionally. The letter in Figure 5.4 may be something you will want to share with parents or it may give you ideas about how to communicate with them.

TABLE 5.2 **Consonant Confusions for English Learners**

B is confused with unvoiced *P* and is difficult in final position.

C is often confused with a hard *G*.

D is pronounced as /th/ in Spanish, so *dog* may be pronounced /thog/.

F is confused with voiced *V*, especially among Arabic speakers. For Japanese speakers, it is confused with /h/.

G may be confused with *K* by speakers of languages like Arabic, French, or Swahili.

H is silent in Spanish. In Chinese it sounds more like /kh/, as in *loch*.

J is pronounced as /h/ in Spanish and may also be pronounced /ch/.

K may be confused with a hard *g* by Spanish speakers.

L may be confused with *R*. A final *L* may be especially difficult.

M may be dropped at the end of words.

N is difficult for speakers of Chinese, especially at the end of words. It may be confused with *L*.

P is easily confused with its voiced mate, *B*.

R is rolled in Spanish and may be spelled with W. It is confused with *L* by speakers of many Asian languages.

S is difficult to perceive in final position.

SH is a sound that does not exist in many languages and is confused with *CH, G,* and *J.*

S blends in Spanish such as *st, sk,* and *sp* are separate syllables that begin with *E* as in *Español.*

T may be confused with its voiced mate, *D,* by Spanish speakers and may not be pronounced at the end of words.

V may be confused with *B* by speakers of Spanish and Korean. It does not exist in many languages.

W is a letter that does not exist in many languages and may be confused with *V.*

Y may sound more like /jh/ in dialects of Spanish.

Z may be confused with *S* and may not be voiced in Spanish.

FIGURE 5.4 Parent Letter About Developmental Spelling

Dear Parents/Guardians,

You may wonder why your child brings home writing with misspelled words. Sometimes these early efforts are called "invented spellings," but they are also known as "developmental spelling" because over time they become more complete and accurate as your child learns to read and develops phonics knowledge. During writing time I ask my students to "spell as best they can" rather than waiting for someone to tell them how to spell a word. This frees them to write about anything that interests them, but also requires them to think about the sounds in the word and to think about the letters they need to represent those sounds. Hearing all the sounds is difficult, so at first they may only represent one sound, spelling *like* as L or K. "Spelling the best you can" requires that children use the phonics knowledge they are learning, and over time I expect to see more complete and accurate spelling. During the school year, watch as your child's spelling includes more letters and sounds—even if it is still not complete.

When your child progressed from crawling to taking steps on his or her own, you were very proud of the development and encouraged your child to walk, even though he or she often stumbled and fell. When children spell *like* as L or LK or LIK, they are taking their first steps into the world of writing, and you should encourage these efforts as well. Don't worry that these early efforts will stick with them and interfere with learning correct spelling. With exposure, practice, and instruction, children continue to develop until they can spell thousands of words correctly without even thinking about it—just like they can run and skip and twirl without thinking about it. However, unlike learning to walk, learning to spell takes many years to master because English is a complicated written language.

Although it is important to accept developmental spelling, I am also constantly working to teach my students the foundations for correct spelling so that by the 3rd or 4th grade they will spell most of the words they need correctly and they will also know strategies for figuring out how to spell the words they don't know.

Encourage your child to write at home. If he or she asks you how to spell a word, say "What sounds do you hear?" rather than simply giving the spelling. Offer praise for what your child figures out and accept what he or she was able to do. When your child brings home something he or she has written at school, ask him or her to read it to you and show that you are proud of how your child is learning to communicate with writing. I am happy to talk with you further about this if you have any questions.

Sincerely,

LETTER NAME–ALPHABETIC STAGE. The prominent use of letter names as a strategy for making letter–sound matches accounts for the name of the second stage of spelling development: **letter name–alphabetic stage**. During this stage, children's phonemic awareness continues to develop, and their representation of sounds will increase. At the same time, with experience and instruction, they learn about conventional letter–sound correspondences, and they begin to move beyond their letter name strategy. Because of the changes across this stage, it is divided into early, middle, and late in order to plan word study most appropriately. Figure 5.5 summarizes the characteristics of this stage.

Early letter name–alphabetic spellers have only partial phonemic awareness and represent the most obvious sounds (initial and sometimes final consonants), usually omitting the vowel in the middle. Like children in the late emergent stage, they frequently confuse voiced and unvoiced letter pairs, perhaps spelling *dig* as TK. Because **consonant blends** consist of two tightly meshed phonemes, they may only represent them partially, spelling *skate* as ST or *climb* as KM. **Consonant digraphs** (*ch, sh, th, wh*) are particularly confusing because they are a single sound spelled with two letters and there is no single letter in the alphabet that makes a match. (See Table 5.3 for a chart of phonics terms.) When children

FIGURE 5.5 Characteristics of the Letter Name–Alphabetic Stage

Early letter name–alphabetic *I PT a HK*	Children have partial phonemic awareness and represent the most salient sounds (usually initial consonants), making substitutions based on letter names and articulation. Spacing between words becomes more common and a few high-frequency words (e.g., *the, is, my*) may be spelled correctly.
Middle letter name–alphabetic *I Patid a chek*	Initial and final consonants, as well as some long vowel sounds, are represented correctly. Short vowels are used but confused, and blends and digraphs are incomplete or confused. Consistent spacing is used between words and many high-frequency words are correct.
Late letter name–alphabetic *I petid a chik*	Children have full phonemic awareness and spell most short vowels, blends, and digraphs correctly. Silent letters are omitted unless words are familiar, as in *like* or *come*. Preconsonantal nasals may still be omitted (e.g., the *m* in *bump*).

TABLE 5.3 **Phonics Terms**

TERM	DEFINITION
Consonants	Most letters of the alphabet represent consonant sounds, which are articulated by obstructing air with the tongue, teeth, lips, and other parts of the mouth. Table 5.2 lists the consonants.
Consonant blends	A unit of two or three letters at the beginning or end of words that combine to make a tightly meshed series of sounds. Each sound is heard, if only briefly, Blends can be grouped by *s* blends (*sc, sk, sn, sm, sp, st, sw*), *l* blends (*bl, cl, fl, gl, pl, sl, spl*), *r* blends (*br, cr, dr, fr, gr, pr, spr, str, scr*), and final blends (*st, sk, sp, ft, rd*). Two blends that don't fall into any of these categories are *tw* and *qu*. Blends can be segmented into individual phonemes as phonemic awareness improves.
Consonant digraphs	Two letters that represent one sound only. The digraphs studied by young children are *ch, sh, th,* and *wh*. Digraphs cannot be segmented into smaller phonemes.
Preconsonantal nasals	When the nasal sounds of *m* and *n* come before consonants such as *p, g,* or *k* (*jump, song, pink*), they are difficult to detect as air escapes through the nose in the process of pronunciation.
Vowels	Speech sounds represented by *A, E, I, O, U,* and sometimes *Y.* Vowels pass through the mouth with little or no obstruction and are formed by squeezing and vibrating the vocal chords.
Short vowels	There are five short vowel sounds, as represented in the middles of the words *cat, net, knit, cot,* and *cut*. The consonant-vowel-consonant (or CVC) spelling pattern in these words signals that the vowel sound in the middle is short.
Long vowels	The five long vowels "say their name," as in *cake, keep, night, coat,* and *cute*. Long vowels are often accompanied by silent letters creating a variety of patterns for each long vowel sound such as *A-E* in *cake* (CVCe), *AI* in *rain* (CVVC), and *AY* in *play* (CVV). These patterns are studied in later stages.
Other vowels	There are other vowel sounds that are neither long nor short such as *r*-controlled or *r*-influenced (*car, her, tore*) and diphthongs (*boy, cow*). These vowels are studied in later spelling stages.
Affricates	A consonant sound that begins with a restriction of air followed by a forceful release, as in the last sound of the letter name of *H* (aitch). The letter sounds /j/, /ch/, and /g/ and the consonant blends *tr* and *dr* are often confused by young spellers because they all create an affricate sound.
Onset and rime	A single syllable word can be split before the vowel into two units (*h-ot, sp-ot,* or *l-ost*). The beginning unit, which is a consonant, blend, or digraph, is the onset. The vowel and what follows is the rime unit.

turn to letter names to represent the *SH* in *dish,* they may select H as the closest approximation (because /ch/ and /sh/ are similar in articulation) to spell *dish* as DH.

In the early letter name–alphabetic stage, children may spell a few words correctly. These are usually **high-frequency words** such as *mom* and *love* that they have seen frequently and have stored completely in memory. As young writers attend to beginning and ending sounds in words, they become aware of word boundaries and begin to leave spaces between words in their writing.

Middle letter name–alphabetic spellers are developing better phonemic awareness. With this comes the ability to segment the **vowel** in the middle of words. The vowel sounds are an unobstructed release of air differentiated by very slight changes in the vocal chords, the shape of the mouth, the openness of the jaw, and the position of the tongue, making them much harder to detect than the more clearly articulated consonants. Figure 5.6 shows the place where vowels can be felt in the mouth. Try saying each front vowel sound, starting with long *e* and moving down to long *i*. Then say the vowels that are formed in the back of the mouth. Can you detect the slight changes in your mouth?

By the middle of the letter name–alphabetic stage, long vowel sounds will be spelled using the letter name (SAM for *same* or LIK for *like*), but silent letters will be omitted unless the word is stored in memory (e.g., *love* or *like*). **Short vowels** pose a problem because even when the child can segment the vowel sound, as in /p/ /e/ /t/, there is no letter–name match. Instead, young children select the closest approximation based on place of articulation. Short *a* is not too far from long *a*, because they are both at the front of the mouth, so *sat* might be spelled accurately. But notice in Figure 5.6 how long *e* is high in the mouth and short *e* is lower and closer to long *a*. Children will often logically spell *pet* as PAT because of this. Typically, vowels at the front of the mouth (*A, E,* and *I*) are confused, and vowels in the middle (short *u*) and at the back (long and short *o*) are confused.

Middle letter name–alphabetic spellers will begin to spell some blends, but the *r-* blends of *dr* and *tr* may pose problems because they really do not begin with /d/ or /t/. Say the words *drive* and *trip*; if you pay careful attention, you may notice they really sound like *jrive* and *chrip*. As a result, they may be spelled JRIV or HRP by young spellers. The sounds for *j*, soft *g* (as in *gym*), *ch*, *dr*, and *tr* are known as **affricates** and are often substituted for each other in letter name–alphabetic spellings.

Late letter–name alphabetic spellers have full phonemic awareness and are able to represent blends and medial vowels. Some children will continue to have problems with short vowels but consistently include a logical substitution, if not the correct vowel. Nasal letters that are part of a final blend such as the *mp* in *jump* or the *nk* in *pink* are the most elusive consonant sounds to be perceived and may still be missing in the late letter name–alphabetic stage. These sounds are known as **preconsonantal nasals**. Try saying *jump* and *pink*; see whether you can segment the *M* and *N*. They are there (compare *jup* and *jump*), but the nasal sounds of *M* and *N* escape out the nose with little articulation.

Many high-frequency words may be spelled correctly by the late letter name–alphabetic stage. Children will have seen a lot of words in their reading, have many words stored in memory, and begin to experiment with silent letters. They will often use but confuse silent *e*, perhaps spelling *wait* as WATE or *fan* as FANE. These are indications that the speller is moving to the next developmental level, known as the **within word pattern stage**, where the many long vowel patterns of English will be studied in depth. If you have spellers at

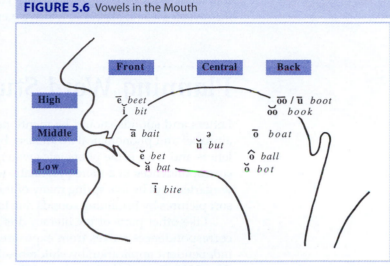

FIGURE 5.6 Vowels in the Mouth

Front   Central   Back

High
Middle
Low

ē *beet*
ĭ *bit*
ā *bait*
ĕ *bet*
ă *bat*
ī *bite*
ə
ŭ *but*
o͞o / ū *boot*
o͝o *book*
ō *boat*
ô *ball*
ŏ *bot*

See Chapter 6 for more information about how the ability to read words follows a similar developmental path.

this stage, we refer you to *Words Their Way: Word Study for Phonics, Vocabulary and Spelling Instruction* (Bear et al., 2012), which covers this stage and upper-level stages in detail.

Planning Word Study

Letters and sounds should be mentioned and modeled in lots of ways in the study of alphabet and phonological awareness, but once children can identify at least some of the letters and have some phonemic awareness, it is time to begin the study of letter–sound correspondences in a more systematic way. This formal study typically happens in kindergarten, but by late spring many of the children in Jackie's preschool classes are able to sort pictures by beginning sounds due to exposure and explanations.

Like other parts of the literacy diet for young children, learning about letter–sound correspondences moves from exposure, explanations, and modeling by the teacher to independent application by children—the gradual release model (Duffy, 2009; Fisher & Frey, 2008; Pearson & Gallagher, 1983).

1. *Exposure and explanation.* There are many opportunities for you to point out letters and talk about their matching sounds throughout the day. For example, after reciting "Mary Had a Little Lamb," you might point to the title on a chart and say, "Look— *little* and *lamb* both start with the letter *L*. Listen. *Little. Lamb.* Do you hear how they sound alike at the beginning? Who has that sound in their name? Yes, *Lisa* starts with that sound." Or, in the housekeeping center, you might emphasize the /m/ sound as you point to the *M* on a box of macaroni.
2. *Recognition and identification.* Children identify or match words that begin with the same letter–sound correspondences. The picture sort with *F* and *B* described at the beginning of this chapter is a good example of this. Or you might say, "Can you find a picture that begins with *F,* like the beginning of *fox*? Listen to the first sound: *fffffffox.*"
3. *Production or application.* Children are able to supply answers to the question, "Can you think of something that begins with the /fffff/ sound made by the letter *F*?" And, most importantly, children use letter–sound correspondences as they learn to read and write words.

Developmental Scope and Sequence

Looking at children developmentally, we see that beginning consonant sounds are the first letter–sound correspondences children begin to master in the late emergent stage, so systematic phonics instruction begins with picture sorts for consonant sounds. Vowels do not make much of an appearance in young children's writing until the middle letter name–alphabetic stage, when children are developing the phonemic awareness needed to segment and isolate sounds in the middle of words, so short vowel sounds are not formally taught until later in the sequence of features. Table 5.4 provides an overview of the developmental sequence and phonics features described in this chapter for word study. Later in this chapter, we will describe assessment tools to help you determine where children fall in this developmental sequence. In general, phonics instruction in preschool is limited to the study of beginning consonants. In kindergarten, standards generally require instruction in beginning consonants, blends, digraphs, and short vowels (*Common Core State Standards for English Language Arts,* 2010). However, we urge you to always consider where children are developmentally and to plan instruction accordingly. Although children progress through these features in a predictable sequence, the rate of their progress will differ and, to be most effective, instruction must match where they are developmentally.

| TABLE 5.4 | **Developmental Sequence of Systematic Word Study in PreK–K** |

STAGE AND FEATURES	PACING
Late Emergent	
Beginning consonant sorts: Contrast two sounds that are very different in articulation such as /m/ and /s/, /f/ and /t/, or /b/ and /r/. Contrast up to four sounds when children are able.	Set a slow pace for preschoolers and early kindergarten, selecting sounds based on words that occur in poems and jingles used for shared reading or letter sounds in children's names.
Early Letter Name–Alphabetic	
Beginning consonant sorts: A fast-paced sequence for children who know most sounds might be as follows: b/m/r/s t/g/n/p c/h/f/d l/k/j/w y/z/v w/y/g/j p/b/d/t	In kindergarten contrast up to four sounds at a time, covering all the consonants systematically and end up by comparing sounds children confuse such as /b/ and /p/ and /d/ as needed. Spend about a week on each set for an introductory pace.
Same-vowel word families (with words and pictures): at an/ad ap/ag op/ot/og et/eg/en ug/ut/un ip/ig/ill	Start out slowly, spending as much as a week on a set, but move more quickly as children catch on to how word families work.
Digraph sorts: s/h/sh c/h/ch h/ch/sh ch/sh th/wh ch/sh/wh/th	Some children will need to spend time comparing digraphs to single consonants (in the first row) but many children can start with the second row of consonants. Digraphs will be reviewed later so complete mastery is not required at this point.
Blend sorts: s/t/st s/p/sp sp/sk/sm sc/sn/sw p/l/pl pl/sl/bl t/r/tr d/r/dr cr/cl/ fl/fr bl/br/gr/gl pr/tr/dr k/wh/ qu/tw	Start by comparing single consonants to blends, but move on quickly to comparing just blends, setting as fast a pace as children can handle. Blends will be reviewed in word families and short-vowel sorts.
Middle Letter Name–Alphabetic	
Mixed short-vowel word families: at/ot/it an/un/in ad/ed/ab/ob ag/eg/ig/og/ug ill/ell/all ick/ack/ ock/uck ish/ash/ush ink/ank/unk ing/ang/ung/ong	At first, spend about a week on each set, as children will need to attend carefully to the medial vowel. Blends and digraphs will be reviewed in these sorts.
Short vowel picture sorts: a/o i/u e/i/o/u	Some children benefit from focusing on the medial sounds using pictures. Use these sorts as needed and combine with word sorts.
Late Letter Name–Alphabetic	
Short vowels in CVC words: a/o i/u e/i/o/u a/i/e with digraphs a/i with blends e/o/u with blends short vowels with final blends short vowels with final digraphs	These sorts begin with simple three-letter words and contrast vowels that are further apart. Then the sorts move toward closer contrasts and include words with blends and digraphs. Not all kindergarteners will get this far.
Word Sorts for Preconsonantal Nasals: n/nk/m/mp g/ng/t/nt m	Use as needed if the children are omitting the nasal.

Teaching Phonics through Sorting

Categorizing is a natural way that we make sense of the world, finding order and similarities across multiple encounters with words, objects, or ideas. The simple process of sorting pictures and words into categories is at the heart of word study. Sorts focus attention on the sounds and letters within words that children can already say in an **analytic** approach

to beginning phonics instruction. In a **synthetic** approach, children are directly taught letter–sound correspondences, including vowels, and then are expected to blend sounds together to decode unknown words. Both approaches have been researched and found to be effective ways to learn phonics (National Reading Panel, 2000), but the analytic approach we take is more sensitive to the young child's development and allows phonics instruction to begin without the mastery of short vowels. During the study of word families, children do learn to blend sounds and when children apply their phonics knowledge in their early writing, they are exercising a synthetic approach as they match letters to sound one by one.

The developmental scope and sequence in Table 5.4 comes from the study of children and what they show us they know and understand. Instruction is differentiated so that children are working with features they are ready to learn. Word and picture sorts are appropriate for young children because they require comparing and contrasting during the active manipulation of materials. In addition, sorting activities can be completed quickly and can be repeated for additional practice using the same materials. In the following section, we describe how to conduct sorting lessons for different phonics features and describe follow-up activities that you and your students will find engaging and effective. Table 5.5 shows the basic lesson plan format used in most sorting lessons.

Beginning Consonant Sorts

Sorts for phonics are designed to focus children's attention on the sounds in words, starting with initial consonants. Ideally children will already know the names of the letters and have the phonemic awareness needed to isolate the beginning sound. However, if kindergarten children are slow in acquiring in these skills, do not delay phonics instruction. Sorting pictures and objects by beginning sound can help them acquire phonemic

---

TABLE 5.5 **Steps in a Teacher-Directed Sorting Lesson**

1. *Provide a context.* When possible, use a poem, song, or simple text to draw attention to letters and sounds as a starting point for a sort. Choose two to four sounds based on words that appear in the text. Often there may be only one word with a particular letter/sound, but ideally there should be several.

2. *Demonstrate.* Identify pictures or objects that will be sorted and establish categories with headers (usually letters) and key words or pictures. Model how to sort a few pictures or words to get started. Explain how to contrast sounds or look for spelling patterns so the children understand what they are listening or looking for as they sort.

3. *Sort and check.* Involve the children in the sort. Correct mistakes if they are likely to cause confusion, but you can also leave a few to be checked and corrected by the children themselves. To check, read down each column after sorting to review the names of pictures, to emphasize the common sound and to make sure all the words are in the right place.

4. *Reflect.* Help the children verbalize how the pictures or words are alike. To get the reflection started, ask, "How are these words alike?" At first, children may not know how to respond to such a question, so reflections will need to be modeled as you introduce new features. You can do this by saying something like, "When I listen to these words [or look at these words] I notice that they sound alike at the beginning [or look the same in the middle]."

5. *Repeat.* Re-sort right away to reinforce the features and review the names of the pictures. Show children how to shuffle by leaving the key words and headers at the top and pushing the others together from the sides (not from the top or bottom). Sort, check, and guide the children to reflect again.

6. *Extend.* Over the next few days, have the children repeat the sort multiple times. This can be done with their own sets of words, with a partner, or in a center. Extensions to sorting include hunting for more words or pictures that fit the features, drawing and labeling pictures, and playing games.

awareness (Bradley & Bryant, 1983) and alphabet letters will be referred to repeatedly in the process. You may already have picture sets to use for sorting, or you can use the resources listed on page 137 to prepare sets of pictures for sorting. Sorting concrete objects is particularly helpful with young children and should be used whenever possible. Lesson 5.1 shows how such a sort is implemented.

See Chapter 6 for more information about the whole-to-part lesson plan that integrates phonics and reading.

LESSON 5.1   Introducing beginning sounds

"Jack and Jill" is a nursery rhyme familiar to many children. It will be used in this lesson to introduce the sounds for *H* (*hill*) and *J* (*Jack, Jill*)—two sounds that are very different in the place of articulation. (CCSS Foundational Skills: 1a, 1d, Print Concepts; 2, 2d, Phonological Awareness; 3a, Phonics and Word Recognition)

Materials

You will need an enlarged copy of "Jack and Jill," objects or picture cards for words beginning with *H* and *J*, and letter cards with capital and lowercase *H* and *J*. Also prepare individual copies of picture sorts or baggies of objects for children to use independently. (A copy of this sort can be found in Appendix B.) Figure 5.7(a) shows what a prepared handout for a picture sort might look like.

Step 1. Context

If your children do not know the rhyme, read and repeat it in preparation for this lesson, and have it printed on a chart, in sentence strips, or projected. Reread "Jack and Jill," pointing to the words as the children read with you. Talk about the meaning of the word *fetch* and try to use it in the classroom during the day (e.g., "Tanya can you fetch me a paper towel?"). Point to the words in the title and ask the children what letter they see at the beginning of "Jack and Jill." Display the capital and lowercase letter *Jj*. Then display the letter *Hh* and ask the children to find a word that begins with *H*. Show the children how to find the word, and then reread to determine what the word is. Verify that *hill* begins with *H* and point to the letter.

Step 2. Demonstrate

Display a collection of pictures and explain that there are lots of words that start with *H* and *J*. Put the picture of the hill under *Hh*, reminding children that *hill* begins with *H*. Then hold up a picture of a juice box and say, "Listen to the first sound in *juice*: jjjjuice. *Juice* begins with the same sound as *Jack* and *Jill*, so I am going to put this picture under the letter *J*. Listen to the first sound in *house*. *House* begins like *hill*, so I will put it under *H*. [*Juice* and *hill* are key words that should be used consistently each time.] Now we are going to name the rest of these pictures and put each one under either *J* or *H*. Here is a jug. Have you seen milk jugs like this? Listen to the sound at the beginning of *jug*. Does *jug* start like *juice* or like *fish*? *Jug* and *juice* start with the same sound, /j/, so I am going to put *jug* under *juice* and the letter *J*." Repeat with a picture for *H*.

Step 3. Sort, check, reflect, and repeat

Ask the children to help you sort the rest of the pictures. Hold up each one, name it, and give it to someone to sort, providing support as needed. "This picture shows someone jumping. Listen to the first sound in *jump*, jjjump. Does *jump* start like *juice* or *hill*? Listen: *jump juice* or *jump hill*?" After all the pictures have been sorted, show the children how to check: "Let's go down each column to name the pictures to see whether we got them all in the right place: *juice, jug, jump* . . . Are there any that we need to move?" The final sort will look something like Figure 5.7(b). Once all the pictures are in the right place, ask the

(*continued*)

LESSON 5.1   Introducing beginning sounds (*continued*)

FIGURE 5.7 A Prepared Sort Sheet and Final Sort for *H* and *J*

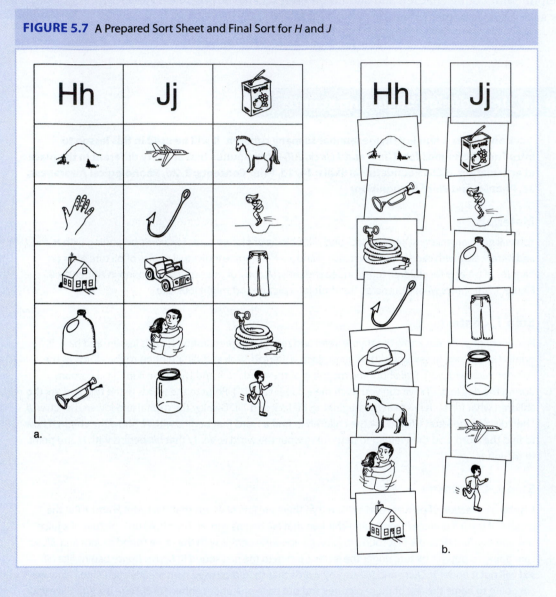

a.

b.

children to reflect on the categories: "How do these words sound alike? They all start with the /j/ sound, made by the letter *J*." Check the *H* pictures the same way. Repeat the sort. Leave up the letters and the picture of juice and hill. Shuffle the rest of the pictures and repeat the sort. You may pass out the pictures or display them and let children choose one to sort. Be ready to name the pictures again, especially if you have English learners.

Step 4. Extend

Give each child a copy of the sort to cut apart after quickly scribbling on the back with different colored crayons to identify the pieces. Or place a prepared sort in a center. Children should repeat the sort over several days (always saying the words as they sort) until they have sorted four to six times and can sort accurately and easily. (Pair up English learners with partners who can supply the name of the pictures.) Using this same nursery rhyme, you could introduce two more sounds on another day such as *W* (*went*, *water*) or *P* (*pail*). After several practice sorts, all four sounds can be combined. Additional practice comes as children engage in follow-up activities and play games. Table 5.6 presents a suggested schedule of activities to do with picture sorts for initial sounds.

GUIDELINES FOR BEGINNING SOUND SORTS. There are a number of things to keep in mind when organizing sorts for initial letter sounds.

1. *Make sorts easier or harder as needed.* Start with two obvious contrasts such as *M* and *S* that feel very different in the mouth; then add one or two more sounds for up to four categories. Look for easy and accurate sorting before moving on. Be ready to drop back to fewer categories if children have difficulty. *M* and *S* would also be good to start with because the sounds can be isolated and elongated without undue distortion (*mmmmoon* and *ssssun*). For English learners, start with sounds that exist in their native languages. See Table 5.2.

2. *Use both a key picture and a letter as headers.* Using the same **key picture** and a letter as a header each time helps students associate the letter and the sound. Compare the sounds in each picture back to the key pictures as you model a sort.

3. *Begin with modeling and explanation.* Discuss both the sound and the letter names, and model the placement of two or three pictures in each category. Be explicit about why you sort the way you do. Say, for example, "Moon—listen to the first sound in *moon*: *mmmmmoon. Moon* and *mouse* start with the same sound, *mmmm*. I will put *moon* under the letter *M*." Over time, as children catch on to what it is they are to attend to, you can use fewer directives.

4. *Use pictures or objects that are easy to name and sort.* Avoid using words with consonant blends or digraphs if you are studying just single consonants (i.e., don't use *frog* for *F*). Single-syllable words are better than two-syllable words because they have fewer sounds that need attention. Introduce the pictures to be sure that children know what to call them, and talk about them a bit if you think the picture is unfamiliar. For example, "This is a picture of a goose. A goose looks sort of like a duck but is larger and has a longer neck."

5. *Correct mistakes in the first few words but allow a few errors to remain.* Show children how to check after sorting by naming the pictures down the columns, emphasizing the beginning sounds. Then ask whether there are any pictures that need to be changed. Ask children to check their own work using the same process, and praise them when they find their own errors. If they do not find an error, prompt them by saying, "There is a picture in this row that needs to be changed. Can you find it?"

6. *Add printed words to sorts.* Words that children know can be added to the pictures in the sort to help make the connection between phonics and reading. For example, familiar words such as *love* and *like* or children's names like *Liam* and *Leslie* could be added to a sort for *L*.

7. *Allow plenty of time for individual practice and follow up activities.* After group modeling and discussion, put sets of pictures or objects in centers or create copies of picture sets for children to cut apart for more sorting. The follow-up activities described in this chapter (such as word hunts through familiar chart stories, nursery rhymes, or little books) are helpful. These application activities require children to recognize, or recall, the same beginning sounds and to judge whether they fit the category. See Table 5.6 for a suggested schedule of activities.

8. *Consider pacing.* In kindergarten you may have children who know no letter–sounds matches, so you must begin with a slow pace, such as that described in Lesson 5.1. However, if children know about half of the matches, you may want to move at a faster pace by doing three or four sounds at a time without trying to match them to particular poems, songs, or other text. (During word hunts or sound hunts, you can return to familiar texts to emphasize the connection between phonics lessons and reading.) Some children may only need to contrast certain letter sounds based on letter name confusions (*y* and *w*, for example) or voiced and unvoiced pairs (*b* and *p*, for example). English language learners may need more sorts that address the confusions

TABLE 5.6   **Suggested Schedule of Activities for Picture Sorts**

This can be modified into a four-day or three-day schedule, depending on the pace you want to set.

Day 1: Introduce the sort in a group. Demonstrate, sort, check, and reflect as described in Table 5.5.

Day 2: Repeat the sort in the group, making sure that the children know the names of the pictures, and ask the children to sort individually or with a partner. Ask the children to name the pictures aloud as they sort (e.g., "Say and Lay") and to check their work after sorting, moving any pictures that might have ended up in the wrong column. Sets of pictures or objects can be placed in a center, or kindergarten children might be given their own sheet of pictures as in Figure 5.7(a) to cut apart for sorting. Before cutting, have the children quickly scribble over the back of their handouts, each one using a different color, as a quick way to identify the sets.

Day 3: Have the children repeat the sort in a center or using their own cut-up pictures. In a small group, brainstorm or search for more words in alphabet books or in familiar reading selections that begin with the same sounds. Children can record these as drawings or cut out pictures and label them individually or on a group chart.

Day 4: Sort pictures again and play games.

Day 5: Re-sort, paste the sort, and label. This activity can also be used as a means of assessment. See Figure 5.9 for an example.

that arise because of sounds that are missing or different in their native language, especially for letter sounds like *b* and *v*.

9. *What about final consonants?* Ending consonants are not included in the sequence of features in Table 5.7 but are targeted in same-vowel word families later on. Generally, learning ending consonants depends on developing the phonemic awareness to

TABLE 5.7   **Suggested Schedule of Activities for Word Family Sorts**

This is only a suggested schedule, and you may abbreviate it to fewer days or add routines to provide more practice as needed.

Day 1: Introduce the sort, making connections to text when possible. Prepare copies of the sort for the children to cut apart and use during the next few days. With young children who are not very good at cutting, you may want to prepare sets of sorts in advance or have students cut them up during non-instructional times such as morning arrival. Have the children quickly scribble over the backs of their handouts, using a different color of crayon for each child, before cutting as a way to identify the words. If pieces get separated, you will simply look for the color on the back. Store the sorts in baggies or envelopes.

Day 2: Repeat the group sort and review the reflections from before ("What do you notice about these words? How are these words alike? Why do we call them a 'word family'?"). If the sort has pictures, remove them and read the words in each column. Support reading the words by asking the children to blend the beginning sound (onset) and family (rime unit). Ask the children to repeat the sort individually or in pairs using their own cut-up sorts.

Day 3: Have the children repeat the sort independently or with partners. Do a small-group activity such as Build, Blend, Extend or Show Me that requires children to blend word parts and spell the words in the family. New words can be introduced at this point; for example, add *stop, not, lot, got, clog, fog,* and *hog* to the word families in Lesson 5.3.

Day 4: Lead a blind sort or a blind writing sort in which you set out one picture or word as a header for each family and shuffle the word cards. Read each word card without showing it for children to sort. After modeling, children should be able to do blind sorts with partners.

Day 5: Assess. Find out whether the children can identify the words by holding them up randomly (without the support of pictures) for them to read. Then administer a simple spelling check by asking the students to write five or six words.

attend to the sounds. If children know the letter–sound correspondences for beginning consonants, they will usually transfer that knowledge to sounds in other parts of the word. However, English language learners often benefit from picture sorts that focus on ending sounds that might be missing or rare in their native language. Some children may have a few remaining confusions even when they are in control of most consonant matches, but do not hesitate to move on. Beginning consonants are reviewed and ending consonants are targeted in same-vowel word families.

Digraph and Blend Picture Sorts

Once children know beginning consonant sounds, they are ready to learn about initial consonant digraphs and blends. Digraphs are often introduced before blends because there is only one phoneme to segment and attend to, but most children can study both at about the same time (Johnston, 2003). We placed the study of digraphs and blends *after* the introduction to same-vowel word families in Table 5.4, but it could come beforehand. For convenience, it's described in this section on beginning consonant sounds.

DIGRAPHS. Consonant digraphs studied by young children include *ch, sh, th,* and *wh.* In each case, two letters are used to spell a single unique sound that cannot be broken down further. The introductory sorts for beginning digraphs suggested in Table 5.4 contrast the digraph with single letters, particularly the letter *H* because children often confuse the letter name of *h* (aitch) with *sh* and *ch. Th* is compared to single *t, sh* to single *s,* and *ch* to single *c.* However, it would be difficult to sort pictures by *w* and *wh* because most words beginning with *wh* do not have a distinctive sound. (Consider *witch* and *which.* When you say them naturally do you use a different beginning sound?). Compare *wh* to *th, sh,* and *ch* in a culminating digraph sort. Digraphs are revisited in the study of mixed-vowel word families and short vowels in both initial and final positions.

BLENDS. Like digraphs, blends studied at this stage consist of two letters, but in blends two sounds can still be heard, although they are tightly meshed and not easily segmented. Young spellers who lack full phonemic awareness will often represent only one of these two letters, perhaps spelling *stem* as SM. Because of this, some of the suggested introductory blend sorts in Table 5.4 contrast single consonants to the blend, such as comparing *S, T,* and *ST* in Lesson 5.2. However, there are a lot of blends and to do this with each one would take a long time. So once children develop the ability to segment the phonemes and understand how consonant blends work, it is important to pick up the pace and group them for study. Blends that begin with *S* (*st, sp, sk, sm, sn, sw*) are the easiest for children to master, perhaps because the *S* can be drawn out, as in *sssssstep.* Blends with *L* and *R* are more difficult for most children, especially *TR* and *DR,* which are sometimes confused with *J* and *CH,* resulting in spellings such as JRAN for *train.* It may be necessary to spend more instructional time on *R* and *L* blends for this reason. You will revisit the study of blends in mixed-vowel word families and short vowels in both initial and final positions, so students' complete mastery is not required before moving on to later features.

PRECONSONANTAL NASALS. A special type of blend is the preconsonantal nasal, which includes a nasal sound (*m* or *n*) right before a final consonant, as in *-ng, -mp, -nt, -nd,* or *-nk.* This is a particularly difficult blend because the nasal is hard to perceive as it passes through the nose. The *-ng* is the most common of these endings with a nasalized sound and can be studied as a word family in words ending in *ang, ing, ong,* and *ung.* Comparing words like *rag, ran,* and *rang* can help children understand that there are two letters at work even though they are impossible to segment. Using letter tiles to move the *N* in and out to change *rag* to *rang* is also beneficial. Preconsonantal nasals are studied at the very end of the letter name stage and are rarely taught to the majority of kindergarten children.

The PDToolkit has some prepared sorts for initial consonants. Go to the Sorts and Games tab and select Letter Name–Alphabetic. Scroll through to find the different sorts. You can also make any combination of letter–sound sorts you need by selecting the Create Your Own button at the top right of that tab.

The PDToolkit has prepared picture sorts and games for blends and digraphs. Select the Sorts and Games tab and then choose Letter Name–Alphabetic Stage. Scroll to find different sorts. You can also prepare your own sorts by clicking the Create Your Own button at the top right of the Sorts and Games page and following the directions.

LESSON 5.2 Introducing the *st* blend

Children need to understand that blends are composed of two sounds that should already be familiar to them. In this lesson *s, t,* and *st* are contrasted for children who are first learning about blends. (CCSS Foundational Skills: 2, Phonological Awareness; 3a, Phonics and Word Recognition)

Materials

You will need picture cards (or objects) that feature words that begin with *s* (sun, six, sink, socks, seal), *t* (tent, tie, tire, tub), and *st* (star, stick, stool, stamp, stump, etc.); cards with the letters in capital and lowercase forms; and individual copies of the picture sort for children to use independently. A copy of this sort can be found in Appendix B.

Step 1. Context

Display or draw an octagon in the shape of a stop sign. Ask children to help you spell the word *stop* as you print it inside the shape. Explain that *stop* begins with two sounds and say the word slowly (*ssssssstop*). Explain that two letters often work together to make a blend and that they can hear each one of the sounds if they say it slowly and listen carefully.

Step 2. Demonstrate

Display the collection of pictures and name them with the children's help, talking about any that might be unfamiliar. Put up the letters for *S, T,* and *ST* and explain that some of the words start with just *S,* some with just *T,* and some with both *S* and *T.* Hold up a picture of the sun and say, "Listen to the first sound in *sun: ssssun.* I only hear the /ssssss/ sound at the beginning, so I will put this under *S.*" Repeat with a picture for *T* such as tent. Then introduce star: "When I say *star,* I hear /ssssss/, but I hear /t/ also. *Star* begins with two sounds: /s/ and /t/. These two sounds are blended together, so I'll put *star* under the blend *ST.* Now we are going to sort the rest of these pictures under either *S, T,* or *ST.* Here is a *stool.* Listen to the sound at the beginning of *stool.* Does *stool* start like *sun, tent,* or *star*? *Stool* and *star* start with the same two sounds blended together, /s/ and /t/, so I am going to put the *stool* under the letters *ST.*"

Step 3. Sort, check, reflect, and repeat

Ask children to help you sort the rest of the pictures. Hold up each one, name it, and give it to someone to sort: "This picture shows a tie. Does *tie* go under *T, S,* or *ST*?" After all the pictures have been sorted, show the children how to check, emphasizing the beginning sound: "Let's go down each column to name the pictures and see whether we got them all in the right place." Ask whether there any that need to be moved. Once all the pictures are in the right place, ask children to reflect on the categories: "How are the words in each column alike?" Then quickly repeat the sort. Leave up the letters and the pictures of the sun, tent, and star. Shuffle the rest of the pictures, pushing them in from the sides if they are on a flat surface. You may pass out the pictures or display them and let children choose one to sort. Ask each child to compare his or her word to one of the key words before sorting. Be ready to name the pictures again, especially if you have English learners. After all the pictures are sorted, call on different children to come forward and model how to check each column and explain how the words in each column are alike, reflecting on the common sound and the letter (or letters) associated with it.

Step 4. Extend

Children should repeat the sort over several days until they have sorted four to six times and can sort accurately and easily. (Pair up English learners with partners who can supply the name of the pictures.) Additional practice comes as children engage in extension activities and games, described next.

EXTENSIONS TO PICTURE SORTS. The most important follow-up activity for picture sorts is simply to have children repeat the sorts individually or with a partner over several days. In kindergarten you might even send the sort home for children to practice with parents. However, there are other activities that teachers have found appropriate for young children to complete in small groups with teacher guidance and eventually as independent activities.

Word or Sound Hunts

To help children see that many words begin with a particular sound or letter, we recommend asking them to look for more words in other materials they have read, such as books, poems, or songs. The children might go on a word hunt around the room, looking for words or objects that start with the targeted sound or letters. Create a chart of the words they find, pointing out the first letter and emphasizing the sound as you record it. Add to these charts as new words turn up, and take time to read them aloud to review. Alphabet books are another good place to look for words that start with the sounds you are studying. Pass out a variety of alphabet books and ask children to find the *J* page and report to the group what they find. The *J* page may feature *jaguar* or *jewels,* so new vocabulary is introduced. Be ready to deal with the fact that creators of alphabet books often include words with digraphs, such as putting *chair* on the *C* page or *shark* on the *S* page. You can use this as an opportunity to briefly introduce these special sounds, explaining that the sound is spelled with a *c* or an *s,* but emphasize that it is a different sound. Words with blends can be accepted (*slide* and *swing* do begin with /s/), but remember that some blends, like *tr,* do not have a clearly distinct beginning sound.

Draw or Cut and Label

After going on word hunts and brainstorming more words that start with targeted letters, ask the children to draw pictures and label them. A sheet of newsprint folded into boxes makes a good template for drawing. (See Figure 5.8.) Children can also look for pictures in magazines to cut out and label. To keep this manageable, tear out pages in advance that contain pictures with the targeted sounds. (Catalogs are particularly useful for this purpose.) The pasting and labeling can be a group project in preschool. In kindergarten it can begin as a group activity; after modeling and practice, children can do it independently.

Paste and Label the Sort

If children have been given their own sets of pictures to cut apart and sort, they can eventually be pasted down into categories. Then encourage the children to label each picture, spelling as best they can. Prompt them to listen for more than the first sound to focus attention on other parts of the word. Do this as a group activity several times before expecting children to do it independently. These pasted sorts can be used to assess children's progress. See Figure 5.9.

FIGURE 5.8 Draw and Label

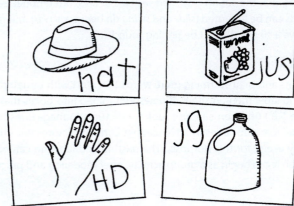

FIGURE 5.9 Paste and Label the Pictures

Alphabet Scrapbooks

For kindergarten children, individual alphabet scrapbooks can be an ongoing project. Prepare a blank book for each child by stapling together seven sheets of paper folded in the middle. As each consonant sound is studied, children can add pictures of things that begin with that letter. Preschoolers might contribute to a class alphabet book in a similar way.

Initial Consonant Follow-the-Path Game

This game is simple enough that even preschoolers can learn the rules, and it can be adapted for other features. Paste a half of a gameboard template from Appendix C on each side of a colored manila folder, leaving a slight gap between the two sides in the middle (so the folder can still fold). Add some color and interest with stickers or cutout pictures to create a theme such as "Trip to the Park" or "The Three Bears Return Home" (see Figure 5.10). Label each space on the path with letters you want to review, using both capital and lowercase forms. Sets of two to six letter sounds at a time is best. Provide a collection of picture cards that correspond with the letters. Mark the backs of the cards in some way (rubber stamps work well) so that lost pieces can be returned to the right folder. Store the pictures and three to four playing pieces in a plastic zip bag inside the folder. The steps to play are simple:

1. All the picture cards are placed face down in a stack.
2. Each player draws a picture in turn and moves the playing piece to the next space on the path with the corresponding beginning consonant.

See Chapter 2 for more information about alphabet books and scrapbooks.

FIGURE 5.10 Follow-the-Path Game

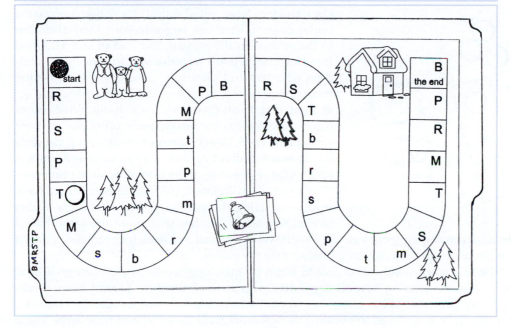

3. The winner is the first to arrive at the destination. Deemphasize competition by encouraging children to play until everyone gets to the end.

   A variation of this game is Follow the Pictures. Rather than writing letters in each space on the game board, paste pictures and then prepare a spinner with the beginning sounds you want to practice. Children spin for a letter and then move to the next picture that begins with that sound.

Letter Spin for Sounds

This is a variation of the letter spin game described in Chapter 2 (see Figure 2.10). Instead of picking up letters, children look for pictures that begin with targeted sounds. This game can be used to review up to eight beginning sounds at a time. Create a spinner divided into four to eight sections, each labeled with a beginning sound. (See spinner directions in Appendix C.) Provide a collection of picture cards that correspond with the letters. Teach children the following steps in small groups before expecting them to play the game independently:

1. All the pictures are placed face up.
2. Two to four players take turns spinning. During each turn, the player selects one picture that begins with the sound indicated by the spinner. If there are no more pictures for a sound, the player must pass.
3. Play continues until all the pictures are gone. Although a winner might be identified by counting the pictures each player holds, winning and losing need not be emphasized. Everyone will get plenty of pictures.

Initial Sound Bingo

In each square of a three-by-three or four-by-four bingo card, randomly write letters for the sounds children have been studying in sorts. Prepare a different card for each child. Chips, pennies, or squares of paper can be used as markers. Children can take turns drawing a picture card from a stack and calling out the picture name. All the children whose card had that beginning sound place a marker on that square. Play continues until someone gets a bingo (three or four in a row) or the board is filled, depending on how long you want play to last. This same game works well with blends and digraphs. Figure 5.11 shows a bingo board set up to review the *s*- blends.

PD TOOLKIT™
for Words Their Way®

Look for ready-to-print games at the PDToolkit under the Sorts & Games tab. Check either Emergent Stage or Letter Name–Alphabetic Stage. Type in "games" and hit the Apply button to go to a list of prepared games. Look for blank gameboard templates under Additional Resources.

Activity

Activity

FIGURE 5.11 Initial Sound Bingo

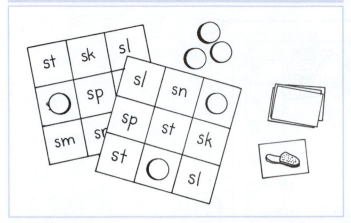

Same-Vowel Word Family Sorts

Once children have initial sounds for single consonants under control, they can begin to turn their attention to the sounds in the middle and end of words. **Word families** offer a good introduction to vowels for children who lack full phonemic awareness, because the medial short vowel is part of the ending **rime** unit (c-**at**, m-**at**, b-**at**, th-**at**) that works as a chunk. What comes before the vowel is the **onset,** made up of one or more consonants (**c**-at, **th**-at). Research with young children has shown that dividing words into onsets and rimes is easier than segmenting them into individual phonemes (Goswami, 2008; Treiman, 1985). Because children have trouble isolating the medial vowel, it is a good idea to compare word families that share the same vowel before contrasting different vowels. To sort words like *mat* and *man,* for example, children must attend to the final consonant rather than the vowel.

The first word family sorts should begin by matching words to pictures, reviewing consonants, and offering support to children who do not know how to read many words and do not have the skill to sound out words by blending the sounds together. However, children can be introduced to blending as they work with the onset and rime units. These same-vowel word family sorts also review and extend the concept of rhyme because children are asked to not only listen for the rhyme sound, but also to look for the letter patterns (the rime) that spell rhyming words. This visual support may be helpful to children who have otherwise struggled to identify rhyming words in phonological awareness tasks.

There is no particular order to the study of word families, but starting with short *a* families (*at, an, ad, ap, ack*) is a good choice because these words are common in early reading materials, and children may already know several words from these families by sight such as *cat* or *can*. In addition, short *a* is the least likely short vowel to be confused when children try to make matches based on letter names and place of articulation. Compare other short-vowel word families in a similar way (*in, it, ip* or *ot, op, og*, etc.) Consider the words that your children know and the kinds of words they encounter in their reading. If you are reading a story with lots of short *u* words, then study a few short *u* families. Lesson 5.3 describes how to introduce a set of short *o* word families and Table 5.7 describes activities to do over several days.

LESSON 5.3   Same-vowel word family sort for *-op*, *-ot*, and *-og*

Pictures provide support in this sort as children work with words they may not be able to read initially. After sorting and matching words to pictures, the pictures are taken away and children are asked to blend the onset with the rime to learn decoding skills. (CCSS Foundational Skills: 2a, 2c, 2e, Phonological Awareness; 3a, 3d, Phonics and Word Recognition)

Materials

You will need picture cards and word cards for *hop, top, mop, pop, cot, hot, dot, pot, dog, log, jog,* and *frog* and copies of the sort for children to cut out to practice individually. A copy of this sort can be found in Appendix B.

Step 1. Context

A book like *Hop on Pop* by Dr. Seuss can be used to introduce the *-op* family. This is really an anthology of short stories featuring word families, so focus on just the one that features the *-op* rime after enjoying the others. Write several sentences from the book on a chart, read them aloud to the children, and then

▶

ask them to look for the words that rhyme with *hop*. Highlight the words and ask the children what they notice about them. Explain that all the words are in a rhyming family, the *-op* family, and you are going to add two more rhyming families—the *-ot* and the *-og* families.

Step 2. Demonstrate the sort

Begin with a rhyming sort using just the pictures. Display the pictures randomly for all three families and name each one. Ask children whether they heard any words that rhymed. Then set up three categories using the pictures for *hop, dot,* and *dog* as headers. Select another picture and model how to compare it with the three headers: "Listen: *log, hop*. Does *log* rhyme with *hop*? No. Does *log* rhyme with *dot*? How about *log* and *dog*? Yes, *log* rhymes with *dog*. They sound alike at the end, so I will put the log under the dog." Repeat with a few more and then have children help you sort the rest. Name the pictures in each column and ask children to tell you how they are alike. (They rhyme or sound alike at the end.)

Next display the word cards in a random fashion where everyone can see them. Explain that you need the students' help to find the words that go with each picture. Point to the picture for *hop*: "Who can find the word *hop*? What does *hop* start with? What do you hear at the end?" Match each word to the right of its picture, as shown in Figure 5.12.

Step 3. Sort, check, reflect, and repeat

Read down the list of *-op* words. Ask the children what they notice about the letters in the words. Children should note that they rhyme, have the same vowel, and end in the same letter (*p*). Explain that it is a rhyming family because the words all end with *o* and *p*, the "op family." Repeat with the other two columns, guiding the children to tell you what they notice about the words. Leave up the pictures and shuffle the word cards. Display them randomly or hand one to each child to match back to its picture. Check after sorting by reading the words and drawing attention to the beginning and ending letters if a mistake was made: "Can this word (*hop*) be 'hot'? It starts with an *h*, but what sound do you hear at the end of *hot*? Let's look again and find a word that starts with *h* and ends with *t*."

Step 4. Extend

Make a copy of the sort for each child or make it available in a center for independent practice. Pair up English learners with partners who can supply the name of the pictures. After introducing the pictures and words, there are several follow-up activities to do over several days, as described in Table 5.7.

FIGURE 5.12 Word Family Sort with Pictures and Words

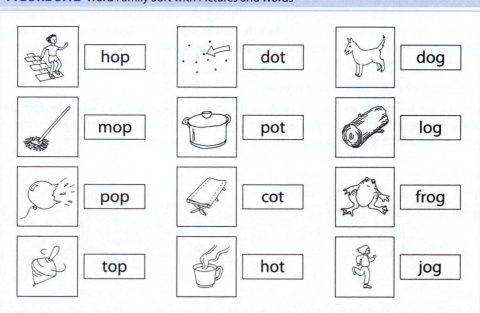

Mixed-Vowel Word Family Sorts

Although the first word family sorts compare words that share the same vowel (*cat, pan, rag*), it is important to work with mixed-vowel families (*top, tip, tap*) to really call attention to the short vowel sounds in the middle of words. These sorts will be more difficult because they lack the support of pictures, so they are most appropriate for children in the middle letter name stage, who are likely to be able to read at least some of the words. Lesson 5.4 provides an example of how to introduce a mixed-vowel word sort.

LESSON 5.4 Mixed-vowel word family sort for -*ag*, -*ig*, and -*og*

In these particular sorts, children are not expected to sound out the word first and then sort. Instead, they sort first and then use the key word, the beginning sound, and their sense of rhyme to support them as they read the new words. Some of these words will be familiar from the same-vowel word family sorts, but here they are contrasted with words that contain different vowels. (CCSS Foundational Skills: 2a, 2c, 2e, Phonological Awareness; 3a, 3d, Phonics and Word Recognition)

Materials

Prepare a set of word cards for the -*ag*, -*ig*, and -*og* families. You can make individual copies for children to cut out using the template in Appendix C. Ask the children to scribble quickly over the back using their assigned color to help identify any pieces that go astray.

Step 1. Context

To provide a context, you might prepare a sentence using a word from each family, such as "The big dog will wag his tail." Read it to the children and have them repeat it after you. Underline *big, dog,* and *wag.* Ask the children how the words are alike. (They all end in *g.*) Remind the children that they have worked with word families before, matching words to pictures, and today they are going to work with word families ending in -*ag*, -*ig*, and -*og*.

Step 2. Demonstrate

Begin by setting out a key word as a header for each family. In this case, *big, dog,* and *wag* are good headers because they have been introduced in the sentence. Hold up another word such as *dig* and say, "Look at this word. What letters do you see in it? I see *i* and *g*, so I will put it under the key word with *i* and *g*—*big*. After I sort it, I will read it and make it rhyme with *big: Big, d-ig.*" Repeat with a word for each family, sorting first and then reading the header and the added word.

Step 3. Sort, check, reflect, and repeat

Ask the children to help you sort the rest. Hold up one word at a time and ask for a volunteer. Each child should sort first and then read from the top of each column down, blending the onset and the rime when necessary to help them identify the new word. The final sort should look something like this:

big	dog	wag
dig	frog	bag
pig	fog	rag
wig	jog	flag
	log	tag

After all the words have been sorted, read down the list of words together in each column to check. Then start the reflection with "How are the words in each column alike?" Talk about the rhyming sound and the ending letters and why they are in the same family. Repeat the sort but, this time, do a blind sort that will require careful attention to the sound of the short vowel. Leave up the same key words as headers for each column. Then explain, "We will sort these words again, but this time you do not get to see the word. I will say it for you and you must listen to the vowel sound in the middle." Call on children to tell you where each word should go and place it in the column, whether it is right or wrong. Once all words are sorted, children will see whether each word is in the right place and can change any mistakes.

Step 4. Extend

Provide the children with their own sets of words to sort. They will probably sort them very quickly just by looking at the spelling of the word, but ask them to read the words down in each column as they sort and at the end when they check. Include a blind sort to do with a partner as an activity during the week and do the other activities listed in Table 5.7.

GUIDELINES FOR WORD FAMILIES. As you implement the study of word families, here are some things to keep in mind:

1. *Do not expect children to begin a sort by sounding out the words.* When working with word families in kindergarten, children are not likely to be able to read all of the words initially. This is why the first word family sorts involve matching words with pictures. When working only with words, it is important to use a familiar word as a header. (Including at least one picture also helps.) Children first sort visually by the spelling of the rime and then read the new word by blending different onsets with the rime.

2. *Include words with digraphs and blends once they have been introduced.* This will not only reinforce the study of blends and digraphs but also increase the number of words that can be studied. For example, the *-op* family can grow to include words like *chop, flop, drop, shop,* and *stop.*

3. *Supply supplemental reading materials.* Many publishers have created little books that are sometimes called **phonics readers** or decodable books that feature a particular family or short vowel. Many of these books, such as the Ready Readers published by Pearson Schools, are simple, but engaging, and can be used as reading materials. Websites such as Starfall and Reading A–Z offer phonics readers or word family books you can download. Such books can also be used as a starting point or as a follow-up for word study, and children can use them to go on word hunts for additional words that follow the same phonics feature. However, text featuring sentences such as "The tan man ran the fan" can be meaningless and confusing, so choose these materials carefully.

4. *Plan follow-up activities.* Some activities and games to use in connection with the study of word families were described earlier, and some additional ones follow. Build, Blend, and Extend; Flipbooks; and Show Me are favorites.

5. *Assess.* See the routines for word families in Table 5.7 that end with assessment. A simple five- to six-word spell check will help you determine whether the children are hearing the sounds in the words. But you can also observe their responses in activities as a way to monitor progress.

Extensions to Word Family Sorts

Plan for children to repeat the sorts over several days. However, you also want children to read and spell the words and the activities that follow will help achieve this goal. Children can learn to do some of these activities with a partner or play games in small groups, while other activities—like Build, Blend, and Extend—are teacher led. Of course, playing teacher is popular and you may find children taking on this role as they direct the activities themselves.

Blind Sort

Once children catch on to the visual patterns in word families, they can sort quickly merely by looking at the medial vowel or ending chunk. To challenge them to really listen for the sounds in words, it is important to add blind sorts to your weekly routines. Leave up the headers for the sort and shuffle the rest of the words. Say the word without showing it and ask a child to indicate where it should be sorted. Lay the word down where directed and let the child check it for accuracy. If it is wrong, it can be put back into the deck for a second try. After modeling this in a group, pair the children up to try it with partners. One reads the word while the other indicates the column and then checks the word as it is laid down. Then they change roles.

Blind Writing Sort

This variation of the blind sort requires children to write the word under the appropriate key word or header before seeing the word. Prepare a paper by writing the headers at the top. Say the word aloud for the child to write before you lay the word down for immediate checking. This can be teacher led or student led and writing sorts can be used for weekly assessment.

Build, Blend, and Extend

This series of steps is designed to reinforce the reading and spelling of the words. Prepare a set of cards like those in Figure 5.13 to be used in a pocket chart or on a tabletop. You can also make additional sets for each child so that they can imitate what you do. Write the targeted onsets and rimes on these cards, keeping the letters of the rime together. For example, to study the -at family, you would have cards with *at, b, c, f, h, m, p, r,* and *s*. As children study digraphs and blends such as *th, ch,* and *fl*, those can be added as well. There are three components:

1. *Building.* This reinforces the patterned spelling of word families. Model how to make a word in the family by putting up two cards, such as *m* and *at*. Explain, "To spell the word *mat,* I will need the beginning letter of *m* and the ending family *-at. m-a-t* spells *mat.*" Then ask the children what letter would be needed to change the word to *sat.* Model how to replace the *m* in *mat* with the *s* to build the new word *sat.* Children should then be invited to build additional words called by the teacher by substituting beginning letters: "Can you build the word *rat?*"

2. *Blending.* This reinforces the reading of word families by blending the onset and rime. Start with a word the children already know, such as *cat,* and then substitute a different beginning letter. Model how to blend the new onset with the familiar rime to read the word: "Let me show you how I read this word by sounding out the parts: *Mmmmmm, aaaaaaat, mat.* The new word is *mat.*" Children are then asked to use the two parts of the onset and rime to sound out and blend the parts of additional words in a family.

3. *Extending.* During the extending part of this activity, use words that are not included in the sort to demonstrate that additional words can be read and spelled once children know how to spell several words in a

FIGURE 5.13 Build, Blend, and Extend Cards

family. This is a time when you might demonstrate using unusual words like *vat* or challenging words with digraphs and blends such as *brag, brim,* or *bran.*

After working with the letter cards, children can be asked to write the words on paper, small whiteboards, or the chalkboard.

Show Me

This is another teacher-led activity that requires children to attend to sounds and manipulate letters to spell words. Each student gets his or her own individual pocket with a set of letter cards. Make the pockets by cutting paper into 7- by 5-inch rectangles. Fold up 1 inch along the 7-inch side; then fold the whole thing into overlapping thirds. Staple at the edges to make three pockets (see Figure 5.14). Cut additional paper into 1.5- by 4-inch cards, making 14 for each student. Print a letter on the top half of each card, making sure the entire letter is visible when inserted in the pocket. A useful assortment of letters for this activity includes the five short vowels and *b, d, f, g, m, n, p, r,* and *t.* You can add blends and digraphs, but too many letter cards can be hard to manage.

To spell same-vowel word families, each child gets a pocket, a single vowel, and an assortment of letters for beginning sounds. Call a word to spell such as *hot.* The children arrange the letters in the pockets and fold it up. When "Show me" is announced, everyone opens their pockets to display their words. Then call another word in the family such as *pot.* Watch to see whether children start over from the beginning or if they simply change the first letter. If you are studying mixed-vowel word families or short vowel words, supply additional vowels and call a series of words such as *pat, pet,* and *pot* that require the children to pay careful attention to the medial vowel.

Word Family Flip Books

Children enjoy working with flip books, as shown in Figure 5.15, to reinforce blending the onset with the rime to read words. Use a piece of tagboard or lightweight cardboard for the base of the book. Write the family or rime on the right half. Cut out pages that are half the length of the base piece and staple to the left side of the base. Write beginning sounds or onsets on each one. Children can draw a picture on the back side of the page to illustrate the word and to use for checking their responses. Pair up children to read each other's flip books.

Follow the Families

This is similar to the follow-the-path game for initial sounds described previously. Create a game board using the template in Appendix B by writing a word from the families you wish to review in each space. Children can turn over a picture or word, or spin a spinner labeled with rimes and progress around the path by moving to a word that rhymes. In order to claim the space, they read the word.

Look for prepared word family games at the PDToolkit. Under the Sorts and Games tab, select Letter Name–Alphabetic Stage, type in "games," and hit the Apply button. This will take you to a list of games for the letter name stage. You can find a prepared Show Me game, Follow the Families board game, and flip books for *-an* and *-at.*

FIGURE 5.14 Show Me Game

FIGURE 5.15 Word Family Flip Book

Word Maker

Create a deck of cards that have onsets on half (single consonants, blends, and digraphs) and short-vowel rimes such as *at, an, it,* and *ig* on the other. For children in the late letter name–alphabetic stage, include rimes with ending blends, digraphs, and preconsonantal nasals such as *ish, ang, ast, amp,* and *all.* In a center, children can work independently with the deck to form as many words as they can, or the cards can be used in a game. The cards will be similar to those shown in Figure 5.13.

1. Each player draws five cards from the deck. With the cards face up, each player creates words and then reads them. You may allow nonsense words as long as the child can read it.
2. Each player in turn then draws one card from the deck. If the child can make a word and read it, that person draws two cards to replace the ones that formed a word.
3. Play continues until the deck is used up.

Roll the Dice

In this activity, children roll cubes or dice and try to generate words. You will need two or three large cubes. On one cube, write four or five rimes that you have studied (e.g., *ag, ig, ug, og, eg*). One side might be labeled "Lose a Turn," and another can be labeled "Roll Again" (see Figure 5.16). On the other cubes, write a variety of onsets such as single consonants, consonant digraphs, or consonant blends. Supply a whiteboard or paper for recording words. The children roll the cubes and then write and read the word or words that can be made by blending the onset from one cube with the rime on the other. Nonsense words (e.g. *dag, lig, shog*) are allowable as long as they can be read.

FIGURE 5.16 Cubes for Roll the Dice

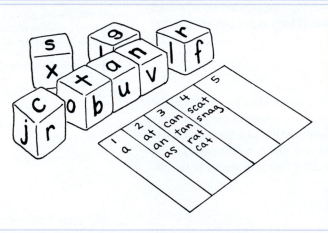

The Study of Short Vowels in CVC Words

If children are spelling half or more of the short-vowel words correctly on a spelling inventory and working with mixed-vowel word families easily and accurately, they are ready for the study of short vowels in non-rhyming words outside of word families. This word study will ask them to look at words in a new way—not as two units with various rimes (*m-ad, fl-ag, tr-ack*), but as three units with a **consonant-vowel-consonant (CVC)** pattern (*m-a-d, fl-a-g, tr-a-ck*): one vowel surrounded by consonants. For the first short-vowel sorts, begin with words your children already know from previous sorts or from their reading of familiar texts.

During the study of short vowels, the **oddball** category is introduced. People do not all pronounce words quite the same way; nor does spelling always match pronunciation. For example, some speakers may hear a short *o* in *dog,* but others will hear a sound closer to /*aw*/. In addition, English has many words that are not spelled the way they sound, and this needs to be recognized early.

GUIDELINES FOR SHORT VOWELS. As you implement the study of short vowels in CVC words, here are some things to keep in mind:

1. *Think about contrasts.* When you first introduce short vowels, plan contrasts that are fairly distinct from each other. For example, compare short *a* to short *i* or short *o,* not to short *e.* Figure 5.6 shows how some vowels are produced closer in the mouth than others; this should be used as a guide.

PD TOOLKIT™

for Words Their Way®

Visit the PDToolkit to watch Ms. Kiernan's first graders sort short-vowel words and learn how they follow a CVC pattern even when there are blends. Click on the Videos tab and select Letter Name–Alphabetic Stage. Select "Sorting Short *e, o,* and *u* with Initial Blends." Ms. Kiernan also talks about classroom organization and schedules for the letter name stage in other videos you will see listed.

2. *Add pictures to focus on sounds.* Most sorting for short vowels will be done with printed words, but pictures can be used as headers and added to sorts to ensure that students are saying and analyzing the vowel sound in the middle, not just visually sorting by the letter in the middle of the word.

3. *Use words children know how to read.* Most of the words in a short-vowel sort should be familiar so that children are analyzing words they can readily pronounce. Go over the words before sorting and lay unfamiliar words aside until after the reflection part of the lesson. Children can then be asked to sound out a few of the unfamiliar words by applying the vowel sounds that have been identified. Be ready to model how to say the sounds and blend them together. You might also support children's efforts by putting a familiar word (such as *bug*) next to an unfamiliar word (such as *bus*).

4. *Include oddballs in sorts.* We recommend adding one or two oddballs to short-vowel sorts, choosing the ones children are most likely to already know how to read. For example, including the word *was* in a short *a* vowel sort requires children to pay attention to the fact that the vowel sound in *was* is not the same as in *wag, fast,* or *flat,* despite the fact that it is a CVC word with an *a* in the middle. These oddballs will keep children on their toes if they try to sort simply by looking at the vowel in the middle. Suggested oddballs for short-vowel sorts include *boy, ball, call, car, for, from, her, how, new, now, put, saw, they, was, what, most, want,* and *walk*.

5. *Pacing.* The study of short vowels in kindergarten need not be rushed, because short vowels will be taught or reviewed in first grade. When planning sorts, start with simple three-letter words that include many of the words studied in word families (e.g., *bag, can, pat*), but then move to the use of more complex words with blends and digraphs at the beginning and end (e.g., *brag, than, path*). Short vowels will be reviewed when they are compared to long vowels in the next stage, so do not expect 100 percent accuracy.

TABLE 5.8 **Suggested Schedule of Activities for Short-Vowel CVC Sorts**

Day 1: Lesson 5.5 provides an example of an introductory sort comparing short *a* and *o*. Introduce the sort in a small group and then give each child a copy of the sort to cut apart and store in an envelope or baggie to use during the next few days.

Day 2: Repeat the group sort as a blind sort, in which you read each word without showing it. Ask the children to repeat the sort individually or in pairs using the sets of cut-up sorts. On day 2, you can also have the children record their sorts by writing words in columns under the key words.

Day 3: Have the children repeat the sort independently and work with a partner to do a blind sort, just as you have modeled for them. The blind sort is important so that children do not simply sort visually without paying attention to the sounds in the words. A blind writing sort requires that children write each word under the appropriate key word as it is called aloud.

Day 4: Do word hunts. It will be fairly easy to find words with short vowels in just about any beginning reading material, because they are very common. Be sure to hunt in texts the students have already read. Also look for two-syllable words with short vowels in CVC syllables such as *funny* or *kitten*. Expect children to not only find, but also record, the words that they find. Do this first as a group activity before expecting them to do it independently in small groups or with partners.

Day 5: Review and do assessments. The extension activities described for word families can be adapted to review short vowels. Administer a simple spell check by asking children to write five or six words.

LESSON 5.5   Short-vowel sort for short *a* and *o*

Following is the basic procedure for sorting words by short vowels. Many of the words in this sort have been introduced in word family sorts, so children should be able to read them using the familiar rime. (CCSS Foundational Skills: 2d, 3a, Phonological Awareness; 3b, Phonics and Word Recognition)

Materials

Make a collection of word cards to model the sort on a table or in a pocket chart. Prepare a handout of the same sort, such as the one in Figure 5.17(a). A copy of this sort can be found in Appendix B.

Step 1. Demonstrate

Begin by setting up **key words** that will be used as headers each time the sort is repeated, and include a header for oddballs. Read each key word and isolate the vowel, covering up the first sound and then the last: "Here is the word *cat*. Listen as I take away the consonant sounds: *cat, at, /a/. Cat* has the short *a* sound in the middle." Repeat using *sock* as an example and isolate the short *o*. Pick up another word such

FIGURE 5.17 Prepared Sort Handout and Final Sort for Short *a* and Short *o*

cat	sock	oddball
jam	sad	map
job	got	top
fox	hop	has
had	ran	box
wag	lot	mop
was	hot	boy
cab	mom	ham

a.

cat	sock	oddball
sad	hop	was
jam	lot	boy
wag	mop	
ham	hot	
ran	fox	
map	top	
cab	box	
has	job	
had	mom	
	got	

b.

as *sad* and say, "I am going to put this word under *cat*. Listen: *s-aaa-d, ca-a-at*. They have the same vowel sound in the middle." Continue to model one or two words in each category, reading each new word and comparing it to the header. Hold up the oddball *was*. Ask children whether they hear the same vowel sound in the middle. Model how to place it in the oddball category, explaining that it does not have the same vowel sound as *cat* or *fast*, even though it has an *a* in the middle.

Step 2. Sort, check, reflect, and re-sort

Ask the children to help finish the sort. Call on someone to read each word, and then sort it by comparing it to a key word as you modeled. If no one can read a word, put it aside to revisit later. Caution the children to listen carefully to the middle vowel sound because there is another oddball that might trick them (*boy*). Once the words are sorted, everyone should read down each column to check and to practice reading the words. Lead the reflection by asking "What do you notice about these words? How are the oddballs different?"

Step 3. Repeat

Do the sort again with the group, but this time make it a blind sort so that children will have to listen carefully to the vowel sound. Leave up the key words as headers. Read each word without showing it, and call on someone to tell you where it should go before you show it. Introduce the children to the CVC pattern by labeling the letters in *cat* and *sock*, as shown in Figure 5.17(b). Point out that *sock* is also a CVC word because *ck* works together. At this point, go over any words that children could not read, and model how to use the key words as a guide to the vowel sound: "Let's try to sound out this word (*had*). I see an *A* in the middle, so let's use the short *a* sound, like in *cat: h –aaaaa-d, had*. We will put this with the other short *a* words."

Step 4. Extend

Give each child a set of words to sort. Because these words are easy to sort just by looking at the middle vowel, remind them to read the words as they sort ("say it and lay it") and to watch out for the oddballs. Always include blind sorting with a partner as a follow-up activity, and consider adding the blind writing sort described previously. Model it several times with the group and then see whether the children can do it independently with a partner.

Assessment for Letter–Sound Correspondences

To plan for word study instruction in phonics and spelling, you will need to determine what children already know and what they are ready to learn. We will describe several assessment tools and how to use the information to identify what spelling stage children are in and what phonics features would be the most appropriate for instruction.

Qualitative Assessments and the Zone of Proximal Development

All assessments we describe are qualitative; that is, children's uncorrected efforts to spell are not simply considered right or wrong, but are analyzed according to three questions: What do they know? What are they using but confusing? What is missing or beyond their understanding? By looking at spellings in this way, teachers can determine a child's **zone of proximal development (ZPD)** (Vygotsky, 1962), where instructions will be most effective. There is no reason to spend a lot of time teaching children what they already know, and trying to teach them something they know nothing about can be an exercise in frustration. Instead we look for what they are using but confusing.

Observing Children's Daily Writing

Children's writing provides ongoing information about what they know about letter–sound matches. You may want to keep writing samples over time to document growth. A Qualitative Spelling Checklist, provided in Appendix A, can guide your assessment of writing. However, children may use a variety of resources when trying to spell words during writing (such as asking for help or copying print from a word wall), or they may limit their writing to only words they know how to spell. For these reasons, their writing may not offer accurate or complete information to plan instruction and we recommend that you use one of the other assessment tools described here several times a year.

Assessment for Beginning Consonants

An easy way to assess young children on their knowledge of beginning consonants is to use the Beginning Consonant Sounds and Letters task found in Appendix A. This task only requires recognition; it asks children to identify a picture that begins with a given letter. With children in pre-K, you may want to administer it individually or in small groups. It is important that you name the letter and pictures for the children and not simply give it to them to complete independently. You will find directions in Appendix A.

PD TOOLKIT™

for Words Their Way®

Spelling inventory forms can be found at the PDToolkit under the Assessment Tools tab. Choose a category or type in the name of the inventory in the search box.

Kindergarten Spelling Inventory

A simple five-word assessment can provide lots of information about what children know about single beginning and ending consonants as well as short vowels. The Kindergarten Spelling Inventory (KSI) is a production task because children will need to write the letters. (It could be done orally with young children in special cases.) After modeling how to spell at least one word by listening for sounds, simply ask children to spell five CVC words as best they can. Directions and the form can be found in Appendix A. In Figure 5.18 you will see an example that shows how the child's form includes a copy of the alphabet as well as a picture for each target word. The scoring grid in Figure 5.18 shows how you will evaluate the children's results by checking off how each sound is represented. Notice that Ian gets credit for using a *k* to represent the *g* in *log* and *g* for the *j* in *jet* because they are logical substitutions, as described earlier in this chapter. However, the *a* at the beginning of log is not counted as logical. Ian was asked to name the second letter in his spelling of *jet* to determine whether it was a *t* or a *j*. If children spell most of the words correctly on the KSI, then you will need to use the inventory described next.

The Primary Spelling Inventory

A spelling inventory designed to be used from kindergarten to third grade is the Primary Spelling Inventory (PSI). It offers a much more complete picture of letter–sound knowledge for children in the letter name–alphabetic stage because it includes words with blends and digraphs. You may have some children in kindergarten who have mastered these features and are spelling words with long vowels and silent letters; this inventory will capture that information as well, because it is designed to assess children up to the within word pattern stage. To administer the spelling inventory, simply call out words for children to spell until they have made about five errors. It is important that children not study or be specifically exposed to these words in preparation for the assessment, because we want to find out what children know and understand, not what they are able to memorize. You may use as few as five words or as many as 26, depending on what children know. A list of the words and complete directions can be found in Appendix A. A **feature guide** is provided to help you analyze the words and a **classroom composite** form

FIGURE 5.18 Sample KSI

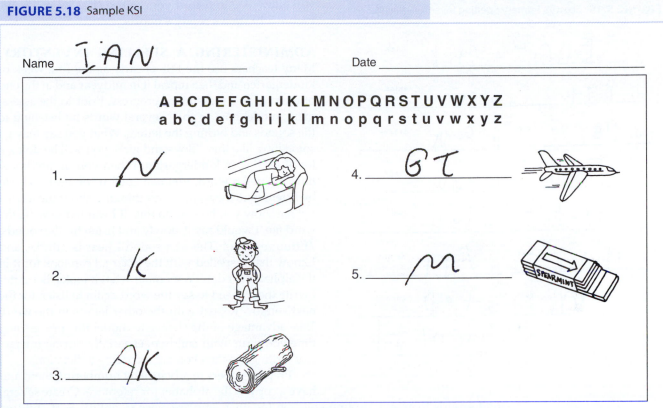

Adapted from PALS Quick Checks, University of Virginia

Fold here ---

Scoring Grid

	Beginning	Middle	Ending	
1. nap	n ✓	a	p	*1*
		e	b	# phonetically acceptable
2. kid	k ✓	i	d	*1*
	c or g	e	t	# phonetically acceptable
3. log	l	o	g	*1*
		i	k ✓	# phonetically acceptable
4. jet	j	e	t ✓	*2*
	g ✓	a	d	# phonetically acceptable
5. gum	g	u	m ✓	*1*
	k or c	o		# phonetically acceptable

Spelling Feature Analysis	Number of Beginning Phonemes	Number of Middle Phonemes	Number of Ending Phonemes	Total Phonetically Acceptable
	3	*0*	*3*	*6* /15

FIGURE 5.19 Scotty's Primary Spelling Inventory Results

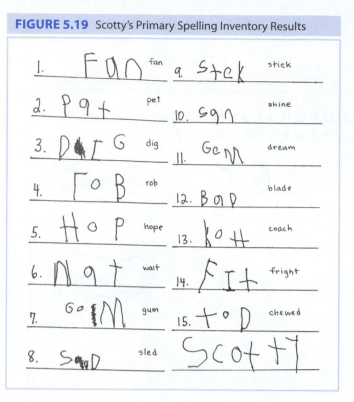

will allow you to record your entire class on one page. Figure 5.19 shows Scotty's efforts.

ADMINISTERING A SPELLING INVENTORY.

Many teachers use the PSI as early as the first week of kindergarten and then repeat it in midyear and at the end of the year as a measure of progress. Prior to the assessment, model how to spell several words by listening to the sounds and writing the letters. What you say may go something like this: "Boys and girls, you will be doing a lot of writing in kindergarten. When you do not know how to spell a word, you can spell it the best you can by listening to the sounds and thinking about the letters. Let me show you how to do this. If I wanted to write the word *fun*, I would say it slowly and listen for the sounds: /ffffuuuunnnn/. The first sound I hear is /ffffff/, and I know that is spelled with the letter *f*. I can look for it in the alphabet if I don't remember what it looks like. After I write the *f*, I need to say the word again to listen for the next sound." Repeat with the other letters in the word. Take advantage of the chance to model this process any time you write with children, especially during interactive writing or when you are recording a dictation.

Prepare papers in advance by numbering them and have a copy of the alphabet for reference. Create several small groups to assess, putting children together who are close in ability. Seat children to minimize copying but keep the atmosphere relaxed. Assure children that you do not expect them to know how to spell the words but you want to see what sounds they can hear. Then call each word, use it once in a sentence, and repeat. (Explain that they do not write the whole sentence, just one word.) Do not stretch out the sounds in the word; say it naturally. Periodically glance over students' papers to see whether you can interpret the children's handwriting and to determine how many words to call aloud. You can stop when a child misspells five words. In early kindergarten, five words is likely to be all you need to call. By late kindergarten, you may keep going up to 15 or even do the entire list for your advanced readers.

SCORING THE PSI INVENTORY.

Analyzing an inventory is more than marking words right or wrong. The feature guide for the PSI will help you systematically analyze the results. See Figure 5.20 for the feature guide that scores Scotty's inventory from Figure 5.19. Beside each word on the feature guide, check off whether the child represented each sound correctly in the boxes to the right. Assign an extra point at the far right if the word is completely correct. If they substituted something logical, like an *a* for the *e* in *pet*, write it in to show that they did hear the sound. A child who spells *pet* as PAT is developmentally ahead of a child who simply spells it PT. After scoring, add the number of checks in each column and then across the bottom to get a total score. Adjust the ratios at the bottom depending on the number of words you call.

Scotty's PSI results are typical of how some children will spell by the second half of kindergarten, using a mixture of capital and lowercase letters. He was only asked to spell 15 words, so a line was drawn on the feature guide to show this. Scotty is solid on initial and final consonants and is consistently representing short vowels. However, many of his short vowels are confused in a predictable way: substituting *a* for short *e*, *o* for short *u*, and *e* for short *i*. He does not represent any digraphs, but he uses *h* for the *ch* in *coach* and uses a *t* for the *ch* in *chewing*. This may seem odd, but if you say the sounds /ch/ and /t/, you should notice that both are formed by the tongue as it touches the front palate right behind the teeth. He spells the *st* blend in *stick* correctly but uses a *g* to represent the sound he hears at the beginning of dream. Again, say /g/ and /dr/ and you will notice

FIGURE 5.20 Feature Guide for Scotty

Words Their Way Primary Spelling Inventory Feature Guide

Student's Name: **Scotty Howerton** Grade: **K** Date: **1-2013**

Teacher: _____ Spelling Stage: **Early–Mid LN**

Words Spelled Correctly: **3 / 26** Feature Points: **18 / 56** Total: **21 / 82**

SPELLING STAGES → Features →	Consonants Initial (LETTER NAME–ALPHABETIC EARLY)	Consonants Final (MIDDLE)	Short Vowels (MIDDLE)	Digraphs (LATE)	Blends (LATE)	Common Long Vowels (WITHIN WORD PATTERN EARLY)	Other Vowels (MIDDLE)	Inflected Endings (SYLLABLES AND AFFIXES LATE)	Feature Points (EARLY)	Words Spelled Correctly
1. fan	f ✓	n ✓	a ✓						3	1
2. pet	p ✓	t ✓	e *a*						2	
3. dig	d ✓	g ✓	i ✓						3	1
4. rob	r ✓	b ✓	o ✓						3	1
5. hope	h ✓	p ✓				o-e *o*			2	
6. wait	w ✓	t ✓				ai *a*			2	
7. gum	g ✓	m ✓	u *o*						2	
8. sled			e *a*		sl					
9. stick			i *e*		st ✓				1	
10. shine				sh		i-e				
11. dream					dr *g*	ea *e*				
12. blade					bl	a-e *a*				
13. coach				ch		oa *o*				
14. fright					fr	igh *i*				
15. chewed				ch			ew	-ed		
16. crawl					cr		aw			
17. wishes				sh				-es		
18. thorn				th			or			
19. shouted				sh			ou	-ed		
20. spoil							oi			
21. growl							ow			
22. third				th			ir			
23. camped								-ed		
24. tries					tr			-ies		
25. clapping								-pping		
26. riding								-ding		
Totals	7/7	7/7	3/7	0/3	1/3	0/7	/7	/7	18/56	3/26

how similar they are in place and manner of articulation. Scotty accurately selects the long vowels in words like *blade* (spelled BAD) and *fright* (spelled FIT), but he lacks knowledge of silent letters or vowel patterns.

COMMON CONFUSIONS. There are a few common confusions about scoring. One is what to do about reversals. Letters reversals are common with young children and are not treated as spelling errors but as handwriting confusions. Record the reversal on the feature guide by writing in what they did, but check it as correct if you feel certain it was a reversal. You can always ask for confirmation: "What sound did you hear at the beginning of *dig*?" Children may also get the letters out of order, spelling *dig* as DGE. They would not get the extra point for a correct spelling, but you should give credit for each of the letter–sound matches that are accurate. Young spellers sometimes get the first letter in a word but cannot determine the others. They may understand that words need more than one letter and add more to fill it in, spelling *dig* as DBRS, but only the first letter would get credit. In general, exercise your judgment and give children credit when possible.

At the beginning of kindergarten, most children will spell very few sounds correctly, and filling in a feature guide for each one is not worthwhile. Instead you may want to use the Emergent Class Record found in Appendix A. This offers a more holistic scoring system, and you can record your entire class on one sheet. If children are representing most consonants and some vowels, the feature guides may be more helpful.

IDENTIFYING FEATURES FOR INSTRUCTION. The general rule of thumb we suggest is that children need to work on features for which they miss more than one out of five to seven attempts. This means that a child who spells three out of five (or 60 percent) of the beginning consonants will benefit from more instruction and practice. Another way to think about this is using four out of five or 80 percent as a criterion score. Below 80 percent, children are in the "using but confusing" zone for that feature and are likely to benefit from instruction. Scotty clearly needs no instruction on initial and final consonants, but digraphs and blends need work. He will also benefit from instruction in short vowels because we know he has the phonemic awareness to isolate them and is using but confusing the letter matches. Referring to the sequence outlined in Table 5.4, it looks as though a step back to the early letter name–alphabetic stage is needed to work on blends and digraphs with pictures before working on mixed-vowel word families listed for the middle letter name–alphabetic stage.

IDENTIFYING THE STAGE OF DEVELOPMENT. Look across the list of spelling stages at the top of the feature guide in Figure 5.20, where you will see early/middle letter name–alphabetic circled. Look across the bottom of the feature guide and you will see that this lines up with where Scotty first missed more than one on a feature, in this case short vowels. You can also refer back to the Figures 5.2 and 5.5, which describe each of the stages. Placement in the early, middle, or late parts of this stage using the spelling inventory depends primarily on how well children spell short vowels. If they do not attempt vowels, they are in the early part of the stage. If they use but confuse vowels, perhaps getting a one or two correct, they are likely in the middle of the stage. If they spell half or more of the short vowels on an inventory, they are in the late letter name–alphabetic stage. However, knowledge of blends and digraphs should also be considered, so Scotty's stage is called conservatively as between early and middle letter name–alphabetic. Don't be too concerned about selecting the stage accurately; concentrate on the phonics features for which the child misses more than one.

COMPLETING A CLASSROOM COMPOSITE. To get an overview of your entire class, you may want to fill in a PSI classroom composite sheet by transferring scores from each child's feature guide to the form provided in Appendix A. Use each child's total score to rank the students in order from highest to lowest before transferring the scores from the bottom row. Look for cells where children miss more than one on a feature to help you identify groups that can work together on the same features. In the sample class composite in Figure 5.21, you can see that three groups have been identified. The

PD **TOOLKIT™**
for Words Their Way®

To see Mrs. Smith talk about how she uses the PSI, go to the PDToolkit. Look under Videos and select Emergent Stage to find the clip "Assessment of Students in the Emergent Stage."

PD **TOOLKIT™**
for Words Their Way®

An electronic version of the PSI can be found at the PDToolkit; you can enter data into a feature guide and a class composite form will be created for you. Select the Assessment Tools tab and then Create under Assessment Application.

FIGURE 5.21 Class Composite for Kindergarten with Three Groups Circled

Words Their Way Primary Spelling Inventory Classroom Composite

Teacher __Smith__   School __—__   Grade __K__   Date __1/15/13__

SPELLING STAGES →	EMERGENT LATE		LETTER NAME—ALPHABETIC			WITHIN WORD PATTERN		SYLLABLES AND AFFIXES		Total Rank Order
	Consonants		EARLY MIDDLE		LATE	EARLY MIDDLE	LATE	EARLY		
Students' Names	Initial	Final	Short Vowels	Digraphs	Blends	Common Long Vowels	Other Vowels	Inflected Endings	Correct Spelling	
Possible Points	7	7	7	7	7	7	7	7	26	82
1. Clair	7	7	7	3	5	0			5	26
2. Jose	7	7	5	2	4	1			5	26
3. Jackie	7	7	5	1	3	0			4	22
4. Brad	7	7	3	2	3	0			3	22
5. Penny	7	7	3	1	2	0			3	20
6. Tawna	7	7	1	1	1	0			1	17
7. Scott	7	7	1	1	1	0			1	17
8. Gabe	7	6	1	1	1				1	17
9. Tina	7	7	1	1	1				1	17
10. Rosa	7	6	0	1	1				0	15
11. Shawn	7	6	1	1	0				0	15
12. Grace	5	4	0	1	1				0	11
13. Emma	6	3	0	0	0				0	9
14. Josh	4	1	0	0	0				0	5
15. Day	3	0	0	0	0				0	3
16. Amy	2	1	0	0	0				0	3
17. Tam	3	0	0	0	0				0	3
18. Carrie	2	0	0	0	0				0	2
19.										
20.										
21.										
22.										
23.										
24.										
25.										
26.										
Highlight for instruction*										

(Handwritten annotations on form: "LLN" and "MLN" and "ELN" marking three circled groups of students.)

*Highlight students who miss more than 1 on a particular feature; they will benefit from more instruction in that area.

early letter name–alphabetic (ELN) group still needs work on initial consonant sounds. The middle letter name–alphabetic (MLN) group is ready to compare same-vowel word families, which will also reinforce consonants (especially final consonants) before working on blends and digraphs. The late letter name–alphabetic (LLN) group looks ready to review blends and digraphs and work with short vowels in CVC words, but they should be assessed on more digraphs because the 15-word list only included three words with digraphs. The progress monitoring spell check described in the next section could be used to gather more information.

PROGRESS MONITORING. Ongoing assessment can be as simple as observing how easily and accurately children sort pictures, or you can have children paste the pictures they have sorted into categories and label them. In addition we provide a series of spell checks that can be used for progress monitoring. Although the spelling inventories test features, the spell checks can be used to assess particular features in depth: initial consonants, same-vowel word families, digraphs, blends, mixed-vowel word families, short vowels, and preconsonantal nasals. There are two forms for each feature: one that can be used before your instruction, and another after. If you have a general idea of what children know about letter sounds, a pretest using the spell checks may be an easier and more exact way to identify the features children are ready to study. For example, you might administer the digraph spell check shown in Figure 5.22 and find that most of the students miss about half of the digraphs with *sh* and *ch*. With this information, you can target instruction to the features children missed. Progress monitoring forms and complete directions can be found online.

FORMING GROUPS FOR INSTRUCTION. With the information you get from the inventory and an overview of your class from the class composite, you can begin to form three to four groups that will target phonics instruction close to your students' ZPDs. Because spelling inventories are highly correlated with other literacy assessments, many teachers find that they are the best way to establish small groups that will work on alphabet, phonics, concept of word, and other reading skills. However, some teachers may prefer to plan phonics instruction at a separate time. Keep your instructional groups flexible, because young children progress at different rates.

Chapter 6 describes a whole-to-part lesson plan for small groups that includes phonics instruction.

for Words Their Way®

Progress monitoring forms for the letter name–alphabetic stage can be found online at the PDToolkit. Select the Assessment Tools tab and choose "Progress Monitoring/ Goal Setting" under Choose Your Category.

FIGURE 5.22 Spell Check for Digraphs

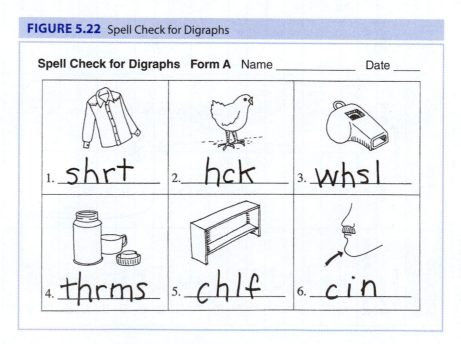

Spell Check for Digraphs Form A Name _____ Date _____

1. shrt 2. hck 3. whsl 4. thrms 5. chlf 6. cin

Resources for Implementing Word Study in Your Classroom

Several sources of materials are available to help you implement developmental phonics instruction.

1. Pictures in Appendix C can be used with the template on page 251 to create your own sorts and games.
2. The supplement *Words Their Way: Letter and Picture Sorts for Emergent Spellers* provides over 30 one-page copies of nursery rhymes, jingles, and poems with ideas about how to use them to introduce beginning consonant sorts.
3. The supplement *Words Their Way: Word Sorts for Letter Name–Alphabetic Spellers* provides a complete curriculum of 50 prepared sorts, beginning with a review of initial consonants, picture sorts for blends and digraphs, word family sorts, and short-vowel sorts. Spell checks are supplied for each of the eight units.
4. The Spanish supplement *Words Their Way: Letter Name–Alphabetic Sorts for Spanish-Speaking English Learners* provides different contrasts and additional practice.
5. Prepared sorts, spell checks, and games are available on the PDToolkit website and you can make more using the "Create Your Own" feature. The website also offers copies of all assessment materials, an online assessment tool, and videos of classroom instruction.

Concept of Word in Text

Lori Helman loves singing with her kindergartners, and she uses lyrics of the songs they sing to develop their concept of word in text—their ability to fingerpoint read a short memorized text. Lori coordinates with the music teacher so that the whole class learns a new song each week. Once the children learn the lyrics by heart, Lori writes out the words to the first verse of the song on chart paper that is always accessible. She uses this text in small-group reading lessons using a whole-to-part framework. This week it's "I'm a Little Teapot."

After acting out the song and discussing the meanings of *stout* and *spout* and how they rhyme, Lori introduces the text. She models how to read it by pointing to each word as she says it slowly, commenting on how she is touching each word from left to right. After careful modeling and print referencing, Lori asks her students to read with her as she points to each word once again. After this choral reading, she asks her students to echo read each line right after her. Then she calls on volunteers to come up to the chart to point to each word with her pointer as the rest of the group recites it once again. Alicia comes up but starts to point from right to left. Lori gently gets her back on track by guiding her pointing, word by word, in the right direction. Jasmine points from left to right, but she gets off track on the word *teapot*, pointing to the word *short* while saying the second syllable, *pot*. She realizes that she is off track and starts over again, this time pointing to *teapot* while saying both syllables. Lori compliments her for getting back on track and then asks her find the word *teapot*. After pointing quickly to the word, Lori asks, "How did you find that word?" Jasmine replies, "I looked for the letter *t*." Darian points to each word accurately and does not get off track at all, even on two-syllable words. When Lori points to several words in the rhyme, Darian can easily identify each one. The children have been introduced to the whole song, but over the next few days they will work with sentences, words, letters, and sounds in small groups with others who are at a similar developmental level using the whole-to-part instructional framework described in this chapter.

Phonological awareness and alphabet knowledge are powerful predictors of children's early reading development, and phonics instruction is also essential for children to learn to read (Adams, 1990; Burgess & Lonigan, 1998; National Early Literacy Panel, 2008). But one of the best indicators of children's progress in emergent reading is their developing concept of word in text (COW-T) (Morris, Bloodgood, & Perney, 2003; Warley, Landrum, Invernizzi, & Justice, 2005). COW-T is a child's ability to match speech to print accurately as he or she touches each word in a memorized song, rhyme, or jingle (Flanigan, 2007). It is a critical component of early literacy development and a "watershed event," because it brings together and solidifies all of the foundational emergent literacy skills we have talked about in the first five chapters of this text (Henderson & Beers, 1980; Morris, 1981). Achieving a COW-T is necessary to develop an initial sight word vocabulary and to start reading in a conventional way.

What Is Concept of Word in Text?

Early definitions of a concept of word (COW) focused mainly on children's *oral* language and their awareness of words as discrete units within a larger phrase or sentence. Children seemed to pay more attention to the rhythm of phrases than to individual words. For example, children would partition "Jack and Jill went up the hill" into four rhythmic chunks as in "Jack / and Jill / went up / the hill" (Holden & McGinitie, 1972). These findings from research in the 1970s were troubling because they raised the question of how children were to learn to read words if they didn't know how to segment the words accurately (Downing, 1979).

Researchers soon discovered that children's perception of oral language structures develops gradually over time from larger units to smaller ones (Chaney, 1989) and that there is a reciprocal relationship between word awareness in speech and word awareness in print. Teachers and researchers observed that while prereaders had difficulty segmenting the speech stream into word units, children who could actually read didn't have this difficulty (Ehri & Wilce, 1985; Morais, Cary, Alegria, & Bertelson, 1979). Furthermore, although prereaders had difficulty separating articles and prepositions from the noun that followed (e.g., *the hill* was considered one word instead of two), readers didn't have this problem either (Templeton & Spivey, 1980; Templeton & Thomas, 1984). Ehri (1975) suspected that readers were better able to analyze the speech stream "as a consequence of viewing the printed forms and learning how speech is represented" (p. 211). Seeing words in print increased the readers' conscious awareness of the units comprising oral language—specifically, awareness of words.

A flurry of new research explored children's COW-T. Clay (1990) noted that prereaders confused the terms *letter* and *word*, and she argued that "reading the spaces" (p. 141)—matching spoken words to written words in text—was an important milestone in early literacy development. Building on Clay's insights, Henderson & Beers (1980) described how children's word awareness in oral language improved in accord with their gradual attainment of a COW-T, as did the phonetic accuracy of their invented spellings. They suggested that a stable COW-T allowed students to conceptualize a word as a discrete unit with a beginning and an end.

Henderson's theory expanded the notion of a simple interaction between word awareness in speech and word awareness in print to include a more complex interaction between COW-T and phonological awareness. This theory was tested in a longitudinal study (Morris, Bloodgood, Lomax, & Perney, 2003) that showed how alphabet knowledge and initial consonant phoneme knowledge led to a COW-T. Once children had achieved a COW-T, they were able to more fully analyze the phonemic structure of words, and their word recognition improved. Morris' theory was validated by Flanigan (2003), who summarized the progression as shown in Figure 6.1. Attaining a COW-T is more than simply making a one-to-one speech-to-print match, though that is certainly the goal. Children must be able to simultaneously isolate the beginning phoneme of a spoken word and match it to a recognized letter at the beginning of the word in running text. So, to attain a concept of word, children must have a certain degree of phonological awareness, automatic alphabet and letter–sound recognition, and other concepts about print. In short, with a COW-T, children can find the individual words on the page and begin to fully analyze and remember them.

The Concept of Word in Text Continuum

A COW-T is not an all or nothing insight but develops over time. The continuum for COW-T may be described according to (1) levels of children's fingerpoint reading accuracy, (2) their ability to identify words in context, and (3) their ability to remember words they have seen in one context when they see them in a different context (Blackwell-Bullock, Invernizzi, Drake, & Howell, 2009). We describe three developmental levels of COW-T:

FIGURE 6.1 The Evolution of Word Recognition

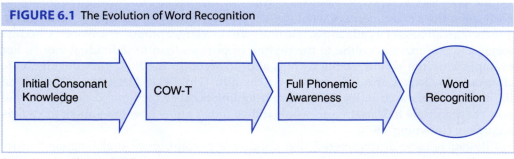

Source: Based on Flanigan (2003).

developing, rudimentary, and *firm.* These levels are highly correlated to the spelling stages described in Chapter 5 (Smith, 2012).

DEVELOPING COW-T. Students who possess little or no COW-T are able to recite the words to a memorized nursery rhyme or jump rope jingle. They cannot, however, accurately point to the words they are saying and, like Alicia in the beginning of this chapter, may not even have mastered left-to-right directionality. Through demonstrations and instructional support like Lori's, left-to-right movement becomes habitualized. As white spaces are noted, children may begin to track rhythmically across the text, pointing to words for each stressed beat. For example, when tracking the traditional five-word ditty "Sam, Sam, the baker man," they might tap the print with each stressed syllable and point four times: "Sam / Sam / the-baker / man," as if keeping time on a tom-tom. Articles (*the, a, an*) may be treated as part of the noun that follows them (e.g., *thebaker*). These students are not able to synchronize their recitation of the words in the rhyme with their fingerpointing because they do not yet have sufficient alphabet and letter–sound knowledge. They may lack other concepts about print such as return sweep or punctuation. Their writing also reflects this developing knowledge: Their scribbled, letter-like forms, or random letters may show no connection to speech sounds or be limited to a few letter sound matches.

> **See Chapter 4 for more information about concepts about print.**

RUDIMENTARY COW-T. Moving along the continuum, students with a *rudimentary* COW-T can accurately point to or track words left to right as they recite from memory, but they may get off track on two- or three-syllable words. For example, in the phrase "Sam, Sam, the baker man," they may point to the word *man* when they are saying the second syllable of *baker,* as shown in Figure 6.2. However, they are frequently able to self-correct by looking at the beginning consonant sound. When they see that *man* doesn't start with the /k/ sound of "ker," they self-correct and are back on track. Jasmine did this when she saw that the word *short* did not begin with a *p.* Children with a rudimentary COW-T are able to identify words in context, but they usually do not remember many of those words outside of that particular context. When teachers point to a word and ask, "What word is this?" children may start at the beginning of a line and count their way up to the word they are asked to identify. In their writing, children make connections between letters and sounds at the beginning and end of a word, and may begin to include some vowels in the middle by letter name.

FIRM COW-T. Students have developed a firm COW-T when they are able to demonstrate three early reading behaviors. First, they are able to accurately and consistently

FIGURE 6.2
Trying to Match Voice to Print

COW-T	POINTING	SPELLING FEATURES	SPELLING STAGE	WORD RECOGNITION PHASE (BASED ON EHRI, 1995)
Firm ↑	Tracks accurately	Includes medial short vowels	Middle letter name–alphabetic	Full alphabetic: Can identify words easily in context and names many words out of context
↑ Rudimetary ↑	Self-corrects when gets off track	Initial and final consonants	Early letter name–alphabetic	Partial alphabetic: Names many words in context and some words out of context, but may confuse words that are visually similar
	Points to words but gets off track on syllables			
	Points to words and says stressed units	Initial consonants	Emergent speller	
		Random letters		
↑ Developing	Understands left-to-right directionality but does not point to words	Letter-like symbols and scribbles		Prealphabetic: May know a few words using visual clues

TABLE 6.1   **COW-T in Relation to Other Literacy Skills**

Source: Based on Blackwell-Bullock, R., Invernizzi, M., Drake, A., & Howell, J. L. (2009). Concept of word in text: An integral literacy skill. *Reading in Virginia, XXXI,* 30–36.

match speech to print when fingerpoint reading a memorized text and are not thrown off track by articles, prepositions, or two-syllable words—as Darian demonstrated with "I'm a Little Teapot." Second, they can quickly and easily identify words in context when they are pointed out randomly by their teacher. Third, and most important, they recognize many of the words when they see them in another context such as a word list, another rhyme, or on word cards.

Even for students who have achieved a firm concept of word, the development of a reading vocabulary will take some time. For words to stick in their memory, students will need many experiences with them in and out of context. Table 6.1 shows the continuum of COW-T development across the three levels (developing, rudimentary, and firm) and the relationship of COW-T development to other early literacy skills such as developmental spelling and word recognition. Children are not able to remember many words out of specific contexts until they have a firm COW-T. This has enormous implications for sight word development.

Sight Word Development

A large and stable reading vocabulary, or **sight word vocabulary,** is the hallmark of an accomplished reader because automatic word recognition makes it possible to read fluently and to devote attention to comprehension rather than to figuring out or guessing at words (Perfetti, 2007). However, the term *sight word* may be problematic, because it is often used for what are better described as **high-frequency words,** such as the words that appear on Dolch's (1936) *List of Basic Sight Word Vocabulary* or on Fry's (1980) *Instant Word List*. High-frequency words like *and, the, in, from,* and *put* are also known as **function words** because their primary role is gluing together all the other words in the sentence. The problem is that function words have little to no meaning in and of themselves. For example, in the sentence "I went to the store to buy some apples," the bulk of the meaning resides in three content words: *store, buy, apples.* These words refer to a concrete place; a concrete action; and a concrete, desirable thing. Images of all three can be easily be conjured up in the mind's eye. This is not the case for the high-frequency function words *to, the,* and *some.* For early learning, there is a clear advantage for concrete, meaningful words over more abstract, less meaningful words (Johnston, 1998). But progress in reading depends on knowing both.

The term *sight word* is also problematic for another reason. It suggests that there are certain words that can only be learned "by sight" because they are not phonetically regular (e.g., *was, of, are,* and *said)* and must therefore be acquired by rote visual memory. This erroneous interpretation can result in ineffective and unpleasant practices for very young children, such as the drill of high-frequency words in isolation from meaningful text— sometimes before children have acquired even a rudimentary COW-T.

The term *sight word* is best defined as *any* word that a reader can recognize immediately, without hesitation, "at first sight." The words *cat* and *caterpillar* can both be sight words once they become very familiar to a particular reader. Understanding how sight words are learned is essential to understanding how it is that children achieve a COW-T.

How Children Learn to Recognize Words

How do children develop the ability to recognize what will eventually become thousands and thousands of words? A number of researchers have investigated the question of how children store words in memory for immediate identification, and various terms have been applied to a series of phases or stages through which children move as this ability develops over time (Ehri, 1995; Henderson, 1992; Juel, 1991). Table 6.1 includes Ehri's terms aligned with other literacy skills. It is important to understand that young readers do not remember words the same way mature readers do, especially when they do not have a firm COW-T or knowledge of letters and their corresponding sounds.

PREALPHABETIC READERS. Children just developing a COW-T may not know all the letters of the alphabet, and they do not know how to use letter–sound correspondences when attempting to match speech to print or to write. Ehri (1995) called such learners *prealphabetic* and Henderson (1981) referred to them as *preliterate.* For such children, memory for a word may be triggered through the use of selective visual cues (Juel, 1991), such as the "tall posts" in the word *yellow* or the golden arches in the logo for McDonalds. They might identify *elephant* because it is a long word or the word *dog* because it has a tail at the end. Such cues are not helpful, however, when children see other long words or other words that end in a *g.* For these reasons, prealphabetic readers can identify few if any words at all.

PARTIAL ALPHABETIC READERS. Moving to a rudimentary COW-T hinges on understanding the alphabetic principle: that letters represent speech sounds in a systematic way. Ehri (1995) referred to this phase of word recognition as *partial alphabetic* because children can begin to identify words with the help of context or memory but use only limited letter–sound matches. For example, a child with only a rudimentary COW-T might be able to read the line "I'm a little teapot" using her memory of the song and and probably recognizes only a few letter–sound correspondences, as if the line were written "I___ a l___ t___ p___." Without context cues, the partial letter cues alone are usually not enough to remember the words when seen out of context. For example, children with only a rudimentary COW-T may incorrectly identify the word *little* as *like* or *light* when presented in isolation, despite the fact they "knew'" it in context. With limited knowledge of letter–sound matches, especially vowels, readers at this stage cannot retain many sight words without getting them confused.

FULL ALPHABETIC READERS. As children achieve a firm COW-T, they start remembering many of the printed words they encounter and are able to retrieve them *on sight*. Full alphabetic readers (Ehri, 1995) begin to use consonant and vowel knowledge to process words from left to right, and the end result is a more complete "orthographic mapping" between letters and sounds. This complete mapping of letters to speech sounds in the beginning, middle, and end positions of words provides the glue for words to stick in memory. Even high-frequency "sight words" such as *was* and *said* are learned the same way as other words. Repeated exposure certainly helps, but to acquire a sight word, readers must make multiple connections between letter sounds, word pronunciations, word meanings, and spellings (Invernizzi & Hayes, 2010). When these are all forged together, words begin to stick in memory and children begin to read conventionally.

Acquiring Sight Words

There are expectations in many school systems that kindergarten children acquire a certain number of high-frequency words before starting first grade. These goals may be attainable, but until children have acquired at least a rudimentary COW-T, trying to teach sight words in isolation is of questionable value. When children do begin to acquire sight words, there is no reason to limit instruction to high-frequency words, which can be the hardest ones to learn. Words targeted for instruction can certainly include some function words, but they should also include many nouns (e.g., *cat, bird, dog, nest*), adjectives (e.g., *red, fast, glad*), and action verbs (e.g. *run, jump, hop*)—words that are concrete, meaningful, and more memorable to children. In the following section, we describe a variety of activities designed to cultivate a COW-T and the acquisition of sight words, both of which are necessary to progress in reading.

Planning Instruction for COW-T

COW-T must be constructed by emergent readers as they coordinate looking for initial letters, listening for beginning sounds, and pointing to individual words in running text. There is no other way to teach COW-T except through practice, practice, practice that is based on enjoyable, memorable, and interesting texts, in combination with the instructional diet outlined in earlier chapters. With repeated practice, children might learn how to accurately point to words in a particular piece of text, but unless they can transfer that fingerpoint accuracy to another piece of text, they have not achieved a firm COW-T. With teacher modeling and the support of memory, this can be accomplished.

How to Scaffold Fingerpoint Reading

To develop a concept of word in text, learners need lots of teacher-scaffolded experiences in which they fingerpoint to simple memorized texts. These experiences should progress from modeling and explanation by the teacher, to guided practice, and then to independent practice by the child in a gradual release model (Duffy, 2009; Fisher and Frey, 2008; Pearson & Gallagher, 1983):

1. *Modeling and explanation:* Beginning in preschool, teachers should look for opportunities to point to words as they read. This is best accomplished when the text is large and relatively short, as in the title of a book or a song written on a chart. Look for opportunities to slow down your speech as you touch each word with your finger or a pointer. Explain what you are doing: "Watch as I point to the words in this title." Explain why you might point to one word more than once: "*Butterfly* is one word, but I have to touch three times, once for each syllable."

2. *Guided practice:* Ask the children to fingerpoint to a familiar piece of text under your close supervision. Continue to offer explanations and model strategies as needed. For example, teach children how to *voice point;* ask them to find a particular word by starting at the beginning of the line and "counting up" as they reread until they get to the word. Model how to think about the letters or sounds in the word as a strategy for finding or naming a word. You might explain, "If I want to find a word, this is what I do. I listen to the first sound and then think about what letter spells that sound. Then I look for a word that starts with that letter."

3. *Independent practice:* Give the children extended practice with short, memorable selections of text. These can be collected in their own personal readers as described later in this chapter. When the children get off track, draw their attention to beginning sounds and letters and explain what might have thrown them off. Pose questions such as "Can this word be *rain*? Why or why not? What would you expect to see at the beginning of *rain*?"

Print Sources to Use for Modeling and Practice

Texts appropriate for developing a COW-T can be poems; songs; nursery rhymes; jump rope jingles; interactive writing selections; dictations; excerpts from predictable patterned story books such as *Brown Bear, Brown Bear, What Do You See?* (by Bill Martin); or the entire text of a simple repetitive book such as *The Cat Sat on the Mat* (by Brian Wildsmith). These selections are introduced in the manner of shared reading, as described earlier, and reread repeatedly with the support of memory. It is very important that the text is large enough for everyone to see comfortably, and "big books" were created for this purpose. However, you can create your own enlarged text on charts or sentence strips. For example, you might print "I'll huff and I'll puff and I'll blow your house down" on a sentence strip, and have the children read it with you whenever you come to those lines as you read aloud *The Three Little Pigs*. You can also use an overhead document camera or an interactive whiteboard to display enlarged selections.

Look for texts that children will enjoy and that can be easily memorized. The words to familiar songs that are commonly used in early childhood classrooms are particularly good, such as "There Was a Little Turtle Who Lived in a Box" and "The Itsy Bitsy Spider Climbed up the Water Spout." The length of the selections will depend on how well students can memorize the text. You might just use one to three sentences, or you might use entire nursery rhymes or multiple verses of songs. Rhythmic texts are particularly appealing to use when children are developing a COW-T, but they may throw children off in their tracking. An eventual move to less rhythmic, less predictable texts may be necessary to achieve a firm COW-T (Cathey, 1991; Mesmer, 2008). Students with limited English generally need shorter selections of text, and they will benefit from using materials in their primary languages whenever possible. A list of resources for rhymes and songs can be found in Table 6.2. You can download printable versions of these and other rhymes by searching online for nursery rhymes. Once these texts become familiar, children can be encouraged to read them from memory, pointing to each word as it is spoken. In this way, children learn how to find the words on the page—an important prerequisite to acquiring a sight vocabulary.

Memorize and Then Read

It is important for children to first learn a rhyme, song, or jingle "by heart," because developing a COW-T is all about matching speech to print. Repeat as many times as needed. Sometimes the selection may lend itself to simple dramatization or finger play. Once the

See Chapter 4 for a list of predictable books and a further discussion of shared reading as a context for developing concepts about print.

 TOOLKIT™

At the PDToolKit, you can watch Jackie use a nursery rhyme with her preK students to develop COW-T. Click the Videos tab and then choose Emergent Stage. Scroll to find the clip entitled "Humpty Dumpty."

See Lesson 5.1 in Chapter 5, in which "Jack and Jill" is used as the starting point for a picture sort for beginning sounds.

TABLE 6.2 **Resources for Rhymes and Songs**

Books of Rhymes and Songs

Bear, D., Invernizzi, M., Johnston, F., & Templeton, S. (2010). *Words Their Way: Letter and picture sorts for emergent spellers.* Boston, MA: Allyn & Bacon. This contains ready-to-print individual illustrated copies.

Cole, J. (1989). *Anna Banana: 101 jump-rope rhymes.* New York, NY: Scholastic.

Cole, J., & Calmenson, S. (1990). *Miss Mary Mack and other children's street rhymes.* Illustrated by Alan Tiegreen. New York, NY: Morrouno.

Helman, L., Bear, D., Invernizzi, M., Templeton, S., & Johnston, F. (2009) *Words Their Way: Emergent sorts for Spanish-speaking English learners.* This contains ready-to-print individual copies in Spanish.

Schwartz, A. (1989). *I saw you in the bathtub.* New York, NY: HarperCollins.

Sierra, J., & Sweet, M. (2005). *Schoolyard rhymes: Kids' own rhymes for rope jumping, hand clapping, ball bouncing, and just plain fun.* New York, NY: Knopf.

Examples of Websites for Rhymes and Songs (some offer ready-to-print versions)

DLTK Nursery Rhymes

Enchanted Learning

First School Nursery Rhymes

KIDiddles

Nicky's Nursery Rhymes

Webbing into Literacy Rhyme a Week

selection is committed to memory, the children should be shown the printed form. An enlarged copy makes it possible to draw attention to individual words and refer to concepts about print such as punctuation or terms like *word* and *sentence*. If you have used a song, it is time to slow it down and read it instead of singing it. Model how to **fingerpoint read** and be explicit about what you are doing. Talk about how you are starting with the first *word* on the left and touching each *word* in the *sentence* as you say it. Make sure all eyes are on the chart paper! Then invite students to recite with you using **choral reading** (in unison) or **echo reading** (you read a line, then they read the same line again). After at least three passes (modeling, choral, echo), call on a few individuals to fingerpoint read, touching each word as they say it. Observe to see how well they are able to track the words. This is the time to observe and provide instructional support, so don't be bashful about guiding students who get off track. Help them get back on track to ensure accurate pointing. There are a number of activities that will help children develop a COW-T.

Read the Room

Activity

It is important for children to fingerpoint read at other times besides group time. An activity known as Read the Room has become popular with teachers of emergent readers. Provide children with pointers and encourage them to read posted charts and displays of print all over the room.

Work with Sentence Strips

Activity

Simply reading and rereading a copy of a text from memory can have limited value unless children are paying careful attention to the print. Working with smaller portions of text like sentence strips and word cards not only makes reading more hands-on and manipulative but also demands a higher level of attention. You can purchase strips of paper or tagboard with ruled lines and use these to write lines or sentences from a selection that was used for shared reading. You can also make your own strips from paper cut into 3- by 16-inch to 3- by 24-inch lengths. Neatly print the words from a rhyme, song, or other text on strips. Place them in a pocket chart with plastic slips, and you will have an enlarged version that can be used for shared reading and for follow-up activities such as rebuilding the sentence or matching word cards to the sentence. Children like to work with the sentence strips independently during center times, so make the strips and word cards available. Lesson 6.1 describes a very concrete activity in which the children "become the words."

LESSON 6.1   Stand up and be counted

As children build a repertoire of known songs, nursery rhymes, and jump rope jingles, use them for COW-T activities that integrate phonological awareness with concept of word in print. This activity is based on research by Lundberg, Frost, and Peterson (1988). (CCSS Foundational Skills: 1, 1a, 1b, 1c, Print Concepts; 2b, Phonological Awareness)

Materials

You will need an enlarged copy of the text and a pointer.

Step 1. Recite

Recall the nursery rhyme, song, or jump rope jingle you have been learning and recite it. Point out the written copy of the verse that you have posted on the wall or chart.

Step 2. Stand up for each word

Go around the circle, having a student stand up for the next word in the nursery rhyme as it is recited. One student would stand up for *Jack,* another for *be,* and a third for the next *nimble,* for example. Watch to see whether two students stand up for a two-syllable word like *nimble* or *over.*

Step 3. Reflect on words and syllables

After everyone is finished standing up for each word, have the students sit down. If appropriate, say, "I think we may have made some mistakes. Did anyone notice?" Some students will notice that perhaps two people stood up for one word. Ask them to explain.

Step 4. Compare speech to print

Say, "Yes, two people stood up for the word *over* but *over* is one word. It has two syllables, but it means one thing—*over* [motion with your hands jumping over something]. Let's clap the word *over.* Hear? *Over* has two syllables, but it's only one word." Go to the chart or wall poster and point out the word *over.* You might also note that it starts with an *o,* ends with an *r,* and is surrounded by white space.

   Variation Have students recite a sentence or rhyme, and add a cube for each word as it is recited. Count the cubes (words). Compare sentences or lines. "Which sentence is longer? How can you tell?" Children can also be given large cards with each word in the sentence and each stand up as his or her word is called.

Rebuild the Selection with Sentence Strips

After reading a selection multiple times, pass out sentence strips to individual children and ask them to help you rebuild the text. Recite each line as a group; then ask who has the corresponding strip. As children come forward, ask them to point to the words on their strip as they tell what it says. Children with a developing COW-T may need to be told what their strips say as you pass the sentence strips out to the class. Personal copies of the selection can also be cut into sentence strips for additional practice. Children can paste these down after getting them back in order.

Cut-Up Sentences

Cutting sentences into words is a very concrete way to work on COW-T. Children first cut apart their sentences by focusing on the spaces between words. Then they must pay attention to the letters in the words to get them back in order to rebuild the sentence. This is a very worthwhile activity that can be modeled in the group and practiced in centers, for seatwork, or for homework.

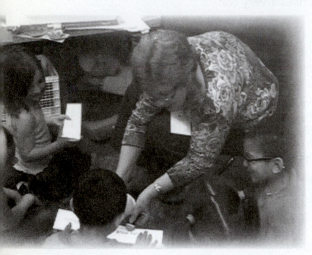

Hand out sentence strips (a smaller version of the one you would use in a pocket chart) and scissors. Call out each word as the children cut it off. The spaces between words are not obvious to children with a developing COW-T, so be prepared to model for them. Then demonstrate how to find the words in order to rebuild the sentence: "What letter would you expect to see at the beginning of *swam*?" The sentences children cut apart can be glued down and perhaps illustrated, as shown in Figure 6.3(a), or the word cards can be put into an envelope with the sentence written on the outside, as shown in Figure 6.3(b), to be used in a center or to take home.

FIGURE 6.3 Cut-Up Sentences

Be the Word

Write a familiar sentence on a chart, sentence strip, or on the board. Start with short sentences such as "Today is Monday" or "I love you." Then write each word from the sentence on a large card. Give each word to a child, naming it for him or her. "Stephanie, you are the word *Monday;* Lorenzo, you are the word *is.*" Then ask the children to work together to arrange themselves into the sentence. Have another child read the sentence to check the direction and order. Leave the words out for children to work with on their own.

Picture Captions and Dictations

An important way to help children make connections between speech and print is to write down what they say in a dictation as you discuss the writing process and then model fingerpoint reading. You might record what the children say about a picture they have drawn or about an experience they have had. These dictations provide an engaging source of text that is easily memorable because they are in the children's own words. Picture captions can be quick and easy forms of dictation.

Picture Captions

While the children are drawing, move around and ask each child to say something about his or her picture. Choose a simple phrase or sentence from the child's oral description and write it verbatim beneath the picture, as shown in Figure 6.4. Say each word as you write it, drawing attention to the sounds and letters and asking questions of the child when appropriate: "What sound do you hear first?" Next, read the caption by pointing to each word. Ask the child to read chorally along with you and, finally, to read it alone while touching each word. Later, the child may attempt to reread the caption to a buddy during sharing time.

Language Experience Approach

Like picture captions, dictated accounts of children's experiences also help them link speech to print. This approach has traditionally been referred to as the **language experience approach** or LEA (Stauffer, 1970). LEA is much like interactive writing (described earlier), but the teacher does the writing to produce a text that is easy to read—something that may not result when children do the writing. However, the same print referencing should take place, and children can be involved in listening for sounds and selecting letters. The motivation and interest that result from using children's self-generated language has revitalized the use of LEA, especially for students learning English as another language (Dorr, 2006).

Science or art projects, cooking activities, playground events, visitors, or class pets all provide opportunities for shared experiences in which children's language will flourish. See more ideas in Table 6.3. Children's observations and comments can be recorded during a group dictation, as shown in Figure 6.5, or children can dictate individual accounts. McCabe (1996) used a technique called "tell a story to get a story," in which the teacher tells a simple two- to three-sentence story and then asks the children whether anything similar has ever happened to them. As children tell their own stories, the teacher writes down their narration and these dictated personal accounts can be reread.

When recording a dictation as described in Lesson 6.2 children's own language should be recorded as closely as possible so that they will be able to read it back. If the language is changed, children may not remember the words as their own. Corrections to grammar should be rarely used and then only with the approval of the child, using prompts like "Good idea! Can we say it this way?" When the dictation is completed, it should be read and reread many times, focusing on words and their boundaries. For example, a child may be asked to locate his or her own name in a group dictation or to find a word that starts with the same letter as his or her own name. Each child should get his or her own copy

FIGURE 6.4 Drawing with Dictated Caption

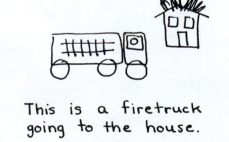

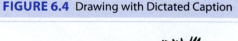

This is a firetruck going to the house.

TABLE 6.3 **Experiences for LEA Dictations**

- Examine foods like apples, oranges, pumpkins, gourds, unshelled peanuts, coconuts, pineapples, pomegranates, or popcorn
- Ask parents or volunteers to demonstrate making foods like tortillas, sushi, pasta, or pizzas
- Observe animals like hermit crabs, gerbils, birds, earthworms, butterflies, turtles, spiders, insects, ants, chicks, or fish
- Explore the senses, magnets, sinking and floating, the parts of a flashlight, color mixing, bubble blowing, soil composition, or the parts of a plant grown from seed
- Talk about the weather, a recent vacation, favorite foods, new clothes, a new student, or a school assembly
- Summarize a story, a field trip, an art activity, or a concept sort
- Interview the school principal, classroom visitors, parents from other countries, parents with interesting jobs, school helpers such as a crossing guard, or every child in turn

of the dictation to practice fingerpointing while reading together chorally and from memory. These copies can go into a personal reader.

Activity

Personal Readers

Children need repeated practice with text, and one of the best ways to accomplish this is to give them copies of familiar selections so they can track the text for themselves after it has been modeled in a group. LEA dictations, rhymes, songs, and other selections children have memorized can be added to a collection called a **personal reader** (Bear, Caserta-Henry, & Venner, 2004). Personal readers are an inexpensive but powerful way to provide early readers with text that they can read with success, keep, and share with parents. To create copies of text that are as readable as possible for early readers, select a large font size (18 to 24 points) and put an extra space or two between words when possible. Sometimes you may leave space for children to draw their own illustration. These one-page copies can be collected into notebooks or folders with pockets. New selections are easily added and numbered. The pockets can hold little books or word cards. Alternatively, selections can be glued into a composition book or a book made from newsprint or blank white paper stapled together.

FIGURE 6.5 Dictated Language Experience Chart

> The Fire Station
> Amanda said, "We went to the fire station yesterday."
> Jason said, "We rode on a big orange bus."
> Clint said, "I liked the ladder truck. It was huge!"
> D. J. said, "The firemen told us how to be safe."
> Beth said, "Firemen wear big boots and a mask."

LESSON 6.2 The Language Experience Approach (LEA)

Materials

You will need chart paper, an overhead projector, smart board, or some other way to display the text so that children can easily follow along as you write the dictation. (CCSS Foundational Skills: 1, 1a, 1b, 1c, 1d, Print Concepts; 2d, Phonological Awareness; 3a, Phonics and Word Recognition; 4, Vocabulary Acquisition and Use; CCSS Language: 1f, 2, 2a, 2b, 2c, Conventions of Standard English; 6, Vocabulary Acquisition and Use)

Step 1. Language and experience

Just like interactive writing (described in Chapter 4), LEA dictations can come from many sources. Often teachers plan hands-on experiences such as a simple science experiment or feeding a baby animal. But you can also take advantage of unexpected events such as the appearance of a rainbow. Begin by introducing and encouraging children to use new vocabulary when appropriate and lead a discussion that will stimulate lots of oral language. At some point, say something like, "We have lots of things to say and I think we should write down some of your ideas."

Step 2. Record dictation

Students dictate an account of the experience and their observations while you record each child's statement on a chart—one statement per line for emergent learners. To help students find their own contributions, you might start each line with the student's name, as in "Shannon said, 'The bunny has soft fur.'" Once children get good at fingerpoint reading single lines of text, begin to write sentences without the line breaks. Crafting children's ideas into a coherent account can take some skill. Don't hesitate to ask a child to hold an idea until a more appropriate place if sequence is important.

Step 3. Print referencing

As you write word by word, model how to say words slowly and listen for sounds, talk about letters, and ask for children's input when appropriate. For example, you might say, "When I say *bunny,* I hear the /b/ sound at the beginning. *Ben* starts with that sound. What letter should I write down first?" Lots of print referencing can take place as you refer to spacing, capitalization, and punctuation. Before starting another sentence, reread the sentence just completed, pointing to each word.

Step 4. Select a title

Select a title for the dictation. Although you might begin by writing a title, we suggest that you do it after the dictation is complete as a way to summarize. Help the children determine what the dictation is about overall by asking "What have we written about today?" Then choose a simple title such as "The Rainbow" or "A Baby Bunny."

Step 5. Read

Once the dictation is complete, reread it entirely and then ask the students to read with you, one sentence at a time, letting the children echo what you read. Then ask them to read it with you in a choral fashion. The goal is to familiarize children with the dictation so that they can rely on memory to support their own reading.

Step 6. Reread and extend

On a second day, chorally reread the entire dictation—several times as needed—and then give students their own copy to illustrate and use for voice pointing practice. Extensions using sentence strips and word cards are recommended over the next few days.

Children can take their personal readers home regularly to share with their families. However, parents should be cautioned that children are reading from memory. Encourage them to praise their child's efforts even though it may not seem like "real" reading. You may want to include a letter to parents like Figure 6.8, explaining the value of pretend reading and some of the things they can do to support children at this stage of their reading development.

Planning Instruction for Sight Word Development

Learning to recognize words and acquiring a COW-T go hand in hand; one supports the other. The goal here is the actual learning of words so that they are stored in memory as sight words to be retrieved when needed. Do not expect children to learn every word from a reading selection. Move on to fresh selections to build a repertoire of familiar text they can reread over time. Children with a developing COW-T will remember few if any words but they can still work with words and learn to look for letter–sound clues.

Supporting Sight Word Development in Context

There are various ways to draw attention to words both in and out of context to increase the chance they will be remembered. These follow-up activities are first introduced using the enlarged copy of text but are even better when each child has his or her own copy and everyone can participate.

Matching Words in Context

Prepare a set of word cards with words that come from a selection you have used for shared reading. Sentence strips can be cut into word cards or you can write words on index cards. Pass out the words to the children. Introduce matching with support by reading through the selection together, stopping word by word to ask who has the word card. Each word can be placed on top of the sentence. You might also hold up a word, name it, and then model for the children how to find a word: "Look at this word from our poem. The word is *me*. I notice that it is a short word that starts with the letter *m*. I am looking back at our poem to find this same word. Can you spot it?" As children begin to take turns looking for the word you hold up and name, ask them, "How did you know that word was *me*?" or "What did you notice about that word?" You might focus on a few high-frequency words, words that start with a particular sound, or concrete words that children will find interesting like *nest* or *worm*.

Finding Words in Context

This is similar to matching words, but you do not show the word. Instead you simply name a word and ask the children to find it. Children can recite and point to words from the beginning to find a word in context, "counting up" to find it. But you should also model how to use sounds and letters: "If I want to find the word *spider* in the title of this song, I can read from the beginning until I get to the word, or I can think about the way it sounds: *sssssspider*. I hear /sssss/, so I will look for a word that starts with *s*. When I find a word that starts that way, I check to see whether other sounds in the word match to the letters." As children take turns, remember to ask them how they were able to find the words. When children have their own copies of a selection, everyone can look for words and they can underline or highlight them.

Identify Words in Context

A third way to work with words in context is to point to words and ask the children to name them or let the children select their favorite words and point to them for others to name. Watch to see whether children can name a word immediately or if they need to count up to figure out what a word is. Words they can quickly identify are good candidates to go into word banks, described in the following section.

I'm Thinking Of . . .

This game is a favorite with Lori's children. She poses a riddle such as "I'm thinking of a word that starts just like the word *cat*. What word am I thinking of?" When a child comes up to point out the answer, Lori asks in astonishment, "What is that word? How did you know that was the word I was thinking of?" Begin with just one line or sentence and choose words with a clear initial consonant sound or blends and digraphs that the children have been learning about. Children can learn to pose the riddles for each other.

Cloze Activity

Cover up one word per line, leaving only the beginning letter visible to use as a clue for figuring out what word you've left out (e.g., "*Four little monkeys jumping on the b___.*" Then uncover the *ed* to let them see whether they were right. Ask them how they knew that *bed* comes next (saw the *b*, starts with a /b/ sound, etc.).

Supporting Sight Word Development out of Context

Words should be introduced in a meaningful context, but taking words out of context and reviewing words over time helps children store them more completely in memory (Ehri & Roberts, 1979; Johnston, 2000). This is probably because young readers attend to the features of the printed word more carefully out of context and, with repeated encounters, remember more of the details. **Word banks** and **word walls** are two ways to take words out of context.

WORD BANKS. Individual collections of words written on little cards that children can identify out of context are known as *word banks*. The words come from familiar reading selections and are reviewed over time to achieve mastery as sight words. Traditionally word banks consist of words that children have selected themselves as being ones that they recognize (Stauffer, 1980). For this reason, no two children have the same words in their word banks. Children enjoy a sense of accomplishment as the number of words they have collected grows (Johnston, 1998).

Harvesting Words for a Word Bank. Here is the basic procedure to use when selecting words to add to individual word banks:

1. Prepare a collection of word cards. Cut 1- by 4-inch cards from cardstock or index cards. Be ready to print each word neatly on the card.

2. After reading their copies of a dictation, poem, song, or jingle, ask the children to find words they think they know. Children may simply point to words, or they can underline words on their personal copy. At first, children may simply underline every word as they read through the text from memory. So teachers should model different ways to select words. Rather than starting at the beginning, the children might be encouraged to scan through the text backward or scan up and down to spot words they know. Some teachers let pairs of students work together with a "word window" to randomly spot check their partner's ability to read the words from a familiar context (see Figure 6.6). With experience, children learn how to select appropriate words.

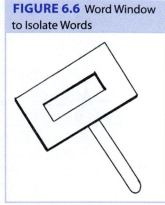

FIGURE 6.6 Word Window to Isolate Words

3. The next step is to see whether the word the child underlined is stored well enough in memory to be recalled. Point to a word and ask the child to name it. If the student names it immediately (without any rereading to use context), write the word on a card for him or her. If the word has been harvested from a personal reader, record the entry number on the back of the card.

4. If you are harvesting words in a small group, give each child a chance in turn to identify three or four words that he or she has underlined. High-frequency words are useful candidates, but include concrete and interesting words such as *helicopter* or *pizza*.

5. Check the choices by showing the printed words to see whether they are identified. New words can then be added to a collection stored in an envelope or baggie that might be kept with a personal reader. These words should then be reviewed, as described in the section on word bank activities.

Go to the PDToolkit to hear Ms. Kiernan talk about personal readers and word banks. Select the Videos tab and then Letter Name–Alphabetic Stage. Scroll through the list of videos to select "Weekly Schedules and Classroom Activities."

An alternative way to harvest words is to write down words from a selection in advance on cards or randomly in a list. Children can then point to the words they can name. This provides a more accurate way to harvest words that children really know. If children are using little books, you can create a list of words from the book or a collection of word cards and keep it in a library pocket in the back. Part of the reading routine can be going over the words as well as reading the book.

Managing Word Banks. One of the advantages of word banks is having a growing collection of words that students can review over time to better secure in memory as sight words. Word banks in kindergarten may grow to 100 words or more once children have a COW-T. But successful review depends on knowing the vast majority of the words. Children at this point in development are usually not able to sound out words they don't know. To avoid frustration and increase the odds of learning the unknown word, have the children go back to their personal readers and match the word back in context. This can be tedious and time consuming if there are more than a few unknown words, so be judicious. If children consistently fail to recognize a word, you might tactfully suggest that it be removed from the word bank by saying something like, "Shall we take out this word since it is such a tricky one to remember? We will add some others that you know."

Activities for Word Bank Review. To reap their full benefits, word banks need to be reviewed regularly. This can be done as a warm up for small-group time or for a seatwork activity or center activity. They can also be sent home for practice.

Independent Review

The children read through their collections of words, putting aside those they cannot remember. If they do not remember a word, they can refer back to the original source in their personal readers or a book to see whether they can identify the word in context, or they may elect to remove it.

My Pile, Your Pile

The children work with a partner (another child or a classroom volunteer) to review their words. Words that the child correctly identifies go in that student's pile and words the child misses go in the partner's pile. Missed words can be matched back to the original source or used to play Pick Up, described next. Words that children consistently miss should be removed.

Pick Up

Lay out a collection of five to eight words that the student does not know or frequently confuses. A teacher or partner names a word, and the child must find it based on letter–sound features and pick it up. If the child has trouble, provide clues such as "What sound do you hear at the beginning [or end] of the word? Children who rely on initial consonants can be asked to distinguish between words such as *me, make, mad,* and *Mom,* which require attention to other letters in the word.

Guess My Word

This is similar to Pick Up, but instead of naming a word, offer clues such as "I am thinking of a word that rhymes with *hat*" or "I am thinking of a word that starts like *ship.*"

Build Sentences

When children have nouns and verbs included in their word banks, they can begin to build sentences. It is fun to add the names of friends to the word bank so they can make sentences such as "I like Rosaria" or "Shantay can run." During writing time, encourage students to use their word banks as a source for words they might want to use. A few words such as "I like to . . ." might get them started when they can't think of things to write about.

Games

Word bank words can be used in a variety of games: Memory, Bingo, and Tic Tac Toe. Because word banks will vary from child to child, the game needs to be tailored to the specific words a child might have.

Sort Words

Once children have 50 or more words in their word bank, they can use them to sort in various ways:

- Put the words in alphabetical order using an alphabet strip or letter cards as headers.
- Sort by concept categories such as animals, people, and actions.
- Sort by beginning consonant sounds. After sorting pictures or objects that begin with *b* and *r*, children can go to their word banks and add the words that begin with those same letter sounds. Note that digraphs such as *th*, *sh*, and *ch* will require some explanation.

WORD WALLS. Word walls, described by Pat Cunningham (2009) as an instructional strategy to support word learning, have been widely adopted in classrooms. Word walls in preK should be limited to children's names accompanied by photographs. (See the photo on page 48 in Chapter 2.) Kindergarten word walls begin by posting children's names. Then 30 to 50 words are added over the course of the year as they are encountered in reading selections. Include concrete, meaningful words like colors, animals, action verbs, and adjectives (*little, big*) as well as a few of those more abstract high-frequency words. Words should be displayed large enough and low enough that young children can not only see them, but go up and touch them. Each week, introduce several new words and spend a little time working with them each day during the week. Here are a few guidelines to "do" a word wall in kindergarten.

1. Create an alphabetic display and leave space to add words over time. Avoid using glossy paper or laminating word cards to reduce the chance of glare that makes it difficult to see the words.
2. Start with children's names as they are introduced in "name of the day" activities (described in Chapter 2) and put them under the appropriate letter.
3. Focus on a few words each week that students have encountered in a familiar text (big books, poems, songs, etc.). Five words are often recommended, but we suggest fewer in the early part of kindergarten so that the total is not overwhelming. Remember that children without a COW-T may not be able to memorize many, if any, words. Prepare neatly written word cards large enough to be easily read from a distance. Practice the new words each day for a week before they are formally added to the wall using word wall activities, described next.

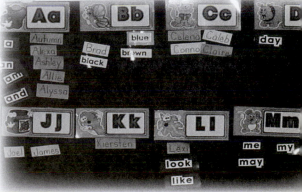

Word Wall Activities. There are lots of activities to do with word wall words. These activities are important to help secure the word in memory so that children eventually will not need to refer to the wall at all. Keep these practice activities fast and fun.

Chant the Letters

Hold up a word or point to it. Ask the children to name the letters with you: "Here is the word *was*. Let's chant the letters—*w-a-s* spells *was*." Add variety by chanting in different voices (whisper, cheer, squeak, growl, baby talk) and with different expressions (excited, sad, puzzled, robotic) or add movements (snap, clap, stretch for tall letters and squat for short letters).

Write the Words

Writing words is a way to help secure them in memory. Children can write on individual chalkboards, whiteboards, or paper. Point to a word and explain, "Look carefully at this word. I am going to hide it and ask you to write it. Can you remember the letters?" (Chant them if you wish.) Cover or hide the word and wait for children to write it. Then reveal it and ask children to check their own writing. Repeat if more than one or two of the students miss the word. Keep this fun and do not put anyone on the spot if they make a mistake.

Model How to Use the Word Wall

Look for opportunities to model the use of the word wall. For example, during writing say, "*Was* is on our word wall. Can someone find it and tell us how to spell it?" or "That word starts with a capital *B*, just like *Beatrice*. Look on the word wall for her name."

Encourage Active Use

Add the words to word banks or children's alphabet books, or create a word wall sheet that can be stapled inside the cover of personal journals for easy reference. This can be updated periodically, and children can add words that they are personally interested in, such as the name of an animal or pet. (An example of this can be seen in Figure 4.3.) In kindergarten Kaitlyn had a list of "star" words she kept in her journal.

Practice Words Frequently

Keep a collection of word wall words in a box or gift bag. Write the words on sturdy cardboard or cardstock. These can be used for many activities:

- When you have a few minutes of extra time, pull out a word and call on someone to name it and find it on the word wall. The child can touch the word with a pointer. This simple activity reminds the students what words are on the wall and helps them learn how to find the words when they need them. Be sure to ask the children how they knew the word selected was the correct word.
- Children can work with a partner or in a small group to take turns pulling out words, naming them, and pointing to them on the word wall. Or they can name a word to spell. They may look at the word wall or—even better—try to spell it without reference to the wall. Then show them the word to confirm their spelling.
- Many alphabet games, like those described in Chapter 2, can be adapted into word wall games simply by replacing letter cards with word cards.

Be a Mind Reader

In this game, children try to guess a word based on five clues. First, each student numbers a paper from one to five to write a guess after each clue. The first clue is always "The word is on the wall." Subsequent clues should narrow the possibilities. For example, the next clue might be "This word has five letters," followed by "This word ends with a *t*" or "This word rhymes with *light*." By the final clue (usually the beginning letter), everyone usually has the correct word. This is a particularly valuable game because, although it only takes a few minutes, the children are actively scanning the word wall for possibilities; this keeps them familiar with what words are on the wall.

WORD IDENTIFICATION GAMES AND ACTIVITIES. Repeated exposure to the words you want your students to review and acquire as sight words can be accomplished with games and activities in centers after they have been introduced in meaningful text. Flash card activities can be useful as long as children are not overburdened with a large number of words they do not know. They must also have access to the original source of the words to support identification in context when the word is not known in isolation. Children should not be expected to sound out flash card words when they lack vowel knowledge.

Build the Words

An easy center activity asks children to build words using letter cards, magnetic letters, letter stamps, or some other material. Children can select words from their word banks, or you can assign particular words for them to build.

Word Books

Staple several strips of newsprint folded in half (3- by 11-inch strips work well) into a little book. Provide a collection of letter stamps so that children can find the letters needed to spell a target word and then illustrate the word or use it in a sentence.

Face-Up Matching

Provide two sets of words and lay them out face up, but scrambled. Children take turns selecting a word, naming it, and finding a match for it. If no one can identify a word, they should refer back to the text from which it came. This can be the first step when introducing the game Memory.

Memory

Make two sets of words to be used for the classic game of Memory, which can be played by two or three children. Scramble the words and turn them face down in rows and columns. Children then turn over two words at a time to find a match. Twelve to 16 cards (six to eight pairs) is a good number for a game that moves quickly.

Word Bingo

Provide children with blank grids of 9 squares (3 by 3) or 16 squares (4 by 4). An easy way to create these is to simply fold newsprint into squares. The children write selected words randomly in the spaces as someone calls words aloud, displaying each so it can be copied accurately. This in itself is a worthwhile activity, but if time is an issue, bingo cards could also be prepared in advance. Remember that each grid should be different. Play bingo in the traditional way. As someone calls words aloud, the children cover the target word with a penny, button, or other marker. The first person to get three or four in a row is the winner and gets to call out the words for the next round.

Wash the Elephant

Draw a simple outline of an elephant on a chalkboard or whiteboard. Write words inside that you want children to learn. Name a word and call on someone to come forward and erase it. The elephant is gradually washed clean as the words are called. Other shapes can be a car, bus, or house.

The Whole-to-Part Five-Day Plan

Now that we have covered the various elements that support the development of COW-T and the acquisition of sight words, we are ready to describe the **whole-to-part framework** in which everything comes together. Holdaway (1979) and McCracken and McCracken (1986) described a sequence of instruction that begins with a whole text and progresses down to its parts. The research of Johnston (2000) established that the sequence supported sight word acquisition. All the components of the early literacy diet are worked into this plan—oral language and vocabulary, alphabet knowledge, concepts about print, phonological awareness, and phonics—all pressed into the service of achieving a firm COW-T and promoting sight word acquisition. The lesson sequence provides scaffolding needed for emergent readers, beginning with the introduction of a whole text through shared reading and then working with smaller parts across five days. In this supportive context, reading from memory with modeling and choral reading progresses to independent reading, which takes students back to the "whole" again.

Overview

Previous chapters have described portions of the whole-to-part plan, but here we pull it together and review activities.

The 15- to 20-minute whole-to-part lesson plan is designed for small groups of five to seven students, grouped by approximate skill levels in COW-T. Table 6.4 offers an overview of the whole-to-part instructional sequence and shows how it can be differentiated. Notice that on day 1, the entire text is introduced and much time is devoted to modeling and practicing how to fingerpoint read the memorized text—something the students will do every day. The whole text is broken down into sentences on day 2, when the focus of instruction is on rebuilding the text, sentence by sentence. On day 3, sentence strips are cut into words and students rebuild their sentence and match word cards back to their counterparts in context. On day 4, students focus on the beginning sounds and letters and use initial consonant sounds to find words in context. On day 5, the students are informally assessed on the accuracy of their fingerpoint reading and their memory for specific words. At this point, word bank words can be harvested.

WHOLE-GROUP INTRODUCTION. Prior to the small-group lessons in which the children will get differentiated instruction, introduce the selection to the whole group by memorizing a rhyme, singing a song, or enjoying a story.

DIFFERENTIATED SMALL-GROUP LESSONS. The specific activities within each day's lesson follow a before, during, and after framework. The exact nature of what you do will depend on where children are in their development. When children have a developing or rudimentary COW-T, the following activities are important.

The *before reading* section of each day's lesson is a brief warm-up, lasting two to five minutes each day. Children with a developing COW-T usually need work on alphabet and phonological awareness and might work on brief game-like activities like those described in Chapter 2 and 3. They might track the alphabet by pointing to each word while singing the song, rebuild their first names with letter tiles, or write letters on dry erase boards, depending on their skill. Draw attention to some phonological awareness aspect, depending on the selection you are using. You might point out syllables if there are long words (e.g., "Let's clap the syllables in *alligator*") or beginning sounds if there is alliteration (e.g., "I hear several words that start with the same sound! *Peas, porridge*! They both start with the /p/ sound!"). If you were using *Five Little Ducks*, you might find rhyming words or brainstorm other words that rhyme with *quack*. Part of the warm-up can also be chorally rereading selections from previous weeks using charts or personal readers. Word banks can also be reviewed during this time if children have a rudimentary COW-T. Keep this section fast and fun, varying the activities across the five-day whole-to-part plan.

TABLE 6.4 **Differentiated Whole-to-Part Sequence for Children with a Developing and Rudimentary COW-T**

	DEVELOPING CONCEPT OF WORD	RUDIMENTARY CONCEPT OF WORD
Whole Class Introduction	Introduce the selection to the whole class by memorizing a rhyme, learning the words to a song, or sharing a book.	
Day 1: The Whole	Review the selection by reciting it, singing it, or acting it out. Introduce one to six lines of printed text using an enlarged copy that everyone can see. Model, echo read, and read chorally. Ask several children to solo read, providing support as needed. Review the phonics sort from the previous week.	
Day 2: Sentences and Individual Copies	Reread the selection chorally and let several children solo. Then have the children rebuild cut-up sentence strips, telling them what the strip pieces say as needed. Pass out individual copies and have the children point as teacher leads. Add a copy to personal readers.	Reread the selection chorally. Then rebuild cut-up sentence strips, giving help as needed. Pass out individual copies and have the children read chorally and then with partners. Add a copy to personal readers. Review word bank words from the previous selection.
Day 3: Words	Reread the selection chorally. Then match word cards with words in one line or sentence of enlarged copy. Rebuild cut-up sentence. Name concrete and/or high frequency words for children to find.	Reread the selection using individual copies so children can touch the words. Then ask the children to match, find, or identify concrete and/or high-frequency words in individual copies that are good candidates for word banks.
New Selection	During the week, introduce a new selection in shared reading with the whole class that will become text for the whole-to-part sequence the following week.	
Day 4: Letters and Sounds	Reread the selection and call attention to letters and sounds. Ask children to find letters and sounds in individual copies that will become the focus of new word study.	Reread the selection and call attention to letter–sound matches. Review previous matches and focus on new matches for word study.
New Word Study	Introduce a new phonics sort based on letter–sound matches in the selection. Continue the sort into the following week.	
Day 5: Assess & Word bank	Ask the children to read individual copies as you observe. Have the children find words and letters in individual copies.	Ask the children to read their individual copies as you observe. Then work with the children to identify two to five words for word banks and/or the word wall.

The *during reading* part of each day is the heart of the whole-to-part lesson and lasts about 10 minutes. It focuses intensely on the development of COW-T through fingerpoint reading selections that have been memorized and then working with increasingly smaller parts of the text. This is also a time for print referencing and a review of vocabulary or concepts introduced in the whole group.

The *after reading* section of the whole-to-part lesson plan provides targeted phonics instruction through beginning sound picture sorts as described in Chapter 5. This portion of the lesson can take anywhere from five to 10 minutes. Do not introduce a new sort until day 4 of the whole-to-part plan so you can focus on initial consonant sounds and example words that come from the selection. Review the previous sort and plan follow-up activities on days 1, 2, and 3 of the next round of lessons.

The Whole-to-Part Instructional Sequence Day by Day

Lessons 6.3 through 6.7 describe the whole-to-part framework and how all parts of the literacy diet can be incorporated. The phonics or word study portion of the plan is described briefly, but refer back to Chapter 5 for more detail. This is a suggested sequence; feel free to modify it to fit your situation and your students' needs.

LESSON 6.3 Day 1: Introducing the whole

Familiar rhymes, songs, jingles, and simple, predictable text are easily memorized and can be used to help children develop a concept of word in text. Many teachers work with a different rhyme or song that the whole class enjoys each week. The selection is introduced to the entire group prior to this lesson. (CCSS Foundational Skills: 1a, 1b, 1c, Print Concepts; 3c, 4, Phonics and Word Recognition)

Materials

You will need an enlarged copy of the text from *Five Little Ducks* or another selection on chart paper or sentence strips, pointer (dowel rod, chopstick, or unsharpened pencil), and the phonics sort introduced previously to review. You might focus on just the first two lines with children who are developing a COW-T. Children with a rudimentary COW-T can handle the entire first verse. You can also prepare number words from one to five and substitute them as you read the other verses, as shown in Figure 6.7.

FIGURE 6.7 Pictures Support the Reading of Sentence Strips

Step 1. Warm up

Do warm-up activities, depending on children's needs (alphabet, phonological awareness, rereading previous selections, reviewing word banks, etc.).

Step 2. Review the selection

Sing the song, chant the rhyme, or reread a big book to review. It is helpful to use pictures for prompts, as shown in Figure 6.7. Highlight any unusual vocabulary and talk about illustrations when appropriate.

Step 3. Focus on the print

Once the selection is committed to memory, the children should be shown the printed form. Model how to fingerpoint as you read to them and reference concepts about print. If you were using *Five Little Ducks*, you might draw attention to the capital and lowercase *Q*.

Step 4. Share the reading

Invite the students to read with you using choral and echo reading. After at least three passes, call on a few individuals to fingerpoint read, touching each word as they say it. Offer instructional support when needed.

Step 5. Children fingerpoint read

Give the students their own copies of the rhyme on a single sheet of paper so that they can get more practice pointing to the words as they read. Tell the children to get their finger ready and follow along together as they read chorally. Then have them read individually. Observe the solo efforts to monitor children's development of COW-T.

Step 5. Phonics

Have the children repeat the sort from the previous week under your supervision and assign seatwork or center activities such as re-sorting with partners, pasting pictures into categories, or looking for more things that start with target letters.

LESSON 6.4   Day 2: Working with the parts: Sentences

The focus of day 2 is to reread the selection from day 1 and work with sentences. The children review phonics features. (CCSS Foundational Skills: 1a, 1b, 1c, Print Concepts; 3a, 3c, 4, Phonics and Word Recognition)

Materials

You will need an enlarged copy of the selection, sentence strips, and individual copies for each child in personal readers.

Step 1. Warm up

Do warm-up activities, depending on the children's needs.

Step 2. Review

Go over the printed selection from day 1 by reading it chorally.

Step 3. Focus on sentences

Explain that you will be working with sentences today. Pass out the sentence strips to individuals or pairs. (Read sentences to children with a developing COW-T as you do this.) Explain that you need help putting the sentences back in order. Recite the selection, pausing to ask who has each sentence after it is said. Provide support when needed by having the children match their sentences back to a whole copy of the selection. Question the children about how they were able to determine what the sentence said. Invite a child to read the selection solo using the pointer to check whether the sentences are in the right order.

Step 4. Assign individual practice

Ask the children to read their own copies and observe how well they are able to point to the words. Pair them up with a buddy to practice fingerpoint reading to each other again. Ask the nonreading buddy to make sure his or her partner is saying and pointing to each word. You may want to give the children their own smaller sets of cut-up sentences to put back in order. Simply cut apart an individual copy into sentences.

(continued)

LESSON 6.4   Day 2: Working with the parts: Sentences (*continued*)

Step 5. Phonics

Children can be assigned to repeat the sort at their seats or in a center. "Draw and label" can be assigned for seatwork after brainstorming words in the group or looking up the beginning sound in alphabet books.

LESSON 6.5   Day 3: Working with the parts: Words

On day 3, words are examined. The phonics part of the lesson includes assessment. (CCSS Foundational Skills: 1a, 1b, 1c, Print Concepts; 3a, 3c, 4, Phonics and Word Recognition)

Materials

You will need an enlarged copy of the selection, personal readers, sentence strips to cut apart into words, and word cards that you have prepared with targeted words. Children with a developing COW-T might focus on concrete words (such as *ducks, five, hills*) in just one sentence or line from the selection, whereas children with a rudimentary COW-T can work with the whole text and a wider variety of words. In the case of *Five Little Ducks,* you might want to focus on the number words from one to five.

Step 1. Warm up

Do warm-up activities, depending on children's needs. Reread the selection and call on one or two children to solo. Explain that everyone will be working with words today.

Step 2. Focus on words

For children developing a COW-T, you might demonstrate how to cut apart a sentence into words, naming each word as it is cut off. Pass out the words and ask the children to help you rebuild the sentence, providing a model of the completed sentence if needed. Ask children with a rudimentary COW-T to match, find, and identify words in context. For example, you might hold up the word *five* and call on someone to find and then identify it. Ask the student to explain how he or she did it. If the children are unable to identify the word after making the match, teach them how to *voice point* by starting at the beginning and reading up to the word in question. Once the word has been identified, call attention to the letters and sounds that will help them identify it (e.g., "This word begins with /ffff/, spelled with the letter *f*"). See different activities for working with words in context described earlier (pages 152–53) such as I'm Thinking Of . . . .

Step 3. Assign individual work with words

Ask the children to find words using their own copies of the text. They can simply point, highlight, or underline target words. Children with a developing COW-T might be given a sentence from the selection to cut apart and then put back together. Ask the children to explain how they know the order in which to place the words. Prompt for beginning sounds and initial consonants.

Step 4. Phonics

Letter hunts or word hunts work well for day 3. For example, if students have been working with the initial consonant *b*, have them look at *Five Little Ducks* and find all the *b* words (*but, back*). This is also a good time to informally assess the letter sounds you have been studying for several days. Watch for accuracy and automaticity as you observe students sorting and as you observe how they label pictures or use beginning sounds in writing. Although you should encourage students to write all of the sounds that they hear in a word, only hold them accountable for what you have taught them.

LESSON 6.6   Day 4: Working with the letters and sounds

On day 4, the focus is on the smallest units of print and a new phonics sequence is begun based on the selection. (CCSS Foundational Skills: 1a, 1b, 1c, 1d, Print Concepts; 2d, Phonological Awareness; 3a, 3c, 4, Phonics and Word Recognition)

Materials

You will need an enlarged copy of the selection, personal readers, and letter and picture cards for sorting by sounds. Select a phonics feature that is appropriate for the developmental level of the children in each group based on words from the selection. Or choose a text selection based on the letter sounds you want to study.) *Five Little Ducks* contains the words *five, far, ducks,* and *day,* so the study of *f* and *d* would be a logical choice. Children with a rudimentary COW-T might also study *l* (*little*), *h* (*hills*), or even *q* (*quack*) for a sort with up to four sounds.

Step 1. Warm up

Keep the warm-up activities brief on day 4 so you have time to introduce the picture sort described for the phonics part of the lesson. If your group has really caught on you might skip the rereading of the selection.

Step 2. Isolate targeted letters and sounds

Begin by saying something like "I'm thinking of a word in our song that starts with the letter *d*. What word am I thinking of? [*Duck*]. Yes, *duck* starts with *d*. Can you find another word that starts with *d* [*day*]?" Repeat with another letter such as *f* and find *five* and *far*. Model this on the enlarged copy, but also ask the children to look for letters and sounds on their own copies.

Step 3. Sort pictures

Follow the introduce, demonstrate, sort, check, and reflect routine described in Chapter 5. For example, explain that there are many more words that begin with *f* and *d*. Put up letter cards for *f* and *d* and place a picture of a duck and the numeral five under the letter headers. Then model how to sort several cards or objects before inviting children to help you finish the sort. Check by reading down each column to ask students to reflect on their sort and say what is the same in each column—by sound and by letter. Repeat the sort: Leave up the headers, mix up the pictures, and pass them out.

LESSON 6.7   Day 5: Review the whole

Day 5 wraps up the lesson sequence and new word bank words are harvested. The phonics feature from day 4 is reviewed. (CCSS Foundational Skills: 1a, 1b, 1c, 1d, Print Concepts; 2d, Phonological Awareness; 3a, 3c, 4, Phonics and Word Recognition)

(continued)

LESSON 6.7   Day 5: Review the whole (*continued*)

Materials

You will need an enlarged copy of the selection, individual copies, and materials for word banks (word cards, marker, and envelopes or baggies to store words).

Step 1. Warm up

Do warm-up activities, depending on the children's needs.

Step 2. Assess fingerpointing

Ask the children to read through their personal copies of the text and point to the words. Observe to see which children do this easily and accurately and which children need to be assessed individually.

Step 3. Assess word recognition

For children with a developing COW-T, assess their word identification in context. Ask one child at a time to read his or her personal copy while pointing to each word. Observe how accurately the student tracks each word. Then point to a few words and ask, "What's this word?" If the student can name any of the words in context without voice pointing, see whether he or she can identify that word in isolation, using a word card. Simple word banks can be started for these children by targeting a few words from the week's selection that everyone will get. For example, for *Five Little Ducks* you might select the words *duck, five,* and *the.* Show each word, and ask the children to find it in their personal copy.

Step 4. Work on word banks

For children with a rudimentary COW-T, focus day 5 on harvesting words for a word bank, as described earlier. Children can be asked to read through their personal copies and underline words. Or you can present them with a list or word cards to identify in isolation. Work with one child at a time to identify a small set of words to go into their word bank. This should go quickly because you are looking for immediate identification of words you point to. (Don't expect the children to sound out any words.) The number you harvest will depend on where the child is developmentally and the time available. There is no need to add every possible word to the word bank. This might also be a time to select a few words that are good candidates to add to the word wall.

While you are working with one child, the other children in the group can be reading previous selections in their personal readers, illustrating the new selection, reviewing their word banks, or cutting out their own sets of words for the phonics sort introduced the previous day.

Step 5. Review the picture sort

Review the sort from day 4 by setting up the headers and then letting children take turns sorting and naming the beginning letters. Then give the children their own copies of the sort. You may send children back to their seats to do this or have them cut while you work with individuals. Ask them to complete the sort independently or with a partner under your supervision. Sorts can also be placed in a center for repeated practice. As you begin a new rotation of whole-to-part lessons, assign follow-up phonics routines on days 1 to 3.

Instruction for Children with a Firm COW-T

Children with a firm COW-T can participate with the whole class in the introduction of shared reading but, as beginning readers, they no longer need all the supports of the whole-to-part routine. With a firm COW-T and a growing sight vocabulary, they are ready to read from little leveled books, predictable story books, and nonfiction picture books with repetitive language structures. Here will we give a brief introduction to small-group differentiated reading instruction for beginning readers, but we also refer you to other sources for more thorough coverage.

A beginning reader lesson is usually conducted in a small group of five to seven children reading at approximately the same level as determined by running records and word list reading. (See one of the beginning reading sources listed in Table 6.5 for more information about determining reading levels.)

It is important to select a book that has just the right amount of challenge—not too hard and not too easy. Books for beginning readers offer a lot of support through the use of pictures, repetitive language structures, and familiar settings and situations. As the books get more difficult, pictures will provide less support and the language will become less predictable. In general, students will read books on the same level of difficulty for a few weeks before moving on to a higher level. Reading lessons for beginning readers are structured in a before-during-after framework.

BEFORE READING. Before introducing a new book, you should prepare a book preview by thinking about the content and anticipating what supports your students will need to read and understand it. First, read the title of the book aloud to the children as you point to the words. Show the cover of the book and discuss the illustration. You might ask the children what they notice about the illustration and ask for a prediction: What do they think the story might be about? If the book is nonfiction, you might offer a brief summary of what the book will be about and ask a few questions to activate their background knowledge; for example, for a book about big machines, ask questions like "Have you ever seen big machines at a construction site?" Take a "picture walk" through the first part of the book and discuss essential concepts and vocabulary your students may be unfamiliar with. For example, point to a picture of a front-end loader and explain what it is and what it's called: "That machine is called a *front-end loader*. Front-end loaders are a kind of tractor that can lift and move very heavy things like huge rocks and boulders or big loads of dirt." Converse with your students using the vocabulary and language patterns of the text. However, if the book ends with a surprise, don't give away the ending by previewing that part. You might find that your students will change their predictions after your picture walk—which means they are thinking and paying attention.

DURING READING. Beginning readers need lots of practice, so avoid round-robin reading, which forces children to wait their turn and breeds inattention. Children get more practice by reading the whole book to themselves in a whisper read—out loud but in a quiet voice. This allows you to listen in to monitor and offer support. Supporting

---

TABLE 6.5	**Additional Resources for Teaching Students with a Firm Concept of Word**

- Fountas, I. C., & Pinnell, G. S. (1996). *Guided reading: Good first teaching for all children*. Portsmouth, NH: Heinemann.

- Johnston, F. R., Invernizzi, M., Juel, C., & Lewis-Wagner, D. L. (2009). *Book buddies: A tutoring framework for struggling readers* (2nd ed.). New York, NY: Guilford Press.

- Mesmer, H. (2008). *Tools for matching readers to texts: Research-based practices*. New York, NY: Guilford Press.

- Opitz, M. F., & Ford, M. P. (2001). *Reaching readers: Flexible & innovative strategies for guided reading*. Portsmouth, NH: Heinemann.

- Tyner, B. (2009). *Small-group reading instruction: A differentiated teaching model for beginning and struggling readers*. Newark, DE: International Reading Association.

TABLE 6.6   **What to Do When a Beginning Reader Needs Help with Words**

1. Don't say anything! Give the child time to figure it out. Offer praise when a child self-corrects.
2. Say, "Try that again. Did that make sense?" or "Something isn't right. Can you fix it?" Sometimes you can simply point to the word. Praise the specifics of the child's problem solving (e.g., "I like the way you used that beginning sound").
3. Draw attention to what the child knows about letter sounds and spelling (e.g., "Slide your finger under this word and look at all the letters" or "Do you see a part of that word that you know?" or "Cover up _____ and try it.").
4. Encourage the use of context (e.g., "Reread that sentence and try that word again" or "What would make sense?").
5. Sometimes you should just give the word: "That's a hard word. It is _____." or "Watch me [as you slide your finger under the word while sounding it out]."

Source: Based on *Book Buddies* (2nd ed.), by F. Johnston, M. Invernizzi, C. Juel, & D. Lewis-Wagner. Copyright 2009 by the Guilford Press. Page 178.

beginning reading is a lot like teaching a child how to ride a bike—you must be prepared to provide support when the child is wobbling, but let go when the child is stable and able to proceed independently. The supports you might offer during reading will depend on what aspect of the text is giving the child difficulty, but the list of prompts in Table 6.6 will give you a good repertoire to get started. Keep a clip board or small white board handy and write down any words that you might want to revisit after reading.

After reading a new book for the first time, beginning readers benefit from reading it again right away. If a child continues to miss more than a few words on the second reading, it may be a book that is just too difficult.

AFTER READING.   After reading the new selection, it's a good idea to talk about the book in a conversational way. Don't quiz the children by asking questions about what they read. If you did a good job of previewing the book, they should have had no trouble understanding it. But if you noticed that all of the students seemed unfamiliar with a particular word, idea, or concept, now would be the time to revisit it, both conversationally and by returning to a given page or picture to discuss it further. After reading is also the time to give your students feedback. Praise their efforts to puzzle out unfamiliar words, and share the different strategies you noticed they used. You might revisit a word that everyone stumbled on and talk about its letter sounds and meaning. Children can also respond to the reading by sharing their favorite part orally or in writing. After each new reading, make the book available for rereading at their desks and in centers throughout the week. Before tackling a new book the next day, warm up by rereading the completed book to get the juices flowing.

Working with Parents

Personal readers can be sent home so that children can share their developing skills. But parents need some suggestions about how to use them. Often parents think that memorizing (instead of "real" reading) and pointing at words are inappropriate behaviors. So be sure to communicate with them about why they should support these early efforts. A letter such as the one in Figure 6.8 can be sent home along with the personal reader or copies of reading selections. Talking about these ideas at back-to-school night and parent conferences is also important. When children have achieved a firm concept of word, they will rely much less on memory, but you should continue to involve parents and get additional practice by sending home the little books used for reading instruction.

FIGURE 6.8 Parent Letter about Reading

Dear Parents/Guardians,

Your child will be bringing home copies of poems, songs, and other short reading selections that we have used in school. It is important that you encourage your child to read to you and that you praise his or her efforts, even though it may not seem like real reading. Your child may have memorized these selections, but this is not a bad thing at this stage of development. It is much like training wheels for learning to ride a bike. Memory offers support and helps children enjoy a sense of accomplishment until they have had a chance to learn a lot of words.

As your child reads, ask him or her to touch the words. Pointing to the words requires paying attention to the print, and this will increase the chances that your child will learn the words. If your child does not know a word, simply point to it and name it. After your child reads to you, make a game of asking him or her to find some words on the page. Here are three ways you can do this:

- Ask your child to find a word such as *hill* in the nursery rhyme of Jack and Jill. Say something like, "Can you find the word *hill*? What letter would come at the beginning of *hill*?"
- Switch places and let your child name a word for you to find.
- You might ask your child to find and touch a word or name that starts with a /j/ sound (*Jack, Jill*) and then ask how he or she found it (letter *J* at the beginning).

Over time, pointing to words and using memory will decrease, so do not worry that these behaviors will interfere with real reading. I will be happy to talk with you about any questions or concerns that you have.

Sincerely,

Assessing COW-T and Word Identification

You should assess COW-T informally all the time as you observe children's efforts to track the words in the selections you provide. However, you may also want to periodically plan a more formal assessment using the special forms and materials supplied in Appendix A. When formally assessing the development of COW-T, be sure to use a rhyme or other text that *has not been used in instruction*. "One, Two, Buckle My Shoe" and "Humpty Dumpty" work well because they have words of more than one syllable. Read the selection to the whole class until the children know it by heart; then call on children individually. The steps in assessment are similar to the steps used in instruction.

MEMORIZE A RHYME. You might use a picture representation of a nursery rhyme to model how to recite the nursery rhyme by pointing to each picture several times while reciting the rhyme. The example we supply in Appendix A uses "Humpty Dumpty." Ask the students to

- Chorally chant the rhyme with you
- Echo chant the rhyme, picture by picture
- Recite the rhyme independently while pointing to the picture prompts

Repeat these steps as many times as necessary until the children know the selection by heart. Remember that text is not used at this point and the student is not yet finger-point reading.

FIGURE 6.9 COW-T Assessment Form

Concept of Word in Text with Humpty Dumpty

Name *Drake*   Date *4/11* Teacher *Smith*

	Pointing	Word ID	Word List	
<u>Humpty</u> Dumpty sat on a <u>wall</u>	6	(2) ✓	on	✓
Humpty Dumpty had a <u>great</u> fall	6	(1) ✓	Humpty	✓
All the <u>king's</u> horses	6	(1) ✓	put	*but*
And all the king's <u>men</u>	6	(1) ✓	horses	—
Couldn't <u>put</u> Humpty together again	5	(1) ✓	sat	✓
			men	✓
			king's	✓
			wall	✓
			had	*has*
			fall	✓
Totals	5.8/6	6/16	7/10	

COW-T: Developing   Rudimentary   (Firm)

Source: Based on PALS Quick Checks. University of Virginia.

MODEL FINGERPOINT READING. Once students know the selection verbatim, use the printed text as you follow this sequence:

- Model how to point to the words while reciting the rhyme.
- Echo read the selection while pointing to each word, line by line. Say "Now we will take turns reading each line. First, I'll read a line and touch each word. Then you will read the same line and touch each word. Ready?"
- Ask the class to join in as you read it chorally. Say, "Now let's read it together. Eyes on the page. Read it with me as I point to each word."

ASSESS. Invite individual children to solo read the selection. Prompt by saying "This time I want you to do what I did. Be sure to touch each word as you say it." Observe each child's pointing. Do they have directionality? Are they pointing to stressed syllables or to separate words regardless of the number of syllables? Do they get off track on two-syllable words? Do they treat articles and prepositions as if they were part of the following noun? The answers to these questions (along with the additional information gathered as described next) will help you determine whether a child is still developing or if that student has a rudimentary or firm COW-T. Figure 6.9 shows an example of the recording form. You can find a template for the form in Appendix A.

ASSESS WORD IDENTIFICATION IN CONTEXT. To assess word identification in context, point to selected words and ask "What word is this?" Students who have to voice point to identify words are probably still developing a COW-T. Students who can identify most words in context immediately, without voice pointing, may do so by using their automatic knowledge of beginning letters and sounds. These students most likely have at least a rudimentary COW-T, and you should assess word identification out of context.

ASSESS WORD RETENTION OUTSIDE OF CONTEXT. If a child is successful at identifying words in context, try assessing words in isolation. Use the word list in Appendix A for "Humpty Dumpty" or select about five to 10 words (both content words and high-frequency words) and write them on a list or on little cards. Point to or hold up each word and ask the child to read them in isolation—without looking back at the context. Remember, don't expect them to decode unknown words at this point by sounding them out. You are assessing whether they know the word at first sight, so only show the word for a few seconds. Record substitutions and note the similarities to the target word. For example, a child might say *has* for *had* or *five* for *fall*. Such errors show that the child is using at least partial alphabetic clues to identify the word. If the child doesn't know the word, you may want to ask him or her to match the word card back to its counterpart in the text. Once the match is made, ask, "How did you know that was the same word?" Continue to ask until the student can tell you that he or she used the first letter and beginning sound as clues to identify the word. Students with a firm COW-T will remember many of the words from a familiar selection when they see them in isolation and will be able to identify them immediately without having to match them back into context.

The Phonological Awareness Literacy Screening for Kindergarten (PALS-K) (Invernizzi, Juel, Swank, & Meier, 2008) uses seven out of 10 words immediately identified in isolation (without decoding) as a criterion, along with perfect fingerpointing and word identification in context, for determining a firm COW-T. The PALS Quick Checks for COW-T Development also contain seven public domain rhymes, picture support for memorization, and scoring rubrics (Invernizzi, 2010).

Classroom Organization in PreK and Kindergarten Settings

In the introduction to this book, we saw how Jackie Dagenet's preK duck theme integrated components of the literacy diet, including vocabulary and concept development, alphabet knowledge, phonological awareness, letter–sound knowledge, and concepts of word and print—all aspects of the literacy diet. Her students sang, waddled, and acted out the song "Five Little Ducks." They read and reread a few lines of the text, pointing along at the words and focusing on letters and beginning sounds. They listened to and talked about other books featuring ducks, and they drew pictures of ducks. Many of the reading and word study activities taking place were connected to the theme that was introduced with oral language experiences. Throughout this book, you have met some of our favorite teachers and have seen how they implement particular components of the literacy diet. In this chapter we widen the lens to investigate how teachers organize their classrooms for instruction.

In the photo at the beginning of this chapter, we see Kilee Christnagel as both she and her student teacher provide literacy instruction in small groups. Kilee is a full-day kindergarten teacher who organizes the literacy diet into a reading block in the morning that includes guided reading and word study, and a writing block in the afternoon. In her guided reading group, she is able to focus in on students who are at a similar developmental level, and she provides

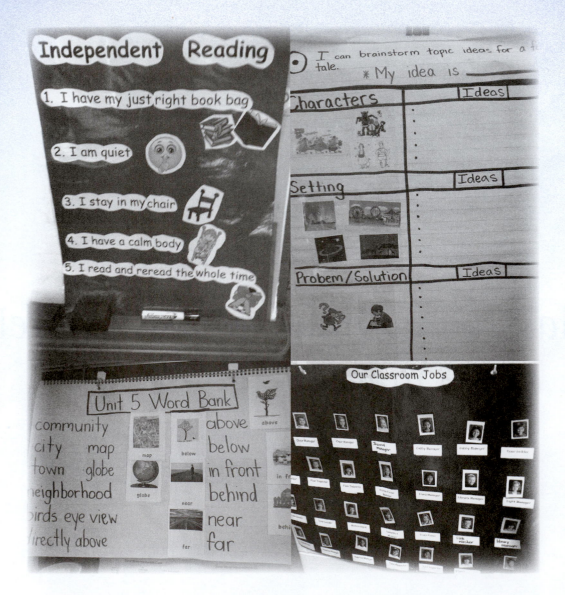

them with support at their "just-right level." Elsewhere in the classroom, children are rereading entries in their personal readers and other familiar reading materials, and listening and responding to books on tape.

There are various reading and writing activities each day that revolve around a theme, and you might hear students using their home languages as they talk about what they are learning. Visitors to this kindergarten classroom see books and charts everywhere. There are books in the classroom library, on the easel in the circle area, in the listening center, and in play centers. On a recent visit to Kilee's class, many charts were on display in this print-rich classroom. Some describe the daily routines, and others describe what students are learning in their studies. The photo collage shows some of the charts you would see in this kindergarten classroom:

- *Job responsibilities chart.* The children's names are inserted below each job. Responsibilities include managing the chairs, journals, library, lights, and cubbies. Other jobs are door holder, sink washer, plant tender, meteorologist, line leader, and floor inspector.

- *Charts for routines and behavior.* There are charts with steps for the daily schedule, expectations for group behavior, morning check-in, rules for lining up, ways to greet your teacher, and a short list of classroom rules that each student has signed. There is also a voice chart that explains the level of voice students can use: "4—Outside Voice, 3—Entire class can hear you, 2—Only people near you can hear, 1—Whisper, 0—No talking, no sound." Several charts include pictures to provide a visual cue to support the print. There is also a pocket chart with assignments for each group during the literacy block.

- *Word bank charts.* Kilee posts charts that list key words and phrases that students have studied and that they use in their writing. For example, there is a word bank chart for writing about birthdays. Another chart lists words related to the community theme, including the content words on the left side of the chart as well as general academic words and phrases on the right.

- *"I can" charts.* There are also charts that chronicle what students are learning in their thematic studies: "I can identify natural and human-made features"; "I can brainstorm topic ideas for a fairy tale"; and "I can describe different ways people learn about the past." Using this framework, children generate ideas for their own tales.

Implementing the Balanced Literacy Diet

PD **pd** TOOLKIT™
for Words Their Way®

On the PDToolkit, several teachers have shared ways they organize instruction. Click the Video tab, choose either Emergent Stage or Letter Name–Alphabetic, and scroll to find "Classroom Organization with Students in the Emergent Stage," "Classroom Organization with Students in the Letter Name–Alphabetic Stage," or "Weekly Schedules and Classroom Activities in the Letter Name–Alphabetic Stage."

The job of an early childhood educator is not only to reveal the alphabetic code of English to children, but also to help them put this new knowledge into practice by structuring daily in-class opportunities to read, write, and spell for authentic purposes. Roskos and Neuman (2001) encourage early childhood educators to see beyond simply "adding" things to the classroom space, and reflect on how physical and social supports work together to guide literacy development. Young children bring a natural curiosity to the classroom, and they are eager to use books and their newly acquired writing knowledge to learn and communicate with others and make sense of the world. The job of the teacher of young children is to help that enthusiasm become productive early literacy learning. In this section, we guide you to integrate the research-based practices discussed throughout this text into your planning and classroom organization.

Young children learn best when the curriculum is presented at their level of understanding and when classroom routines are clear and developmentally appropriate. The informal assessments that have been discussed throughout this text will help you plan the content of your curriculum. Your students' developmental literacy levels will likely vary significantly, so it is important to plan for small-group instruction that helps students build on their emerging capabilities, no matter where they are starting. When students are not working with an adult, they can engage in familiar tasks that they have practiced before. In partnerships or on their own, young children who have been taught a set of independent activities and routines can spend their time engaged in learning.

Organizational Elements for Literacy

Organizing print-rich classrooms in which students follow consistent routines and engage in meaningful literacy activities takes time and planning. Classroom organization cannot be purchased at the educational supply store! Teachers are constantly working to integrate the elements of the literacy diet as described throughout this text, while balancing how to work with small groups at their instructional level and make sure other students experience productive independent time.

Classroom organization is about how space, time, and interactions are structured in the classroom. Teachers take stock of the physical space and the key areas of their classrooms, and build workspaces and daily schedules. Coordination of space, time, and interactions with students is the mortar that holds all of the bricks of classroom life together. Throughout this chapter, we will describe five essential elements to include when organizing your classroom. Literacy learning takes place in (1) print-rich classrooms and (2) during the language arts block, of course, but is also integrated into (3) classroom routines, (4) units of study, and (5) centers, as summarized in Table 7.1.

The Print-Rich Classroom

A print-rich environment welcomes children into the world of literacy. They are invited to read texts of many kinds; write to share their ideas; and use letters, words, sentences, and stories to communicate and learn with others. When you walk into a classroom, it should be evident whether it is a print-rich environment. There will be many interesting things to read; access to a variety of writing materials; and meaningful lists, charts, or directions. The walls and surfaces in an exemplary literacy preK or kindergarten classroom are seen as instructional space to encourage interaction with print. Display a variety of printed resources around the room, but be sure that the print serves a real purpose and does not simply become clutter. Later in this chapter, we provide an extensive checklist of what you might find in a print-rich early literacy classroom. Here are some essentials:

- Alphabet charts can be colorful and fun and can be useful in a variety of places—not just posted over the board. Display at least one alphabet chart, posted at a level where children can easily touch the letters. Include a chart or alphabet strips in the writing center. If you have students learning English as a new language, it is helpful for them to have consistent and easy-to-understand pictures to represent the words of the alphabet.

TABLE 7.1	Five Elements of Organization

- **Print-rich classrooms.** Literacy is fully integrated in all areas and activities.
- **Classroom routines.** Students need to know how and when to do things, and many of these routines incorporate literacy for practical purposes.
- **Thematic units.** Students are actively involved in activities that are authentic studies relating to a concept or learning focus.
- **Language arts block.** Whole-group literacy activities introduce the literacy curriculum and materials that students will study more carefully in small, teacher-guided groups.
- **Literacy and dramatic play/learning centers.** There are special areas for students to read and write and use literacy materials.

- Word walls are a type of alphabet chart with children's names and other useful words. In kindergarten, a word wall will encourage students to have access to the important beginning sight words they are learning, and will help them write letters, messages, or stories using their peers' names. Consider posting the words in such a way that children can take them down to copy them, sort them, or work with them in various ways. This can be accomplished by attaching magnets to the back of each card or placing an extra copy of the word in a paper pocket. Pocket charts can also be a great way to display important words.

See Chapter 6 for ideas about how to "do" a word wall.

- The daily schedule, calendar, job chart, and classroom reminders such as rules and procedures should be referred to throughout the day as a way to help children understand how print serves many practical functions.

- Children's work should be displayed prominently. Jackie creates a space on her bulletin board for each child so parents and friends know where to look for current writing and artwork. Photos are also posted of the child, sometimes with dictations that describe what they were doing when the photo was taken.

- Display books you have read aloud or books that you plan to read to build anticipation. Children should always be given access to books you have read to them so they can look through them on their own. You may want to have a special place to display such books. Books that relate to a particular theme or unit of study may be placed in a center. Share your own love of books and treat them as valued objects. Take the time to model and talk to children about how to care for books, how to turn the pages, and how to store the books properly. Books should be displayed with the cover facing out. A number of creative solutions for displaying books can be found at the hardware store, including the use of rain gutters or wooden molding that has a small lip for books to rest on. Simple stands that hold decorative plates can also be used to display books.

Room Organization

Effective room design helps students to get materials easily and safely without disturbing others, increases time on learning activities, allows the teacher to move around and work with all students, and allows children to operate independently while engaging in a print-rich environment (Belvel, 2010; Cambourne, 1988; Kohn, 1996). Planning ahead to provide easy access to materials and to arrange classroom spaces for whole-group time, small-group lessons, and independent reading and writing is important for preventing confusion or distraction later (Evertson, 1987). Room design helps support small-group differentiated instruction for Kilee while the rest of her class is engaged in independent reading activities.

A reading center, a writing center, a listening center, computers, smart boards, or electronic tablets should be available for guided literacy activities and independent practice. In addition, an area of the classroom can be used for dramatic play to encourage learning about the world as well as developing language and early literacy skills. This area may rotate among a series of mini-environments such as home, the post office, a police station, a doctor's office, a restaurant, a fire station, or other environments related to your classroom studies. Then, literacy-related items, such as signs, menus, and notepads, can be brought into the play area so that students are reading and writing as they engage in thematic learning (Schickedanz, 1999). Centers are part of the print-rich environment but will be described in more detail later in this chapter.

8:30		Breakfast/Jobs
9:00		Morning Meeting
9:20		Writer's Workshop
9:55		Math Workshop
10:40		Art
11:40		Lunch
12:15		Reader's Workshop
1:15		Recess
1:50		Social Studies
2:20		Active Learning
2:45		Clean up/Peace Paws
3:05		Dismissal

Kindergarten teachers need to think ahead about having enough table or floor space to accommodate all of the students and their assigned literacy tasks. Materials should be spread around the room so that there is not a crunch for access as students begin their work. In kindergarten classrooms, teachers are also likely to have leveled boxes of books in their library so that students can easily access texts of a range of difficulty. The photo at left shows two students in Kilee's kindergarten classroom as they read a book together. You can see how she provides plenty of leveled (and nonleveled!) reading materials, as well as a word wall to post the sight words students are learning.

Materials

To support the engaging activities that will take place during literacy learning, the early childhood classroom teacher needs to be a good scavenger and collector of reading and writing materials. Some of these materials will last for years, such as books for the classroom library and alphabet puzzles. Other materials, such as book-making materials or magazine pictures for writing projects, are used up as students create projects or messages. In addition to a wide variety of books and other print materials, a well-equipped early literacy classroom has plenty of writing tools such as pencils, crayons, and markers and a range of materials for students to write on for a variety of purposes, including book making, letter writing, and note taking. Paper, staplers, glue, old magazines to cut up, rubber stamps, stickers, scissors, envelopes, and post-office paraphernalia add to the excitement of the writing center. Props such as pointers, clipboards, pocket charts, an author's chair, and cozy furniture also support an interest in reading. For language development, think about having flannel board or pocket chart materials that have pictures of the characters from familiar stories and songs such as "Old MacDonald Had a Farm."

There are ways to access many of these hands-on materials for little cost, such as looking for recycled materials, asking for materials from parents or the community, spending discretionary supply funds wisely, and applying for small materials grants. Many corporations and nonprofit organizations are anxious to support early literacy learning with donations of children's books. Don't be afraid to ask around—you may be surprised what will come your way when others know that you need it!

Integrating Language and Literacy into Daily Routines

Preschool and kindergarten classrooms present endless opportunities for children to engage in literacy and language activities for practical and social purposes. From morning check-in to following the daily agenda, reading and writing opportunities abound. Students can sign up for classroom activities, check out materials, or record lunch choices. Some of these processes can help the classroom work in a more orderly fashion as children take responsibility for managing materials and completing tasks. In Jackie's classroom, the class guinea pig becomes the center of numerous literacy experiences, such as procedure charts, sign-up lists, and displays of information. By building on what students want to know, Jackie motivates them to interact with print in a purposeful way.

Table 7.2, based on a list created by Jackie, presents examples of how literacy practices can be implemented in daily tasks throughout the school day. This list does not include specific literacy activities such as those described in the content chapters of this text, but instead focuses on routines that take place all year. Children need lots of modeling and support to master these routines, but they should gradually be given more responsibility. For example, at first you may use photographs instead of, or in addition to, printed labels for supply areas; these can be cut back over time so that children come to rely on the print itself.

TABLE 7.2 **Daily Routines for Literacy and Language Development**

Arrival

- Have the children sign in every day to facilitate attendance checking. The procedure evolves across the year, moving from simply findings one's name card in a pocket chart to writing one's name on a clipboard.

- Let the children make their own lunch choices using pictures and labels. Again, this changes from simply using a name card to signing one's name to indicate a choice.

- When there is a waiting list for favorite activities or centers, have the children sign up.

- Keep personal items in baskets or cubbies and make the children responsible for finding their own cubbies each day by identifying their names.

- Greet each child individually with "Good morning. How are you today?" and expect them to use a similar pattern of greeting in return. Ask questions to facilitate conversations.

Breakfast and Lunch Times

- If food is served in the room, post a sign to indicate when breakfast or lunch is ready. One side reads "open" and the other reads "closed." If children inquire about whether it is time to eat, refer them to the sign.

- Post choices of cereal, juice, or other options so the children can decide in advance what they want to eat. If they chose as they signed in earlier, refer them to the sign-in list when it's time for them to pick up their food and drink.

- When the children ask for help opening milk, juice, or other containers, point out the instructions (e.g., "open here").

- Post signs indicating where trash and recycling should be placed.

- Have adults in the classroom (teachers, teacher assistants, and parent volunteers) spread around to different tables to engage the children in conversation. Encourage the children to talk to each other. Meals are a time to model forms of friendly verbal exchanges.

Morning Group Time

- Go over the attendance record, reading all the names, to determine who is present and absent.

- Teach the children to turn and greet their neighbors and engage in a brief interchange that is first modeled by the teacher. Children might be taught greetings in different languages, especially if children in the class speak those languages.

- Refer to posted schedules and job charts to orient children to the day's activities and responsibilities.

- Share items from a morning newspaper related to the weather, interesting pictures, local events, and so forth.

- Check the calendar for special events such as birthdays. Calendar activities can include reciting the days of the week and the months of the year and looking for words on the calendar. For example, point to Wednesday and ask what day of the week starts with *W*. Remember to keep calendar time short and active.

- Read at least one book.

- Refer to printed charts as children recite rhymes, sing songs, or review daily reminders.

Transitions

- Line the children up or move them to centers in various ways. For example, instruct them to "Stand up if your name [starts with a particular sound or letter, or rhymes with a given word]."

- Draw name cards to indicate who can transition.

- Refer to sign-up procedures to see who goes to certain centers.

- Use "Closed" or "Under Construction" signs to indicate centers that are not available.

- Use a stop sign to indicate where the children line up to wait for a turn.

- Sing familiar songs or recite poems as you wait for all students to transition to the rug for whole-group time.

- Read a short, familiar book to lure students to group time.

Clean Up Routines

- Post a chart showing the steps children must follow as they wash their hands, and refer to it as needed. Use pictures and labels.

- Refer to posted jobs when a specific helper is needed. Over time, expect the children to help each other identify helpers.

- Encourage the children to use posted labels when they put materials away. Be ready to model how to create these labels when a new one is needed.

Rest Time

- Post a chart that shows the items children need for rest time: a cot or mat, covers, or a book to look at. Refer to the chart regularly.

- Assign the children a number (posted at their cubby) that corresponds to a cot or mat, a cover, and a designated area of the classroom. It is their responsibility to find their cot and cover, to place it in the designated area, and to return things to the storage area after rest time.

- Have adults in the classroom (teachers, teacher assistants, and parent volunteers) move about during rest time to read quietly to individual children. Children who do not sleep can look at books alone.

Preparing to Go Home

- Review the events of the day with "What do you want to tell your family about today?" This might be the time of the day to write a daily message together or write individual messages to take home. It can also simply be an oral rehearsal to help children answer that inevitable question, "What did you learn in school today?"

- Create a folder or notebook for each child that can go back and forth every day. This serves as a way to communicate with parents and keep materials organized. The folder can hold special messages (that are read to the children) as well as printed copies of songs and rhymes the children are learning. In kindergarten, such folders might include simple homework assignments such as repeating a picture sort done in the classroom.

- Allow children in kindergarten to take home their personal readers at least once a week.

- Let the children check out books to take home. This is especially important if your school library has limits on the number of books children can check out each week. Frequent book check-outs help children experience many new books on a regular basis.

Classroom Procedures and Expectations

Creating a well-organized classroom environment goes a long way toward helping students succeed academically (Evertson, 1987). Children who know what they should be doing when, have the appropriate materials, and are not wasting too much time during transitions spend more time on the productive academic tasks that lead to learning (LePage, Darling-Hammond, Akar, Gutierrez, Jenkins-Gunn, & Rosebrock, 2005). In addition to setting up an organized physical environment, it is also important to clearly communicate the procedures and expectations for how students should be participating in learning activities and interacting with materials (Belvel, 2010). Modeling procedures and setting clear expectations are useful for all students, but are especially helpful to children who may be less accustomed to school environments or students who are learning English as a new language. Procedures can cover a range of classroom activities, such as participation in morning meeting, what to do during independent reading, use of the writing center, or how to operate the listening center.

Simple routines can be posted and referred to regularly. The morning check-in chart hanging in Kilee's kindergarten classroom illustrates what students do when they arrive in the morning. She models and practices these activities with children for many days until they learn the routine well. The easy-to-read chart with pictures serves as an ongoing reminder in case anyone forgets the procedure. The chart also becomes a way to keep classroom talk positive; if students are not behaving appropriately, a teacher can point to the chart to guide them to "what they should be doing now."

To write procedures for young children, remember to think about your expectations regarding *where* students will work, *how many* will work together, *what* particular behaviors will be needed, and *what* they will accomplish. Keep phrases as simple and clear as possible, and use icons or photos to show what you mean. Jackie uses photographs she has taken of the children to illustrate the charts she prepares for daily routines and center directions. If you find that students are having difficulty being independent at a certain center, it is probably time to review and practice the procedures with the group. If difficulties persist, you may need to simplify the tasks at the center. Smoothly running centers are key to free up the teacher to work with small groups in order to teach the students at their varying developmental levels.

Integrating Literacy into Units of Study

A meaningful way to structure the classroom learning environment for young students is to present the curriculum in units of study, or themes. Children are interested in themselves, their families and friends, animals, nature, how machines work, and much more. One of the reasons that thematic studies work well is because they represent concrete experiences, people, places, or things in the real world. The letter *D* and the sound /f/ are abstract concepts that young children are not likely to see as important in and of themselves. But learning how to care for a pet, creating a shopping list and going to the store, and keeping track of the weather are intrinsically meaningful to children. Therefore, one of the goals of early literacy instruction is connecting letters, sounds,

reading, and writing to purposeful tasks in the real world. Besides its value in literacy instruction, "out-of-school" knowledge is also valuable for its own sake, giving young children skills that will be useful in their home lives.

In Jackie's preschool class, the children study birds and their nests, and the teacher brings in books and real objects to connect literacy with world knowledge. Similarly, in Kilee's kindergarten class, students learn about weather and the snow that has piled up outside their classroom window. They read books and write about their own experiences with the wintery weather that is so much a part of their daily lives.

Purposeful literacy tasks that connect especially well to units of study include the following:

- Reading to get information about a topic
- Writing notes about a topic
- Writing letters to someone who knows about a particular topic
- Making shopping lists or lists of suggestions
- Creating informational posters
- Creating dictations of content information that have been learned
- Looking at books about the topic with a friend for enjoyment
- Following a recipe
- Following a how-to chart to create something
- Reading and singing the words to a thematic song
- Dramatizing an event being studied
- Inviting students' family members to tell, draw, or write about their experiences related to the theme being studied
- Making a class book about new learning to put in the book corner or share with families

When these purposeful literacy activities are used within a unit of study that is relevant to young learners, the classroom stage is set to motivate children to understand, try out, and independently practice their emerging reading and writing skills.

Planning the Language Arts Block

When planning the language arts block of your classroom program, you may feel like you need a long menu of mini-activities; we suggest creating a regular weekly routine that revolves around a unit of study that brings together the short instructional activities. This thematic hub could be related to the content of your current science or social studies curriculum, or a concept in math or literature. Examples of themes for preK and kindergarten classrooms include using the senses, community helpers, geometric shapes, and fairy tales. Words related to this topic should be used to do a concept sort, phonological awareness activities, and alphabet or letter–sound study. Texts related to the topic should be used for lessons that develop concept of word in print. And literature can be connected to your unit of study. Some of these activities should follow the whole-to-part instructional sequence outlined in Chapter 6.

In the following example, a group of four- to five-year-old preschoolers is learning about one of the early childhood life sciences principles: that living things have basic needs. To make this more understandable to the students, the teacher has organized a study of pets. In addition to conducting several science lessons in which students gather and record information using their senses, the teacher also connects the weekly language arts activities to the topic. Over the course of a week, the teacher will involve students in multiple opportunities for concept sorting, playing with sounds, learning about the alphabet, reading and writing connected text to develop concept of word, and making connections to quality literature and nonfiction books. A simplified version of her week's plans is outlined in Table 7.3.

TABLE 7.3 **A Sample Week Focused on "Pets as Living Things"**

1. *Concept sort.* Animals can be sorted as pets or not pets. The teacher first conducts the sort in a whole-group setting, sharing pictures of a number of animals that are common pets and some that would not be good pets. Students practice new vocabulary words as the pictures are introduced, and the group discusses each animal and why it would make a good pet or not. As a follow-up throughout the week, students use small picture cards to do their own pet/not pet sorts.

2. *Phonological awareness activities.* As described in Chapter 3, there are many different ways to play with the sounds of language in the early childhood classroom. Depending on students' developing understandings, activities might include listening for or producing rhyming words, hearing syllables in words, or identifying beginning sounds. In this sample week of study, the teacher invents a simple game using pictures of common pets such as a dog, cat, bird, and fish. Students play an "I like" game, in which they attempt to match pictures of objects that start the same as the pet. For example, the students might say "Dog likes to play with dirt: *dog-dirt.* Dog likes to play with doll: *dog-doll.* But dog does not like to play with book: *dog-book.*" Each day, the teacher chooses a different pet word and asks the students to listen to the beginning sound to see whether they match.

3. *Alphabet or letter study.* A number of alphabet activities take place on a regular basis in the classroom, including singing the alphabet song, playing with alphabet puzzles, and reading ABC books. This week, the teacher adds a font sort with *D* and *C* because of a focus on the words *dog* and *cat.* In this sort, students categorize *D*'s and *C*'s in a range of fonts to gain additional familiarity with these shapes throughout their world.

4. *Concept of word.* The teacher uses connected texts to develop concept of word. Big books or pocket chart stories or rhymes are excellent ways to share books with students and help them memorize simple stories. With repeated readings, students get opportunities to practice left-to-right sweep, move from line to line, and point to individual words. This week, the teacher chooses a focus book with a simple rhyming pattern and an animal theme: *I Went Walking* by Sue Williams. Students read and point to words along with the teacher at first, and later read the memorized text on their own, getting practice in concept of word. The teacher also gives students a sheet for making their own story pages that use the sentence pattern "I saw a _____ looking at me." Each student draws an animal picture and does his or her best to fill in the blank. This page can be added to the students' personal readers to share with other students, teachers, and families.

5. *Literature connection.* Throughout the week, the teacher shares a number of informational texts related to what pets need to be healthy. She also has several books in her classroom and school library that touch on the theme of pets. Many of these read-aloud books provide a great opportunity to engage and motivate students about literacy and learn new concepts and vocabulary (see Chapter 1). One book that the teacher particularly enjoys sharing during this unit is *A Pet for Petunia* (by Paul Schmid), which is about a spunky girl who is obsessed with having a pet skunk. This book and others like it help the class laugh, build community, and experience the joy of books.

Organizing Centers

To keep your early literacy classroom active and focused on learning, it is essential to plan varied types of groupings throughout the day. Short whole-group lessons, well-paced small-group rotations, and opportunities for partner or independent exploration and practice will add up to an efficient use of instructional time throughout the day. If students are asked to spend too much time sitting and listening to the teacher talk, behavior management is likely to become an issue that may reduce quality instructional time. As experienced teachers of young students know, short, focused lessons followed by quick engagement activities such as songs, stretches, or games, will help the class stay attentive and focused on learning.

A great way to get beyond a reliance on whole-group lessons in your class is to organize centers. During center time, teachers can work with a small group of students with similar instructional needs while students who are not with the teacher can do independent, hands-on activities. Centers may focus specifically on literacy, or literacy may be incorporated into the centers through dramatic play. In Kilee's kindergarten class, students work in groups of about six students and rotate through a schedule that includes guided reading, word work,

TABLE 7.4	Independent Activities for Students during Literacy Center Time

Things to Do on Your Own or with a Partner

- Reread books from your personal reader, the book box, or the classroom library.
- Reread poems and songs on charts and in big books introduced in shared reading.
- Work with sentences and word cards in the pocket chart.
- Read the room—take a pointer and read everything you can around the room.
- Illustrate a response to a book you listened to or read.
- Write a story, book, or letter at the writing center.
- Hunt for letters or words you are studying around the room and in books.
- Complete word study sorts and extensions.
- Do an alphabet puzzle.
- Make letters or words with clay, pipe cleaners, or Wikki Stix.
- Write letters or words in salt or sand trays.
- Make words with letter tiles or magnetic letters.
- Write words you are learning on a small whiteboard.
- Listen to a story on the computer or disc player.
- Play literacy games on the computer.
- Match picture cards to words.
- Use props in the drama center to reenact familiar stories.

independent reading, listening center, and writing. The literacy centers provide meaningful practice for those students who are not in the small group that the teacher is currently working with. Table 7.4 lists some of the purposeful activities that students can be doing during literacy center time when they are not working with a teacher. During another part of the day, children go to dramatic play or learning centers such as the science station, housekeeping area, or sand table, where literacy is integrated in many ways.

Literacy Centers

Every classroom should have a reading center and a writing center that are available every day all year long. It is important, however, that the books and materials change every few weeks. These changes can reflect themes, seasons, or holidays. For example, in early February the writing center should be supplied with materials to make Valentines. If you have the space and furniture, you might set up designated areas of the classroom for centers, but this is not always possible. For example, Jackie does not have a designated writing center, but each day she brings out different materials for children to use at the same tables where they eat breakfast and lunch, and an adult is usually stationed there to interact with the children. Basic writing materials are kept in a central location where children can access materials to use in any center.

ALPHABET OR LETTER CENTER. An alphabet or letter center can include alphabet strips, plastic letters, alphabet books, and much more. See Chapter 2.

PHONICS/WORD STUDY CENTER. Some teachers place sorts in a center rather than giving every child a copy of a sort to cut out. Sorts can be stored in colored envelopes—using a different color for each developmental group—and reused over and over. Games and activities, like those described in Chapter 5, can be placed in the center to provide additional practice. Individual word study notebooks or folders that children paste, illustrate, or write their words in can also be stored in the center.

READING/LIBRARY CENTER.

A reading center is designed for students' independent exploration of books, and it encourages them to retell stories or information they have learned. In addition to a variety of interesting reading materials, there should be related materials such as flannel board pieces, puppets, or stuffed animals. These materials, as well as small photo cards or illustrations, stimulate language production and encourage children to sequence events or retell books they have heard. Students can also do buddy reading or share a book with a stuffed animal friend.

The reading center should be located in a quiet area and have comfortable seating such as beanbag chairs, child-sized furniture, pillows, and a rug. Display as many of the books' covers as possible so they attract students. Provide books that children can access easily in bins, baskets, or crates. These bins might be arranged by categories such as alphabet books, information books related to a particular theme, pattern books, or books by an author you are studying. Books that have recently been read aloud to children will be especially enticing for them to explore on their own. Copies of books made by the whole class or individual children are also sure to be well loved.

WRITING CENTER.

Children need opportunities to explore writing in many ways: letters, lists, stories, posters, and more. While writing "the best they can," children practice phonemic awareness, letter–sound knowledge, the alphabet, and their language skills. The writing center should have child-sized tables and chairs and a variety of materials for children to write: notepads, stationery, greeting cards, blank cards made from folded cardstock, envelopes, chalkboards, magic slates, magnetic drawing boards, or whiteboards. A variety of writing implements (e.g., pencils, colored pencils, pens, crayons, markers, and chalk) ensures that children have many ways to express themselves on paper. Although basics such as pencils and paper should always be available, rotating other materials throughout the year will keep the children interested.

It is helpful to have bins with children's journals nearby, as well as an alphabet poster or smaller alphabet cards and a chart with children's names and photos. Having word cards or a nearby word wall can also stimulate students' writing. Many teachers collect whatever materials they can scavenge for the writing center—from old catalogs, magazines, or stickers to use for illustrations, to rubber stamps with letters, dates, or pictures.

Finally, there are many materials that encourage bookmaking at the writing center: staplers, hole punches, blank paper, scissors, tape, and glue sticks. Small books can also be pre-made for students to fill in. Posted charts in the center can guide students to create a variety of mini-books by folding or stapling various sizes of paper. Many of these materials are included in the print-rich classroom checklist in table 7.8 on page 186.

LISTENING CENTER.

Set up a nook within the classroom where students can listen to audio books. Supply a tape player, CD player, tablet, or computer. Hang a procedure card nearby so that students know the proper steps in operating the machines. Provide multiple copies of the text and encourage students to follow along with the text as they listen. Encourage them to respond to the book after they have finished listening to it.

NAME CENTER.

Identify a spot to display the pictures and written names of students, teachers, and pets in the classroom. Provide name cards and pictures for children to match. Set up mailboxes and encourage children to leave messages or artwork for each other. (Empty beverage boxes from a grocery store work well when turned on their side, because they have internal dividers.)

TECHNOLOGY CENTER. A computer or tablet center is a ready-made spot to listen to stories, write or draw, play ABC games, and much more. Demonstrate and practice using the technology prior to expecting students to operate programs and devices on their own. This might be a good place to station a parent volunteer or "big buddy" to help solve technical issues. Because of this center's popularity, a waiting list to sign up will likely be a must!

Dramatic Play/Learning Centers

Thematic centers such as pretend restaurants, fire stations, post offices, and zoos are excellent opportunities for integrating meaningful literacy practices into the daily lives of preK or kindergarten children. In these areas, students work with classmates to accomplish tasks such as delivering pretend meals, mailing letters, or tending to animals. Brainstorm ways to bring in paper, pencils, books, or electronic notebooks that serve a meaningful purpose in these settings in the real world. Ideas for literacy materials for specific centers are suggested in Table 7.5.

TABLE 7.5 Literacy Materials in Dramatic Play/Learning Centers

Science

- Information books related to artifacts such as bones, plants, live animals, and insects
- Notebooks or notepads to write observations
- Charts to record changes in plant growth or results of experiments
- List of vocabulary words adults should use when talking with children at the center

Housekeeping

- Telephone and notepad with pencil and phone book (Children can make their own phone book.)
- Magazines, newspapers, catalogs, and other print found in the home
- Cookbooks and recipe cards (Supply simple cookbooks designed for children or involve the children in making their own cookbook.)
- Books about babies and families
- Empty food containers with labels typically found in a kitchen

Block Area

- Labeled shelves or bins with blocks, vehicles, figures, etc.
- Signs and materials for making signs (cardstock, markers, tape, popsicle sticks)
- Books about vehicles, buildings, and construction workers
- Pictures of buildings mounted and labeled to serve as ideas
- List of vocabulary words adults should use when talking with children at the center

Sand Table or Water Table

- Label bins for containers, figures, vehicles, etc.
- List of related vocabulary words (e.g., *sift*) adults should use when talking with children at the center

Retail Store or Shop

- Store-specific items such as empty food containers with labels for a grocery store (The store can change throughout the year and materials will change, depending on whether it is a flower shop, pet shop, barber shop, bookstore, etc.)
- Coupons
- Advertising flyers
- Price lists
- Receipt book

Post Office

- Envelopes and pretend postage stamps
- Rubber stamps
- Mailboxes for students and teachers

Medical Office, Hospital, or Veterinarian's Office

- Magazines or newspapers
- Posters of systems of the human body (e.g., skeletal, circulatory)
- Posters of various kinds of animals (for veterinarian's office)
- Reference books
- Literature about how to be healthy

Restaurant

- Coupons
- Menus and pads for taking orders
- Advertisements for foods
- Books about nutrition

It is very important that teachers and assistants circulate and take the time to sit and talk with children in these centers. Model things to do with the materials and engage the children in conversation as you introduce and reinforce relevant vocabulary. Some teachers post a list of key vocabulary words in the center as a reminder to use them in conversations with children. Take photos of children in the play centers, print them out, and mount them on paper. Then write a sentence dictated by the child about what he or she was doing. Post the photo dictations in the play centers or a bulletin board, or collect them in a book and read them frequently, to give other children ideas about what to make or do.

Creating a Learning Community

A key to establishing the kind of productive classroom environment we are describing in this chapter is ensuring that each child feels included and valued. Developing an inclusive learning community has been associated with higher performance, greater connectedness to peers and teachers, and fewer discipline problems (LePage et al., 2005; Hamre & Pianta, 2005). In such a community, students know that they are held to high standards, that they are missed when they are absent, and that the goal is for everyone to learn to the best of their abilities. When such an environment is established, students will keep each other on task, take on mentoring roles, and proudly share their accomplishments. Developing strong relationships with families aids in this effort.

The Classroom Community

How can a teacher encourage little ones to feel empowered as members of their classroom learning community? As described previously, an important step is to set up the physical environment and provide procedures so that materials are easy to access and take care of. When students learn how to appropriately use their classroom materials and are held accountable for respecting them, everyone becomes an "owner" of the class. If someone damages classroom materials, it is an affront to the whole community. Additionally, each member of the classroom must be held to the same high expectations. All students need an equal opportunity to experience engaging curricula, to share their voices in class, and to see their family backgrounds and cultures reflected in the classroom environment. If students speak languages other than English, these languages should be respected and viewed as an asset and part of the identity of the child (Helman, 2012).

A job chart is one way to allow all children to be "owners" of the class. Each child has a job every week, ranging from line leader to meteorologist to sink washer. By holding responsibility, each person feels important and contributes to the functioning of the class. It is one way to value everyone's participation in the classroom.

An important way to develop a classroom learning community is to make sure that there are strong student-to-student relationships as well as student-to-teacher relationships. These bonds are built in a number of ways, including making sure each member of the classroom feels safe, appreciated, and connected to others in the group. Table 7.6 provides some beginning ideas for how to strengthen these interpersonal relationships.

Extending the Community to Include Families

An important way to positively influence students' literacy learning is for teachers to engage with their families and caregivers to learn about what students bring to school and to share how families can support school-based learning. All families want the best for their children, and they will do what they can to support their success. In turn, educators

TABLE 7.6 **Ways to Build Relationships within the Classroom Community**

Help Students Connect to Each Other

- Learn and use each other's names
- Use collaborative learning strategies such as partner sharing
- Share affirmations when children help each other
- Maintain an atmosphere that is free of "put-downs"

Build Student-to-Teacher Bonds

- Greet individuals as they enter each day
- Show an interest in students' families and outside experiences
- Share personal experiences with students so they learn about you
- Show compassion and treat students equitably

Include Students' Languages and Cultures in Class

- Address differences in language and culture openly and positively
- Invite families and community representatives to share about their cultures
- Have some books and signs in students' home languages in the classroom
- Respect the cultural practices used in students' homes

Help Students Identify with the Whole School

- Introduce key members of the school team such as principal, secretary, specialist teachers, and facilities personnel
- Create support materials for learning the names of school personnel: matching photo and name cards, class books, or games
- Introduce and use the school mascot on classroom artifacts to ensure that students feel included as members of the larger community
- Participate in school-wide beautification projects such as cleaning up trash or decorating the hallways of the school

TABLE 7.7	Bi-Directional Connections between Families and Schools

FROM HOME TO SCHOOL	FROM SCHOOL TO HOME
Set up informal social events for families to come to school to share their ideas and talents.	Schedule family literacy nights for families to come to school to learn about reading and writing activities they can do at home.
Create structures for getting to know families, such as asking them to send in photographs, write in a class journal, or make an "all about me" page.	Create a take-home reading program for sharing books with families.
Attend family events involving your students so you can engage outside of school.	Send home a weekly alphabet or word study sort or game for families to play with their children.
Make home visits to get to know your students' families.	Provide interpreters for conferences and school meetings, and translate your classroom notes for families who speak languages other than English.

will do best when they welcome, honor, and connect with families around student learning (Mapp, 2003).

The good news for preK and kindergarten classrooms is that parents are often more present than at other grade levels. An early education teacher has a greater likelihood of meeting parents face to face. If this is the case in your school, you can take advantage of these opportunities by being approachable, taking time to share about what is going on with students in your class, and inviting parents to visit or participate in the classroom program. As you build connections with families, informally chat about the strengths of the children, and offer compliments and suggestions that will support each child's learning. If you don't speak the same language as the families of your students, consider bringing in a community liaison periodically at drop-off or pick-up time, or be brave in using nonverbal communication skills to share ideas.

Students will feel a greater sense of belonging in class if they know that their teachers and parents have similar goals for their learning. This partnership can be shared by accepting children's language attempts, having culturally representative materials on hand, and being interested in what children share in speech and writing about their families. A thematic unit (as described earlier in this chapter) on diverse families will go a long way to building a classroom community that is inclusive and respects where each child comes from.

Table 7.7 describes the two-way flow of information that is necessary to build on what students bring with them to school and enhance their academic progress. It is through strong bonds between teachers and families that young children receive a foundation for early language and literacy success.

Assessing the Physical Environment of Your Classroom

The materials and room arrangement of your classroom contribute immensely to children's access to literacy opportunities. Although no room will have every artifact we have discussed in this chapter, we do encourage you to use the print-rich classroom checklist in Table 7.8. It provides a quick overview of possible literacy support materials, and may help you self-evaluate and set next steps for your environment.

TABLE 7.8 **The Print-Rich Classroom Checklist**

Name _____ School _____ Date _____

Communication
____ Check-in area for parents
    ___ Message board for parents
    ___ Pens and paper to write messages such as notes for children
    ___ Mailboxes
____ Independent check-in area for children
    ___ Attendance or sign-in sheet
    ___ Lunch count
    ___ Sign-up sheet for centers or activities
    ___ Question of the day or choices to make
    ___ Mailboxes for each child
____ Daily schedule posted
____ Message board with classroom news
____ Other

Labels and Directions
____ Personalized storage for each child
____ Classroom supplies in labeled storage areas
____ Center signs and directions
____ Art work displayed and labeled
____ Phrases in other languages, such as greetings
____ Directions for standard routines such as washing up, rest time, or snack

Interactive Displays
____ Job charts
____ Calendar
____ Word wall
____ Pocket chart with sentence strips and word cards
____ Other

Literacy Displays
____ Alphabet strip
____ Color words
____ Number words
____ Seasonal or thematic words
____ Children's names
____ Children's writing
____ Interactive group writing
____ Charts or posters of rhymes and songs
____ Books used for recent read-alouds
____ Photos of children with dictated captions
____ Group dictations
____ Individual dictations
____ Pointers
____ Other

Class Library
____ Picture storybooks (record number for each)
____ Folktales and other traditional literature
____ Information books
____ Alphabet books and picture dictionaries
____ Poetry books
____ Wordless books
____ Leveled books for beginning readers
____ Magazines
____ Child-made books
____ Other

Reading Area
____ Quiet carpeted partitioned area
____ Comfortable soft seating
____ Recently read books available to look at
____ Books displayed with covers out
____ Book collections grouped and labeled by topic, genre, or author
____ Rotating displays or collections
____ Signs and posters that feature book titles or authors
____ Props to dramatize stories or encourage retellings (puppets, flannel board)
____ Check-out system to borrow books
____ Other

Centers
____ Signs
____ Books related to center themes
____ Phone book
____ Posters
____ Directions for use of center
____ Lists of related vocabulary words
____ Catalogs
____ Magazines
____ Writing supplies (notepads, pencils, markers, cardstock for signs)
____ Play money
____ Other

Writing Supplies Available for Children's Use at Centers or around Room
____ Journals stored for easy access
____ Access to computer and/or typewriter
____ Variety of paper (lined, unlined, colored, blank books, stationery, note cards)
____ Variety of writing surfaces (chalkboards, magic slates, whiteboards)
____ Variety of writing tools (markers, chalk, crayons, colored pencils, rubber stamps)
____ Bookmaking materials (stapler, hole punch, yarn, scissors, glue)
____ Clipboards
____ Other

TABLE 7.9 **Online Resources to Support Enhanced Literacy Environments**

WEBSITE NAME	DESCRIPTION
Center for Early Education and Development	Presents resources on child development and early literacy environments, including an overview of the Classroom Assessment Scoring System (CLASS) with videotaped examples.
National Association for the Education of Young Children	Website for the professional organization committed to bringing high-quality early education to young children. Offers standards and position statements, conferences, professional development opportunities, and publications.
Ontario Institute for Studies in Education, University of Toronto: The Balanced Literacy Diet	Provides a framework for understanding and teaching literacy, including at the preK and kindergarten levels. Includes virtual room tours, lessons, and video examples.
Phonological Awareness Literacy Screening, University of Virginia	Includes tools for assessment, activities for classrooms, and a guide to planning literacy workstations.

Another source of support for enriching your classroom environment is your state's educational standards document. These standards often include items relating to setting up the physical environment, promoting social development and a safe classroom community, using routines and procedures to support positive behaviors, and effectively using instructional time (*c.f.,* CA Commission on Teacher Credentialing, 2009). These classroom environment standards, along with your state's literacy standards, are a good place to begin to gather information about how to enhance what is going on within your classroom. In addition, a number of resources are available online to learn more about how to set up engaging literacy environments for your young students. Many of these sites offer video tours or photographs of actual classrooms that you can explore. Table 7.9 lists some of the sites you may want to explore.

In addition to our checklist and the online resources we have listed, various environmental surveys and checklists are available that can help you evaluate the quality of your early literacy environment. These checklists generally document aspects of the print-rich classroom and students' access to and interaction with materials (Wolfersberger, Reutzel, Sudweeks, & Fawson, 2004). Examples of these observation/survey tools include the Early Language and Literacy Classroom Observation (ELLCO) (Smith & Dickinson, 2002) and the Classroom Literacy Environmental Profile (CLEP) (Wolfersberger et al., 2004).

In this chapter, we have presented a number of examples and ideas for organizing your classroom to integrate a balanced literacy diet. Many aspects of early literacy learning—such as vocabulary and concept development, phonological awareness, print concepts, the alphabet and letter sounds, and concept of word in text—can come together through well-planned thematic lessons and a variety of whole-group, small-group, and independent activities. Taking the time to create routines and procedures that support a classroom in which students take responsibility and ownership is essential to this process. Making connections with families will increase buy-in from students, help you build on students' background knowledge, and extend academic learning beyond the school walls. Putting together all these pieces will help you create a research-based, developmentally appropriate, and engaging early literacy classroom community for your students.

APPENDIXES

....

Assessment Summary Sheet

Name _____ Date _____ Teacher _____

ALPHABET:
Recitation and Tracking observations:

ALPHABET RECOGNITION: Capitals	**ALPHABET RECOGNITION:** Lowercase
M P S O X N A F G K L T U C Y B I V D J E Q R Z H W	m p s o x n a f g k l t u c y b i v d j e q r z h w
Number correct _____ /26	Number Correct _____ /26

PHONOLOGICAL AWARENESS:

1A Syllable Sort _____ /10
1B. Rhyme Identification with Pictures _____ /9
2A. Syllable Segmentation _____ /8
2B. Rhyme Production _____ /8

---

1. cat _____	2. back _____	3. wet _____	4. hop _____
5. bug _____	6. will _____	7. king _____	8. tap _____

1C. Alliteration—Beginning sound match _____ / 8
1D. Segment sounds with counters _____ / 8
2C. Segment initial sound _____ / 8

2D. Spelling Task: Kindergarten Spelling Inventory

Initial Phonemes _____ / 5	Middle Phonemes _____ / 5	Final Phonemes _____ / 5	Total Phonetically Acceptable _____ / 15

CONCEPTS ABOUT PRINT:
See separate assessment form

PHONICS:
Beginning Consonant Sounds and Letters: _____ / 16
Primary Spelling Inventory: See feature guide

CONCEPT OF WORD:
Pointing score average: _____ / 6 _____ Developing (0–3) _____ Rudimentary (4–5) _____ Firm (6)
Word identification in context: _____ of _____ Word list identification: _____ of _____
Observations:

Alphabet Assessments

Alphabet Recitation and Tracking

Teach the alphabet song and sing it often. Slow it down and model pointing to the letters on a chart as it is sung. Observe to see who is able to sing along. Look for students who

- Know the song and handle *lmnop* in punctuated fashion
- Need the support of the group but can keep up
- Need more practice with the song

Assess students individually to see who can point accurately as they sing or recite the letters. Prepare an alphabet strip like the one on page 222.

INSTRUCTIONS   Ask students to touch and name each letter. Record the results on the Assessment Summary Sheet on page 190.

Alphabet Recognition: Capitals

To assess students' recognition of capital letters, pull students aside individually. Prepare a copy of page 192, or download an enlarged copy from the PDToolkit.

INSTRUCTIONS   Say to students, "Put your finger on each letter and say the name of the letter. Skip the letter if you do not know its name." As the children point and name the letters, record their responses on the Individual Assessment Summary Sheet. Indicate substitutions by writing in what the student says. If the child identifies *O* as "zero" or *I* as "one," ask the student what letter it could be. You can time students if you wish.

Note the ease with which students are able to name the letters. Do they respond quickly and confidently, or do they hesitate and perhaps recite the alphabet to help them recall the name of the letter? Students who score at least 16 are ready to be assessed on the lowercase recognition task that follows.

Benchmarks   At the end of preK, students on average know the names of 20 of the 26 capital letters. Kindergarten children usually know them all. Students who know more than nine letters can be considered ready to study beginning consonant sounds through picture sorts. The time it takes students to name the letters with benchmark accuracy may range from 20 to 40 seconds.

Alphabet Recognition: Lowercase

Use page 193 to assess students' knowledge of lowercase alphabet recognition, or download an enlarged copy from the PDToolkit. Record the results on the Assessment Summary Sheet. Pull students aside individually. You can time students if you want.

INSTRUCTIONS   Say, "Put your finger on each letter and say the name of the letter. Skip the letter if you do not know its name." As the children point and name the letters, record their responses. If the child identifies *l* as "one," ask the student what letter it could be. Write down what the student says if he or she makes a substitution such as *b* for *d*. Expect that reversals will be common with young children learning the lowercase letters.

Benchmarks   According to PALS benchmarks, kindergarten students on average know the names of 20 lowercase letters in the fall and all by spring. The time it takes students to name the letters with benchmark accuracy may range from 20 to 40 seconds.

Alphabet Production

If students seem to know most letters, you can ask them to write the alphabet without looking at a model to assess how well they can produce the letter forms. Note whether they write capitals, lowercase, or both.

Alphabet Recognition: Capitals

M P S O X

N A F G K

L T U C Y

B I V D J

E Q R Z H

W

Alphabet Recognition: Lowercase

m p s o x

n a f g k

l t u c y

b i v d j

e q r z h

w

Assessments for Phonological Awareness

Children are not likely to be successful with these assessments until they have seen them modeled and participated in similar activities such as those described in Chapter 3.

1A: Syllable Sort

INSTRUCTIONS   Make a copy of the sort on page 198.

Model   Lay out the numbers and explain that they will stand for the number of syllables in a word. Pick up the picture of the kitten and say "Listen: *kit-ten.*" Tap or clap as you say the syllable. "When I say *kitten,* I hear two syllables, so I will put this under the number 2. I will do another one." Pick up the picture of the motorcycle and say "Listen to the syllables in motorcycle: *mo-tor-cy-cle.*" Tap or clap as you say each syllable. "I hear four syllables, so I will put it under the number 4."

Your Turn   Name each picture and clap out the syllables; then put the picture under the number of syllables it has. Count the number of correct responses in the next 10 choices. Record the score on the Assessment Summary Sheet.

2	3	4
kitten	kangaroo	motorcycle
zipper	umbrella	thermometer
turtle	newspaper	watermelon
pencil	ladybug	

2A: Syllables Segmentation (Oral Production Task)

INSTRUCTIONS

Model   "I am going to say a word and break it into syllables as I clap. Let me show you with the word *zipper.* Break the word *zip-per* as you clap each syllable. *Zipper* has two syllables. Let me show you another one. I will say the word slowly and break it into syllables: *yes-ter-day.* Clap for each syllable.

Your Turn   "Now I want you to do the same thing. I will say a word. You break it into syllables and clap for each syllable."

   Say each word below. Record the number correct on the Assessment Summary Sheet. If the child cannot do the first few items, do not continue.

   1. peppermint (3)   2. birthday (2)   3. kindergarten (4)   4. table (2)

   5. october (3)   6. funny (2)   7. whisper (2)   8. celebrate (3)

1B: Rhyme Identification with Pictures

Make a copy of the assessment on page 199 for each student. Fold it in half so that only one side shows at a time. You can conduct this individually or in small groups. Enter the score on the Assessment Summary Sheet.

INSTRUCTIONS

Model Tell the child that you want him or her to find some rhyming words. First, demonstrate the procedure by modeling with the first item. "Put your finger on the picture of the duck. Next to the duck is a ball and a truck. What are the two pictures that rhyme? Listen: *duck, ball truck*. Which ones rhyme or sound the same at the end? *Duck* and *truck* rhyme. Circle the two pictures that rhyme." Help students complete the sample item.

Your Turn "Now you will put a circle around the others that rhyme on your own. Look at the bear, the keys, and the cheese. Circle the two things that rhyme. Listen: *bear, keys, cheese*. Circle the two that rhyme." Name the pictures each time for students to be sure they use the correct labels and guide them in the completion of this assessment.

Record the number correct on the Assessment Summary Sheet. If the child cannot do the first few items, do not continue. The picture words used in the Rhyme Identification assessment are as follows. The first row (marked with an *) is the practice rhyme done in the Model step. Correct responses are underlined.

*duck	ball	truck
1. bear	keys	cheese
2. bed	bread	sock
3. mop	jar	shop
4. box	bell	shell
5. bug	rug	cat
6. snake	cake	fish
7. feet	pan	man
8. clock	rock	fan
9. star	glass	car

2B: Rhyme Production (Oral)

INSTRUCTIONS

Model "I am going to ask you to think up some rhyming words. Listen while I do one. The word is *jump*. I need to think of a word that rhymes with *jump*. *Jump, bump*. Can you think of one? What else would rhyme with jump?" Give feedback. "Yes, *dump* rhymes with *jump*." "Let's try another one. The word is *rock*. What rhymes with *rock*? *Rock* and *sock* rhyme. Can you think of one?" Give feedback. If the child is successful, continue with the assessment.

Your Turn "Listen to the word I say. Tell me a word that rhymes with it."

1. cat
2. back
3. wet
4. hop
5. bug
6. will
7. king
8. tap

Record responses on the Assessment Summary Sheet. Accept nonsense words such as *gat* for *cat*.

1C: Alliteration—Beginning Sound Match

Make a copy of the assessment on page 200 for each student. You can conduct this individually or in small groups. Do not do it immediately after the rhyme assessment, because students will find it confusing to shift their attention to the beginning of the word after listening to the end. Enter the score on the Assessment Summary Sheet.

INSTRUCTIONS

Model "We are going to find pictures that begin with the same sound. Let's do one together. Put your finger on the sun. Say the word *sun*. Now look at the pictures beside the sun. Say them with me: *book, soap, jet*. Which one begins with the same sound as *sun*? *Sun* and *soap* begin with the same sound. They begin with /s/." Say the sound, not the letter. "Circle the picture that begins with the same sound as the first picture." Help the children complete the sample item.

Your Turn "You are going to do the rest by yourself, but we will name the pictures together." Name the rest of the pictures to be sure they use the correct labels and guide them in the completion of this assessment. Say the words naturally and do not overly elongate the initial sound. Record the number of correct responses on the Assessment Summary Sheet.

The picture words are as follows. Correct responses are underlined.

*sun	book	<u>soap</u>	jet
1. nose	fan	kite	<u>nine</u>
2. rabbit	<u>rug</u>	dog	leaf
3. lamp	cat	toes	<u>log</u>
4. watch	<u>web</u>	zero	van
5. belt	kitten	yoyo	<u>bird</u>
6. pie	<u>pig</u>	ball	gum
7. zebra	key	<u>zipper</u>	hand
8. dog	jet	leaf	<u>desk</u>

2C: Segment Initial Sound (Oral)

INSTRUCTIONS

Model "I am going to say a word and listen for the first sound. The word is *five*. I say the word slowly and listen for the first sound: *fffffffive*. *Five* start with /f/." Say the sound, not the letter. "You try one. Say the word *wet*. What is the first sound you hear in *wet*?" Give feedback and assistance as needed.

Your Turn "I will say a word. Then you say the word again and tell me the first sound you hear."

Say each word below naturally. Do not draw out the first sound. Record the number correct on the Assessment Summary Sheet. If the child cannot do the first few items, do not continue.

What is the first sound you hear in . . .

1. soap
2. duck
3. mouse
4. fire
5. book
6. jump
7. give
8. nose

1D: Segment Sounds with Counters

INSTRUCTIONS   You will need four chips, blocks, or some other counter for the child to push for each sound. Do not name letters—only say the sounds.

Model   "I am going to say a word and listen for all the sounds. As I say the word and break it into sounds, I will push a counter for each sound I hear. The word is toe: /t/ /o/. *T-oooe.* I hear two sounds in *toe,* so I push two counters: one for /t/ and the other for /o/. Let me do another one. The word is *stop. Sssss-t-ooooo-p.* I hear four sounds in *stop,* so I'll push four counters: /s//t//o//p/."

Your Turn   "I will say a word. Then you say the word and break it into sounds as you push a counter for each sound."

Say each word below naturally. Do not break them into sounds. Record the number correct on the Assessment Summary Sheet. If the child cannot do the first few items, do not continue.

1. sun (3)
2. zoo (2)
3. mat (3)
4. nest (4)
5. hoe (2)
6. flag (3)
7. rug (3)
8. sled (4)

2D: Spelling Task

Use the Kindergarten Spelling Inventory (KSI) (page 209) to assess the ability to segment the sounds in words. This task demands more than phonemic awareness because children also have to produce letters and match those letters to sounds. But any child who represents the sounds in a logical way has the requisite phonemic awareness. For children who know their letters, a phonetic spelling task is an excellent way to assess their phonemic awareness.

You may also use the Primary Spelling Inventory (PSI), but it does not give credit for logical substitutions that indicate a child's ability to segment phonemes and assign a phonetically acceptable letter.

Phonological Awareness Assessment 1A: Syllable Sort

Phonological Awareness Assessment 1B: Rhyme Identification with Pictures

INSTRUCTIONS Circle the two pictures that rhyme.

Name _____

Date _____

*Practice item

Phonological Awareness Assessment 1C: Alliteration—Beginning Sound Match

INSTRUCTIONS *"Put your finger on the sun. Say the word* sun. *What picture sounds like* sun *at the beginning?* Book, soap, jet. *Circle the picture that sounds like the first picture."* Name the pictures for students to be sure they use the right labels and guide them in the completion of this assessment.

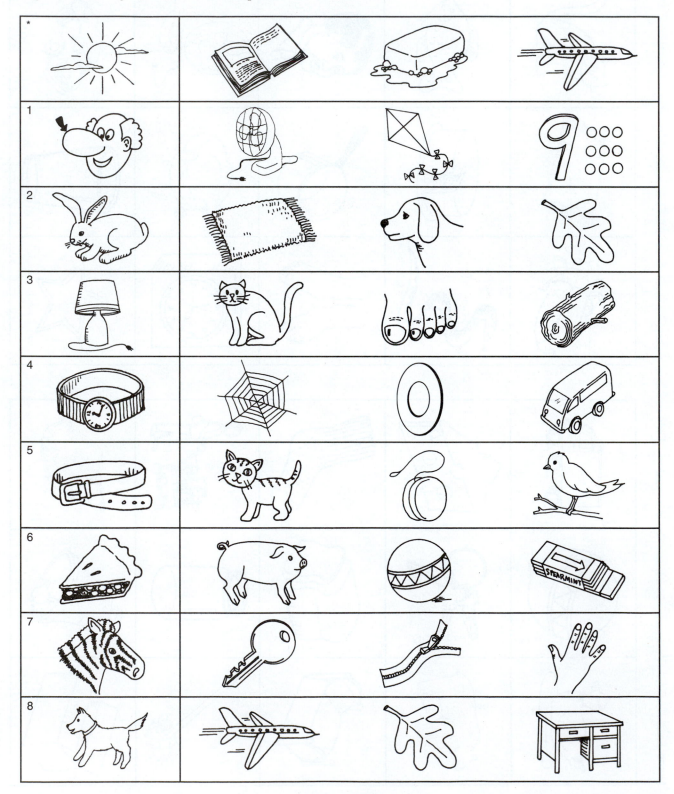

Assessments for Concepts about Print

Name Writing Assessment

DIRECTIONS   Provide a sheet of unlined paper and say to the children, "Draw a picture of yourself and then write your name." If children respond that they do not know how to, encourage them to do the best they can or to "pretend." Before collecting the papers, ask the children to point out their name on the paper and, if they have used letters, ask them to identify them. Figure 4.6 has examples to help you assign points. Record scores on the CAP assessment form to track children's development over time.

ASSESSMENT OF WRITING   Writing samples collected from children can be analyzed in a manner similar to name writing. Assign points and record on the CAP assessment form (page 202). Samples can be found in Figure 4.7.

ASSESSING CONCEPTS ABOUT PRINT   Check off concepts children understand by posing questions during read-alouds or shared reading. For individual assessments, sit down with one child at a time and use a simple book that has at least one question. Explain that you are going to be reading the story but you will ask him or her to help. Sample questions and directives follow. Responses can be recorded on the CAP assessment form.

1. What do people do with this? [Hold up a book.]
2. Show me the front of this book [Hand the book to the child with the spine facing him or her.]
3. Where is the title of the book?
4. Where would I start reading? Here or here? [Point to the print and picture.]
5. Where would I go next? [Point to the end of a sentence that continues below.]
6. Where is the top of the page? Where is the bottom of the page?
7. Point to one word on this page.
8. Show me the first letter in that word. Show me the last letter in that word.
9. Can you find the letter *T*? [Select any letter.]
10. Can you show me a capital letter? A lowercase letter?
11. Can you show me a sentence?
12. Can you show me a period?
13. Can you show me a question mark?

Concepts about Print Sorts: "Picture, Letter, Word, or Sentence?"

INSTRUCTIONS   Enlarge the prepared sort on (page 203) and cut it apart.

Model   Do the entire sort with groups of children before assessing one child. Introduce the headers. Say something like "Here is picture of a shoe and here is the word *shoe*. Words have letters that we read. Here is a letter. Here is a sentence. I can tell it is a sentence because there are words with spaces between them." Model another letter and another word and explain your thinking in the same way.

Your Turn   "You sort the rest of these. Sort it under the picture, the letter, the word, or the sentence." Encourage the children to explain their sorting, but do not insist. Record the number of correct responses out of the 10 remaining items on the CAP Assessment Form.

Concepts about Print (CAP) Assessment

Name _____ Teacher _____ Year _____

Name Writing Assessment:

Ask the child to draw a picture and write his or her name.

Record dates below.

Assign a point or check for all features to the right that apply.	Name separate from drawing	Linear	Segmentation into units	Letter-like forms	First letter	Symbol salad	At least half of letters	All letters	Left to right with no reversals	Names letters	Total Points
1.											
2.											
3.											
4.											

Emergent Writing Assessment:

Evaluate independent writing samples

Record dates below.

Assign a point or check for all features to the right that apply.	Identified as writing	Message assigned	Linear orientation	Separate symbols	Symbol salad	Salient sounds	Beginning and ending sounds	Some vowels	Spaces between words	Total Points
1.										
2.										
3.										
4.										

Concepts About Print:

Assign a point or check for concepts child knows

Date	What is a book for?	Front and back	Title	Where to start reading	Where to go next	Top and bottom	Word	First and last letter	Find a letter	Capital and lowercase	Sentence	Period	Question mark	Total Points
1.														
2.														
3.														
4.														

Number correct _____

Concepts about Print Sort: "Picture, Letter, Word, or Sentence?"

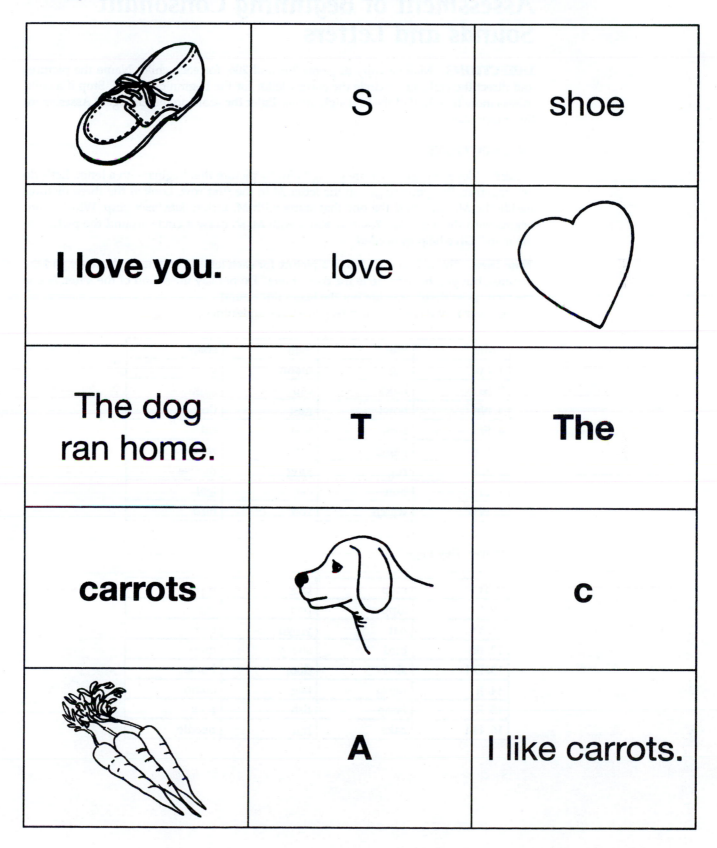

Assessment of Beginning Consonant Sounds and Letters

DIRECTIONS   Make a copy of pages 205 and 206, for each child. Name the pictures and direct the children to circle the correct letter for the beginning sound. Stop if a child misses more than half of the first eight items. Enter the score on the Emergent Assessment Summary Sheet.

INSTRUCTIONS

Model   "Boys and girls, we are going to find a picture that begins with a letter. Let's do one together. Put your finger on the letter *M* in the first row. Look at the three pictures beside the *M*. Let's find the one that starts with *M*. Listen: *kite, man, soap*. Which word begins with the letter *M*? Yes, *man* starts with *M*, so draw a circle around the picture of the man." Give help as needed.

Your Turn   "Now you will choose a picture for each letter. I will name the letter and the pictures, but you have to circle the correct one.' Do not say the sound of the letter. Name the pictures without drawing out the beginning sound.

Answer Key Page 1 (correct responses are underlined)

* Mm	kite	man	soap
1. Pp	pig	moon	gum
2. Ss	block	cap	sink
3. Nn	bowl	nest	dog
4. Ff	sock	foot	cat
5. Gg	game	seal	rabbit
6. Kk	rug	king	mouse
7. Ll	bun	car	leaf
8. Ww	watch	zoo	bird

Answer Key Page 2

9. Tt	map	tack	rope
10. Cc	zipper	pan	cat
11. Yy	bat	yo-yo	fork
12. Bb	bird	sheep	mop
13. Dd	sled	door	horse
14. Jj	jump	bag	comb
15. Rr	lamp	fish	rock
16. Hh	cake	hill	needle

Beginning Consonant Sounds and Letters

Name _____ Date _____ Correct _____

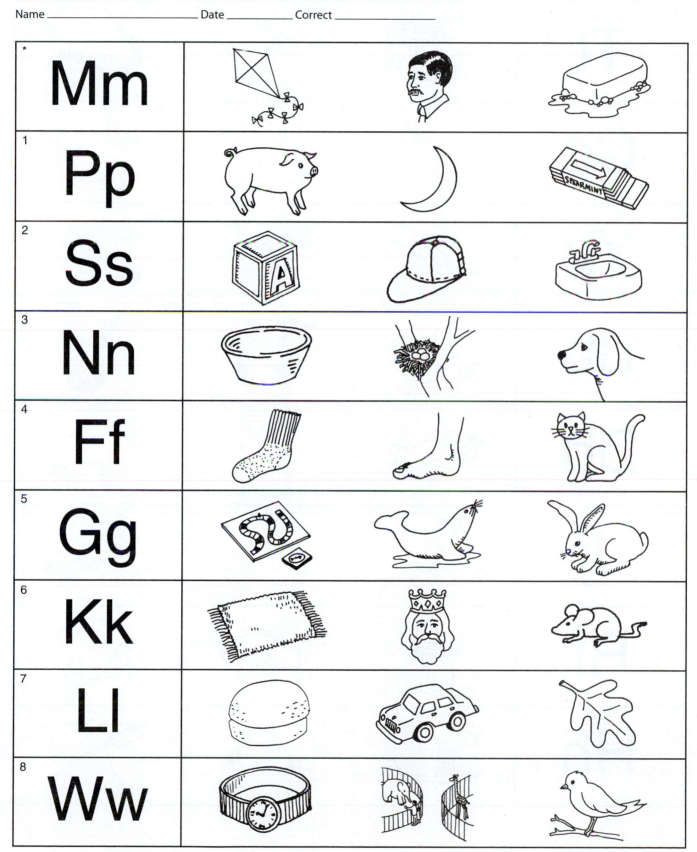

Name _____ Date _____ Correct _____

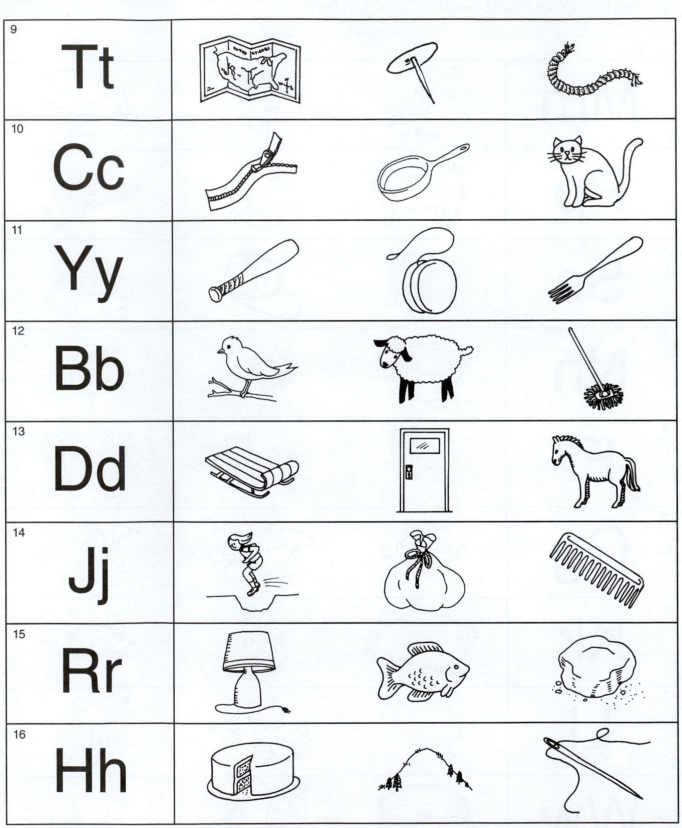

Kindergarten Spelling Inventory (KSI)

Make a copy of the form on page 209 for each student. Note that the bottom half of the form should be folded up so that it is out of sight while students are writing the words. The KSI gives you information about students' ability to segment phonemes (i.e., break words into sounds) and choose phonetically acceptable letters to represent the beginning, middle, or ending sounds of simple short vowel words. If a child scores 10 points or more, use the Primary Spelling Inventory (PSI) to collect information about blends and digraphs.

- To prepare children for this assessment, model how to spell "as best you can" several times as a whole-class activity using a variety of words but not the words on this assessment. Do **not** pre-teach these words and do **not** have them displayed during testing.
- Most teachers find it easiest to administer this assessment in small groups. Seat students so that they cannot see the papers of their classmates. Manila folders propped on end can provide a screen.
- On the day of assessment, model *mat* as a practice item, helping students to focus on the letter sounds by stretching out or repeating the sounds made by the letters. Sounds are indicated in the directions between slash marks / /. Do not demonstrate the sounding-out process beyond the *mat* example. You may prompt the student by saying, "What else do you hear? Do you hear any other sounds in the word _____?"
- Observe as children write. If you are not sure about the intended letter due to poor letter formation, ask the child what letter he or she has written or ask the student to point to the letter on the alphabet strip he or she meant to write. To help with scoring, write the intended letter above the student's attempt.

INSTRUCTIONS

Model Tell the students that you want them to spell some words. First, demonstrate the procedure by thinking aloud, on a blackboard or chart paper. Say, "We're going to spell some words. I'll go first. The word I want to spell is *mat*. I am going to begin by saying the word slowly: *MMM-AAA-TTT*. Now I'm going to think about each sound I hear. Listen: *MMM*. I hear a /m/ sound, so I will write down the letter *m*. *MMM-AAA*. After the /m/, I hear an /ah/ sound, so I will write down the letter *a*. *MMM-AAA-TTT*. At the end of the word, I hear a /t/ sound, so I will write down the letter *t*." Repeat with another word such as *sun* if needed.

Your Turn Say, "Now I want you to spell some words. Put down a letter for each sound you hear. You can use the alphabet strip at the top of your sheet if you forget how to make a letter. Ready?" Ask the student to spell the following words in this order:

1. nap
2. kid
3. log
4. jet
5. gum

A picture of each word is next to the line where it should be written. These pictures are additional support for identifying the word you are saying. The picture is not a substitute for your oral dictation.

SCORING Please note that spelling is scored based on phonetically acceptable letter–sound matches to determine whether children are able to segment the individual phonemes and choose a logical letter to represent it. Compare students' spelling to the boxes on the scoring grid at the bottom on the page, checking off letters that match the child's effort. Only one check per column is possible for each word and leave a box blank if there are no matches. Total the number of boxes checked in each column beside "Spelling Feature Analysis," and then add across for the "Total Phonetically Acceptable" score. Remember that static reversals, in which the student writes a mirror image of a single letter, and self-corrections are **not** counted as errors.

Benchmarks   A score of 12 out of a possible 15 points is the benchmark for the end of kindergarten.

You can create a classroom profile of all students on one page by using the Emergent Class Record Form on page 211.

Kindergarten Spelling Inventory

Name_____   Date _____

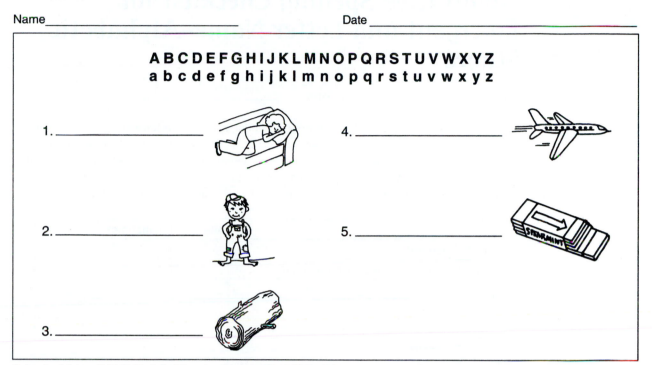

1._____

2._____

3._____

4._____

5._____

A B C D E F G H I J K L M N O P Q R S T U V W X Y Z
a b c d e f g h i j k l m n o p q r s t u v w x y z

Adapted from PALS Quick Checks, University of Virginia

Fold here ---

Scoring Grid

	Beginning	Middle	Ending	
1. nap	n	a	p	_____
		e	b	# phonetically acceptable
2. kid	k	i	d	_____
	c or g	e	t	# phonetically acceptable
3. log	l	o	g	_____
		i	k	# phonetically acceptable
4. jet	j	e	t	_____
	g	a	d	# phonetically acceptable
5. gum	g	u	m	_____
	k or c	o		# phonetically acceptable

Spelling Feature Analysis	Number of Beginning Phonemes	Number of Middle Phonemes	Number of Ending Phonemes	Total Phonetically Acceptable
				/15

....
Qualitative Spelling Checklist for Emergent and Letter Name–Alphabetic Stages

Name _____ Dates _____ _____ _____

Use this checklist to analyze children's uncorrected writing as a way to estimate spelling stage. Select *yes* if a child uses a feature consistently, check *sometimes* if a feature is used but confused, and check *no* if the feature is rarely, if ever, observed. The stage is determined by where checks fall into the *sometimes* category. This form can be used three times by using different colors to check the boxes. You can create a classroom profile of all students on one page by using the Emergent Class Record Form.

	Yes	Sometimes	No
Early Emergent			
Does the child scribble and call it writing?	__	__	__
Are letter-like forms arranged linearly?	__	__	__
Middle Emergent			
Are letters used randomly in pretend writing?	__	__	__
Late Emergent			
Are some sounds represented—usually the first sound of a word or syllable?	__	__	__
Early Letter Name–Alphabetic			
Are initial consonant sounds represented consistently but with predictable confusions?	__	__	__
Are final sounds attempted?	__	__	__
Middle Letter Name–Alphabetic			
Are beginning and ending consonant sounds represented conventionally?	__	__	__
Is spacing between words consistent?	__	__	__
Are long vowels represented with their letter names?	__	__	__
Are blends and digraphs represented partially?	__	__	__
Are short vowels attempted but predictably confused?	__	__	__
Late Letter Name–Alphabetic			
Are short vowels represented conventionally?	__	__	__
Are blends and digraphs spelled conventionally?	__	__	__
Are preconsonantal nasals represented?	__	__	__

Emergent Class Record

Class Record to Assess Emergent and Letter Name – Alphabetic Stage Spelling, Pre-Kindergarten – Kindergarten

Directions: Check boxes or date entries over several observations. A check minus (√–) indicates features used occasionally. A check plus (√+) indicates consistent use.

Teacher _____ Class _____ Grade _____ Date(s) _____

SPELLING STAGES →	Emergent Stage						Letter Name–Alphabetic Stage				
	Early	Middle		Late		Early		Middle			Late
↓ Name of Student / Spelling Features →	Random Marks	Linear Scribbles	Letter-like Writing	Random Letters	Beginning Consonants	Final Consonants	Logical Vowel Substitutions*	Consonant Digraphs	Consonant Blends		Correct Short Vowels

*Logical vowel substitutions show how a student would use a letter name strategy to spell long vowels (as in HOP for *hope*) or short vowels (PAT for *pet* or DEG for *dig*)

Primary Spelling Inventory

If children know most of their letters and are using them to represent at least beginning and ending consonant sounds, you may elect to use the Primary Spelling Inventory (PSI), which is administered much like a traditional spelling test. However, children should **not** study the words in advance of testing.

The inventory consists of a list of 26 words ordered by difficulty. For early kindergarten, you may call out only the first five words, unless a child spells more than one correctly. By late kindergarten, call out at least 15 words so that you sample digraphs and blends; use the entire list if children are spelling most features correctly. Prepare a numbered paper and assess in small groups in order to closely monitor children.

Here is a possible introduction to the assessment. "I am going to ask you to spell some words. Spell them the best you can. Some of the words may be easy to spell; some may be difficult. When you do not know how to spell a word, spell it the best you can."

Call each word aloud and repeat it. Say each word naturally, without emphasizing phonemes or syllables. Use it in a sentence, if necessary, to be sure children know the exact word. Sample sentences are provided along with the words.

1. fan — I could use a fan on a hot day. *fan*
2. pet — I have a pet cat who likes to play. *pet*
3. dig — He will dig a hole in the sand. *dig*
4. rob — A raccoon will rob a bird's nest for eggs. *rob*
5. hope — I hope you spell these words the best you can. *hope*
6. wait — You will need to wait for the bus. *wait*
7. gum — I stepped on some bubble gum. *gum*
8. sled — The dog sled was pulled by huskies. *sled*
9. stick — I used a stick to poke in the hole. *stick*
10. shine — He rubbed the coin to make it shine. *shine*
11. dream — I had a funny dream last night. *dream*
12. blade — The blade of the knife was very sharp. *blade*
13. coach — The coach called the team off the field. *coach*
14. fright — She was a fright in her Halloween costume. *fright*
15. chewed — The dog chewed on the bone until it was gone. *chewed*
16. crawl — You will get dirty if you crawl under the bed. *crawl*
17. wishes — In fairy tales, wishes often come true. *wishes*
18. thorn — The thorn from the rosebush stuck me. *thorn*
19. shouted — They shouted at the barking dog. *shouted*
20. spoil — The food will spoil if it sits out too long. *spoil*
21. growl — The dog will growl if you bother him. *growl*
22. third — I was the third person in line. *third*
23. camped — We camped down by the river last weekend. *camped*
24. tries — He tries hard every day to finish his work. *tries*
25. clapping — The audience was clapping after the program. *clapping*
26. riding — They are riding their bikes to the park today. *riding*

SCORING THE INVENTORY USING THE FEATURE GUIDES

1. Make a copy of the feature guide (page 214) for each child (or use the Emergent Class Record when children have few correct responses). If you call fewer words than the total number draw a line under the last word called and adjust the possible total points at the bottom of each feature column.
2. Score each word by checking off the features spelled correctly that are listed in the cells to the right of the word. For example, if a student spells *bed* as *bad*, he gets a check in the initial *b* cell and the final *d* cell, but not for the short vowel. Write in the vowel

used (*a*, in this case), but do not give any points for it. If a student spells *train* as *trane*, she gets a check in the initial *tr* cell and the final *n* cell, but not for the long vowel pattern. Write in the vowel pattern used (*a-e*, in this case), but do not give any points for it. Put a check in the "Correct" column if the word is spelled correctly. Do not count reversed letters as errors, but note them in the cells. If unnecessary letters are added, give the speller credit for what is correct (e.g., if *bed* is spelled *bede*, the student still gets credit for representing the final consonant and the short vowel), but do not check "Correct" spelling.

3. Add the number of checks under each feature and across each word, double-checking the total score recorded in the "Feature Points" column. Modify the ratios in the last row depending on the number of words called aloud.

INTERPRETING THE RESULTS OF THE SPELLING INVENTORY

1. Look down each feature column to determine instructional needs. Children who miss only one can go on to other features. Children who miss two or three need some review work; children who miss more than three need careful instruction on a feature. If a child does not get any points for a feature, earlier features need to be studied first.
2. To determine a stage of development, find the columns where students first make two or more errors. Move up to the stage listed at the top of the feature guide. Circle this stage.

USING THE CLASSROOM COMPOSITE FORM

1. Staple each feature guide to the student's spelling paper. Arrange the papers in rank order from highest total points (or number of words correct) to lowest total points.
2. List students' names in rank order in the left column of the PSI classroom composite on page 215. Transfer each student's feature scores from the bottom row of the individual feature guides to the classroom composite. If you did not call out all the words, adjust the totals on the bottom row of the classroom composite.
3. Highlight cells where students made two or more errors on a particular feature to get a sense of your groups' needs and to form groups for instruction.

Words Their Way Primary Spelling Inventory Feature Guide

Student's Name _____ Teacher _____ Grade _____ Date _____

Words Spelled Correctly: ____ / 26 Feature Points: ____ / 56 Total: ____ / 82 Spelling Stage: _____

SPELLING STAGES →	EMERGENT LATE		LETTER NAME–ALPHABETIC			WITHIN WORD PATTERN		SYLLABLES AND AFFIXES		
	Consonants		Short Vowels	Digraphs	Blends	Common Long Vowels	Other Vowels	Inflected Endings	Feature Points	Words Spelled Correctly
Features →	Initial	Final	(EARLY/MIDDLE)	(LATE)		(EARLY/MIDDLE)	(MIDDLE)	(LATE/EARLY)		
1. fan	f	n	a							
2. pet	p	t	e							
3. dig	d	g	i							
4. rob	r	b	o							
5. hope	h	p				o-e				
6. wait	w	t				ai				
7. gum	g	m	u							
8. sled			e		sl					
9. stick			i		st					
10. shine				sh		i-e				
11. dream					dr	ea				
12. blade					bl	a-e				
13. coach				ch		oa				
14. fright					fr	igh				
15. chewed				ch			ew	-ed		
16. crawl					cr		aw			
17. wishes				sh				-es		
18. thorn				th			or			
19. shouted				sh			ou	-ed		
20. spoil							oi			
21. growl							ow			
22. third				th			ir			
23. camped								-ed		
24. tries					tr			-ies		
25. clapping								-pping		
26. riding								-ding		
Totals	/7	/7	/7	/7	/7	/7	/7	/7	/56	/26

Words Their Way Primary Spelling Inventory Classroom Composite

Teacher _____ School _____ Grade _____ Date _____

SPELLING STAGES →	EMERGENT LATE		LETTER NAME—ALPHABETIC			WITHIN WORD PATTERN				SYLLABLES AND AFFIXES			
	Consonants		EARLY	MIDDLE	LATE	EARLY	MIDDLE		LATE	EARLY			
Students' ↓ Names	Initial	Final	Short Vowels	Digraphs	Blends	Common Long Vowels	Other Vowels		Inflected Endings	Correct Spelling		Total Rank Order	
Possible Points	7	7	7	7	7	7	7		7	26		82	
1.													
2.													
3.													
4.													
5.													
6.													
7.													
8.													
9.													
10.													
11.													
12.													
13.													
14.													
15.													
16.													
17.													
18.													
19.													
20.													
21.													
22.													
23.													
24.													
25.													
26.													
Highlight for instruction*													

*Highlight students who miss more than 1 on a particular feature; they will benefit from more instruction in that area.

....
Concept of Word Assessment

Children's ability to accurately track or point to the words of something they have memorized is easily assessed in daily classroom activities when you ask them to point as they read. Below are some guidelines about how to do this more formally. A scoring rubric for "Humpty Dumpty" is provided, and a blank form is also provided on page 221 so you can do this with any short text that students have memorized.

INSTRUCTIONS

Model   Teach a rhyme such as "Humpty Dumpty" as a whole-class activity. Enlarge or project the pictures on page 219 to teach the rhyme. Practice until children have memorized it. Make a printed copy of the rhyme (page 219) or write it on a chart or sentence strips and present it so that all can see. Explain: "This time, as I say the rhyme I am going to point to the words." Model saying the rhyme slowly enough to point to each word. Then ask the students to say it along with you as you point again.

Your Turn   Assess concept of word with one child at a time. Provide a copy of the poem for the student to read and a copy of the word list (page 220). Make a copy of the assessment form (page 218) for each student. If you are not sure whether children have memorized the poem, have them recite it using the pictures as prompts before they are asked to read it. Have each student read the poem. Say, "Read 'Humpty Dumpty' to me and point to the words as you read." Note whether the student has accurately tracked each line, and use the rubric to score each child's efforts from 0 to 6 for each line. Score each line of the rhyme and then compute an average. Transfer this to the Individual Assessment Summary Sheet and check "Developing," "Rudimentary," or "Firm." See an example of this in Figure 6.9.

SCORING

DEVELOPING COW

0   No left-to-right directionality established. May go right to left or change directions.
1   Points left to right, but pointing is vague or random with no consistent units.
2   Points to a letter for each syllable or rhythmic beat.
3   Points to words for each rhythmic beat or syllable, getting off track.

Rudimentary COW

4   Points to words accurately, but gets off track on two- or three-syllable words.
.   Points to words accurately. Gets off track, but self-corrects.

Firm COW

6   Points to words accurately.

Word Recognition in Context

Point to the selected words on the child's copy of "Humpty Dumpty." (They are underlined on the teacher recording sheet.) Say, "Can you tell me this word?" Give one point for each word that is correctly identified. Note strategies used by the student. Did the student reread to figure out the word or did he or she name it immediately? Don't hesitate to ask how the student knew a word. He or she may say, "I knew it was *horses* because it started with *h*."

Word List Reading or Recognition in Isolation

If a student's concept of word score is 4 or better, you can also assess recall of words in isolation. Use the list of words from page 220 for "Humpty Dumpty," or create a similar list if you are using a different rhyme. Point to each word in turn, and ask students to say the words they can read in the list. Note correct responses on the right side of the COW assessment form; then transfer scores to the Individual Assessment Summary Sheet.

OBSERVATIONS Use the space at the bottom of the recording form to write in any observations you made. How readily does the child identify words in context? What strategies are used when the word is not identified immediately? When reading words in lists, do errors resemble the word, such as reading *house* for *horse* or *pet* for *put*?

Benchmarks At the beginning of kindergarten, most children in the early emergent stage will score 1 to 3 on concept of word and will identify few (if any) words, even in context. By the end of kindergarten, most students should have a rudimentary concept of word and score 4 to 5 (pointing to words but occasionally getting off track). They will be slow and hesitant about identifying words you point to, but will know some of them. Students who consistently score 5 to 6 have a full concept of word and are probably in the letter name–alphabetic stage of spelling. They should be able to identify nearly all words quickly in context (6 of 7) and will identify most of the words in the list (7 of 10).

Concept of Word in Text: Recording Form for "Humpty Dumpty"

Name _____ Date _____ Teacher _____

	Pointing	Word ID	Word List
<u>Hump</u>ty Dumpty sat on a <u>wall</u>		(2)	on
Humpty Dumpty had a <u>great</u> fall		(1)	Humpty
All the <u>king's</u> horses		(1)	put
And all the king's <u>men</u>		(1)	horses
Couldn't <u>put</u> Humpty together again		(1)	sat
			men
			king's
			wall
			had
			fall
Totals	/ 6	/ 6	/ 10
COW-T: Developing	Rudimentary	Firm	

Scores for pointing: Score each line of the poem and compute the total.

Developing	0	No left-to-right directionality established. May go right to left or change directions.
	1	Points left to right, but pointing is vague or random with no consistent units.
	2	Points to a letter for each syllable or rhythmic beat.
	3	Points to words for each rhythmic beat or syllable, getting off track.
Rudimentary	4	Points to words accurately, but gets off track on two- or three- syllable words.
	5	Points to words accurately. Gets off track, but self-corrects.
Firm	6	Points to words accurately,

Scores for word identification: Point to underlined words on the child's copy. Put a check for each one named correctly.

Scores for word list reading: Ask the child to read from the list of words. Put a check for each correct one. Write in substitutions.

Totals: Compute the totals and circle the COW-T level.

Observations:

"Humpty Dumpty"

Name_____   Date/Story Number_____

Humpty Dumpty

Humpty Dumpty sat on a wall.

Humpty Dumpty had a great fall.

All the king's horses

And all the king's men

Couldn't put Humpty together again!

Word Recognition in Isolation for "Humpty Dumpty"

on

Humpty

put

horses

sat

men

king's

wall

had

fall

Concept of Word in Text: Recording Form Template

Name _____ Date _____ Teacher _____

	Pointing	Word ID	Word List
Totals	/6	/6	/10
COW-T: Developing Rudimentary Firm			

Scores for pointing: Score each line of the poem and compute the total.

Developing   0   No left-to-right directionality established, may go right to left or change directions.

                1   Points left to right, but pointing is vague or random with no consistent units.

                2   Points to a letter for each syllable or rhythmic beat.

                3   Points to words for each rhythmic beat or syllable, getting off track.

Rudimentary   4   Points to words accurately, but gets off track on two- or three- syllable words

                5   Points to words accurately. Gets off track, but self-corrects.

Firm   6   Points to words accurately.

Scores for word identificaton: Point to underlined words on the child's copy. Put a check for each one named correctly.

Scores for word list reading: Ask the child to read from the list of words. Put a check for each correct one. Write in substitutions.

Totals: Compute the totals and circle the COW-T level.

Observations:

APPENDIX B

Alphabet Materials and Sample Sorts

Alphabet Strip

Aa	Bb	Cc	Dd	Ee	Ff	Gg	Hh

Ii	Jj	Kk	Ll	Mm	Nn	Oo	Pp	Qq

Rr	Ss	Tt	Uu	Vv	Ww	Xx	Yy	Zz

Alphabet Cards

A	B	C	D	E
F	G	H	I	J
K	L	M	N	O
P	Q	R	S	T
U	V	W	X	Y
Z				

a	b	c	d	e
f	g	h	i	j
k	l	m	n	o
p	q	r	s	t
u	v	w	x	y
z				

Rhyming Sort

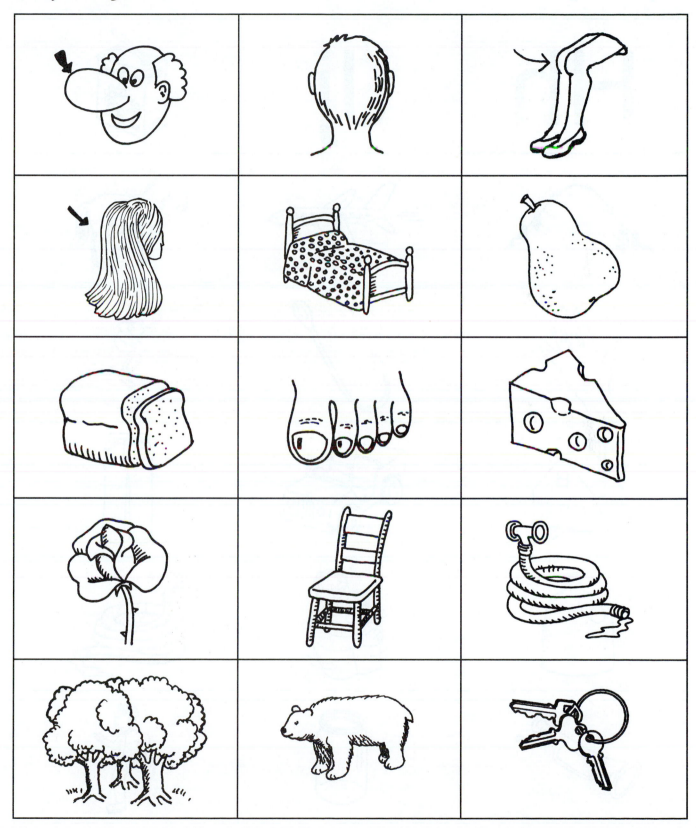

Beginning Sound Sort for *H* and *J*

Word Family Sort

pot	dog	cot	hop
log	frog	top	jog
mop	dot	hot	pop

Blend Sort

Short Vowel Sort

cat	sock	*oddball*
jam	sad	map
job	got	top
fox	hop	has
had	ran	box
wag	lot	mop
was	hot	boy
cab	mom	ham

APPENDIX C Pictures and Templates

Pictures for Sorts and Games

The pictures that follow can be used in a number of ways. You may want to make a complete set of the pictures for modeling, small-group work, and centers. Enlarge the pictures to the desired size and color if you wish. For durability, glue pictures to card stock and laminate. The collection of pictures can be used as clip art to create handouts. Make copies and cut out the pictures you need (comparing two, three, or four sounds) and glue them to a template such as the one on page 251. You will probably want to enlarge the pictures about 50 percent. The pictures are grouped by initial consonants, digraphs, blends, and vowels.

If you want to create sets of rhyming pictures, refer to the list below. The pictures in bold type can be found among the vowel pictures; the others can be found by their beginning sound.

tape	game	soap	beach	deer	slide	fire	vine	bone	pear
cape	frame	rope	peach	spear	bride	tire	nine	cone	chair
moon	toad	cube	bead	heel	suit	peas	glue	gate	school
spoon	road	tube	read	seal	fruit	cheese	shoe	plate	stool
					flute	keys	zoo	skate	spool
snake	jeep	hive	rose	coat	three	hay	cane	pie	whale
cake	sheep	five	nose	boat	bee	pay	rain	tie	tail
rake	sleep	dive	toes	goat	knee	pray	chain	fly	mail
lake	sweep	drive	hose	float	tree	tray	plane	cry	snail
				note	key	play	train	fry	pail
									nail
									scale
glass	lamp	four	trunk	duck	switch	mitten	book	jump	cut
grass	stamp	door	skunk	truck	witch	kitten	hook	stump	nut
wig	car	sun	box	gum	bed	kick	dog	hen	pot
pig	jar	bun	fox	drum	sled	stick	log	men	dot
dig	star	run	socks	thumb	shed	chick	jog	ten	hot
					bread	brick	frog	pen	cot
net	shell	can	cat	king	sock	bag	pill	mug	
pet	bell	man	bat	swing	rock	rag	hill	bug	
jet	well	fan	hat	ring	lock	wag	mill	jug	
vet	smell	pan	mat	wing	clock	flag	spill	tug	
		van	bat	sting	block	tag	drill	rug	
						cap	grill	plug	
						map			
						nap			
						trap			
						clap			
						snap			
mop		jack		zip					
hop		sack		lip					
top		pack		rip					
pop		shack		ship					
chop		quack		whip					
shop		track		skip					
stop		crack		clip					
				drip					
				flip					

Pictures for Sorts and Games
Initial Consonants

		Cc			
					Dd
Bb					

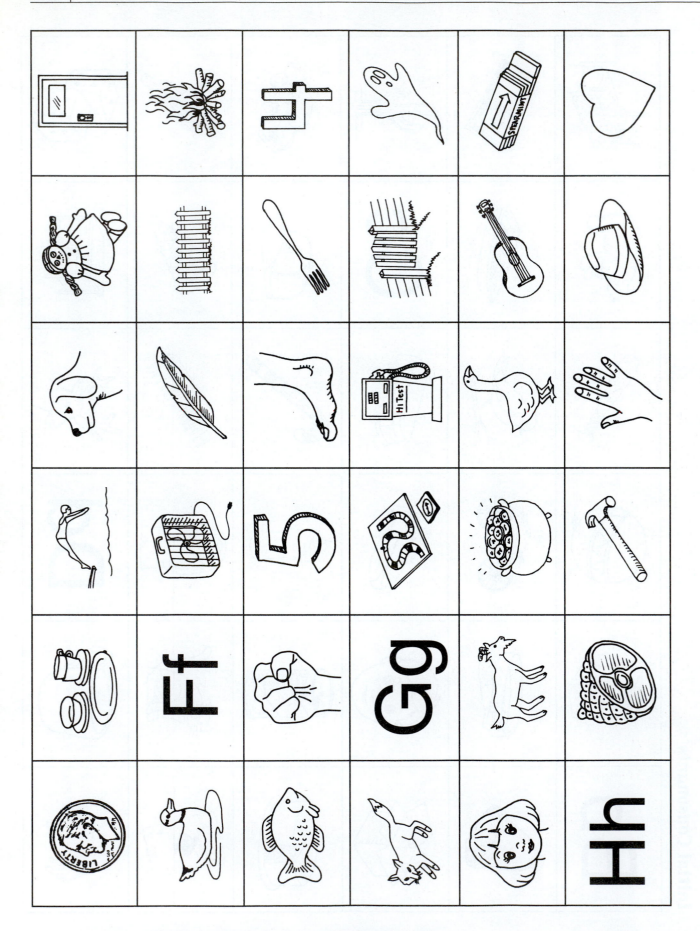

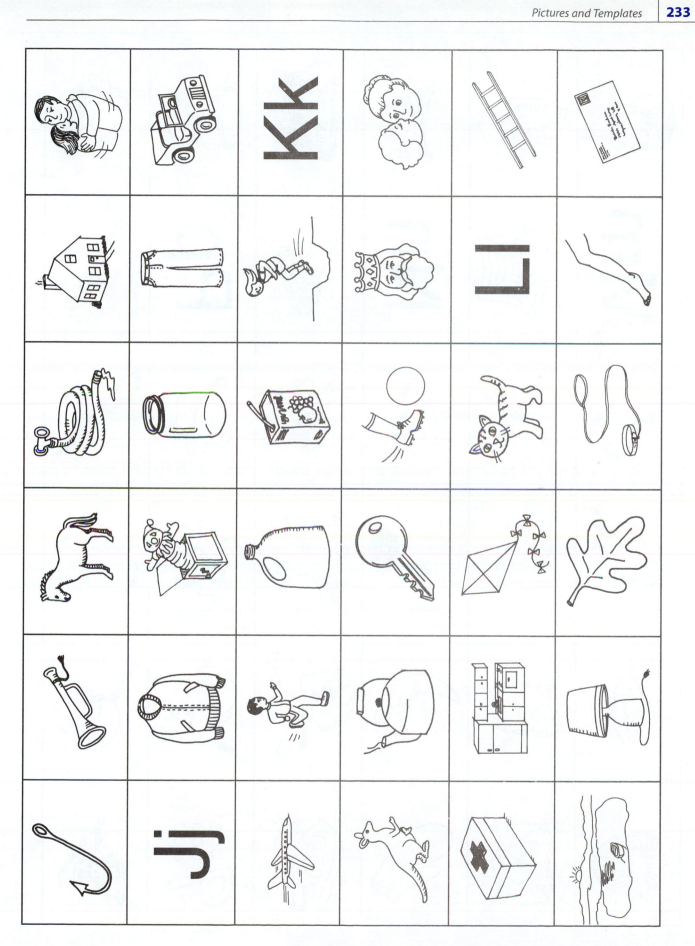

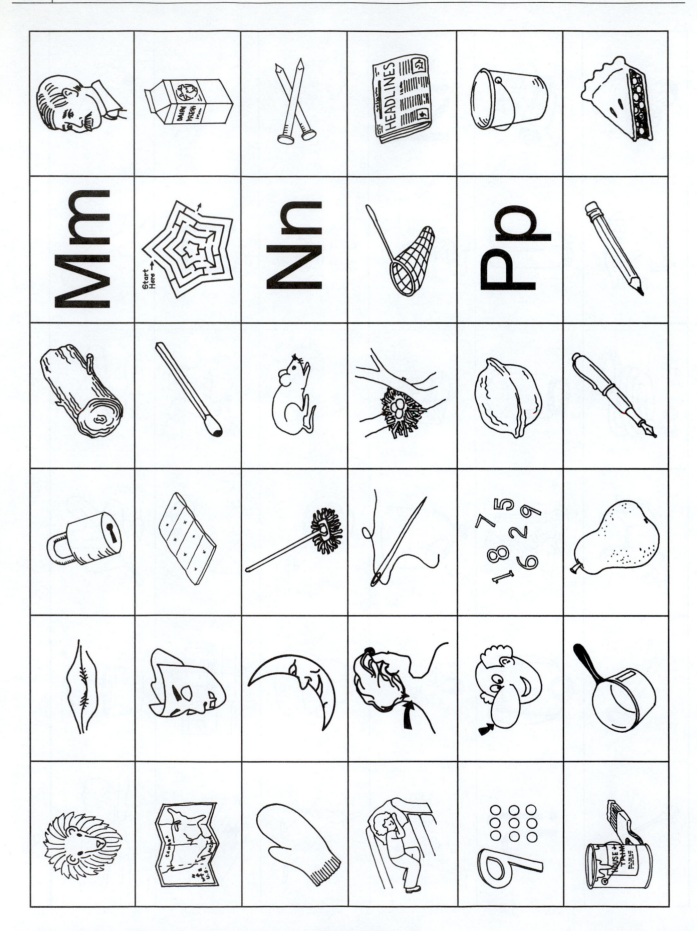

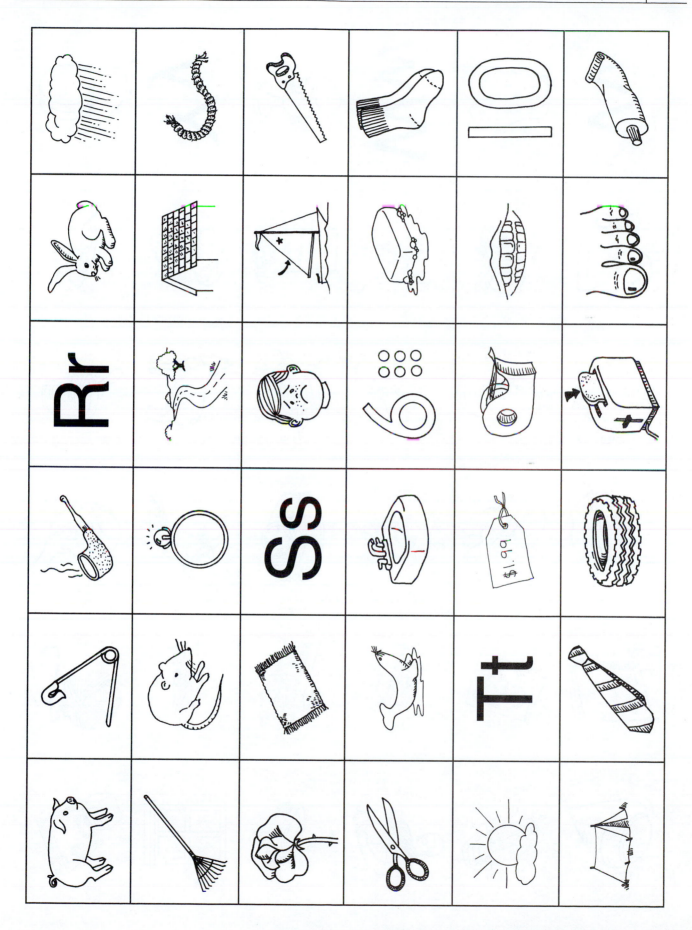

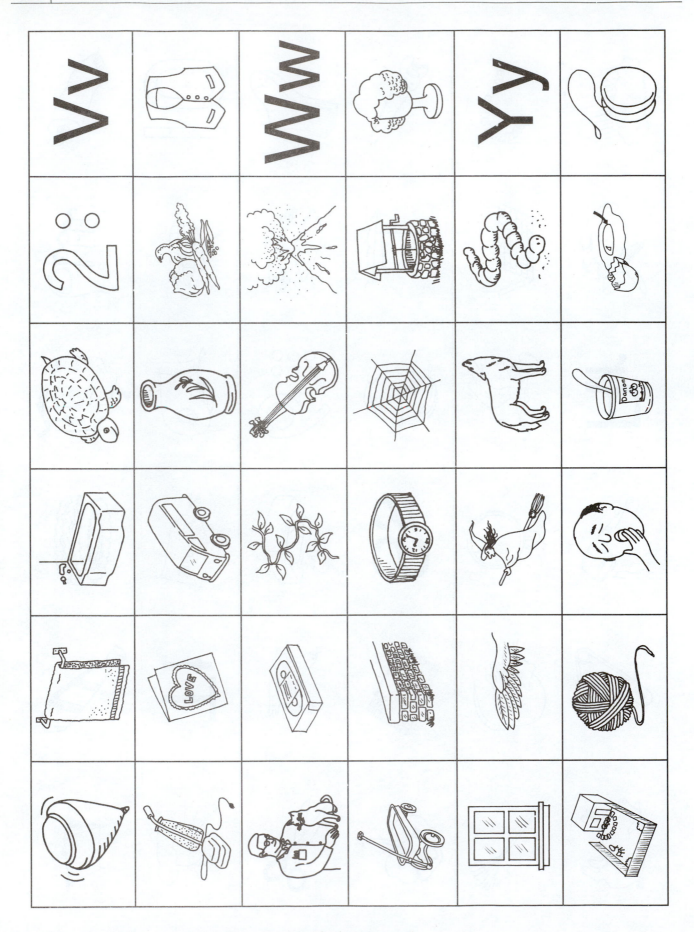

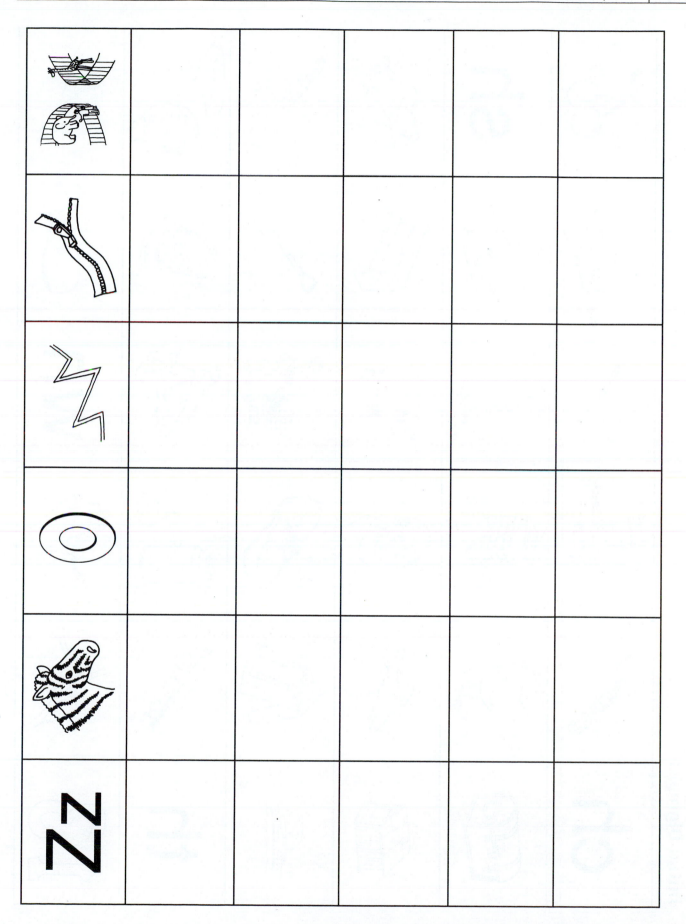

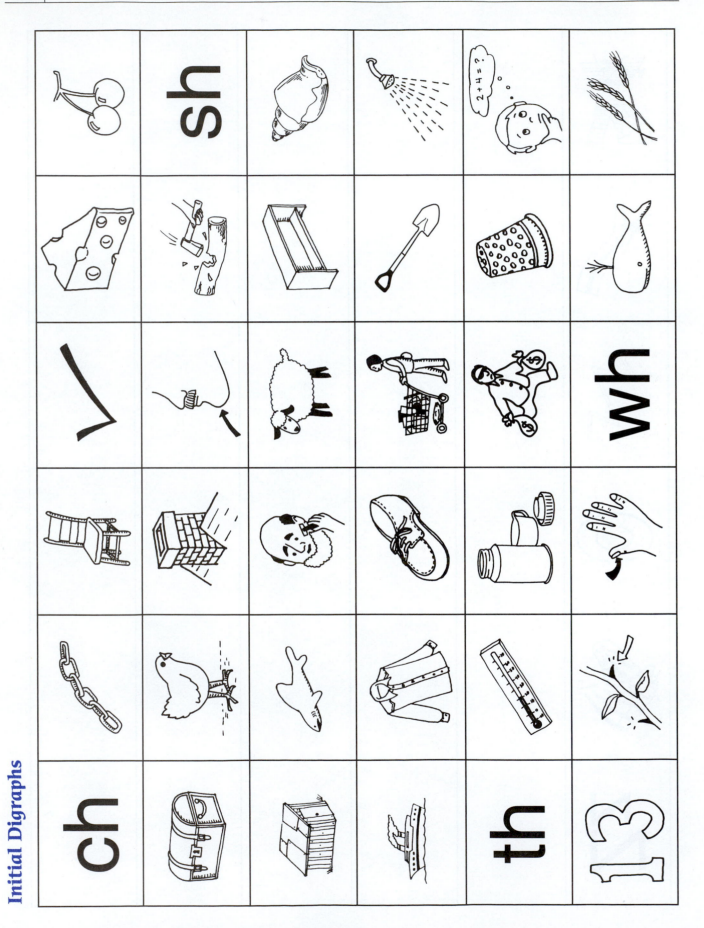

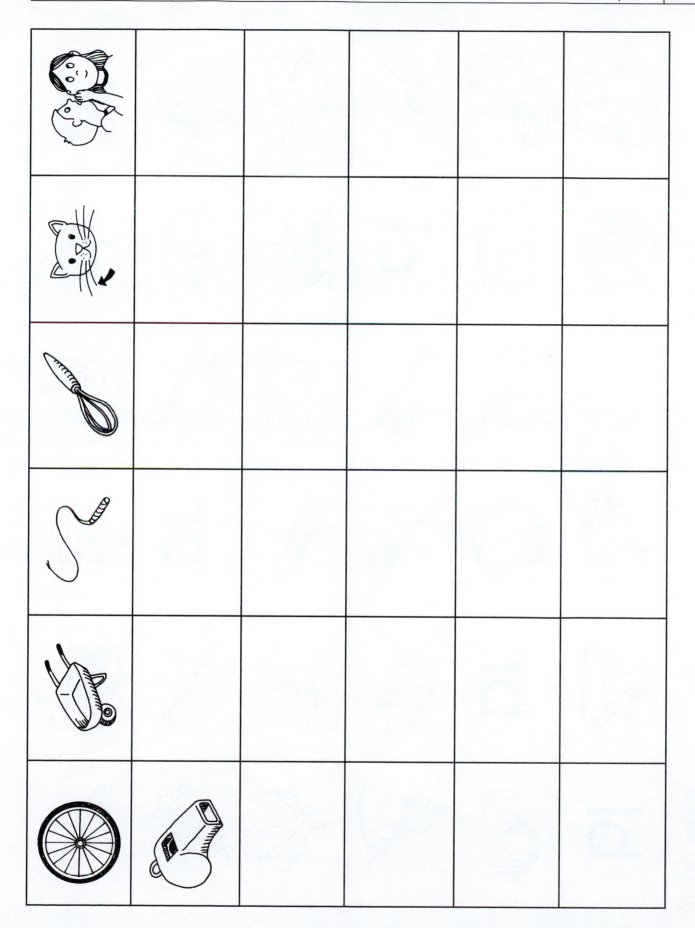

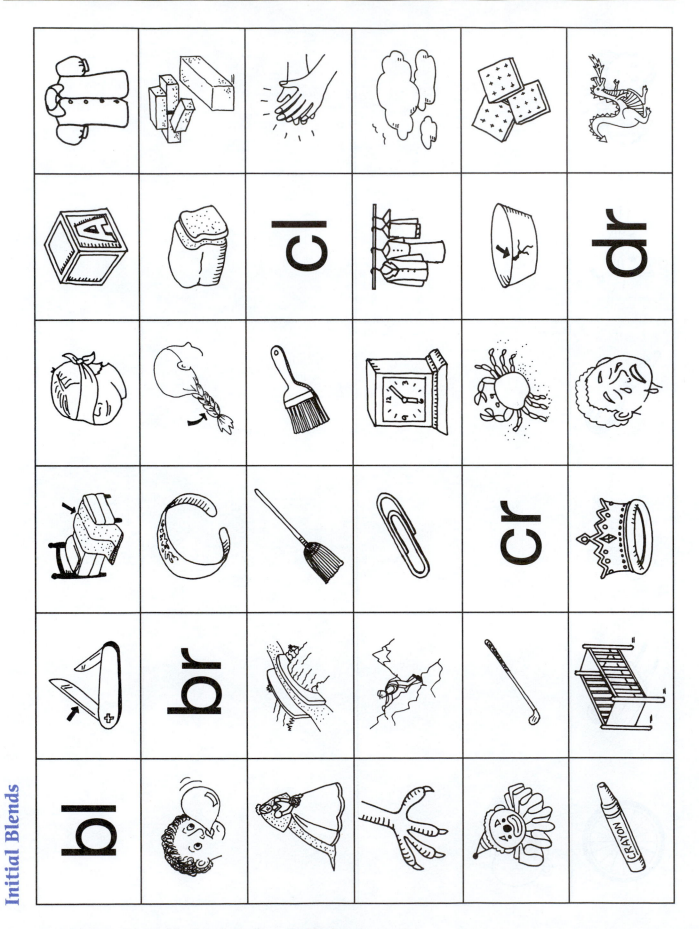

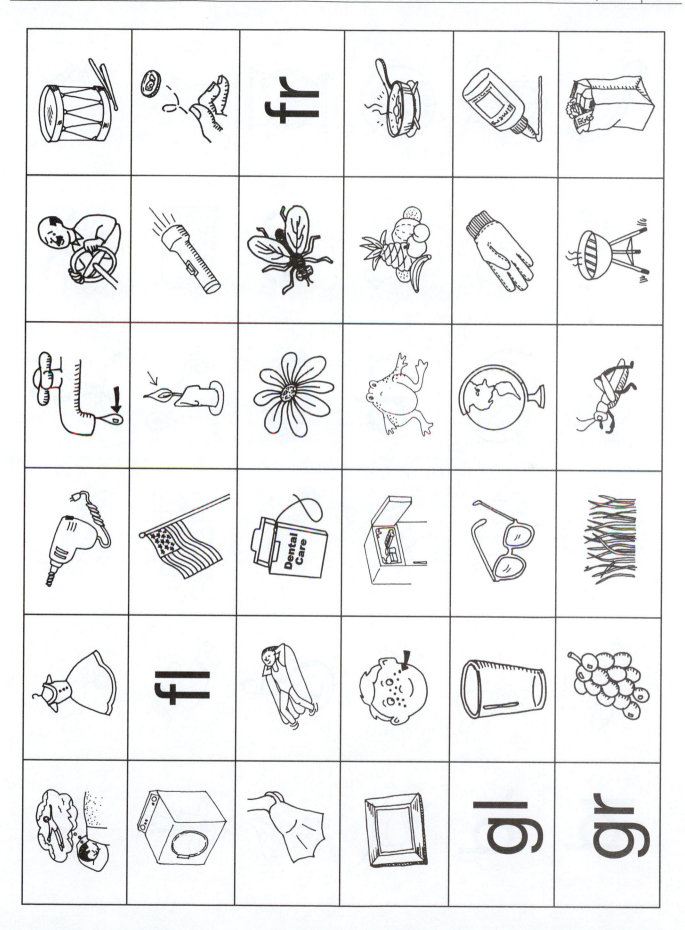

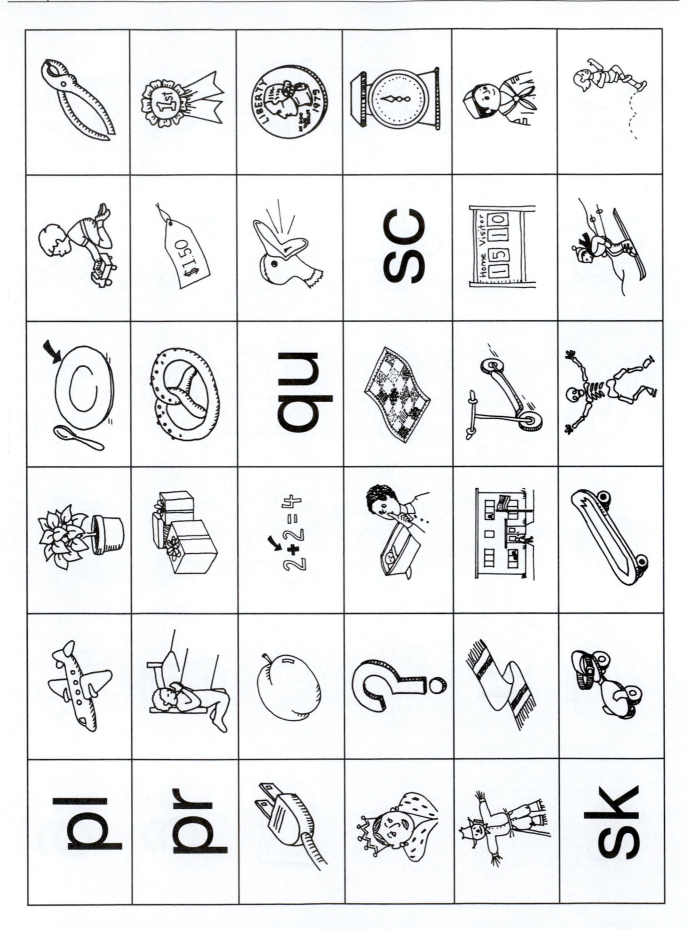

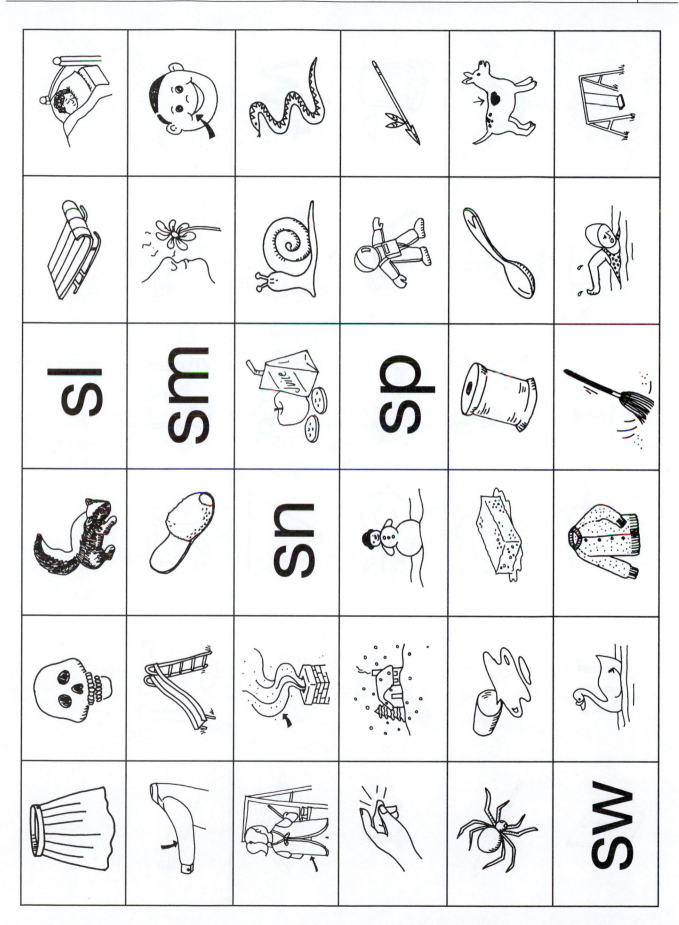

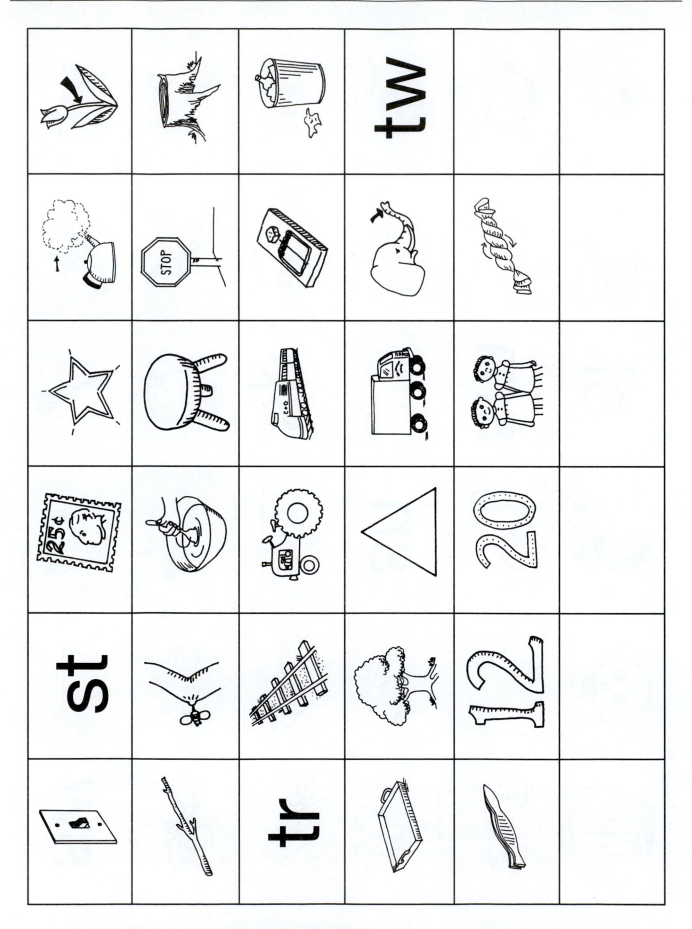

Initial Short Vowel Sounds

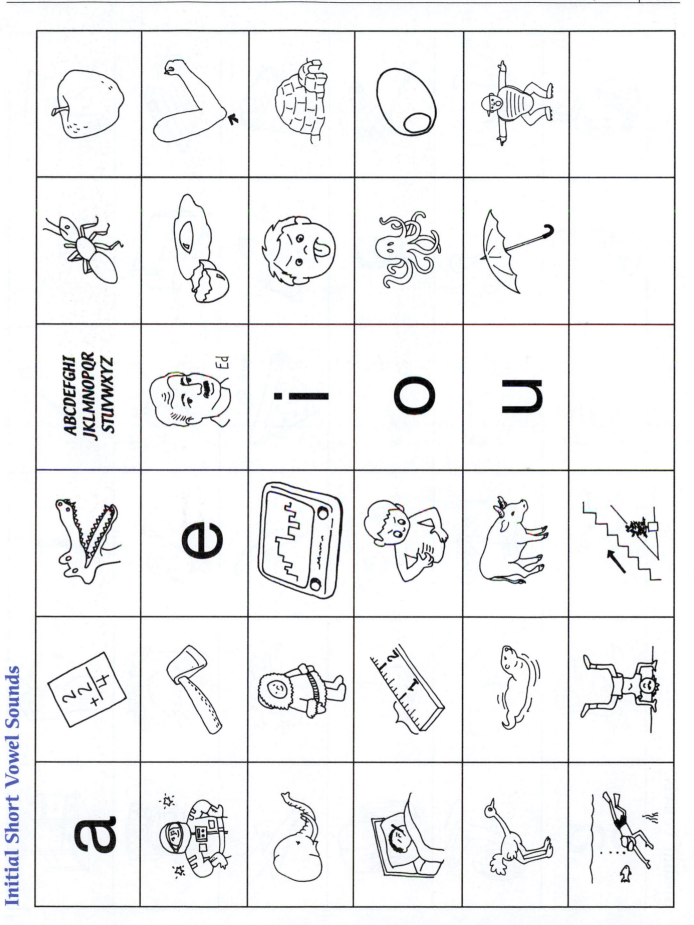

Medial Vowels

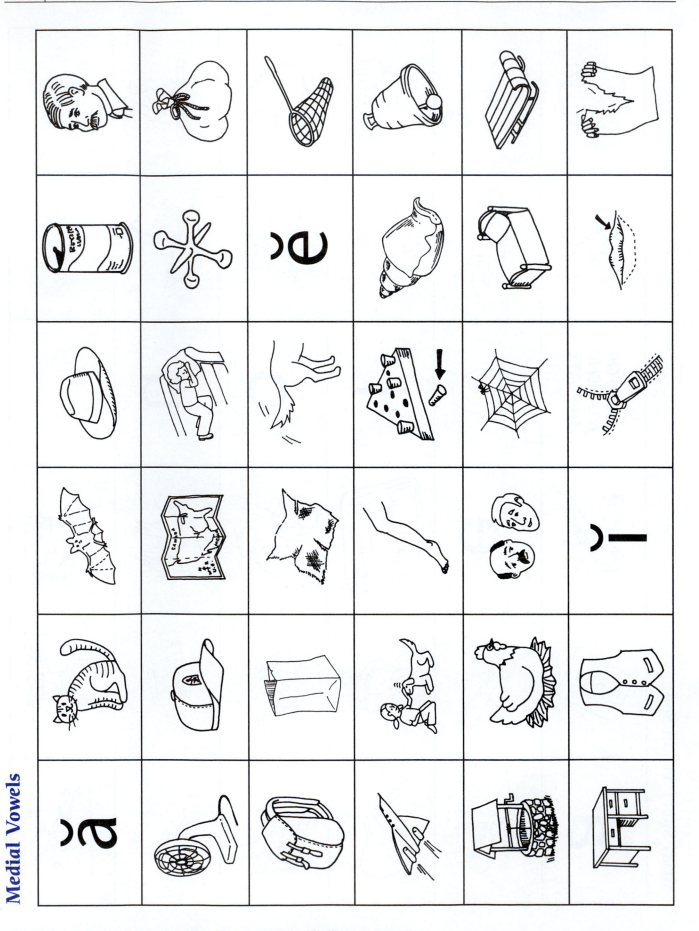

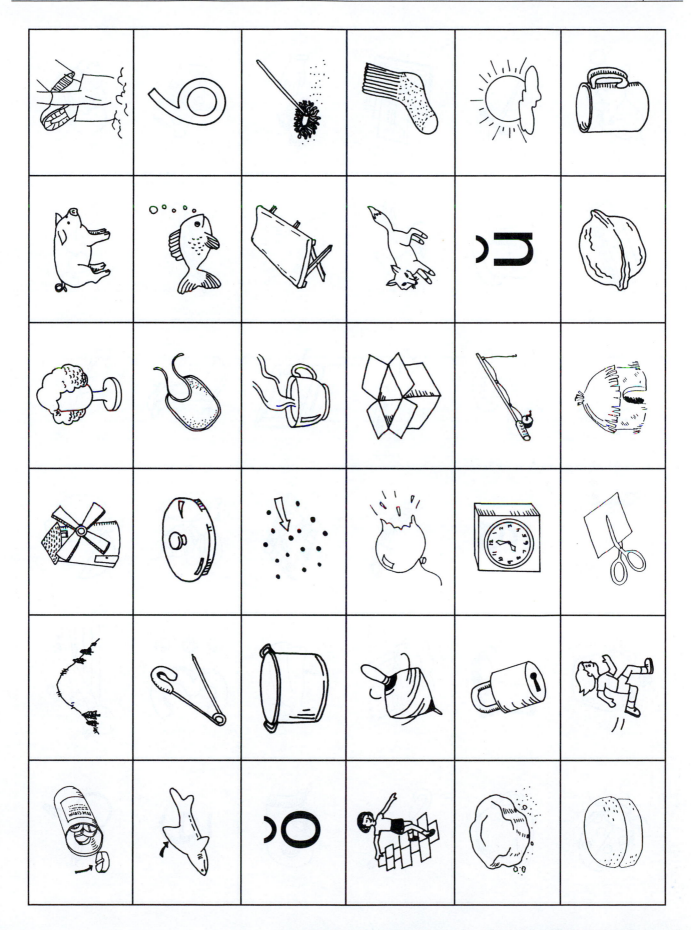

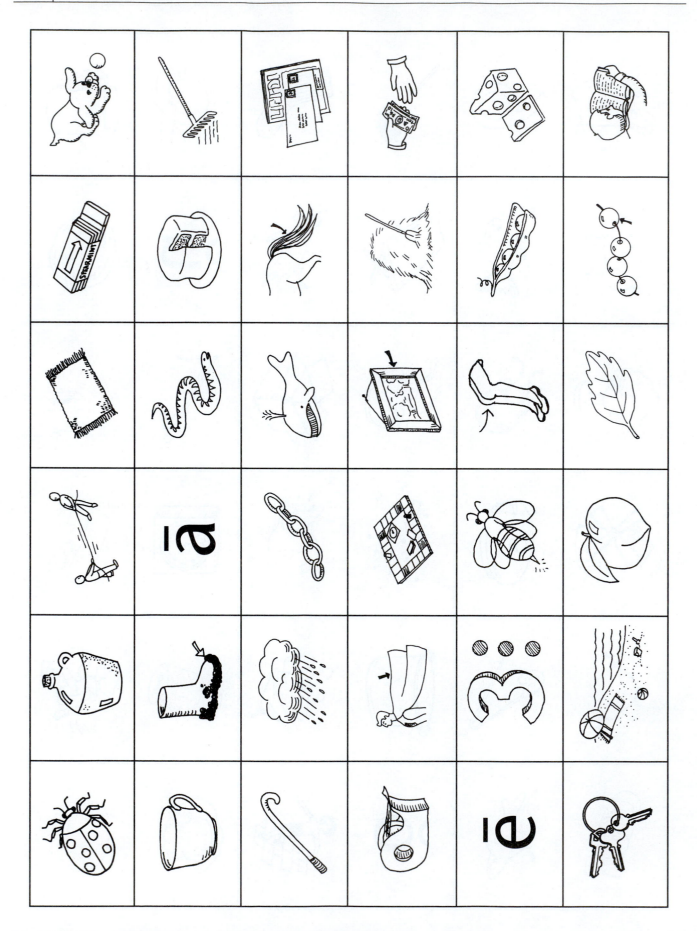

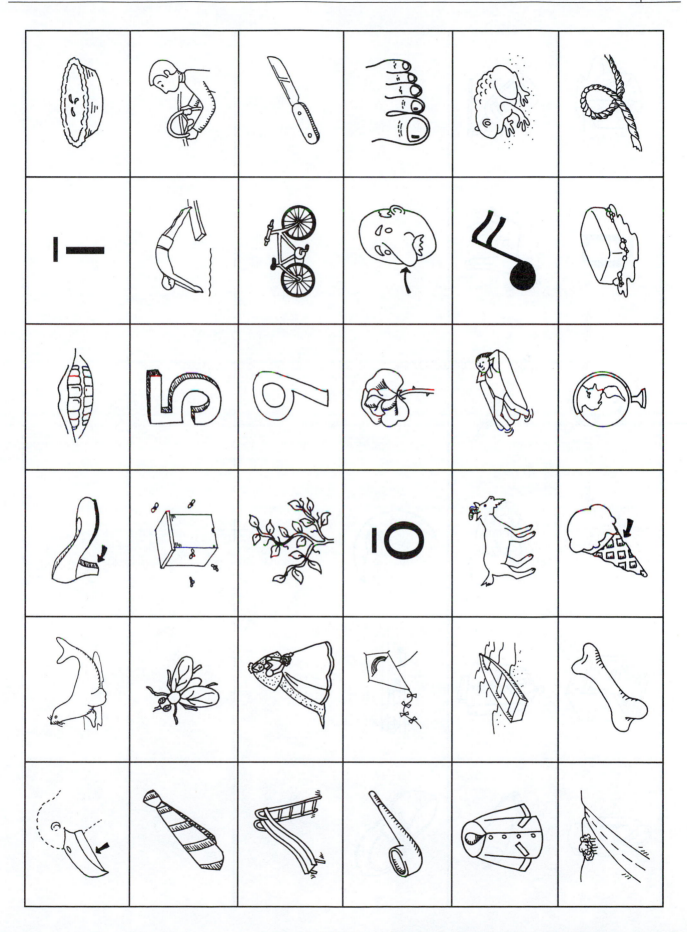

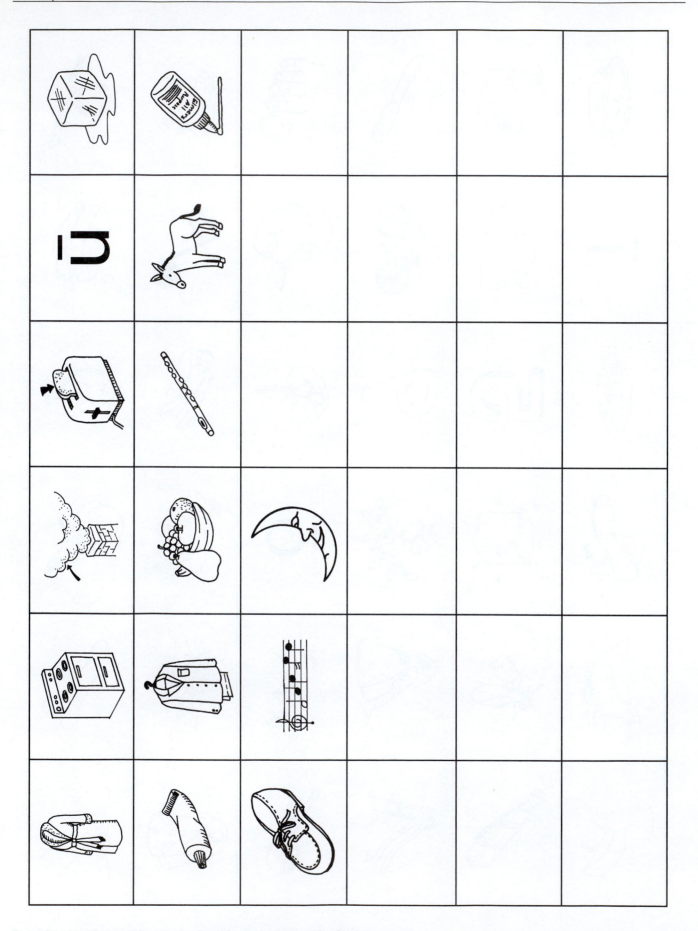

Templates for Sorts

Template for Picture Sorts

Template for Word Sorts

Templates for Game Boards

U Game Board (left)

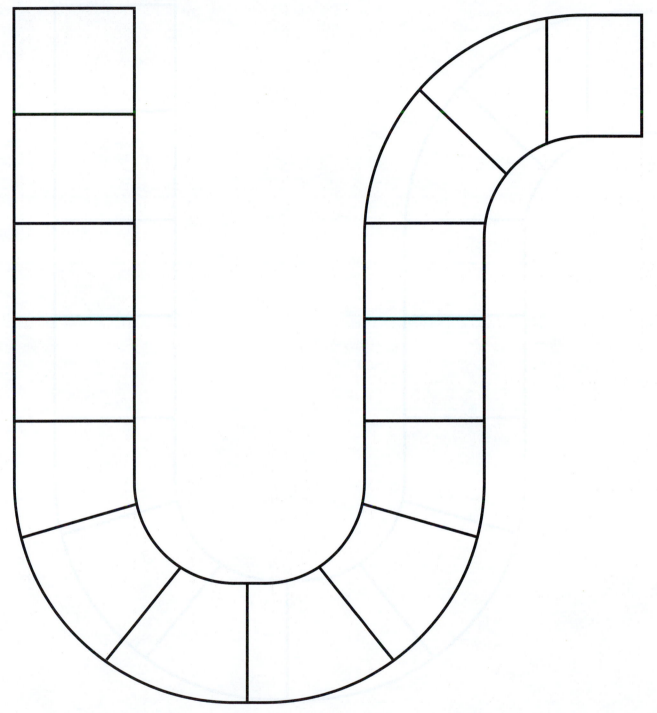

U Game Board (right)

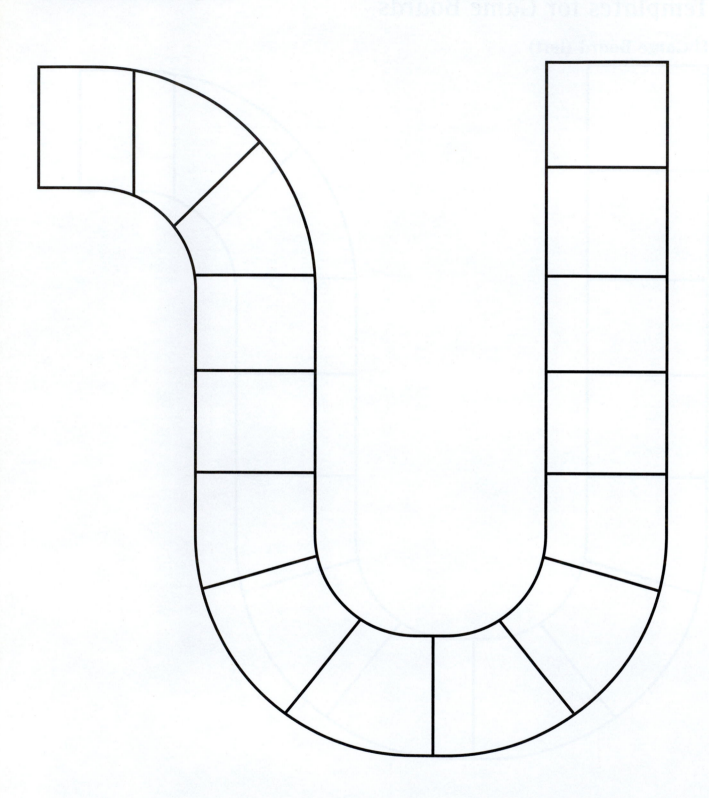

S Game Board (left)

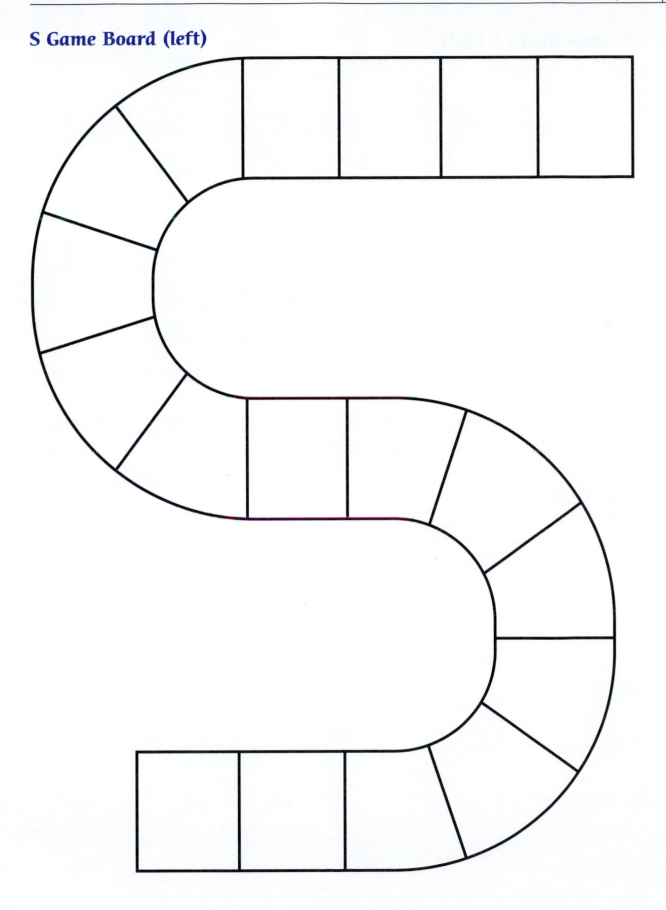

S Game Board (right)

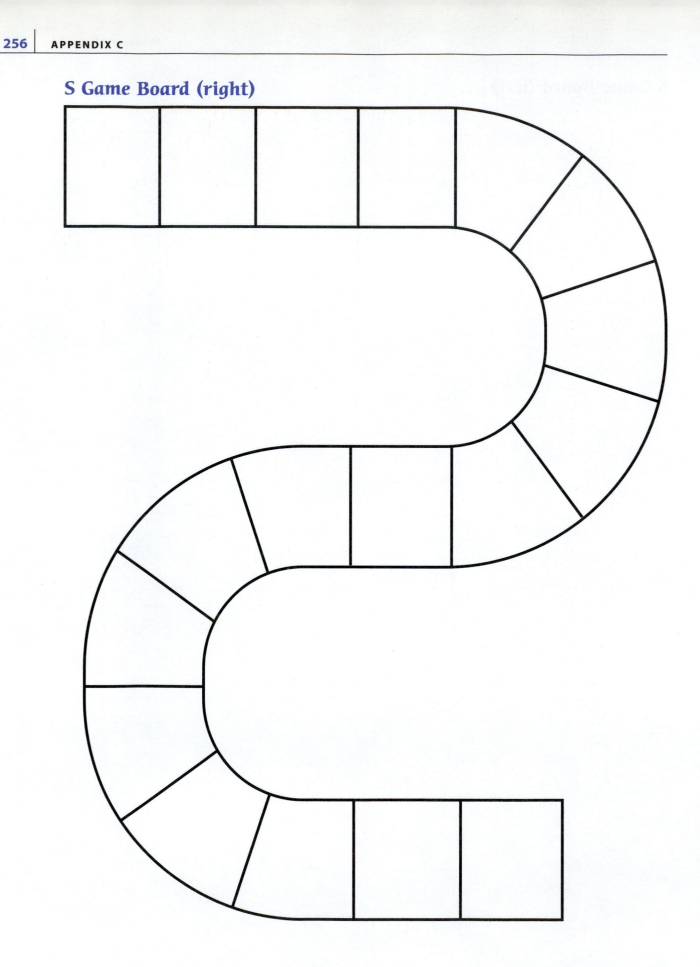

Directions for Spinner

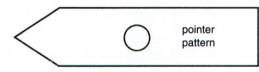

1. Glue a circle (patterns or cutouts to the right) onto a square of heavy cardboard that is no smaller than 4" × 4". Square spinner bases are easier to hold than round bases.

2. Cut a narrow slot in the center with the point of a sharp pair of scissors or a razor blade.

pointer
pattern

3. Cut the pointer from soft plastic (such as a milk jug) and make a clean round hole with a hole punch.

4. A washer, either a metal one from the hardware store or one cut from cardboard, helps the pointer move freely.

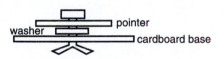

washer — pointer — cardboard base

5. Push a paper fastener through the pointer hole, the washer, and the slot in the spinner base. Flatten the legs, leaving space for the pointer to spin easily.

GLOSSARY

affricates Speech sounds produced when the breath stream is stopped and released at the point of articulation, usually where the tip of the tongue rubs against the roof of the mouth just behind the teeth, such as when pronouncing the final sound in the word *clutch* or the beginning sound in the word *trip*.

alliteration The occurrence in a phrase or line of speech of two or more words having the same beginning sound, as in "Simon sells seersucker suits."

alphabetic principle The concept that letters and letter combinations are used to represent phonemes in written language. English and Spanish are alphabetic writing systems. Chinese is not.

analytic Phonics instruction that begins with whole words and then divides them into their elemental parts through analysis.

blend An orthographic term referring to a sequence of two or three letters that are blended together. There are *l*- blends (*bl, cl, fl, gl, pl, sl*), *r*- blends (*br, cr, dr, fr, gr, pr, tr*), and *s*- blends (*sc, scr, sk, sp, st, squ, sw*). Although the letter sounds are blended together quickly, each one is pronounced.

choral reading Oral reading done in unison with another person or persons.

classroom composite A class profile that groups children into instructional groups by features to be taught.

concept book A simple book designed for young children to teach a single basic concept such as colors, shapes, numbers, alphabet, or opposites. Such illustrated books typically have limited text, if any, and may be in the form of board books.

concept of word The ability to match spoken words to printed words as demonstrated by the ability to accurately point to the words (including two-syllable words) of a memorized text.

concepts about print The conventions, orientations, and language of printed text such as use of punctuation and capitals, directionality, and tracking words.

concept sort A categorization task in which pictures, objects, or words are grouped by shared attributes or meanings to develop concepts and vocabulary.

consonant blends See *blend*.

consonant digraphs See *digraph*.

consonant A letters that is not a vowel (*a, e, i, o,* and *u*). Whereas vowel sounds are thought of as musical, consonant sounds are known for their noise and the way in which air is constricted as it is stopped and released or forced through the vocal tract, mouth, teeth, and lips.

consonant-vowel-consonant (CVC) Refers to the pattern of consonants and vowels within a syllable. The spelling pattern for the word *mat* would be represented a *CVC* pattern. The spelling pattern for the word *mail* would be represented as a *CVVC* pattern.

developmental spelling Spellings produced by young children who have not learned to spell in conventional ways. They are also called *invented spellings* because children generate spellings for words they do not have stored in memory based upon what they know about letter–sound relationships. Developmental spelling changes in predictable ways as children learn more about the spelling system.

digraph One sound represented by two letters. There are consonant digraphs and vowel digraphs, but the term most commonly refers to consonant digraphs. Common consonant digraphs include *sh, ch, th,* and *wh*.

directionality The left-to-right and top-to-bottom directions used for reading and writing English.

echo reading Oral reading in which the student echoes or imitates the reading of the teacher or partner. Echo reading is used with very beginning readers as a form of support.

emergent stage The period of literacy development ranging from birth to beginning reading. This period precedes the letter name–alphabetic stage of spelling development.

environmental print Words and graphic symbols found in the physical environment and in media such as signs, logos, advertisments, packaging labels, and billboards. Environmental print serves many functional purposes in the real world.

feature guide A tool used to score and classify students' errors on spelling inventories to assess students' knowledge of specific spelling features at their particular stage of spelling development. The guide is used to plan word study instruction to meet individual needs.

fingerpoint read Reading in which emergent and beginning readers use a finger to point to each word as it is spoken.

function words   Words that have little meaning of their own but establish grammatical relationships, such as conjunctions (*and, or, then*), articles (*a, an, the*), or prepositions (*of, in*).

high-frequency words   The most common words readers encounter in print. 100 words (such as *of, the, is was*) account for about 50 percent of words in texts.

invented spelling   A term coined by Charles Read to refer to young children's efforts to spell. Invented spellings are generated by any speller when the word is not stored in memory.

key picture   A pictures placed at the top of a category in a picture sort. Key pictures act as headers for each column.

key words   Words placed at the top of each category in a word sort. Key words act as headers for each column.

language experience or language experience approach (LEA)   A method of teaching reading in which students read about their own experiences recorded in their own language. Experience stories are dictated by the student to a teacher, who writes them down. Dictated accounts are reread in unison, in echo fashion, and independently.

letter name–alphabetic stage   The second stage of spelling development, in which students represent beginning, middle, and ending sounds of words with phonetically accurate letter choices. Often the selections are based on the sound of the letter name itself, rather than abstract letter–sound associations. The letter name *h* (aitch), for example, produces the /ch/ sound, and is often selected to represent that sound (HEP for *chip*).

letter–sound correspondences   The systematic matches between letters and sounds. They are also known as *graphophonics, grapheme–phoneme relationships,* or *phonics.*

literacy diet   A comprehensive daily curriculum for preschool and kindergarten that includes vocabulary and concept development, alphabet knowledge, phonological awareness, phonics, concepts about print, and a concept of word.

long vowel   A vowel whose sound says its letter name. The vocal cords are tense when producing the long-vowel sound. Because of this, the linguistic term for the long-vowel sound is *tense.* See also *short vowel.*

mock linear   Writing characterized by a linear arrangement of letterlike shapes and squiggles.

nasal   A sound produced when the air is blocked in the oral cavity but escapes through the nose. The first consonants in the words *mom* and *no* represent nasal sounds.

oddball   A word that does not fit a targeted feature in a sort.

onset   The initial consonant sound in a single syllable or word. The onset of the word *sun* is /s/. The onset of the word *slide* is /sl/.

personal reader   An individual book of reading materials for a beginning reader. Group experience charts, dictations, and rhymes comprise the majority of the reading material.

phoneme   The smallest unit of speech that distinguishes one word from another. For example, the *t* of *tug* and the *r* of *rug* are two phonemes.

phonemic awareness   The ability to consciously manipulate individual phonemes in a spoken language. Phonemic awareness is often assessed by the ability to tap, count, or push a penny forward for every sound heard in a word like *cat*: /c/ /a/ /t/.

phonics   The systematic relationship between letters and sounds.

phonics reader   A beginning reading book written with controlled vocabulary that contains recurring phonics elements.

phonological awareness   An awareness of various speech sounds such as syllables, rhyme, and individual phonemes.

preconsonantal nasals   Nasals that occur before consonants, as in the words *bump* or *sink.* The vowel is nasalized as part of the air escapes through the nose during pronunciation. See *nasals.*

predictable   Stories or texts that are easy to predict and memorize because the langauage is simple, patterned, and supported by illustrations.

prephonetic   Writing that bears no correspondence to speech sounds; literally, "before sound." Prephonetic writing occurs during the emergent stage and typically consists of random scribbles, mock linear writing, or hieroglyphic-looking symbols. See *mock linear.*

print referencing   An instructional strategy used with emergent readers to direct their attention to the orientation and conventions of print using the language of print such as *letter, word, sentence,* and *left-to-right.*

productive vocabulary   Words that are understood and used correctly by a speaker.

receptive vocabulary   Words understood when used by other speakers. Children's receptive vocabularies are larger than their productive vocabularies.

rime   A unit composed of the vowel and any subsequent consonants within the syllable. For example, the rime unit in the word *tag* would be *ag.*

salient sound   A prominent sound in a word or syllable that stands out because of the way it is made or felt in the mouth, or because of idiosyncratic reasons such as being similar to a sound in one's name.

semantic field   A collecton of words that are related by meaning. Cats, dogs, hamsters, and gerbils might be part of the semantic field of pets or of small mammals.

shared reading   An instructional setting in which the teacher first reads a memorable text aloud and then a group of children read along on subsequent readings using memory as a support.

short vowels   Vowels whose sound is produced when the vocal cords are more relaxed, in comparison to when producing the long-vowel sounds. Because of this, short-vowel sounds are often referred to as *lax*. The five short vowels can be heard at the beginning of these words: *apple, Ed, igloo, octopus,* and *umbrella*. See also *long vowel*.

sight word vocabulary   Words recognized and pronounced immediately "at first sight." The term *sight words* does not necessarily mean high-frequency words or phonetically irregular words. A sight word is simply any *known* word, regardless of its frequency or phonetic regularity.

syllable   A unit of spoken language that consists of a vowel that may be preceded and/or followed by several consonants. Syllables are units of sound and can often be detected by paying attention to movements of the mouth.

synthetic   Phonics instruction that begins with individual sounds and the blending of sounds to form words.

track   Fingerpoint reading a text, demonstrating concept of a word.

unvoiced   A sound that, when produced, does not cause the vocal cords to vibrate. See also *voiced*.

voiced   A sound that, when produced, vibrates the vocal cords. The letter sound /d/, for example, vibrates the vocal cords in a way that the letter sound /t/ does not. See also *unvoiced*.

vowel   A speech sound produced by the easy passage of air through a relatively open vocal tract. Vowels form the most central sound of a syllable. In English, vowel sounds are represented by the following letters: *a, e, i, o, u,* and sometimes *y*. See also *consonants*.

whole-to-part   An instructional framework for teaching beginning reading that first introduces the whole text, which is read aloud as shared reading. Then attention is directed to smaller and smaller parts, moving from sentences to words to letters and sounds.

within word pattern stage   The third stage of spelling development, in which spellers have mastered the basic letter–sound correspondences of written English and grapple with letter sequences that function as a unit, especially long-vowel patterns. Some of the letters in the unit may have no sound themselves. These silent letters, such as the silent *-e* in *snake* or the silent *-i* in *drain*, serve as important markers in the pattern.

word bank   A collection of known words harvested from frequently read texts such as little leveled books, dictated stories, basal preprimers, and primers. Word bank words are written on small cards. Words students can recognize with ease are used in word study games and word sorts.

word families   Words that share the same rime (e.g., *fast, past, last, blast,* all share the *ast* rime). See also *rime*.

word study   A learner-centered, conceptual approach to instruction in phonics, spelling, word recognition, and vocabulary.

word wall   A display of words that children are expected to use in reading and writing. Typically a word wall contains a large number of high-frequency words that are introduced gradually over the course of a year.

zone of proximal development (ZPD)   A term coined by the Russian psychologist Vygotsky referring to the ripe conditions for learning something new. A person's ZPD is that zone which is neither too hard nor too easy.

REFERENCES

Adams, M. J. (1990). *Beginning to read*. Cambridge, MA: Harvard University Press.

Adams, M. J., Foorman, B. R., Lundberg, I., & Beeler, T. (1998). *Phonemic awareness in young children: A classroom curriculum*. Baltimore, MD: Paul H. Brookes.

American Heritage First Dictionary, The. (2007). Boston, MA: Houghton Mifflin Harcourt.

Asher, A. V. (2006). Handwriting instruction in elementary schools. *Journal of Occupational Therapy, 60*, 461–471.

August, D., & Shanahan, T. (Eds.). (2006). Developing literacy in second-language learners: Report of the National Literacy Panel on Language-Minority Children and Youth. Mahwah, NJ: Lawrence Erlbaum.

Bara, F., & Gentaz, E. (2011). Haptics in teaching handwriting: The role of perceptual and visuo-motor skills. *Human Movement Science, 30*, 745–759.

Barrentine, S. J. (1996). Engaging with reading through interactive read-alouds. *The Reading Teacher, 50*, 36–42.

Bates, E., Marchman, V., Thal, D., Fenson, L., Dale, P., Reznick, J., et al. (1994). Developmental and stylistic variation in the composition of early vocabulary. *Journal of Child Language, 21*, 85–123.

Bear, D., Caserta-Henry, C, & Venner, D. (2004). *Personal readers for emergent and beginning readers*. San Diego, CA: Teaching Resource Center.

Bear, D. R., & Helman, L. (2004). Word study for vocabulary development: An ecological perspective on instruction during the early stages of literacy learning. In J. F. Baumann & E. J. Kame'enui (Eds.), *Vocabulary instruction: Research to practice* (pp. 139–158). New York, NY: Guilford.

Bear, D. R., Invernizzi, M., Johnston, F., & Templeton, S. (2010). *Words Their Way: Letter and picture sorts for emergent spellers*. Boston, MA: Allyn & Bacon.

Bear, D. R., Invernizzi, M., Templeton, S., & Johnston, F. (2012). *Words Their Way: Word study for phonics, vocabulary, and spelling instruction* (5th ed.). Boston, MA: Pearson.

Beck, I. L., McKeown, M. G., & Kucan, L. (2002). *Bringing words to life: Robust vocabulary instruction*. New York, NY: Guilford.

Beck, I. L., McKeown, M. G., & Kucan, L. (2008). *Creating robust vocabulary: Frequently asked questions and extended examples* (Vol. 10). New York, NY: Guilford.

Beck, I. L., McKeown, M. G., & Kucan, L. (2013). *Bringing words to life: Robust vocabulary instruction* (2nd ed.). New York, NY: Guilford.

Belvel, P. S. (2010). *Rethinking classroom management: Strategies for prevention, intervention, and problem solving* (2nd ed.). Thousand Oaks, CA: Corwin Press.

Berninger, V. (1999). Coordinating transcription and text generation in working memory during composing: Automatic and constructive processes. *Learning Disabilities Quarterly, 22*, 99–112. Cited in Puranik, Lonigan, & Kim (2012).

Bhattacharyya, R. (2010). *The castle in the classroom: Story as springboard for early literacy*. Portland, ME: Stenhouse.

Biemiller, A. (2005). Size and sequence in vocabulary development: Implications for choosing words for primary grade vocabulary instruction. In E. H. Hiebert & M. L. Kamil (Eds.), *Teaching and learning vocabulary: Bringing research to practice* (pp. 223–242). Mahwah, NJ: Lawrence Erlbaum.

Biemiller, A., & Boote, C. (2006). An effective method for building meaning vocabulary in primary grades. *Journal of Educational Psychology, 98*(1), 44–62.

Biemiller, A., & Slonim, N. (2001). Estimating root word vocabulary growth in normative and advantaged populations: Evidence for a common sequence of vocabulary acquisition. *Journal of Educational Psychology, 93*, 498–520.

Blachman, B. A. (1994). What we have learned from longitudinal studies of phonological processing and reading, and some unanswered questions: A response to Torgenson, Wagner, and Rashotte. *Journal of Learning Disabilities, 27*, 287–291.

Blachman, B. A., Ball, E. W., Black, S., & Tangel, D. M. (1994). Kindergarten teachers develop phoneme awareness in low-income, inner city classrooms: Does it make a difference? *Reading and Writing: An Interdisciplinary Journal, 6*, 1–18.

Blackwell-Bullock, R., Invernizzi, M., Drake, A., & Howell, J. L. (2009). Concept of word in text: An integral literacy skill. *Reading in Virginia, XXXI*, 30–36.

Blevins, W. (1997). *Phonemic awareness activities for early reading success*. New York, NY: Scholastic.

Bloodgood, J. W. (1999). What's in a name? Children's name writing and literacy acquisition. *Reading Research Quarterly, 34*, 342–367.

Bradley, L., & Bryant, P. (1983). Categorizing sounds and learning to read: A causal connection. *Nature, 30*, 419–421.

Bradley, B. B., & Jones, J. (2007). Sharing alphabet books in early childhood classrooms. *The Reading Teacher, 60*, 452–463.

Burgess, S. R., & Lonigan, C. J. (1998). Bidirectional relations of phonological sensitivity and prereading abilities: Evidence from a preschool sample. *Journal of experimental child psychology, 70*(2), 117–141.

Button, K., Johnson, M. J. & Furgerson, P. (1996). Interactive writing in a primary classroom. *The Reading Teacher, 49*, 446–454.

Cabell, S., Justice, L., Kaderavek, J., Pence, K., & Smith, A. (2009). *Emergent literacy: Lessons for success*. Plural Publishing.

Cabell, S. Q., Tortorelli, L. S., & Gerde, H. K. (2013). How do I write . . .? Scaffolding preschoolers' early writing skills. *The Reading Teacher, 66*(8), 650–659.

CA Commission on Teacher Credentialing. (2009). *California standards for the teaching profession (CSTP; 2009)*. Sacramento, CA: Commission on Teacher Credentialing.

Cambourne, B. (1988). *The whole story*. New York, NY: Scholastic.

Carey, S. (1978). The child as a word learner. In M. Halle, J. Bresnan, & G. Miller (Eds.), Linguistic theory and psychological reality (pp. 264–293). Cambridge, MA: MIT Press.

Carpenter, K. (2010). *The relationships among concept sorts, storybook reading, language-based print awareness, and language proficiency in the vocabulary learning of kindergarten children*. Unpublished doctoral dissertation, University of Nevada, Reno.

Cathey, S. S. (1991). *Emerging concept of word: Exploring young children's ability to read rhymic text*. Doctoral dissertation, University of Nevado, Reno, UMII #9220355.

Chaney, C. (1989). I pledge a legiance tothe flag: Three studies in word segmentation. *Applied Psycholinguistics, 10*(3), 261–82.

Clark, E. V. (2003). *First language acquisition*. Cambridge: Cambridge University Press.

Clay, M. (1985). *Early detection of reading difficulties* (3rd ed.). Auckland, New Zealand: Heinemann.

Clay, M. M. (1990). *Reading: The patterning of complex behavior*. Portsmouth, NH: Heinemann.

Clay, M. (1993). *An observational survey of early literary achievement*. Auckland, New Zealand: Heinemann.

Clay, M. (2001). *Change over time in children's literacy development*. Portsmouth, NH: Heinemann.

Common Core State Standards for English Language Arts & Literacy in History/Social Studies, Science, and Technical Subjects. (2010, March). Retrieved January 25, 2011, from www.corestandards.org/assets/CCSSI_ELA%20Standards.pdf

Coxhead, A. (2000). A new academic word list. *TESOL Quarterly, 34*(2), 213–238.

Cunningham, A. E., & Stanovich, K. E. (2003). Reading matters: How reading engagement influences cognition. In J. Flood, D. Lapp, J. Squire, & J. Jensen (Eds.), *Handbook of research on teaching in the English language arts* (Vol. 2, pp. 857–867). Mahwah, NJ: Lawrence Erlbaum.

Cunningham, P. (1988). Names—A natural for early reading and writing. *Reading Horizons, 23*, pp. 114–122.

Cunningham, P. M. (2009). *Phonics they use: Words for reading and writing* (6th ed.). New York, NY: Pearson.

De Houwer, A. (1995). Bilingual language acquisition. In P. Fletcher (Ed.), *The handbook of child language* (pp. 219–250). Oxford: Blackwell.

Dickinson, D., McCabe, A., & Essex, M. J. (2006). A window of opportunity we must open to all: The case for preschool with high-quality support for language and literacy. In D. K. Dickinson & S. B. Neuman (Eds.), *Handbook of early literacy research* (Vol. 2). Baltimore, MD: Paul H. Brookes.

Dolch, E. W. (1936). A basic sight vocabulary. *The Elementary School Journal, 36*(6), 456–460.

Dorr, R. E. (2006). Something old is new again: Revisiting language experience. *The Reading Teacher, 60*(2), 138–146.

Downing, J. (1979). *Reading and reasoning*. New York, NY: Springer-Verlag.

Duffy, G. G. (2009). *Explaining reading* (2nd ed.). New York, NY: Guilford.

Duncan, G., Dowsett, C., Claessens, A., Mangnuson, K., Huston, A., Klebanov, P., et al. (2007). School readiness and later achievement. *Developmental Psychology, 43*(6), 1428–1446.

Durgunoglu, A. Y., Nagy, W. E., & Hancin-Bhatt, B. J. (1993). Cross-language transfer of phonological awareness. *Journal of Educational Psychology, 85*(3), 453–465.

Ehri, L. C. (1975). Word consciousness in readers and prereaders. *Journal of Educational Psychology, 67*(2), 204.

Ehri, L. C. (1993). How English orthography influences phonological knowledge as children learn to read and spell. In R. J. Scales (Ed.), *Literacy and language analysis* (pp. 21–43). Hillsdale, NJ: Lawrence Erlbaum.

Ehri, L. C. (1995). Phases of development in reading words. *Journal of Research in Reading, 18*, 116–125.

Ehri, L. C. (1997). Learning to read and learning to spell are one and the same, almost. In C. Perfetti, L. Rieban, & M. Fayol (Eds.), *Learning to spell: Research, theory, and practice across languages*. Mahwah, NJ: Lawrence Erlbaum.

Ehri, L. C., & Roberts, K. T. (1979). Do beginners learn printed words betters in context or in isolation? *Child Development, 50*, 675–685.

Ehri, L., & Roberts, T. (2006). The roots of learning to read and write: Acquisition of letters and phonemic awareness. In D. K. Dickenson & S. B. Neuman (Eds.), *Handbook of early literacy research* (Vol. 2). New York, NY: Guilford.

Ehri, L. C., & Wilce, L. S. (1985). Movement into reading: Is the first stage of printed word learning visual or phonetic? *Reading Research Quarterly, 20*(2), 163–179.

Elkonin, D. B. (1973). U.S.S.R. In J. Downing (Ed.), *Comparative reading*. New York, NY: MacMillan.

Ericson, L., & Juliebo, M. F. (1998). *The phonological awareness handbook for kindergarten and primary teachers*. Newark, DE: International Reading Association.

Evans, M. A., Bell, M., Shaw, D., Moreti, S, & Page, J. (2006). Letter names, letter sounds and phonological awareness: an examination of kindergarten children across letters and of letters across children. *Reading and Writing, 19*, 959–989.

Evertson, C. M. (1987). Creating conditions for learning: From research to practice. *Theory into Practice, 26*(1), 44–50.

Ferreiro, E., & Teberosky, A. (1982). *Literacy before schooling*. Exeter, NH: Heinemann Educational Books. (Originally published 1979.)

Fink-Chorzempa, B., Graham, S., & Harris, K. R. (2005). What can I do to help young children who struggle with writing? *Teaching Exceptional Children, 37*, 64–66.

Fisher, D., & Frey, N. (2008). Better learning through structured teaching: A framework for gradual release of responsibility. Alexandria, VA: Association for Supervision & Curriculum Development.

Fitzpatrick, J. (1998). *Phonemic awareness: Playing with sounds to strengthen beginning reading skills*. Cypress, CA: Creative Teaching Press.

Flanigan, K. (2007). A concept of word in text: A pivotal event in early reading acquisition. *Journal of Literacy Research, 39*(1), 37–70.

Flanigan, K. W. (2003). A concept of word in text: A watershed event in early reading acquisition. Ph.D. diss., University of Virginia. Retrieved from http://search.proquest.com/docview/305304092?accountid=14678

Fuchs, L. S., Fuchs, D., & Maxwell, L. (1988). The validity of informal reading comprehension measures. *Remedial and Special Education, 9*(2), 20–28.

Fry, E. (1980). The new instant word list. *The Reading Teacher, 34*(3), 284–289.

Gill, S. R., & Islam, C. (2011). Shared reading goes high-tech. *The Reading Teacher, 65,* 224–227.

Gillet, J. W., & Kita, M. J. (1979). Words, kids and categories. *The Reading Teacher, 32*(5), 538–542.

Goswami, U. (2001). Early phonological development and the acquisition of literacy. In S. B. Neuman & D. K. Dickinson (Eds.), *Handbook of early literacy research* (Vol. I, pp. 111–125). New York, NY: Guilford.

Goswami, U. (2008). Reading complexity and the brain. *Literacy, 42*(2), 67–74.

Graham, S., Berninger, V., Abbott, R., Abbott, S., & Whitaker, D. (1997). The role of mechanics in composing of elementary school students: A new methodological approach. *Journal of Educational Psychology, 89,* 170–182.

Halliday, M. A. K. (1975). *Learning how to mean: Explorations in the development of language.* London, England: Edward Arnold.

Halliday, M. A. (1993). Towards a language-based theory of learning. *Linguistics and education, 5*(2), 93–116.

Halliday, M. A. K. (2002). Relevant models of language. In B. M. Power & R. S. Hubbard (Eds.), *Language development: A reader for teachers* (2nd ed., pp. 49–53). Upper Saddle River, NJ: Merrill.

Hammill, D. D. (2004). What we know about correlates of reading. *Exceptional Children, 70*(4), 453–468.

Hamre, B. K. & Pianta, R. C. (2005). Can instructional and emotional support in the first-grade classroom make a difference for children at risk of school failure? *Child Development, 76*(5), 949–967.

Harste, J. C., Woodward, V. A., & Burke, C. L. (1984). *Language stories and literacy lessons.* Porstmouth, NH: Heinemann.

Hart, B., & Risley, T. R. (1995). *Meaningful differences in the everyday experience of American children.* Baltimore, MD: Paul C. Brookes.

Helman, L. (2004). Building on the sound system of Spanish: Insights from the alphabetic spellings of English language learners. *The Reading Teacher, 57,* 452–460.

Helman, L. (2012). *Literacy instruction in multilingual classrooms: Engaging English learners in elementary school.* New York, NY: Teachers College Press.

Helman, L., Bear, D. R., Invernizzi, M., Templeton, S., Johnston, F. (2009). *Words Their Way: Letter name–alphabetic sorts for Spanish-speaking English learners.* Boston, MA: Allyn & Bacon.

Henderson, E. H. (1981). *Learning to read and spell: The child's knowledge of words.* Dekalb: Northern Illinois Press.

Henderson, E. H. (1992). The interface of lexical competence and knowledge of written words. In S. E. Templeton & D. R. Bear (Eds.), *Development of orthographic knowledge and the foundations of literacy: A memorial festschrift for Edmund H. Henderson.* Hillsdale, NJ: Lawrence Erlbaum.

Henderson, E. H., & Beers, J. W. (1980). *Developmental and cognitive aspects of learning to spell: A reflection of word knowledge.* Newark, DE: International Reading Association.

Holdaway, D. (1979). *The foundations of literacy.* Sydney, Australia: Ashton Scholastic.

Holden, M. H., & McGinitie, W. H. (1972). Children's conceptions of word boundaries in speech and print. *Journal of Educational Psychology, 63*(6), 551–557.

Hildreth, G. (1936). Developmental sequences in name writing. *Child Development, 7.* 291–303.

Huang, F., & Invernizzi, M. (2012). The case for confusability and other factors associated with lowercase alphabet naming. *Applied Psycholinguistics.* DOI: http://dx.doi.org/10.1017/S0142716412000604.

Invernizzi, M. (2010). PALS Quick Checks for Progress Monitoring. Retrieved from https://pals.virginia.edu/tools-quick-checks.html

Invernizzi, M., & Hayes, L. (2010). Developmental patterns of reading proficiency and reading difficulties. *Handbook of Reading Disabilities Research,* 196–207.

Invernizzi, M., & Huang, F. (2011). Phonological Awareness Literacy Screening for Kindergarten (PALS-K): Technical Report Prepared for the Virginia Department of Education, Charlottesville, Virginia.

Invernizzi, M., Juel, C., Swank, L., & Meier, J. (2004). *Phonological awareness literacy screening—kindergarten (PALS-K): Technical reference.* Charlottesville: University of Virginia Printing Services.

Invernizzi, M., Juel, C., Swank, L., & Meier, J. D. (2008). *PALS: Phonological awareness literacy screening: Kindergarten.* Charlottesville: University of Virginia Printing Services.

Invernizzi, M., Justice, L., Landrum, T., & Booker, K. (2004). Early literacy screening in kindergarten: Widespread implementation in Virginia. *Journal of Literacy Research, 36*(4), 479–500.

Invernizzi, M., Sullivan, A, Meier, J., & Swank, L. (2004). *Phonological awareness and literacy screening preK.* Charlottesville: University of Virginia Printing Services.

Johnston, F. R. (1998). The reader, the text, and the task: Learning words in first grade. *The Reading Teacher, 51,* 666–675.

Johnston, F. R. (2000). Word learning in predictable text. *Journal of Educational Psychology, 92,* 248–255.

Johnston, F. R. (2003, December). The Primary Spelling Inventory: Exploring Its Validity and Relationship to Reading Levels. Paper presented at the National Reading Conference, Scottsdale, AZ.

Juel, C. (1991). Beginning reading. In P. D. Pearson, R. Barr, M. L. Kamil, & P. Rosenthal (Eds.), *Handbook of reading research* (Vol. 2). New York, NY: Longman.

Juel, C., Biancarosa, G., Coker, D., & Deffes, R. (2003). Walking with Rosie: A cautionary tale of literacy instruction. *Educational Leadership, 60*(7), 12–18.

Justice, L. M., & Ezell, H. K. (2004). Print referencing: An emergent literacy enhancement technique and its clinical applications. *Language, Speech, and Hearing Services in Schools, 35,* 185–193.

Justice, L. M., Kaderavek, J. N., Fan, X., Sofka, A., & Hunt, A. (2009). Accelerating preschoolers early literacy development through classroom-based teacher child story book reading and explicit print referencing. *Language, Speech, & Hearing Services in Schools, 40,* 67–85.

Justice, L. M., & Pullen, P. (2003). Promising interventions for promoting emergent literacy skills: Three evidence-based approaches. *Topics in Early Childhood Special Education, 23,* 99–113.

Kearns, G., & Biemiller, A. (2010/2011). Two-questions vocabulary assessment: Developing a new method for group testing in kindergarten through second grade. *Journal of Education, 190*(1–2), 31–41.

Kim, Y., Petscher, Y., Foorman, B., & Zhou, C. (2010). The contributions of phonological awareness and letter name knowledge to letter-sound acquisition—A cross-classified multilevel model approach. *Journal of Educational Psychology, 102*, 313–326.

Kohn, A. (1996, September). What to look for in a classroom. *Educational Leadership,* 54–55.

Lane, H. B., & Allen, S. A. (2010). The vocabulary-rich classroom: Modeling sophisticated word use to promote word consciousness and vocabulary growth. *The Reading Teacher, 63*(5), 362–370.

Lawrence, J. F., & Snow, C. E. (2011). 14 Oral Discourse and Reading. In M. L. Kamil, P. D. Pearson, E. B. Moje, & P. P. Afflerbach (Eds.), *Handbook of reading research* (Vol. IV, pp. 320–338). New York, NY: Routledge.

LePage, P., Darling-Hammond, L., Akar, H., Gutierrez, C., Jenkins-Gunn, E., & Rosebrock, K. (2005). Classroom management. In L. Darling-Hammond & J. Bransford (Eds.), *Preparing teachers for a changing world: What teachers should learn and be able to do.* San Francisco, CA: Jossey-Bass.

Levin, I., & Aram, D. (2004). Children's names contribute to early literacy: A linguistic and social perspective. In D. Ravid & H. Shyldkrot (Eds.), *Perspectives on language and language development* (pp. 219–239). Amsterdam, The Netherlands: Kluwer.

Longman Elementary Dictionary, The. (2010). Harlow, England: Pearson Longman.

Lonigan, L., & Shanahan, T. (2009). *Developing early literacy: Report of the National Early Literacy Panel: A scientific synthesis of early literacy development and implications for intervention.* Washington, DC: National Institute for Literacy.

Lundberg, I., Frost, J., & Peterson, O. P. (1988). Effects of an extensive program for stimulating phonological awareness in preschool children. *Reading Research Quarterly, 23*(3), 263–284.

Mapp, K. L. (2003). Having their say: Parents describe why and how they are engaged in their children's learning. *The School Community Journal, 13*(1), 35–64.

Mashburn, A. J., Justice, L. M., Downer, J. T., & Pianta, R. C. (2009). Peer effects on children's language achievement during pre-kindergarten. *Child Development, 80*(3), 686–702.

Mayer, K. (2007). Emerging knowledge about emerging writing. *Young Children, 62*, 34–40.

McBride-Chang, C. (1999). *The ABC's of the ABC's: The development of letter-name knowledge. Merrill-Palmer Quarterly, 45*, 285–308.

McCabe, A. (1996). *Chameleon readers: Teaching children to appreciate all kinds of good stories.* New York, NY: McGraw-Hill.

McCarrier, A., Pinnell, G. S., & Fountas, I. C. (2000). *Interactive writing: how language & literacy come together, K–2.* Portsmouth, NH: Heinemann.

McCracken, R. A. & McCracken, M. J. (1986). *Stories, songs and poetry to teach reading and writing.* Winnepeg, Ontario: Pequis.

McGee, L. M., & Richgels, D. J. (2012). *Literacy's beginnings: Supporting young readers and writers* (6th ed.). Boston, MA: Pearson/Allyn & Bacon.

McGinty, A. S., & Justice, L. M. (2010). Language facilitation in the preschool classroom: Rationale, goals and strategies. In M. C. McKenna, S. Walpole, & K. Conradi (Eds.), *Promoting early reading: Research, resources, and best practices.* New York, NY: Guilford.

McKenzie, M. G. (1985). Shared writing: Apprenticeship in writing. *Language Matters,* 1–2, 1–5.

Mesmer, H. (2008). *Tools for matching readers to texts: Research-based practices.* New York, NY: Guilford.

Metsala, J. L. (2011). Lexical reorganization and the emergence of phonological awareness. In S. B. Neuman and D. K. Dickinson (Eds.), *Handbook of early literacy research* (Vol. III, pp. 66–84). New York, NY: Guilford.

Morais, J., Cary, L., Alegria, J., & Bertelson, P. (1979). Does awareness of speech as a sequence of phones arise spontaneously? *Cognition, 7*(4), 323–331.

Morgan, R. K., & Meier, C. R. (2008). Dialogic reading's potential to improve children's emergent literacy skills and behavior. *Preventing School Failure, 52*, 11–16.

Morris, D. (1981). Concept of word: A developmental phenomenon in the beginning reading and writing processes. *Language Arts, 58*(6), 659–668.

Morris, D., Bloodgood, J. W., Lomax, R. G., & Perney, J. (2003a). Developmental steps in learning to read: A longitudinal study in kindergarten and first grade. *Reading Research Quarterly, 38*, 302–328.

Morris, D., Bloodgood, J., & Perney, J. (2003b). Kindergarten predictors of first- and second-grade reading achievement. *The Elementary School Journal, 104*(2), 93–109.

Murray, B. A., Stahl, S. A., & Ivy, M. G. (1996) Developing phoneme awareness through alphabet books. *Reading and Writing: An Interdisciplinary Journal, 8*, 307–322.

National Center for Family Literacy. (2003). *Synthesis of scientific research on development of early literacy in young children.* National Early Literacy Panel (NELP).

National Early Literacy Panel (NELP). (2008). *Developing early literacy: Report of the National Early Literacy Panel.* Retrieved from www.nifl.gov/earlychildhood/NELP/NELPShanahan.html

National Reading Panel (NRP). (2000). *Teaching children to read: An evidence-based assessment of the scientific research literature on reading and its implications for reading instruction.* Washington, DC: National Institute of Child Health and Development.

Opitz, M. F. (2000). *Rhymes and reasons: Literature and language play for phonological awareness.* Portsmouth, NH: Heinemann.

Otto, B. (2010). *Language development in early childhood.* Upper Saddle River, NJ: Merrill.

Pearson, P. D., & Gallagher, M. (1983). The instruction of reading comprehension. *Contemporary Educational Psychology, 8*, 317–344.

Pentimonti, J. M., & Justice, L. M. (2010). Teachers' use of scaffolding strategies during read alouds in the preschool classroom. *Early Childhood Education Journal, 37*(4), 241–248.

Perfetti, C. (2007). Reading ability: Lexical quality to comprehension. *Scientific studies of reading, 11*(4), 357–383.

Piasta, S. B., Justice, L. M., McGinty, A. S., & Kaderavek, J. N. (2012). Increasing young children's contact with print during shared reading: Longitudinal effects on literacy achievement. *Child Development, 83*(3), 810–820.

Pufpaff, L. (2009). A developmental continuum of phonological sensitivity skills. *Psychology in the Schools, 46*(7), 679–691.

Pullen, P. C., & Justice, L. M. (2003). Enhancing phonological awareness, print awareness, & oral language skills in preschool children. *Intervention in School & Clinic, 39*(2), 87–98.

Puranik, C. S., & Lonigan, C. J. (2011). Scribbles to scrabble: Preschool children's developing knowledge of written language. *Read and Writing, 24,* 567–589.

Puranik, C. S., Lonigan, C. J., & Kim, Y. S. (2011). Contributions of emergent literacy skills to name writing, letter writing, and spelling in preschool children. *Early Childhood Research Quarterly, 26*(4), 465–474.

Read, C. (1971). Preschool children's knowledge of English phonology. *Harvard Educational Review, 41*(1), 1–34.

Reutzel, D. R. (2008). Effective Letter Recognition in Kindergarten and First Grade: Lessons Learned from Research and from Working with Early Readers in High Poverty Settings. Paper presented at the International Reading Association Convention, Atlanta, GA.

Reutzel, D. R., & Wolfersberger, M. (1996). An environmental impact statement: Designing supportive literacy classrooms for young children. *Reading Horizons, 36,* 266–282.

Richgels, D. J. (2001). Invented spelling, phonemic awareness, and reading and writing instruction. In S. B. Newman & D.K. Dickenson (Eds.), *Handbook of early literacy* (pp. 142–155). New York, NY: Guilford.

Roskos, K. A., & Neuman, S. B. (2001). Environment and its influences for early literacy teaching and learning. In S. B. Neuman & D. K. Dickinson (Eds.), *Handbook of early literacy research* (pp. 281–294). New York, NY: Guilford.

Schickedanz, J. A. (1999). *Much more than the ABCs.* Washington, DC: National Association for the Education of Young Children.

Scott, J. A., Skobel, B. J., & Wells, J. (2008). *The word-conscious classroom: Building the vocabulary readers and writers need.* New York, NY: Scholastic.

Share, D. L. (2004). Knowing letter names and learning letter sounds: A causal connection. *Journal of Experimental Child Psychology, 88,* 213–233.

Slaughter, J. P. (1993). *Beyond storybooks: Young children and the shared book experience.* Newark, DE: International Reading Association.

Smith, R. (2012). An Examination of the Relationship between the Development of Concept of Word in Text and Other Early Literacy Measures. Paper presented at the 62nd annual conference of the Literacy Research Association (LRA), San Diego, CA.

Smith, M. W., & Dickinson, D. K. (2002). *Early language and literacy classroom observation (ELLCO) toolkit* (research edition). Baltimore, MD: Paul H. Brookes.

Smith, S. B., Simons, D. C., & Kame'enui, E. J. (1995). Synthesis of research on phonological awareness: Principles and implications for reading acquisition. (Tech. Rep. no. 21). Eugene OR: University of Oregon. National Center to Improve the Tools of Educators.

Smolkin, L. B, Yaden, D. B., Brown, L., & Hofius, B. (1992). The effects of genre, visual design choices, and discourse structures on preschoolers responses to picture books during parent-child read-alouds. In C. K. Kinzer & D. J. Leu (Eds.), *Literacy research, theory, and practice: Views from many perspectives* (41st yearbook of the National Reading Conference (pp. 291–301). Chicago, IL: National Reading Conference.

Snow, C. E., Burns, M. S., & Griffin, P. (Eds.). (1998). *Preventing reading difficulties in young children.* Washington, DC: National Academy Press.

Soderman, A. K., Gregory, K. M. & McCarty, L. T. (2005). *Scaffolding emergent literacy* (2nd ed). Boston, MA: Pearson.

Stahl, K. A., & Stahl, S. A. (2012). Young word wizards! Fostering vocabulary development in preschool and primary education. In J. F. Baumann & E. J. Kame'enui (Eds.), *Vocabulary instruction: Research to practice* (2nd ed., pp. 72–92). New York, NY: Guilford.

Stauffer, R. G. (1970). *The language-experience approach to the teaching of reading.* New York: Harper & Row.

Stauffer, R. (1980). *The language-experience approach to the teaching of reading* (2nd ed.). New York, NY: Harper & Row.

Templeton, S. (2009). Foreword. *Curious George's Dictionary.* Boston, MA: Houghton Mifflin Harcourt.

Templeton, S., & Gehsmann, K. M. (2014). *Teaching reading and writing: The developmental approach.* Boston, MA: Pearson/Allyn & Bacon.

Templeton, S., & Spivey, E. M. (1980). The concept of "word" in young children as a function of level of cognitive development. *Research in the Teaching of English, 14,* 265–278.

Templeton, S., & Thomas, P. W. (1984). Performance and reflection: Young children's concept of "word." *Journal of Educational Research, 27,* 139–146.

Treiman, R. (1985). Onsets and rimes as units of spoken syllables: Evidence from children. *Journal of Educational Psychology, 77*(4), 417–427.

Treiman, R., & Broderick, V. (1998). What's in a name: Children's knowledge about letters in their own names. *Journal of Experimental Child Psychology, 70,* 97–116.

Treiman, R., & Kessler, B. (2003). The role of letter names in the acquisition of literacy. In R. Kail (Ed.), *Advances in child development and behavior* (Vol. 31, pp. 105–135). San Diego, CA: Academic Press.

Treiman, R., Weatherston, S., & Berch, D. (1994). The role of letter names in children's learning of phoneme-grapheme relations. *Applied Psycholinguistics, 15,* 97–122.

Turnbull, K. L. P., Bowles, R. P., Skibbe, L. E., Justice, L. M., & Wiggins, A. K. (2010). Theoretical explanations for preschoolers' lowercase alphabet knowledge. *Journal of Speech, Language & Hearing Research, 53,* 1757–1768.

Verhoeven, L., van Leeuwe, J., & Vermeer, A. (2011). Vocabulary growth and reading development across the elementary school years. *Scientific Studies of Reading, 15,* 8–25.

Vygotsky, L. S. (1962). *Language and thought.* Cambridge, MA: MIT Press.

Ward, A. (2009). *A formative study investigating interactive reading activities to develop kindergartners' science vocabulary.* Unpublished doctoral dissertation, University of Virginia.

Warley, H. P., Landrum, T. J., Invernizzi, M. A., & Justice, L. (2005). Prediction of first grade reading achievement:

A comparison of kindergarten predictors. In *Yearbook—National Reading Conference* (Vol. 54, p. 428). Oak Creek, WI: National Reading Conference.

Wasik, B. A., Bond, M. A., & Hindman, A. (2006). The effects of a language and literacy intervention on Head Start children and teachers. *Journal of Educational Psychology, 98*(1), 63.

West, S., & Cox, A. (2004). *Literacy play.* Beltsville, MD: Gryphon House.

Whitehurst, G. J. (1979). Meaning and semantics. In G. J. Whitehurst and B. J. Zimmerman (Eds.), *The functions of language and cognition* (pp. 115–139). New York, NY: Academic Press.

Whitehurst, G. J., Arnold, D. S., Epstein, J. N., Angell, A. L., Smith, M., & Fischel, J. E. (1994). A picture reading intervention in day-care and home for children from low-income families. *Developmental Psychology, 300,* 679–689.

Whitehurst, G. J., Zevenbergen, A. A., Crone, D. A., Schultz, M. D., Velting, O. N., & Fischel, J. E. (1999). Outcomes of an emergent literacy intervention from Head Start through second grade. *Journal of Educational Psychology, 91*(2), 261–272.

Williams, C., Sherry, T., Robinson, N., & Hungler, D. (2012). The practice page as a meditational tool for interactive writing instruction. *The Reading Teacher, 65,* 330–340.

Wolfersberger, M. E., Reutzel, D. R., Sudweeks, R., & Fawson, P. C. (2004). Developing and validating the Classroom Literacy Environmental Profile (CLEP): A tool for examining the "print richness" of early childhood and elementary classrooms. *Journal of Literacy Research, 36*(2), 83–144.

Worden, P., & Boettcher, W. (1990). Young children's acquisition of alphabet knowledge. *Journal of Reading Behavior, 22,* 277–295.

Zucker, T. A., & Landry, S. H. (2010). Improving the quality of preschool read alouds: Professional development and coaching that targets book-reading practices. In M. C. McKenna, S. Walpole, & K. Conradi (Eds.), *Promoting early reading: Research, resources, and best practices* (pp. 78–104). New York, NY: Guilford.

INDEX